Michèle Longino examines the ways in which Mediterranean exoticism inflects the themes represented in French Classical Drama.
Longino explores plays by Corneille, Molière, and Racine, including *Médée*, *Le Cid*, and *Le Bourgeois gentilhomme* among others. She
considers the role the staging of the near Orient played in shaping a
sense of French colonial identity. Drawing on histories, travel journals, memoirs, and correspondences, and bringing together literary
and historical concerns, Longino considers these dramatizations in
the context of French–Ottoman relations at the time of their production. She argues that what goes on in the cultural space of the
theatre speaks to the compelling domestic and international issues
of the time, with important repercussions in our own post-colonial
era. These plays continue to loom large in French cultural production even today, perpetuating a notion of "Frenchness" that is
meanwhile being increasingly put into question by the very demographics of France.

MICHÈLE LONGINO is Associate Professor of French Studies in the
Department of Romance Studies at Duke University. She is the
author of *Performing Motherhood: The Sévigné Correspondence* (1991).

CAMBRIDGE STUDIES IN FRENCH 69

ORIENTALISM IN FRENCH
CLASSICAL DRAMA

CAMBRIDGE STUDIES IN FRENCH

GENERAL EDITOR: Michael Sheringham (*Royal Holloway, London*)
EDITORIAL BOARD: R. Howard Bloch (*Columbia University*), Malcolm Bowie
(*All Souls College, Oxford*), Terence Cave (*St John's College, Oxford*), Ross Chambers
(*University of Michigan*), Antoine Compagnon (*Columbia University*), Peter France
(*University of Edinburgh*), Christie McDonald (*Harvard University*), Toril Moi
(*Duke University*), Naomi Schor (*Harvard University*)

Recent titles in this series include

A complete list of books in the series is given at the end of the volume.

ORIENTALISM IN FRENCH CLASSICAL DRAMA

MICHÈLE LONGINO

Duke University

CAMBRIDGE
UNIVERSITY PRESS

PUBLISHED BY THE PRESS SYNDICATE OF THE UNIVERSITY OF CAMBRIDGE
The Pitt Building, Trumpington Street, Cambridge, United Kingdom

CAMBRIDGE UNIVERSITY PRESS
The Edinburgh Building, Cambridge CB2 2RU, UK
40 West 20th Street, New York, NY 10011-4211, USA
10 Stamford Road, Oakleigh, VIC 3166, Australia
Ruiz de Alarcón 13, 28014 Madrid, Spain
Dock House, The Waterfront, Cape Town 8001, South Africa

http://www.cambridge.org

First published 2002

Printed in the United Kingdom at the University Press, Cambridge

Typeface Baskerville Monotype 11/12.5 pt.   *System* LATEX 2$_\varepsilon$ [TB]

A catalogue record for this book is available from the British Library

ISBN 0 521 80721 2 hardback

This book is dedicated to my parents,
Helen I. and James C. Longino,
who shared with me their love for the Mediterranean,
to my sisters, Helen and Virginia, and my brother Jim,
with whom I first knew that world,
and to my son Nick
who came to love it also.

Contents

ix

Illustrations

Acknowledgments

Lectures from this book in progress were presented at various meetings and at universities in the United States and in Europe. Many thanks to all of my colleagues and friends for their interest and enthusiasm. I owe deep thanks to Duke University, the National Endowment for the Humanities, the Camargo Foundation, the National Humanities Center, and the Mellon Foundation for the support that freed me to pursue the research and do the writing for this book. Sincere thanks to the colleagues who supported the project from its inception: Marcel Gutwirth, Philip Lewis, John Lyons, English Showalter. I also am grateful to my seminar students at Duke University for their enthusiasm and insight as I worked through the challenges this study presented. And I am especially indebted to three friends for generous gifts of time and helpful readings: Peter Jelavich, Alice Kaplan, and Volker Schröder were my key readers; I couldn't have hoped for keener observations or more intelligent suggestions, and I owe a special thanks to Peter for his sharp critical eye. Mary Campbell and Harriet Stone read the manuscript at earlier stages, and offered invaluable critiques. Karen Barkey, Cyril Breward, Marshall Brown, Barbara Fuchs, Ross Chambers, Tom Farrell, Michael Fischer, Paol Keineg, Claude Reichler, George Saliba, Jay Smith, Vicky Spelman, Georges Van Den Abbeele, Ken Wissoker, and the members of the Carolina French Cultural Studies Seminar saw chapters or offered useful guidance at various stages, and their comments were extremely helpful. Richard Hurley expertly and graciously assisted with all of the photography for the illustrations. My thanks here also to the Bibliothèque nationale de France, to the Brown University library, to the Harvard University library, to the Bibliothèque interuniversitaire des langues orientales, and to the archives of the Ministère des affaires étrangères for their assistance and permission to use their materials. Stephanie O'Hara did the translations and Julie Singer provided much fine-tuning of the manuscript, and I am profoundly grateful for their assistance. I owe a great debt to Michael Sheringham, Linda Bree, and to my readers at Cambridge University Press for their generous care in seeing this book to print. My son Nick Farrell was especially understanding and supportive of this project (and me) over recent years as it dictated the shape of much of our life together. To these people, and to the many more who helped out along the way, my heartfelt thanks. And of course, any shortcomings of this book are mine alone.

Early versions of chapters or sections of chapters in this book appeared previously in the following publications, but they have been radically recast or translated here. I am grateful to the editors and publishers for permission to use them; from chapter 1 "Médée and the Traveler Savant" in *EMF: Studies in Early Modern France*, vol. 7 ("Strategic Rewriting"), edited by David Lee Rubin and Julia Douthwaite (Charlottesville: Rookwood Press, 2001); "Creüse: Corneille's Material Girl" in *La femme au dix-septième siècle*, edited by Richard Hodgson, Biblio 17 (Tübingen, forthcoming 2001); "Pollux: Modèle cornelien du nouveau voyageur savant, ou la 'naissance' de l'anthropologue" in *Actes du CIR 17*, edited by Giovanni Dotoli (Tübingen, forthcoming 2001). From chapter 2: "Le Cid: la politique sur scène" in *Littérature et exotisme, XVIe–XVIIe siècle*, edited by Dominique de Courcelles (Paris: Bibliothèque de l'Ecole des chartes, 1997): 35–59; from chapter 5: "Bajazet à la lettre" in *L'Esprit Créateur*, 38 (Summer 1998), "Racine," edited by Harriet Stone: 49–59; "*Mithridate*, or "*La France turbanisée*" in "La Rochefoucauld, Mithridate, Frères et soeurs, les Muses soeurs," edited by Claire Carlin, *Actes du 29e congrès de la North American Society for Seventeenth-century French Literature*, The University of Victoria April 3–5, 1997, Biblio 17, 111 (Tübingen: Narr, 1998): 137–46.

Introduction

Vous me demandez, ma chère bonne, ce que nous lisons . . . Avant les Etats, nous avions lu, avec mon fils, des petits livres d'un moment. Mahomet second, qui prend Constantinople sur le dernier des empereurs d'Orient. Cet événement est grand, et si singulier, si brillant, si extraordinaire qu'on est enlevé.

Correspondance, 1676 Madame de Sévigné to her daughter[1]

[You ask, my dear, what we are reading . . . Before the Estates General met, we had done some light reading, along with my son. Mohammed the Second, which talks about Constantinople under the last of the Oriental emperors. This event is so grand, so singular, brilliant, and extraordinary, that one is quite carried away.]

Sa Majesté m'ordonna de me joindre à Messieurs Molière et Lulli pour composer une piece de théâtre où l'on pût faire entrer quelque chose des habillements et des manières des Turcs.

Mémoires [1670], le chevalier d'Arvieux[2]

[His Majesty ordered me to join Messieurs Molière and Lulli in composing a play which would present something of Turkish dress and manners.]

In the seventeenth century, the domain of the exotic significantly captured the French imagination.[3] This fascination would represent a crucial phase in the development of a collective French identity. It set the operative terms for a colonial mentality, which, in turn, provided key grounding for the articulation of a national consciousness. Essential to the shaping of a sense of "Frenchness" was the signaling of what it was not, the construction of the necessary "other" against which it could define itself. While frontiers, boundaries, and markets were being staked, mapped out, claimed, negotiated, and disputed in the political realm, cultural lines of demarcation and attitudinal markers were being formalized as well, especially in places like the theatre.

I

The theatre in seventeenth-century France functioned as a locus of entertainment and site of artistic expression, but it also forged bonds of common culture. It brought urban dwellers of various classes together, organized them economically and socially through seating arrangements into a stratified but coherent population and concentrated their attention around its dramatic discourse.[4] Their shared experience as audience reinforced a sense of collective identity that was being articulated diplomatically, commercially, and militarily, as the state apparatus was consolidated around the figure of the absolutist monarch, Louis XIV.[5] This was a space of high culture where the elite dominated and set the taste, the tone and the desires of the general public. But it was also the domain of the "parterre" where a more popular audience participated in determining the reception of given plays. The theatre was at once a space of contestation and of consensus-building.[6]

During this period, despite the beginnings of a newspaper culture, the mirroring and shaping of public opinion still took place largely in communal spaces where groups of people gathered, focused on shared concerns, and participated in conversation.[7] While one of these traditional spaces, the Church, retained its position of moral authority, the secular theatre offered a less ritualized and more participatory arena. People congregated as well, but less effectively, in smaller salon gatherings and amid the distractions at court. But especially in the theatre, political and cultural messages were conveyed and exchanged, and the theatregoer discovered a sense of official national purpose as "la mission civilisatrice" gradually enlarged its focus from a religiously motivated Crusader vision to embrace the more diffuse realm of a market-driven culture.

At this time, France needed new but sanctioned stories from which to invent and legitimate new behavior. For the nation, spurred by an accelerated and intensified mercantilist drive, broke out of the hexagon and became a colonial power during the seventeenth century. The entrepreneurial French would not only be exploring but actually settling in worlds new to them and imposing themselves and their ways on indigenous peoples. They would be exploiting territories that produced crops or yielded goods for profitable exchange back in Europe, and they would be promoting slave-based economies. They would occupy strategic points for stamping the fleur-de-lis on maps and in minds. Toward the beginning of this era, France had begun by establishing footholds in the Chesapeake Bay (Annapolis, 1603), in Quebec (1608), in Guyana (1609); this act of expansionism spread to Senegal (1626), several Caribbean islands (Saint Christophe, Martinique, Guadeloupe, Barbados, Saint-Domingue), Madagascar, and by the end of the century France had also set roots in Louisiana, the Antilles, Pondichéry, and Chandernagor.[8] This new colonial venturism represents a major shift, involving personal, social, financial, and institutional transformation, not simply abroad but at home as well. Such profound systemic change called for and came out of a consensual narrative, and the process of shaping the nation's story became a significant function of the theatre. Plays served as the ideal vehicle for nurturing a coherent early colonial mentality.[9]

But the French had long been honing their colonial skills and grounding the legitimacy of their eventual world enterprise. The Mediterranean basin was the privileged arena, at once familiar and exotic, that positioned them with the heritage of example and the sense of entitlement necessary to carry their mission forth into the greater world.[10] Theatre stories organized around the French Mediterranean connection prepared the way for negotiating the pressures of the colonial project. However, this staged Mediterranean narrative did not correlate precisely with the plotting necessary for taking on the rest of the world. For the "Middle Sea" was an old theatre of operations, where contacts were daily and contexts for them went back centuries and through layers of civilizations. The local exoticism practiced here harked back to old traditions of "neighborly" "Othering," and corresponded to the dynamics of a relation of proxemics; this sea basin was a "contact zone."[11]

Proxemics has been defined by human geographers and psychologists, specifically by Edward Hall, as an "elaborate and secret code that is written nowhere, known by none, and understood by all,"[12] having to do with territoriality – at the "face-to-face, architectural, and urban space levels." Cultures each have their own proxemic systems, and differences between them are often sites of conflict, but they can also be sites of enriching hybridization. Proxemics is a useful concept for thinking about areas where different ethnic groups touch on each other, as in the Mediterranean. A more recently formulated concept, developed by Mary Louise Pratt, is of the "contact zone:" "social spaces where disparate cultures meet, clash, and grapple with each other, often in highly asymmetrical relations of domination and subordination – like colonialism, slavery, or their aftermaths as they are lived out across the globe today."[13] In these arenas, communities must contend with differing sets of habits not only around space, but also competing notions of virtue. Neighbors inevitably evaluate one another; as Tzvetan

Todorov puts it: "Human beings have judged themselves as the best
in the world, and they have declared others bad or good according
to the degree of their proximity. Or conversely, [. . .] they have found
that the most distant peoples were the most fortunate and the most
admirable, whereas they have seen only decadence in themselves."[14]
Todorov points up the paradox that proximity is an unreliable indicator
of attitude – people may despise what is too close to them, and idealize
the distant, or just as easily prize and prefer familiarity as opposed
to the unknown and far-away. I see both of these attitudes at play
simultaneously around the seventeenth-century Mediterranean. Despite
rigid political positions, alliances, affinities, and identities could be quite
fluid, depending on the needs of the moment. The Mediterranean
world bears the marks of the violent contact zone, but also the rich
heritage of hybridization, with communities clashing occasionally even
as they touch on and inspire one another. It is in this zone that distinct
cultures first met and negotiated shared space. The history of these
encounters would be both formative and instructive in the shaping of
more far-flung ventures.

The important role of the theatre as a public space for the airing of
current concerns around expansionism and the shaping of public opinion
about the "Other" led me to detect a unified project in seven classical
plays that have never been examined as a group. Corneille's *Médée* (1635),
Le Cid (1637), *Tite et Bérénice* (1670), Molière's *Le Bourgeois gentilhomme*
(1670), Racine's *Bérénice* (1670), *Bajazet* (1672), *Mithridate* (1673) are the
best-known plays from the repertoire most marked by concerns with
"Other"ing that centre on the Mediterranean world. However, they are
by no means the only works to treat the topic. All manner of like-spirited
texts proliferated at this time – novels, histories, newspaper articles, and
many other plays as well.[15] But I focus on these particular plays for the
very reason that they are well known; even today (with the exception of
one which is simply overshadowed by its Greek and Latin versions), they
continue to dominate the French classical stage; their messages still have
resonance for today's post-colonial audience.

   These are star plays – canonical works at the very heart of the official
version of French culture. Having withstood the test of time, they are still
performed regularly – both reverently and iconoclastically – in national,
experimental, school, and municipal theatres. And these masterpieces
are a standard feature of the core curriculum in French state-regulated
classrooms today, even those located in former French colonies, and in

French literature classrooms anywhere. Grandparents recite verses to their grandchildren, audiences murmur verses in anticipation or along with the actors, the odd citation pops out here and there in proverbial fashion to suit the occasion. Of course, this is a good deal more likely in a bourgeois or intellectual milieu, where literary tradition is readily integrated into social discourse. As consecrated in the French repertoire, these plays officially represent, even today, for the French and to the world, along with other works from the seventeenth century, not merely handy clichés, but the apogée of French linguistic and esthetic expression – classicism, and hence "Frenchness." However interpreted, they are not to be ignored. They occasion the recitation of the collective imaginary, the national litany.[16]

1998 statistics for the years since 1944 from the Library of the Comédie Française, the state run and traditional showcase theatre for the classics, give us a sense of the continuing importance of these plays:[17]

authors	titles	Stagings since 1944
Corneille	*Médée*	0
	Le Cid	464
	Tite et Bérénice	36
Molière	*Le Bourgeois gentilhomme*	788
Racine	*Bérénice*	253
	Bajazet	101
	Mithridate	109

We must consider these as mere baseline figures, for, in addition, all over Paris, throughout France, and wherever French culture is prized in any way, these plays are constantly in performance. If we note that Corneille's *Médée* has not been featured at the Comédie, we are wrong to conclude that the play has not been performed at all. Outdone by the Euripides and Seneca (and even the Anouilh) versions, Corneille's story of the wronged and murderous outsider woman has nonetheless appeared on other distinguished French stages, such as that of Ariane Mnouchkine's innovative Théâtre du soleil. And these figures do not take into account the recent Racine tricentennial commemoration (1999) which occasioned the proliferation of productions of this author's plays all over the world. Corneille, Molière, and Racine – this is the sacred trinity of French High Culture.

I am interested in the ideological freight of these plays. As cultural artifacts, they bear an investment of the French imaginary, and point to a constructed and ongoing sense of French collective identity, of "Frenchness." The constitutive characteristic of this "Frenchness" that most interests me here is "Other"ness. Fascination with heavily loaded, and by now almost invisible (so familiar) notions of East and West has been transmitted unquestioningly through the continued circulation of this fixed canon, with serious implications for a France currently reckoning with its legacy as a colonial power. Despite their enduring appeal, these plays are marked by the times that produced them, and this was a time when France was coming to terms with its "Others."

To date, studies of this moment in the sociology of the theatre have concentrated particularly on the ways in which the king's power was symbolized and represented on the stage.[18] Here I look at another as-pect of the organization taking place through the mediation of spectacle: the simultaneous invention of a French and a foreign people. The cat-egory of exoticism that was being developed, refined, and displayed on stage contributed to shaping a sense of French cultural solidarity and, eventually, national superiority.

By exoticism, I mean any signals from within normative French dis-course pointing to, defining, and relating to, worlds, cultures, and lan-guages outside itself. In the seventeenth-century theatre repertoire these are numerous and various, but in keeping with the constraints that gov-erned classical theatre, they invoke most often a specific terrain. They project a consistent image of the Orient understood primarily as the eastern and southern rims of the Mediterranean basin. In some cases, these signals are still directly derived from the geographic politics of the ancient Greek state as reflected in its classical theatre. In others, they are grounded in the affective and military politics of the Roman Imperium, or in the history of relations between the Christians and the Muslims in the area; in yet others, in actual political tensions existing between France and the Near East (the Ottoman Empire, specifically: Anatolia, the Levant, and North Africa) at the time the plays were being writ-ten and performed. Hence, we are considering here a "local" exoticism, a distinctly other cultural world (indeed an amalgam of other cultural worlds) with which nonetheless the French were in regular contact.[19]

Further, the exotic displayed in these plays is various, but none of it is new; it is all recycled material; nor is it uniquely French. It comes from familiar Greek classical myths, or from ancient Latin historical sources; it is an appropriation of a medieval Spanish epic poem, or is gleaned from gossip, letters and diplomatic accounts about Constantinople. Greek, Spanish, Roman, Ottoman – this consideration of sources points up the interesting fact that the core of the French national literature consists largely in a borrowing and cobbling of other people's stories. Paradoxically, the very corpus that features "Otherness" and thereby shapes the idea of "Frenchness" is itself made up and out of the "Other."[20]

The French classical stage does not easily admit of a world beyond the confines of its claimed lineage, the Greek and Roman civilizations; nor, in keeping with the classical tradition, does it (except in comedy) encourage reference to religion, with the exception of mythology.[21] Therefore we are looking at a secular Mediterranean basin. However, in the seventeenth century, this space was dominated by the Ottoman Empire, a powerful Islamic agglomeration, and so the immediate everyday referent with regard to the "Other" for the French was the muslim Turk, and an implicit and specific religious tension informs the articulation of the distinction between self and other. Thus, although we may speak broadly of an exoticist fashion in seventeenth-century cultural production, what we witness in the French theatre at this time is a manifestation of early modern Orientalism. This was more than a mere fashion; it was an aggressive mind-set for comprehending and managing the Other which prepared the way for the full-blown orientalist movement by the end of the eighteenth century. It provided the ideological underpinning necessary to justify eventual French hegemony and dominion over its colonial territories.

"Orientalism," as Edward Said and his many fellow critics have more than amply established, represents an entire apparatus for essentializing, objectifying, classifying, and fantasizing the unfamiliar, for constructing and communicating the "unknown" / the "different" / the "Other" as a body of knowledge that can be controlled and manipulated at will. What can be manipulated on paper can be manipulated in the field. The telling and the event, the pedagogic and the performative, go hand in hand, as the post-colonialist theorist Homi Bhabha has argued.[22] Most often, Orientalism is not dated as early as the seventeenth century. For example, although Said traces a long history of Orientalist thought and production since Aeschylus, he enters into his own analysis of Orientalism only in the late eighteenth century with the full institutionalization of colonialism.[23] However, in our post-colonial era, it is crucial to look behind the heyday of Orientalism, and to examine its initial groundings; we must recognize and revisit the stories that first nurtured this mindset. The classical plays under scrutiny here each constitute important facets of France's "Official" story. They represent illuminating moments in the shaping of an idea of the Orient that in practice proved useful to the early modern French state and beyond. This "story" requires dismantling or at the least close scrutiny if colonialism is truly to be relegated to the past.

This book considers each of the seven plays mentioned above as opportunities for reading documentary texts and events, accessing current concerns and getting at the mentality of the day, and for finding through the contemporary sources new ways to think about these plays. That is, it attempts to reconstruct an ideational reality that bridges fact and fiction, and endeavors to read the documents and plays together as pre-texts and sub-texts of one another, as part of a shared discourse that theatregoers might have experienced at some level as one. Reading through this lens, and through this tension, I examine what I see as formative attitudes, practices, and roles of the "French" *vis-à-vis* the "Other." I seek to produce a suggestive understanding of aspects of French seventeenth-century cultural practices of "Other"ing through this process of contextualizing reading. My aim is to extend the idea of the "stage" metaphorically, and to understand these varied works as integral to a discourse of colonialism that the French were in the process of elaborating for themselves and acting out in the Mediterranean basin.

I situate this study at the conjuncture of various traditional disciplines in that space broadly known as "culture." I attempt to read these plays as one might read Anouilh's *Antigone* or Sartre's *Les mouches* as commentary on contemporary events and concerns occasioned by the Second World War, viewing these same events and concerns as occasions for these plays. Here, however, I need to say a word about what I understand as "culture." Unfortunately, I must renounce Dollimore's inclusive picture of culture, useful as I find the definition for dismantling the preeminence of "high culture": "the whole system of significations by which a society or a section of it understands itself and its relations with the world."[24] Nor is the circular understanding of culture as an interchange between taste and education, or, in Bourdieu's terms "the state of that which is cultivated and culture as the process of cultivating," helpful here.[25] "System," "state," and "process" fail to capture the disparate, messy, sporadic, uneven, and hardly consciously consensual yet necessarily participatory dynamic of culture building.

It would be tempting to examine these plays from the perspective of a "reflection" or a "centrality" theory, given that in the seventeenth-century French theatre space, audience and performance were generally organized around the person of the Monarch. But it would be presumptuous to claim that literature "mirrors" its culture, that it condenses and essentializes a culture's experience. This perspective would posit the homogeneity of culture and the primacy of literature as expression of that culture. Rather, I subscribe, if guardedly, to the notion that literature is merely one of many equally significant facets of a "raggle-taggle after-the-fact construction that we call 'culture',"[26] as Ross Chambers reminds us, or, as Bhabha puts it, merely a shifting collection of some of "the scraps, patches and rags of daily life [which] must be repeatedly turned into the signs of a national culture."[27] But we cannot ignore the evidence: some "rags" endure and serve longer than others, so long and so well as to translate into monuments for their culture. And so, while I attend here to various facets of texts, documents, and events that I consider to speak to one another arbitrarily and roughly, but significantly, through a relation of approximate synchronic production, my eye is on these revered plays. I believe I can then consider them most productively by juxtaposing and weaving them into what of course ultimately is only my own narrative, my own version, my own signifying. This study would like to be able to claim a unifying principle behind the prismatic effects of its various facets, but such a simile infers an impossible notion of coherence. Classical French theatre is indeed "High Culture," but here it is even more than that: it is the equivalent of a national pledge of allegiance – it is a political position.

In the five chapters that follow, reading the plays for the French "Orient," I trace the connections between the staging of cultural "Other"ness and the construction of French collective identity. In the broadest of terms, I map out the practical apparatus (or the spectrum of ideological symptoms) that was necessary to enable the very possibility of a colonial, and hence a national situation. I first sketch out a profile of the traveler-informant / nascent civil servant / anthropologist (*Médée*). I then examine the usefulness of the "Other" as the alien yet essential coalescing force in mediating domestic politics (*Le Cid*). Following this, I study the crucial tools of translation, diplomacy, commerce, and the regulating of class (*Le Bourgeois gentilhomme*). I next consider the phenomenon of gendered geography in the articulation of East–West relations (the two Bérénice plays). In the last chapter, I look at the key role of long-distance correspondence, at lines of contact and demarcation, and the development of the double standard (*Bajazet*); and here also, finally, I take stock of the place of military might and strategizing, hero-building, Realpolitik, and ambivalent alliances, in defining France's sense of self

(*Mithridate*). So integral to the workings of all of these plays is the question of gender, that I do not focus on it as a topic apart, but as a constitutive element in the broader construction of colonial thinking, and it crops up consistently throughout my study.[28]

To summarize, I speculate on the preoccupations the French audiences might have brought to the theatre, and how these concerns might have illuminated and even given shape to aspects of the plays less striking to us today, but crucial to understanding the formation of colonial thinking. By closely examining aspects of seventeenth-century relations between the French and the Ottomans, and by locating resonances of these relations in key French theatre productions of the times, I attempt to ground historically and consider critically the uses and purposes of early modern Orientalism in the cultural construction of the support apparatus of colonial France.

Classical French cultural expression, built by and around the King, came to epitomize for the French, and for the world, its identity, and still does, to this day. Classicism functions even today as the strongest marker of "Frenchness." This identity is most readily assumed by those who have the greatest investment in maintaining a status quo favorable to their interests – i.e. the aristocracy and the bourgeoisie. Here, however, I hope to tease out how not-so-"high" culture is un-wittingly just as bound up in fixing France's image, how the everyday "raggle-taggle" struggle of life and material interest around the Mediter-ranean played a major role in establishing France's production of France.

Several theoretical frameworks have informed this study: of these, "The New Historicism" or "Cultural Poetics,"[29] "Cultural Materialism"[30] or "Cultural Studies,"[31] "Post-colonial Theory,"[32] and especially "Orientalism,"[33] discussed earlier, have influenced my thinking over the course of recent years, as I was deep into archival work and into my reading of the plays. I have found these theories illuminating and useful, but have avoided a programmatic application of any one approach. My main concern has been to study the plays as motors of French mentality and not merely as products or symptoms.

The "new historicists" renegotiated understandings of and relations between what traditionally had been considered the discrete fields of "literature" and "history." They forged ahead with the understanding that these two disciplines were defined by false distinctions – that text and context were inextricable; and that the end project was not to contribute to the "grand narrative" of history, or to the "history" of literature, but through discrete readings, to assert synchronic but hardly exhaustive constructions of cultural systems.[34] They attempted to map out discursive fields in which "discourse" is understood as patterns of thought – ideas, emotions, fears, anxieties – that are coterminous with practice. The place of the critic here was a highly self-conscious and present one.[35]

"Cultural Materialism" and "Cultural Studies" have shared less text-bound and more comprehensive concerns. They have both sought to define their approaches not so much as inter-disciplinary, but rather anti-disciplinary. When they came into their own, "history" and "literature" were still fields; objects and behaviors were not yet quite the texts they have become; and texts were just beginning to be considered as the material things they are. Most usefully, for my purposes, these new endeavors have put into question the touchstone of "culture" that the New Historicism tended to take for granted. They borrow heavily from recent developments in sociology, cultural anthropology, and privilege such non-methodological methodologies as "bricolage" and "thick description." They are resolutely and rigorously undisciplined. They defy class, race, gender, sexuality markers, and national boundaries, and champion the oppressed and marginalized. They are politically leftist, even in the wake of Marxism.

"Post-colonial theory," despite its umbrella welcome by "Cultural Studies," retains an independent specificity and project: it examines the experiences and consequences of colonization, colonial life, and decolonization for colonizers and colonized alike. From this vantage, presuppositions invisible even from the "Cultural Studies" perspective have been exposed, theories exploded, and political agendas further radicalized. In particular, the major blindspot of ethnocentrism has been identified, and the world of literary criticism and theory has awakened to the political implications of privileging certain cultural traditions over others. Post-colonial theory has initiated a major revision of received ideas concerning literary value, honed from familiar Western European canons, by encouraging the discovery and acknowledgment of other ways of apprehending and assigning value to human experience. By considering past and, even more urgently, current political practice in an increasingly globalized world, it has opened conversation to a greater plurality of voices than ever before. These voices do not speak idle words in a disembodied world; they address a world where words matter.

These recent movements have burgeoned largely in American and English academic circles; I am not a card-carrying member of any of

them, but my work is certainly influenced by them. To the degree that
these currents have marked my thinking, they point to the stimulating
and healthy challenge for the American scholar of French Literature
teaching in an American academic setting. The conversation at hand inevitably, and always profitably, enters into our work, just as we contribute
our continental intellectual orientation to that conversation, and are,
"in the best of all possible worlds," carriers back to France as well. The
territoriality of "fields" on the American campus has been challenged,
as signaled by the institutionalizing of such accommodating umbrella
agencies as Cultural and Area Studies Centers, and so it is inevitable,
even desirable, that a hybrid project, such as my own, should be the
result.

However, to the extent that I subscribe to any method, I need to flag
the fact that I am a scholar of French Literature, a "dix-septièmiste,"
examining French seventeenth-century "artifacts," canonical and otherwise. My training as a French literary critic prevents me from altogether
distancing my reading from the canonical texts of my repertoire. The
texts were there first, as it were; my acquaintance with them dates from
high school, even grammar school days.[36] They came then, and still do,
not only in handsome, scholarly, leather-bound volumes, but in neatly
packaged, readily available and affordable pedagogical editions, "Les
Classiques Larousse." We are old friends. In all honesty, I cannot pretend
to put them on a footing with manuscripts of memoirs, correspondences,
unearthed relatively recently at the archives, documents in many cases
too fragile to photocopy, available only to the scholar fortunate to get to
them and willing to assume the arduous role of scribe. Over the years,
I have come to love these plays. I value them for their complexity, their
ambiguity, their richness, and, by now, for their very familiarity.

Working against this too cozy relationship, I have sought, through the
process of reading for the "Orient" in the plays of Corneille, Molière,
Racine, in tandem with archival material, and under the general shadow
of pressing post-colonial issues (immigration, identity, nation, globaliza-
tion), to produce a work of defamiliarization. From this perspective, the
plays signify differently than in their canonical isolation. I am open to
exploring these classical artifacts not only as embedded in their first contexts, but looking to see what has happened to them over time, how they
have been put to use, and in whose interest, remaining self-conscious
all the while about the limited scope of my views and materials. And,
freed of the constraints of a "methodology," the practices of "bricolage,"
"cobbling," "juxtapositioning," "thick description," and "counterpoint"

allow for weaving, meshing, reading for the "clue" and for "detail" and for using my training as a "close reader" at will. The end-product aims to provide a suggestive space of speculation; it hopes to engage the reader's participation in the ongoing project of making new sense out of old texts and events.

The pages that follow can, and I'm sure will be, read in myriad ways, but they do beg one indulgence: that is, the willing suspension of traditional disciplinary criteria. For this is a book about seventeenth-century French literature, but also a book that reaches into various domains – plays, letters, memoirs, histories, the present, the imaginary, the technical, the theoretical, etc. It is a little of all of these and none of them all at once. It has not been possible to do justice to the considerable and distinguished bibliographies already established in the many directions that this study takes. Here again, I beg understanding. Nor is this necessarily a book with a beginning and an end. The chapters can be read separately, as essays, or they can be read together, in which case the cumulative effect and message will certainly be more powerful than the lone chapter. Summaries of each of the plays are offered at the beginnings of each of the chapters to assist in following the argument, and a few provocative questions are intended to assist the reader in entering into the spirit of each chapter's enquiry.

Orientation

French travelers to the Levant in the seventeenth century at once satisfied and fuelled curiosity at home about this part of the world. In their myriad capacities, as merchants, collectors, diplomats, linguists, they provided an abundance of information for armchair travelers back in Paris. They wrote letters home, they produced translations, they bought up old manuscripts, they imported goods, they invented stories, they sent diplomatic messages and military reports, they compiled histories of the Ottoman Empire, and they penned accounts of their travels. Thus seventeenth-century French theatregoers had numerous kinds of textual and material contact with the Ottoman world, as well as their own lived experiences, or those of their children, friends, and relatives. And they brought to the theatre knowledge gleaned and opinions formed from these sources. The plays addressed current concerns and the audiences expected them to. France's notion of itself took shape out of the staged stories that were privileged and told again and again.

The French entertained a clear idea of the "Ottoman" or "Turk" at this time. Derisive colloquial expressions abounded, making it clear that the Turk loomed large, and most often negatively, in the French imaginary. Furetière's 1690 *Dictionnaire universel* definition for the term "*Turc*" lists usage examples that spell out the connotations:

On appelle generalement *Turc*, tous les sujets du Grand Seigneur, que le peuple appelle *Grand Turc* . . . Je suis très humble serviteur à son altesse *Turque*, dit le Bourgeois Gentilhomme dans la Comedie de Molière . . . On dit proverbialement qu'un enfant est fort comme un *Turc*, quand il est grand et robuste pour son âge. On dit aussi, Traiter de *Turc* à More; pour dire, à la rigueur & en ennemi déclaré. Prétendez-vous traiter mon coeur de *Turc* à More? MOL. On dit aussi en voulant injurier un homme, le taxer de barbarie, de cruauté, d'irreligion, que c'est un *Turc*, un vrai *Turc*, un homme inexorable, qu'il vaudrait autant avoir à faire à un *Turc*: il est Turc la-dessus. MOL.[1]

[*Turk* generally refers to all the Grand Lord's subjects, who refer to him as the *Grand Turk*. . . . I am the very humble servant of his *Turkish* Highness, says the Bourgeois Gentleman in Molière's play . . . It is said of a child in proverbial fashion that he is as strong as a *Turk*, when he is tall and robust for his age. The expression "to abuse like a Turk and a Moor" is also used, meaning to treat someone or something harshly and like a declared enemy. "Do you mean to abuse my heart like a Turk and a Moor?" MOLIERE. To insult a man, to accuse him of barbarism, cruelty, and irreligion, he is described as a *Turk*, a real *Turk*, a man without pity, one might as well be dealing with a *Turk*: he is a Turk as far as that is concerned. MOLIERE.]

And just below, the entry *"Turquerie"* reads: "Manière d'agir cruelle et barbare, comme celle dont usent les *Turcs*." ["Turquerie [Turkishness]: cruel and barbarous behavior, like that of the *Turks*."]

To see how pervasive and deeply ingrained anti-Turk attitudes were, one has but to consult the language of Molière's comic characters, who had not necessarily been formally educated, but rather, and more likely, socially indoctrinated in their prejudices. Dom Juan's valet Sganarelle would slur his master as "un enragé, un chien, un diable, *un Turc*."[2] ["a crazed man, a dog, a devil, *a Turk*."] And the rascally Scapin would not invent but borrow the clichéd plot of a kidnapping by Turks – a common enough event at the time – to collect a ransom for his own empty pocket.[3] The foppish Mascarille preciously feigns fear of being treated viciously, "de *Turc* à More."[4] ["abused like a Turk and a Moor."] Molière's *Le Sicilien* features a troupe of Moors and another of slaves.[5] Léonor's servant Lisette, in *L'Ecole des maris*, asserts the superiority of French social mores with regard to women: "Sommes-nous chez les *Turcs* pour renfermer les femmes? / Car on dit qu'on les tient esclaves en ce lieu, / Et que c'est pour cela qu'ils sont maudits de Dieu."[6] ["Are we among *Turks*, that lock women up? / For it's said that there they are held as slaves / And this is why they are cursed by God."] At the end of a long string of epithets to describe the meanness of the miser Harpagon, his valet La Flèche culminates with: "Il est *Turc* là-dessus, mais d'une *turquerie* à désespérer tout le monde."[7] ["He's acting like a *Turk* in all this, with a *Turkishness* that makes everyone despair."] However here, in this last example, as with the first quotes, I am not citing Molière directly from one of his plays, but from a dictionary. And this time the citation is an example for the usage of "Turc" from an edition as recent and a text as willfully definitive as the 1985 *Grand Robert Dictionary*.

Molière's staged version and rhetoric of the Turk, then, has played a key role in setting an enduring attitude toward Turks in France. Thus we see that the French collective imagination would be saturated over the centuries with fixed and lasting ideas about the Turks and what French relations might or should be with them. But the French attitude toward the Ottoman was not wholly one of unadulterated hostility or derision. Just as Sganarelle spoke of his master Dom Juan in terms both of fear and of admiration, so did the French generally contemplate these formidable "Others" with ambivalence. If the "Grand Turc" struck terror in their hearts, so did he inspire respect.

In his *Journal* entry of May 7, 1672, the traveler Antoine Galland offers an example of the wonder with which the French beheld the Ottoman display of might and splendor. After describing in minute detail the magnificent pomp of the Sultan's triumphal sally forth from Adrinople as he undertook a military campaign, Galland had to conclude that if the French were to read this account in a French novel that prided itself in plausibility, they would find it more extravagant than any possible flight of authorial fancy:

Si Mademoiselle de Scudéri avoit pu se forger dans l'imagination quelque chose de semblable, et qu'après l'y avoir représenté avec le crayon de son élégante plume, elle luy eut donné place dans quelque endroit de ses ouvrages, tous ceux qui y prennent plaisir à cause du vraisemblable qu'elle a tousjours taché d'y observer, n'en feroient plus la mesme estime apres avoir leu ce morceau, qui bien loin de leur paroistre vraisemblable à l'ordinaire, leur paroistroit encore au-dessus des extravagances des paladins et de nos Amadis de Gaule. Cependant, il n'y a rien de si vray que ceste sortie estoit la plus belle chose que j'aye jamais veue en ma vie, et j'ay de la peine à croire que dans aucune cour de l'Europe, si on excepte celle de France, on puisse rien entreprendre de si beau.[8]

[If Mademoiselle de Scudéry had been able to imagine something similar, and after having described it with her elegant pen she had inserted it somewhere in one of her works, all those who take pleasure in the verisimilitude which she has always taken care to observe would no longer hold her in esteem after reading such a piece, which, far from seeming typically credible, would seem to outdo the extravagances of our paladins and our Amadis of Gaule. However, nothing is truer than the fact that this triumphal sally was the most beautiful thing I have seen in my life, and I have trouble believing that in any European court, excepting that of France, one could undertake something so beautiful.]

Galland's observation that this actual scene exceeded the gifted Mademoiselle de Scudéry's embellishing flourishes and even those of the fanciful *Amadis de Gaule*, clearly constitutes an admission on his part that France, despite the requisite disclaimer, has produced nothing so splendid as to compare with this Ottoman parade. This sort of panegyric, ever loyal to the belief in French supremacy, but clearly overwhelmed, expressed both great admiration and deep dread – in a word, awe. The consequence of this complex sentiment would be envy. The profound ambivalence the French felt toward the Turks would be such that if they disparaged them it was only by way of consolation for what they perceived to be their own comparative inadequacy. They were being outdone in the very areas of pomp and might in which they prided themselves. Hence their rhetoric of censure was a shield raised not only against difference but also against threatening competition; it took on a thickness and a weight, a predictability so strong as to become a prejudice.

Nor did this prejudice take shape overnight. Since the days of the crusades, the antagonism between Christians and Muslims had been strong; but only since the fall of Constantinople in 1453 had the French set their sights on the Ottomans.[9] In the sixteenth century, under Francis the First, a mixture of admiration and terror informed French feelings toward the Ottomans: admiration for Soliman the Magnificent (as he was known to the French) on the one hand; terror of his Admiral Barbarossa on the other. Hostility toward the Turks surfaced in texts such as Rabelais's that (like Molière's plays) participated in the transmission of popular expression and gave reliable testimony to general sentiment.[10] However, throughout this same period, admiring Renaissance scholars eagerly sought out knowledge from Islamic sources and scholars in the empire, and especially hunted for manuscripts.[11] Ottoman power was at its zenith under Soliman, but the naval battle of Lepanto in 1571 marked the end of the glory days. By the seventeenth century, anti-Turk feeling, local strategic interest, mercantile expansionism, and cultural acquisitiveness in France set the field for the development of the social, bureaucratic, diplomatic mechanisms necessary for advantageously negotiating this "neighborly" relationship. On a greater scale, this early and familiar foreign relations paradigm established the domestic attitude for eventual dealings with French colonial domains (albeit in modulated forms, according to the place and the people), and set in operation the supporting apparatus which would enable the French to pursue their imperialist ambitions down the road.

In the continuance of the Renaissance project, characterized by the same vein of interested inquisitiveness, the seventeenth-century French reading public was avid for information on the Orient. Among many caterers to this taste, the Paris-based journalist Donneau de Visé responded, producing news accounts of events of interest in

Constantinople. In the opening flourish of his 1688 story of the recent demise of Mahomet IV (1648–87), he offered an apology to his readers. The press could barely keep up with demand for information about affairs in Constantinople, and was reduced to publishing unpolished texts in order to satisfy the eager reading public:

La précipitation avec laquelle se font ces sortes d'ouvrages pour satisfaire l'avide curiosité du public, ne permettant pas de les polir, parce qu'une feuille lorsqu'on a achevé de l'écrire, est enlevée aussi-tost par l'imprimeur, on ne doit pas s'étonner si on ne s'attache qu' à la vérité de l'Histoire, sans chercher à luy donner l'embellissement qu'elle pourroit recevoir du stile.[12]

[The hurry in which these sorts of works are produced, in order to satisfy the public's avid curiosity, does not allow any time for them to be edited, because as soon as one page is written it is taken away immediately by the printer; it should not be surprising that we concern ourselves only with the truth of History, without seeking to give it the stylistic embellishment it might otherwise have.]

The readers and consequently the printers were so pressed as not to allow time for Visé to polish his text. Such enforced rush of course also furnished a handy excuse for poor style. At the same time, it did attest to French interest in the Ottoman world.

According to the traveler-savant, Jean Thévenot, the public was made up not of armchair travelers, but of readers who would have preferred to go and see for themselves.[13] Thévenot describes this public and its entrancement with travel, and counts himself as one of the privileged who, inspired by accounts of the Orient, actually made his way there:

Le désir de voyager a toujours esté fort naturel aux hommes, il me semble que jamais cette passion ne les a pressez avec tant de force qu'en nos jours: le grand nombre de voyageurs qui se rencontrent en toutes les parties de la terre, prouve assez la proposition que j'avance, et la quantité des beaux voyages impriméz, qui ont paru depuis vingt ans, oste toute raison d'en douter; il n'y a point de personnes qui ayent l'inclination aux belles choses qui ne soient touchez de celles dont ils instruisent, et il y en a peu, s'ils n'estoient retenus par des attaches pressantes, qui ne voulussent eux mesmes en estre les témoins et les spectateurs: Ce sont ces belles Relations qui m'ont donné la premiere pensée de voyager . . .[14]

[Men have always had a natural desire for travel, it seems to me that never has this passion so strongly driven them as in our time: the great number of travelers to be met with all over the globe, well proves my point, and the quantity of wonderful travel narratives published in the last twenty years erases further doubt on the subject; few people drawn to beautiful things are not touched by what these narratives have to say, and there are few who, if they were not detained by more pressing matters, would not want to see for themselves what

is described. It was these beautiful Narratives that first inspired me to think of
traveling . . .]

Books stimulated and then did not satisfy this desire. The public wanted
to see for themselves, to be "témoins et spectateurs" themselves. Not only
did the French want to be the audience in the Orient; once there, they
also desired to take on the role of actors. We can see how the Orient was
appropriated by them as a space where they played out their fantasies
for their own benefit in mirroring behavior that at once fed on and failed
to take notice of the profound otherness that surrounded them.

An example of the thespian quality of French contact with the
Ottoman world is offered in an anecdote recounted by Thévenot. He
describes how he (along with another Frenchman, first refused) essayed
several roles in order to gain entry to the spectacular audience of the
Persian Mogol's ambassador with the Ottoman Sultan:

Toutefois ce gentilhomme Français ayant parlé en Turc à un de ces Capidgis,
n'en fut pas traité fort rudement, seulement il luy dist qu'il ne nous pouvoit
pas laisser entrer, ce qui nous fit espérer que nous entrerions: je commençay à
parler aussi en Turc à ce même Capidgi, moy qui à peine à lors en sçavois deux
mots, je luy representay que j'estois estranger, et que je souhaitais fort de voir
cela, il me disait toujours que je n'entrerais point, . . . je ne désistais point, et me
taisant lorsqu'il se fachait, je faisais à peu près le même personnage que font les
pauvres honteux lorsqu'ils demandent l'aumosne, . . . enfin après luy avoir bien
rompu la teste de mon Turc à la mode, qui consistoit presque tout en ces mots,
allaï feuerfen, qui veut dire, pour l'amour de Dieu, il envoya un de ses camarades
à leur Colonel, qui estoit sous le porche, pour lui demander permission de nous
laisser entrer, ce que le Colonel accorda facilement. (p. 161)

[However, this French gentleman having spoken in Turkish with one of these
Guards, was not very rudely treated, only told that we could not be allowed in,
which made us hope that we could still gain entrance. I began to speak in Turkish
as well, to this same Guard, I who hardly knew two words of the language, I
conveyed to him that I was a foreigner, and that I very much desired to see this, he
kept telling me that I could not enter . . . I did not desist, and quieting down when
he began to get angry, I began to act somewhat like a shameful beggar when
he asks for money, . . . Finally, after having driven him crazy with my Turkish,
which almost entirely consisted of the words *allaï feuerfen*, which means "for the
love of God," he sent one of his comrades to their Colonel, who was under the
porch, to ask him for permission to let us in, which the Colonel readily granted.]

Attempting to capitalize first on his obvious role as a foreigner (which,
of course, he was), then making the supplicatory gestures of a beggar, he
represented himself. He fashioned his demeanor in a deliberate manner,
stumbling with his limited knowledge of the language, intent on gaining

Map of the seventeenth-century Mediterranean Basin.

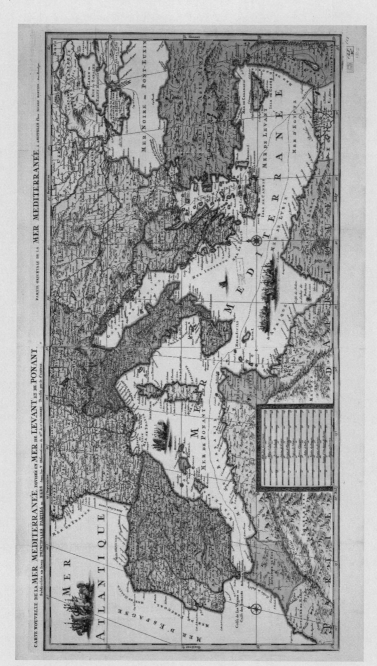

Map 2 of the seventeenth-century Mediterranean Basin.

entry to a place where he was not welcome. The first step in assuming a role here is that of attempting to speak the foreign language: that act already sets up a split within Thévenot between what he thinks and what he says, not to mention what he is able to say. Yet, he is not intent on translating his thoughts, or even on communicating. He is merely hoping to produce the right sounds, or the "open sesame" speech act ("pour l'amour de Dieu") that will gain him entrance to the Divan, the designated chamber of the seraglio where formal government audiences took place, and hence synonym for elaborate ceremony. Even using a foreign language – the language of the Other – by extension, body language, accent, intonation, voice pitch, can be understood as a form of acting for the traveler. Also as the first potential stumbling block. Clothing and hair must be rethought as costume, disguise. It is particularly telling that Thévenot's acting is registered around a moment of forbidden access, a moment that condenses and emblematizes intensely the more general experience of seeking entry to a foreign land, introduction to the mores of another people.

Further, theatricality and disguise appeared a part of the Ottoman mentality as well. Thévenot reports that the Sultan would also masquerade, in his case so that he might pass incognito and inspect the order of his realm: "Le Grand Seigneur va quelquefois par la ville, déguisé et sans suite, comme un particulier, pour épier si on observe exactement ses ordres" (p. 118). ["The Sultan sometimes goes about the city disguised, and without attendants, like a private citizen, in order to see if his orders are being followed exactly."] The knowledge that this was a habit of his generalized into widespread caution and self-conscious behavior throughout the city, since one could never be sure of his whereabouts. The place of acting was materially represented in the architecture of the seraglio: in the main consultation chamber, the Divan, a screened window affords a view from the Sultan's private apartments of all that takes place in that space:

Le Grand Vizir estant entré en meme temps par une autre porte dans la salle du Divan, ils se saluèrent, et demeurèrent debout en se faisant compliment. Ce ministre prit sa place vis à vis de la grande porte de cette Salle, sur un banc couvert de brocard d'or. Une fenêtre fermée d'une jalousie, donnoit presque sur ce banc. Cette fenêtre est commode au Grand Seigneur, qui peut voir de là ce qui se passe au Divan.[15]

[The Grand Vizier having entered the Divan at the same time, by another door, they greeted each other, and remained standing as they exchanged pleasantries. This minister took his station *vis-à-vis* the main door of that Room, on a banquette covered in gold brocade. A window covered by blinds stood very close to this banquette. This window is useful to the Sultan, who can see from there what is happening in the Divan.]

Sometimes the Sultan observed from behind the screen, sometimes not; but those in the chamber needed to behave, in the face of this material reminder, as if he were watching, that is, they had self-consciously to act out their prescribed roles and demonstrate appropriate behavior at all times. Thus role-playing, according to the French observer, was an important element not only of French comportment in Constantinople, but among the Ottomans themselves.

More broadly, the physical site of the Orient was envisaged, indeed appropriated, as the space of performance. Here the literal and figurative senses of the term "theatre" – the military and the performative – collapse into each other. The seventeenth-century historian Mézeray writes of the Venetians' plans to "stage" another victory over the Turks:

C'estait à peu près le temps qu'ils espéraient de celebrer l'anniversaire de la défaite des Turcs, par une autre plus signalée au détroit des Dardanelles, lieu qu'ils avaient choisi comme un illustre et heureux théâtre de leur valeur.[16]
[It was about that time that they hoped to celebrate the anniversary of their defeat of the Turks with an even bigger one, at the strait of the Dardanelles, a place they had chosen as an illustrious and happy theatre for their valor.]

However, those Frenchmen who traveled as would-be spectators ran the risk of getting caught up in the action and becoming dramatis personae themselves. The ambassador de la Haye's confessor, Robert de Dreux, re-counts in his memoirs the story of "un jeune gentilhomme des meilleures familles de Paris" ["a young gentleman from one of the best families in Paris"] who in tourist fashion had traveled "*voir* le siège de Candie" ["*to see* the siege of Candia"] (my emphasis) and his fate: "le vaisseau où il était fut pris et lui-même fut vendu à un Turc vanier . . ."[17] ["the vessel on which he found himself was captured and he himself was sold to a Turkish basketmaker"] Thus, while the Orient was a stage with the Ottoman "Other" featured as center attraction, it was at the same time a highly participatory space where the French were confronted with and forced to negotiate their own identity as potential "Other" as well. It was the space of the performative encounter.

It was commonly held, without reflection, that off-stage theatrics played an integral, even necessary, role in Franco-Ottoman contacts, and in the way France related to the space of the Other. Nevertheless, act-ing could still be and was labeled as superficial and deceptive behavior, but only when Europeans commented on their Turkish counterparts. In 1672, the German philosopher–mathematician Leibniz, who never visited the Orient, traveled from Mainz to Paris to present a proposal to Louis XIV. This mission was neither a self-appointed nor an official démarche, but a little of both. Leibniz never saw the king or even met with the foreign minister. But his proposal serves as an eloquent example of the virulence of anti-Ottoman sentiment at the time.

In this document, Leibniz sought to persuade the king to undertake the equivalent of a final crusade and to defeat the Ottomans decisively. His purported aim disguised his real concern to divert Louis's military activity away from Europe. In his attempt to whip up enthusiasm for such a campaign, Leibniz demonizes the Ottomans, and he specifically accuses them of acting, as if it were a crime: "Il fait nuit dans leurs âmes serviles; sortis de leurs déserts, ignorant le monde, ils vivent, pour ainsi dire, au jour le jour: on dirait qu'ils jouent un rôle sur un théâtre . . ."[18] ["It is dark in their servile souls; having emerged from their desert, ignorant of the world, they live, so to speak, from day to day: it could be said that they are playing a role onstage."] Here, the metaphor of theatre is enlisted to levy an accusation of ignorance and falseness that would dehumanize the Turks and thus legitimate a campaign to eliminate them. Leibniz constructs a sweeping condemnation of the Turks, ultimately dismissing them as unreal, like theatre: "En un mot, la vie, dans ce pays, est aussi désordonnée qu'en rêve, et ne paraît pas plus vraisemblable qu'une comédie" (p. 154). ["In short, life in that country is as disorganized as in a dream, and seems no more real than a play."]

Leibniz's inability or unwillingness respectfully to grant to the Ottomans their otherness marked a failure to appreciate their culture on its own terms. He evaluated it instead according to the European model, and according to his immediate political agenda, and produced an image not of the Ottoman world, but of a European model staged and gone topsy-turvy.[19] Here the Ottoman world is relegated by Leibniz to the chaotic world of bad dreams, seen as no more real than a play. This assigned unrealness was to justify Leibniz in preaching that the French had a mission, to impose their reality and to eradicate the dream.

Yet it is the very notion of theatricality that enabled the French to penetrate that world. Other Europeans, the French here, who entered into direct contact with the Ottomans – linguists, diplomats, merchants – readily assumed their roles as actors. They penetrated that world and found there one not unlike their own, or at least took cognisance of those aspects of this other society that found resonance in their own cultural

Map of seventeenth-century Constantinople.

repertoire. They made sense out of the unfamiliar by applying the grid of their native knowledge. They deliberately assumed, manipulated and put to use key signals of identity. Ottoman dress was as codified as in France – for example, turban colors mattered, they signaled special roles and relative importance in Constantinople, just as in Paris, ribbon colors counted and served the same purpose. The French knew how to read and make the local code work for them. If Thévenot saw fit to comment on the Ottoman Sultan's surveillance system, was it not because he recognized in it the French king's? He had available, in his own culture, a model from which to read.[20]

The seventeenth-century staging of exoticism takes place, then, not only in the Paris and Court theatres, but wherever Europeans and

Map of the prospect of Constantinople. From Guillaume Joseph Grelot's *Relation nouvelle d'un voyage fait au Levant* (1680).

26

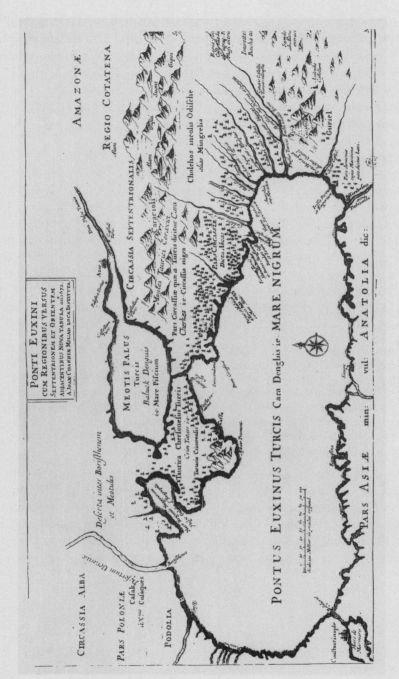

Map of the Black Sea.

27

Ottomans enter into daily contact and must negotiate their cultural identities. Throughout the Mediterranean world, interactions take place which are self-consciously enacted, as if on stage. And these encounters, as reported, are eagerly read back in Paris by roughly that same public that constitutes the theatre audience, which in turn includes some of the actual or near participants in French–Ottoman events. The French will examine and discover themselves in, through, and against the foil of the Other – the local oriental Other – the Ottoman.

If the French classical theatre offers an organized view of France's pre-occupations with itself, it is equally marked by France's pragmatic desire to come to terms with the Orient and its possible relations with this world. These concerns together articulate a move toward the establishment of a heightened sense of "Frenchness." Thus, the theatre here figures, beyond the literal Paris stage as well as beyond the more figurative Orient one, as the shared mental space in which the French forge for themselves, out of their contact with the Other, a collective identity, and develop a notion of themselves as members of an "imagined community."[21]

Said's by now celebrated observation finds its quintessential attestation in the behavior of the seventeenth-century French in the Ottoman world:

The idea of representation is a theatrical one: the Orient is the stage on which the whole East is confined. On this stage will appear figures whose role it is to represent the larger whole from which they emanate. The Orient then seems to be, not an unlimited extension beyond the familiar European world, but rather a closed field, a theatrical stage affixed to Europe. An Orientalist is but the particular specialist in knowledge for which Europe at large is responsible, in the way that an audience is historically and culturally responsible for (and responsive to) dramas technically put together by the dramatist.[22]

All the world was indeed a stage, and the flair for the theatrical among the Ottomans was not to be ignored either. But, for the French, the Mediterranean Orient furnished a practice laboratory theatre permitting them to play out and thus shape their role. Having honed their export identity and put their props in place, they readied to take on their colonial identity, which in turn would assist them in staging their "Frenchness."

CHAPTER I

Médée *and the traveler-savant*

SUMMARY

Corneille's Médée *(1634–5)*

Jason and his wife Médée, a foreigner from Colchis (Asia), have come to Corinth to seek refuge after Médée has committed an atrocity against Jason's enemy Pélie in Jason's kingdom Thessaly (both Corinth and Thessaly are Greek kingdoms and thus in the "West").

Jason's fellow argonaut and friend Pollux arrives in Corinth from Asia after a long absence, and Jason brings him up to date. He tells him he is leaving Médée for the Corinthian king Creon's daughter, Creüse.

Pollux is horrified at Médée's act, but also dismayed at Jason's self-serving philandering. Having spent a prolonged time in Médée's part of the world, he knows her and the ways of her people well. He warns Jason against Médée's powers and her sure revenge. Jason uses the alibi of their children's security as reason for his need to part from Médée.

Jason asks Creüse to intervene with her father Creon and secure safe haven for his children, and Creüse agrees to provided that he do her a favor.

Médée launches into a tirade and consults with her confidante Nerine. She still loves and wants Jason. She is torn between fierce anger and enduring passion. Nerine counsels her against any rash behavior.

Creon officially banishes Médée. He is willing to keep her children, but she must go. She argues her case unsuccessfully, but she obtains the reprieve of a full day, time enough to avenge herself.

Creon and his daughter, along with Jason, consult together. Another pressing issue before them is Aegée's wooing of Creüse. Creüse prefers the young hero Jason to the aging king of Athens. When Jason expresses gratitude for her preference, she exacts her price both for this and the saving of his children: she wants Médée's golden robe. Jason hesitates to wrest the robe, Médée's only patrimony, from her, but unheroically plots to enlist Nerine's assistance in securing it for Creüse.

Creüse officially refuses Aegée.

Nerine and Jason discuss Médée's situation and Jason brings up the matter of her robe. Médée arrives and the couple confront each other directly for the first time.

29

She argues her case again, and presents her plight as the result of all she has done for him. Again, Jason uses the children as alibi. They need a safe haven, says he. Médée repeats her love for him, and warns him directly that she will take revenge.

Médée reacts to Nerine's presentation of Creüse's request for the robe. Now she sees there will be no change and gives full rein to her anger. She concocts a magical poison and soaks the garment in it. She instructs Nerine to take both the robe and her children to Creüse.

The spurned Aegée had tried to storm Creon's palace and remove Creüse by force, but Creon, aided especially by the heroic Pollux, managed to take him prisoner instead. Médée intervenes with her magic, comforts and frees Aegée, and in return he offers her safe haven in Athens when she leaves Corinth.

One of Creon's soldiers, under Médée's spell, reports to her that Creon and Creüse have been destroyed by the gift-robe. Jason doesn't yet know this since he is off saying good-bye to Pollux who is leaving town. Médée decides to complete her revenge, to punish Jason both as lover and as father by killing his children.

Creon and Creüse are dying as Jason finds them. Furious, he vows to punish Médée for their murder by killing the children he now calls hers.

Jason and Médée have their second and final confrontation: Médée announces that she has killed their children – the final vestige of their love. She takes flight in her chariot and Jason kills himself.

Questions to ponder

(1) Why does Corneille replace the traditional chorus of all earlier versions with the character Pollux? What is gained? What is lost?

(2) Why does Corneille's Creüse covet and ask for Médée's robe, when in all earlier versions it is Médée's idea to give it to Creüse? What is gained? What is lost?

(3) Why, in Corneille's later play, La Toison d'or (1661), which represents the earlier story of the Argonauts, does Pollux not appear at all, although the playwright had taken the trouble to invent him in 1635 and cast him as Jason's close friend?

On peut concevoir des mythes très anciens, il n'y en a pas d'éternels; car c'est l'histoire humaine qui fait passer le réel à l'état de parole, c'est elle et elle seule qui règle la vie et la mort du langage mythique. Lointaine ou non, la mythologie ne peut avoir qu'un fondement historique, car le mythe est une parole choisie par l'histoire: il ne saurait surgir de la *nature* des choses.

[We can conceive of very old myths, but there are no eternal ones; for it is human history which turns reality into speech-act, it alone regulates the life and death of mythic language. Distant or not, mythology can have only a historical grounding, for myth is a speech-act chosen by history: it cannot come from the "nature" of things.] (Roland Barthes, *Mythologies*)[1]

In the seventeenth century, at least eight different versions of the Medea myth appeared, in the form of translations, tragedies, and operas.[2] This is not unusual. The story has long had a fascination for Western European culture.[3] The plight of the exotic woman imported from another world, along with other forms of plunder from that same place, submitted to local politics and mores, with dire consequences for all, organizes the core of these versions and resonates through time.[4] The unspoken lesson appears to warn that the introduction of foreign women into a given culture is dangerous to that culture's stability. Exogamy extends only so far as the edges of a set community. But what of the operational features of endogamy?

Even today, minority female populations, women who perceive themselves to be either excluded from the dominant culture or admitted only along the edges, identify readily with the plight of Medea. In the United States, Constance Carroll speaks of the empathy the figure of Medea inspires among the black women students reading Euripides in her college-level classics course:

Black women students, much more than white women students, understand and can identify with the situation of Medea . . . The black woman in higher education is not unlike Medea. She is inexperienced in the system, just as most of her peers and family have traditionally been excluded from it. Black even more than white women need "magic," that is, superior ability, in order to receive equal opportunities.[5]

At the same time, the German author Christa Wolf also identifies with Medea with regard to her own doubly fraught role as a woman intellectual and her forcibly politicized outsider status as she negotiates her complicated former East German past in *Médée, voix*.[6] And the pied noir Marie Cardinal, in her introduction to a recent popular paperback version of the Euripides *Medea* finds in this outsider's status not only the expected parallel with North African women of the French colonies who find themselves imported into France, but also with women of French origin (like herself) brought up in North Africa and then repatriated into the hexagon they have never known, where they are strangers in their homeland.[7] Such women, be they of colonized or of colonizing background, suddenly find themselves uprooted, demonized, and having to cope in the alienating space of the righteous metropole where they are the "Other." Both exploitation and exile exact their price. In this era, Medea proves to be a useful shorthand for women who don't fit in or belong comfortably to the society which nevertheless is their given milieu and with which they must contend. They are doubly "Other."

At different historical junctures, some aspects of this particular story are highlighted and others played down. Innovations crop up and then disappear, in keeping with preoccupations and moods of the day. The obvious example is that Euripides's Greek *Medea*, composed during Pericles's golden reign, stresses pathos and evokes complicated feelings of pity, whereas Seneca's Roman version, marked by the degenerate reign of Nero, focuses on fury and provokes horror. Corneille claims to have been inspired primarily by Seneca, and this surface resemblance is substantiated in a line-by-line comparison of the versions. But, as we shall see, his adaptation is different in important respects.[8]

A number of recent critical studies of Corneille's seventeenth-century *Médée*, produced closely together in the past twenty years, offer varied critiques of his version and attest to a resurgence of interest in the play. The witchcraft trials of 1634, anthropological concerns with the role of the gift, current psychoanalytic debates, feminist studies of woman as outsider, the shaping of the political institution in Early Modern France, the construction of the Corneillian hero, and the primacy of pleasure over morality in the world of art – all of these current topics find grounding and focus in Corneille's *Médée*.[9]

Despite this scholarly attention, Corneille is not remembered by the public today for his *Médée* the way he is for *Le Cid* and a few of his other plays. The Medea story continues to be invoked and celebrated regularly in Western discourse, and so does Corneille's oeuvre generally, but not his *Médée*. His version has not been definitive. While the fact that the handy pedagogical Classiques Larousse series does not carry an edition of the play is no sure indicator of obscurity, it does tell us that *Médée* is not in high demand among students.[10] Of course, the classical corpus generally is suffering a diminishing presence in the French classroom, where the French theatre public is formed. *The New York Times* of January 3, 1999 reported that lycée students were once required to read several plays by Corneille and Racine each; but today, students in France are required to know only one play from the combined corpus.[11] Hence the odds, already poor (if not nil), have significantly diminished that they would be reading Corneille's *Médée*.

This suggests that *Médée* does not support France's official story about itself, the preferred version that French school children are required to ingest as part of their indoctrination into their cultural heritage, their lesson in "Frenchness" (*Le Cid* or *Phèdre* remain key readings, for example). However, with ongoing attention to the discourse of Orientalism as symptom of a major Western blindspot, and with the conflation of the status of women with the Orient in the male Occidental economy, the questions raised in Corneille's *Médée* are highly pertinent to today's world, and this play, coupled with the many critiques of East–West relations now available, offers a key point of entry into debate on this concern.[12]

Why did Corneille revisit the Medea myth in 1634–35? What was the attraction of the story for him, for the audience he wanted to please? To which of their concerns did he address his version? For what contemporary message did this old story serve as a useful vehicle? One could speculate that this young playwright was simply claiming pride of place alongside Euripides and Seneca. But even then, why this particular play and not another? To venture an answer to this question, we need to look not only at what was available to him in the received story, what he did with it, and how he made it speak to his contemporaries. We also need to look at what was going on in his environs at the time he undertook to write this play.

Corneille's *Médée* features significant preoccupations and an important innovation that bear the particular mark of the early French seventeenth century and set it apart from all preceding and subsequent versions. It speaks eloquently of a moment in a story of France that the country does not care to dwell on. It is this eruption and insertion of history into myth that interests me here. I contend that the early decades of the seventeenth century prepared the way for the institutionalizing of France as a colonial power under Louis XIV's minister Colbert.[13] I believe that Corneille's play bears witness to and contests the construction of the *mentalité* necessary to this project.

Well before the systematization of commerce that would take place under Colbert, Louis XIII's minister Richelieu had studied the state of the French economy and decided to take action. In examining the mercantile economies of Genoa and of Holland, he had recognized that their wealth was highly disproportionate to their size, and that France would do well to follow their example. In 1626–27, he legislated against barriers and set in place incentives that would stimulate maritime trade. Nobles were traditionally not meant to "work," but Richelieu aimed to remove the threat of derogation to those who would, specifically with trading companies or in founding their own. He also offered titles of nobility to commoners who would finance for at least five years a ship of two hundred to three hundred tons, as well as to merchants who served abroad as consuls.[14] He summarized the new policy in these few words: "Donner prix au trafic, et rang aux marchands" (336). ["To make commerce a worthy pursuit and to ennoble merchants."]

With this new incentive for both the nobility and the bourgeoisie, the way was set for greater participation and a significant increase in French maritime trade. In the next few years, more and more Frenchmen would be plying the waters of the Mediterranean and more distant seas, and would need new codes of behavior as they took up interests and professions no longer governed by their traditional roles. As they engaged in commerce and French representation abroad, they would be wrestling personally with the very issues that Corneille's play would address. Hence, *Médée* was a timely production with useful lessons for these new merchant travelers and diplomats.

One marginal nobleman who pursued such a career under the new Richelieu dispensation was the traveler, linguist, and diplomat Laurent D'Arvieux (1635–1702). He was born in the year of the staging of *Médée*. This was also the year of the founding of the Académie française, the ambitious purpose of which was: "que les sciences et les arts y fleurissent et que les lettres y soient en honneur aussi bien que les armes." ["That the arts and sciences may flourish there, and that letters may be honored as much as arms."] The flourishing of the sciences, arts, and arms depended precisely on the mercantile wealth which Richelieu had moved to stimulate. The editor of D'Arvieux's *Mémoires*, Jean-Baptiste Labat explained his subject's choice of career as a direct consequence of Richelieu's new law:

Il [D'Arvieux] considera que le commerce en gros qui se fait au Levant, étoit le seul moyen qui fut ouvert aux Gentilshommes pauvres pour rétablir leurs familles; que les maisons les plus considerables de Marseille & de la Provence s'étoient établies par cet endroit, sans avoir dérogé à leur noblesse par le privilege special que le Roi leur a accordé, & souvent réïteré, de pouvoir faire le commerce en gros, & de faire valoir leur argent dans les Echelles du Levant, comme les Nobles le font à Venise, à Gennes, à Florence, à Livorne, & autres Villes d'Italie, & comme ils le font encore en Angleterre, et en bien d'autres Endroits.[15]

[He realized that the wholesale trading which took place in the Levant, was the only way for gentlemen of limited means to re-establish their families; that the most considerable families of Marseille and Provence had established themselves in this way, without compromising their nobility, thanks to the special privilege granted them by the King, a privilege often renewed, which was to be able to conduct trade and risk their wealth in the trading posts of the Levant, as noblemen do in Venice, Genoa, Florence, Leghorn, and other Italian cities, and as they still do in England, and in many other places.]

As if to offer a useful model to this new population of seafaring and trading Frenchmen, Corneille introduces into the traditional plot a completely new character, Pollux. This is the only place in his *oeuvre* that Corneille uses this character. By 1661 he will take up the Jason story again, when, working backwards in the myth cycle, he will produce *La Conquête de la Toison d'or*. Pollux disappears here, although traditionally – and even within the text of Corneille's own *Médée*, along with his brother Castor – he had been cast as one of the Argonauts, and so should have remained essential to the plot. This disappearance is doubly curious since, in the earlier *Médée*, Pollux is a crucial, if not a major, figure, and he is cast as Jason's great friend as well. Nor will Pollux figure ever again in plots by any other playwrights. He is Corneille's unique one-time invention as the playwright accords cultural attention to the new Richelieu laws and the new social profile they call for. Pollux plays an obvious pivotal role in *Médée*: he negotiates the binary tension between Jason and Médée, between the smug Greek state and the destabilizing exotic other. But he does more than that: he enfigures the noble profile of the traveler-savant who brings his knowledge – a specific product of travel abroad – home. Corneille thereby stages the idea of knowledge as a negotiable commodity and of travel as directly useful to the state. Pollux heralds the important entry onto the stage of the traveler returned home who will offer his knowledge of other people to the service of his own kin. He represents the formation and introduction of the collector of human knowledge into literary consciousness. This Pollux marks the emergence of the early and incidental anthropologist. The world where he has done his "field work" is Asia, the world of the Other, the "barbare."[16]

We might consider Corneille's foray into Medea's country as an act poetically sympathetic with his character Pollux's, and politically consonant with that of many of the travelers of his time. Corneille also brought the Orient home. Here, in his adaptation of the Medea story, he actively debates and challenges the assignation of "barbare" to the East, and explores the modalities of the term. He offers a critique of the Western distinction between insider and outsider, civilized and uncivilized, just at that moment when the edges are about to be at once blurred and reinscribed. He discretely sketches out the profiles of the new creatures who would be the agents of that blurring and reinscription, particularly in the figure of Pollux, the world-wise traveler and adviser to the state. At the same time, he discredits the plunderer and the fugitive Jason. There is a new brand of heroism in the making and a new taxonomy of the traveler taking shape, in keeping with Richelieu's program.[17] And Corneille stages an idealized model of this traveler in Pollux before he assimilates and becomes merely another strand in the fabric of society.

It is by highlighting the function of Pollux that we can access the historicity of Corneille's version and appreciate it in the immediate context of its production. Corneille does not make much at all of his invention of Pollux, and in fact he plays it down. But perhaps it is precisely through our least self-conscious gestures that history speaks itself.

"BARBARE" – MÉDÉE ON TRIAL

In 1634–35, Corneille's staging of *Médée* actively challenged her traditional status as either pitiful victim or vicious harridan, and attempted to portray her in a more neutral light, with an important and firm legal argument of her own, even within the Western dispensation. She is brought once again to trial on stage, and then to print. In his "Dédicace," Corneille refrains from casting judgment on her and from disposing the audience favorably or unfavorably toward her.[18] He slips ironically between the received story of the character Médée and his production of her – his play: "Je vous donne [*Médée* / Médée] toute méchante qu'elle est, et ne vous dirai rien pour sa justification. Je vous la donne pour telle que vous la voudrez prendre, sans tâcher à prévenir, ou violenter vos sentiments par un étalage des préceptes de l'art" (535). ["I give you [*Médée* / Médée] in all its/her wickedness, and I will not attempt to justify it/her. I give it/her to you for such as you want to take it/her, without trying to predict or violate your feelings by setting forth the precepts of dramatic art."] The playwright suspends and solicits judgment. If Corneille invites the audience's position on the staging / the case of [*Médée* / Médée], it is because he is sure of his craft – the play will evoke a positive response – and because there is no obvious answer – the virtue of Médée and her general predicament are open to debate. In fact, conflicting and even self-contradictory opinions must mark any ethical discussion in a cross-cultural world.[19]

Médée's virtue is the focus of the play's debate. The traditional Médée, from Colchis on the southeast shore of the Black Sea, was considered by the Greeks to be a "barbare," or stranger, with all that the term connotes.[20] This epithet was crucial to the role she had been assigned in the earlier classical plays. Corneille's Médée was also from Colchis. But, what matters in his adaptation is not merely that she is a stranger, but the compounded fact that she is a stranger and a woman, from Asia, hence doubly, if not triply, suspect.[21] Corneille invites the public to take the position of judge, to serve as jury, and to decide on the case of the heroine and of his tragedy at once, while he disappears and constructs his plea, seeking if not exoneration at least comprehension for her, and certainly applause for himself. His precocious presentation of this troubling outsider and her dilemma – spurned and abandoned in a country not her own – anticipates the development of anthropological sensibility over time and the revaluation of Médée that has taken place in the twentieth century. Corneille's Médée is not simply a mute topic of discourse; she talks back and has as much to say about the people of Corinth as they have to say about her and her world. She is as much a participant–observer in the world of Corinth as Pollux, the neo-anthropologist, has been in hers.[22]

Corneille's presentation follows in the tradition of such recent precursors as Montaigne with regard to its close scrutiny and arguing of the term "barbare."[23] While denoting "outsider," it also connotes "savage" or "uncivilized" as an epithet. Fluidly, it can apply as readily to the "insider" culture as to the "outsider"; Corneille challenges the fixity of its assignment. Creon will use the term "barbare" as an insult, a negative passport, as he lists for Médée all of her crimes:

> Barbare, as-tu si tôt oublié tant d'horreurs?
> Repasse tes forfaits avecque tes erreurs,
> Et de tant de pays nomme quelque contrée
> Dont tes méchancetés te promettent l'entrée.
> Toute la Thessalie en armes te poursuit,
> Ton père te déteste, et l'univers te fuit.
>
> (2.2.383–88)

[Barbarian, have you so quickly forgotten so many horrors? / Think on your crimes and your errors, / And among so many lands name me one country / Where your wickedness will allow you entry. / All Thessaly, up in arms, pursues you / Your father loathes you and the universe flees you.]

Médée will return the insult, in more sweeping terms, and turn it on the supposedly civilized Corinthian population represented by their king, as she rebuts his wrenching offer to keep her children when she is banished:

> Barbare humanité qui m'arrache à moi-même,
> Et feint de la douceur pour m'ôter ce que j'aime!
>
> (2.3.493–94)

[Barbaric humanity which tears me from myself / And feigns kindness in order to take those I love away from me!]

Thus Corneille, through Médée, presents the Greek westerners as "barbares" here in an ethical sense, and in so doing stands the geographical term on its head. When Médée confronts Jason, she reminds him that in the early days of their liaison, he was not at all put off by the idea of a foreigner. When she speaks of herself, she uses the term "barbare" ironically, as if citing her Greek detractors. She shifts cynically then in mimicry style, echoing back but recasting "une Scythe" (Scythia being the land of Colchis), which once referred simply to her in relation to her place of provenance, and was the innocent name of a people rather than the loaded epithet it has become in Jason's new usage:

> Tu n'étais point honteux d'une femme barbare:
> Quand à ton père usé je rendis la vigueur,
> J'avais encor tes voeux, j'étais encor ton coeur;
> Mais cette affection mourant avec Pélie
> . . .
> Une Scythe en ton lit te fut lors un affront.
>
> (3.3.817–25)

[You were in no way ashamed of a barbarian wife / When I restored your weary father's vigor to him / I still had your troth, I was still your true love / But when this affection died, along with Pelias / . . . / A Scythian woman in your bed became an affront.]

In Furetière's *Dictionnaire universel* of 1690, the two definitions of "barbare" illustrate how the term came to signify in the French seventeenth century.[24] The first conflates completely the connotational components of "stranger," "cultural difference," and "cruelty" without any reflection on the biased nature of the understanding: "(1) Barbare: Estranger qui est d'un pays fort éloigné, sauvage, malpoli, cruel, et qui a des moeurs fort différentes des nôtres... Les Grecs appelloient Barbares tous ceux qui n'étoient pas de leur pays, et ce mot ne signifie en leur langue qu'estranger." ["Barbarian: Foreigner who comes from a very distant, savage, rude, cruel country, and who has customs very different from ours... The Greeks used the term Barbarians for those who were not from their country, and this word in their language only means foreigner."]

The second definition, and, for our purposes the most pertinent, focuses specifically on the sense of "cruelty:" "(2) Barbare: signifie aussi seulement cruel, impitoyable, qui n'écoute point la pitié, ni la raison. Un père est barbare, quand il n'a point de tendresse pour ses enfants, un prince est barbare, qui tyrannise ses sujets. *Médée faisait des actions barbares.*" ["Barbaric [adj]: also simply means cruel, pitiless, someone who is deaf to pity and reason. A father is barbaric when he has no tenderness for his children, a prince who tyrannizes his subjects is barbaric. *Medea committed barbaric actions.*"] The hypothetical examples here feature generic males in conceivably current domestic ("un père") and then in state ("un prince") situations, but, ironically, when it comes to furnishing concrete examples, to naming, the scapegoat woman – the specific female from the East, from the past and with a past – Medea is invoked. If Corneille had attempted to put into question the connotations of the term "barbare," and to loosen the hold of Médée's reputation in the Western mind-set in 1634–35, by 1690, Furetière had put her back in her place. She is cited as the very example of the "barbarie" she herself had condemned in the Greeks. Medea is always already irredeemably and necessarily the "Other," by a profound ideological economy that needs for her to be just that, along with the category of woman in general. Evidently, to judge by the authoritative dictionary definition, Corneille's critique of the conflation did not prevail; the myth was more powerful than his version of the story. The French literate readership still subscribed to the "barbare" / "étranger" / "cruel" tautology, and Médée still served as its handy epitome.

TURKS ON TRIAL

If the mythical Médée from the East was on trial on the French stage at this time, the actual Ottoman from the East also was being scrutinized in a more generalized discourse. The staged and unresolved trial of Médée resonates with opinions that would be articulated by the French about the Turks, their contemporary "Others," throughout the century. As we have seen, increased contact with the Levant on the part of merchants, travelers, scholars, adventurers, and missionaries at the time of Corneille's invention appeared to produce conflicting, but always judgmental, opinions of the Turks. "Different" to the French was a tenuous category; whereas they had no difficulty with "good" or "bad." Some opinions tended to be revisionist, challenging common negative prejudice. However, even when writers expressed positive opinions about the Turks, they would frame them in the more widely held and negatively charged discourse. For example, the traveler Jean Thévenot contrasted common belief with informed opinion, falling back on a safe pre-Christian, pre-Islamic ethic:

Beaucoup croient en Chrestienté que les Turcs sont de grands diables, des barbares, et des gens sans foy, mais ceux qui les ont connus et conversés en ont un sentiment bien différent, car certain que les Turcs sont bonnes gens [sic], et qui suivent fort bien ce commandement qui nous est fait par la Nature, de ne rien faire à Autruy que ce que nous voulons qui nous soit fait.[25]

[Many in Christendom believe that the Turks are great devils, barbarians, people without religion, but those who have known them and spoken with them have a very different sentiment, for it is certain that the Turks are good people, and who follow the commandment given to us by Nature, to do unto another as we would have him do unto us.]

And another traveler, Monsieur du Loir, attempted to disabuse his countrymen of their negative ideas about the Turks – all the while reiterating them, and expressed positive sentiments expansively, making a claim for their essential goodness:

Je vous dirai donc quant aux Turcs, qu'il ne faut pas les croire si grossiers et si brutaux que plusieurs se les sont imaginés, et certainement si l'équité est plus considérable que la politesse dans les moeurs, ils ne sont pas moins gens de bien que nous.[26]

[I will tell you then, with respect to the Turks, that you must not believe them as coarse and brutal as imagined, and certainly, if integrity in manners is more important than politeness, they are no less good men then are we.]

The French priest, Robert de Dreux, went so far as to admire the Turks' religiosity rather than dismiss it as fanaticism.[27] The traveler–merchant Jean Chardin reported that among seasoned diplomats, Ottoman governance inspired great admiration. The Venetian ambassador Quirini considered their political style an excellent model for Europeans, on the one hand because founded in common sense and at the same time (and here was a back-handed compliment!) precisely because of its un-European character – its inscrutable workings.[28] Chardin further noted the outstanding fairness of the Turks with regard to the treatment of diplomats and the tradition of immunity and tax-free supplies for their establishments in Constantinople.[29] And when Donneau de Visé in Paris put together his third-hand version of the sultan Mahomet IV's demise, he insisted (to give his story some positive value) on the virtue of at least some Turks: "Vous ne serez pas surpris[e] qu'il y ait des Turcs, dont le caractère soit humain. L'humanité est de tout pays, et il se trouve de la vertu parmy les Peuples les plus barbares."[30] ["You will not be surprised that there may be Turks of a human character. Humanity is a quality found in every land, and virtue is found among the most barbaric peoples."]

But just as French travelers – both of the active and of the armchair variety – were combating blind prejudice and ages-old hostility against the Turks (generically subsumed as "infidels"), tentatively reconstructing them to be good, refined, moderate, and intelligent people, so were others reiterating and finding more fuel for their distrust and dislike of them.

In 1670, the historian Ricaut attempted a dissection of the Ottoman state that might serve as a guide for the Europeans' political strategizing. Absolutism might be fine for the French, but was unacceptable elsewhere. Rhetoric such as his set the official record:

Quand j'examine de prés la constitution du Gouvernement des Turcs, [. . .] je vois une puissance tout-à-fait absolue dans un Empereur, sans raison, sans vertu et sans merite, dont les commandements, quelque injustes qu'ils soient, font des loix: les actions, quoy qu'irreguliéres, des exemples: et les jugemens, sur tout dans les affaires d'Etat, des resolutions auxquelles on ne se peut opposer.[31]

[When I closely examine the set-up of the Turkish government, [. . .] I see a quite absolute power in an emperor, without reason, without virtue and without merit, whose commandments, as injust as they are, make the laws: whose actions, although irregular, set the example: and whose judgments, on all matters of State, provide resolutions which cannot be opposed.]

The most obvious targets of criticism were the doubly "Other" Turkish women. Thévenot engaged in ambivalent attempts to habilitate the Turks' reputation, but he found in their women an outlet for his combined prejudice and misogyny. In describing these women's indolence, he sketched out a viciously detailed portrait:

Or ces femmes sont fort superbes, elles veulent presques toutes estre vestues de brocart, quoy que leur mary ayt à peine du pain, cependant elles sont extremement paresseuses, passant toute la journée assises sur un divan sans rien faire, si ce n'est qu'elles brodent des fleurs sur quelque mouchoir . . . Cette grande oisiveté fait qu'elles sont vicieuses, et qu'elles appliquent toutes leurs pensées à trouver les moyens de se divertir.[32]

[Now, these women are quite proud, almost all of them want to dress in rich clothes, although their husband may hardly have any bread, nonetheless they are extremely lazy, spending all day sitting on a sofa without doing anything, other than embroidering flowers on some handkerchief . . . This great laziness makes them depraved, and they devote all their thoughts to finding ways to amuse themselves.]

At the same time, to his credit, he considered them to have vices not inherently, but as a consequence of the particular ways in which they were regarded and treated. While passing harsh judgment on them, he attempted to understand the conditions of their life that might account for their supposed depravity:

Les Turcs ne croyent pas que les femmes aillent en Paradis, et à peine les estiment-ils animaux raisonnables, aussi ils ne les prennent simplement que pour leur service, comme ils feraient un cheval. (107)

[The Turks do not believe that women go to Heaven, and they barely consider them animals capable of reason, therefore, they merely make use of them for their services, as they would a horse.]

But Thévenot vacillated as he passed judgment on the Turkish men. In one breath he extolled the virtue of moderation as practiced among the Turks with regard to drinking, violence, and gambling, and in the next he excoriated their homosexuality: "Ils sont fort amoureux, mais d'un amour brutal; car ils sont grands Sodomites"(p. 113). ["They have a very amorous temperament, but a brutal one, for they are great sodomites."]

Thévenot castigated the Turks in a most intolerant tone for their own degree of intolerance toward people from other cultures, apparently ignoring the fact that Constantinople was one of the most cosmopolitan cities of the time, and choosing to ignore the Catholic–Protestant tensions of his own country, not to mention various ongoing prejudices against Jews and others. He apparently did not fully appreciate the highly diverse composition of Constantinople in the mid-seventeenth century. At this time, ten thousand neighborhoods (or "quartiers") were Muslim; three hundred and four were Greek; six hundred and fifty-seven were Jewish; twenty-seven were Armenian; and seventeen were European (or "Francs").[33] Thévenot picked up only on prejudice. As he saw it, the Turks did not manifest a sufficiently cosmopolitan attitude and were altogether too arrogant for European taste:

Quant à leurs vices, ils sont fort superbes, s'estimans plus qu'aucune autre Nation; ils se croyent les plus vaillans de la terre, et il semble que le monde ne soit fait que pour eux; aussi méprisent-ils en gros et en general celles qui ne suivent pas leur Loy, comme les Chrestiens et les Juifs; et ils appellent ordinairement les Chrestiens chiens. (p. 112)

[With respect to their vices, they are very proud, esteeming themselves above any other nation; they think themselves the most valiant on earth, it seems to them that the world was made only for them; thus they hold in general contempt those who do not follow their law, such as the Christians and the Jews; and they typically refer to Christians as dogs.]

Thévenot reduced not only the Turks' attitude toward, but the content of, their knowledge to one sole sentence. He decried their lack of intellectual curiosity while in a way demonstrating his own, and evidently was unaware of the important cultural exchanges that had flourished under Francis the First and Soliman the Magnificent:

Les Turcs cultivent peu les Sciences, et ils se contentent d'apprendre à lire et à escrire, et estudient souvent l'Alcoran, dans lequel est compris leur Droit Civil et leur Droit canon; quelques-uns s'appliquent encore à l'Astrologie, et peu à d'autres Sciences. (p. 112)

[The Turks make little attempt to cultivate knowledge, and content themselves with learning to read and write, and they often study the Koran, which contains their civil and canon law; some still devote themselves to astrology, and very little to other sciences.]

The intellectual curiosity that had accompanied increased wealth and fueled the Renaissance, occasioning a lively circulation of texts and ideas between Europe and the Orient, appears here to give way to a flat and highly judgmental attitude *vis-à-vis* the Turk.[34]

In 1661, François de Mézeray would punctuate the second volume of his authoritative *Histoire des Turcs* with the expression of a vaguely collective wish for a renewal of the Crusades against the Turks:

Tous les gens de bien souhaitent ardemment que la Paix générale réunisse tous les princes Chrétiens et les oblige de tourner leurs forces contre ce barbare ennemi de la liberté et de la Religion.[35]

[Every worthy person ardently wishes that the general peace might reunite all the Christian princes and force them to direct their energy against this barbarian enemy of liberty and of religion.]

As so often in the past, religion, the convenient (not at all to say insincere) European blindspot, was harnessed to serve as a rallying cry to muster European forces against the East.

Even the philosopher–mathematician Leibniz, as we saw in the "Orientation," while strategizing to distract Louis XIV from waging war in Europe, had only the most virulent of words concerning these people. In his argument to persuade the French king to mount a final crusade against them, he insisted on their depravity, playing on popular European iconographic cliché:

Ce pays est en quelque sorte la patrie des ténèbres et de la barbarie; et le Sultan, plongé lui-même dans l'ignorance, traîne sur le trône, parmi des troupeaux de femmes et d'eunuques, sa robe de Sardanapale.[36]

[This country is, in a way, the land of darkness and barbarism; and the Sultan, himself sunk in ignorance, trails his Sardanapalian robe on the throne, among the troops of women and eunuchs.]

By the end of the seventeenth century, in the preface to his important systematizing *Bibliothèque orientale*, the orientalist Herbelot de Molainville would offer an entire classification of the accumulated common beliefs about the Oriental part of the world. He would denounce the negative reputation of the Turks as a "grande injustice," but his reinscribing and contrasting of it with current more positive opinions about other cultural groups to the east, such as the Persians and the Arabs, hardly succeeded in rectifying popular belief. Indeed, one has to wonder what his purpose was in repeating such cultural slander. In any event, the Turks appeared to have acquired a fixed reputation:

Il faut dire la vérité, on fait quelque grace aux Arabes, et ils passent pour avoir autrefois cultivé les Sciences avec grande application. On attribue de la politesse aux Persans, et on leur fait justice. Mais, par leur nom seul, les Turcs sont tellement décriés, qu'il suffit ordinairement de les nommer pour signifier une Nation barbare, grossière, et d'une ignorance achevée, et sous leur nom, l'on entend parler de ceux qui sont sous la domination de l'Empire Ottoman.[37]
[The truth must be told, we make some concessions towards the Arabs, and they pass for having formerly cultivated learning to a great degree. We attribute politeness to the Persians, and we are right to do so. But by their very name, the Turks are so decried, that normally it suffices to name them in order to refer to a barbarous nation, vulgar, and completely ignorant, and by their name we mean all those who are under the domination of the Ottoman Empire.]

Herbelot's remarks attest to two strands of contradictory discourse that appear to run through the conversation: the Ottomans are either good or bad people – they cannot be both, or simply different. Like Médée, they are ever on trial, and their merit among the French is an ever-ready topic for debate. How to explain such opposed views? Although not without exception, a general observation holds that merchants and those who dealt directly with the Ottomans without language barriers tended to be disposed to have relatively favorable impressions. The pragmatic grounding of barter and trade set value on heterogeneity and difference not only with regard to goods, but also to their purveyors. The merchants' concerns were of a more neutral sort, since they were intent primarily on making relationships work in order that their business flourish. Aristocrats and travelers directly under the French king's patronage were rather more baffled by the structure of the Porte (the Sultan's Constantinople palace and site of government), which both mirrored the French court society in its ostentation and at the same time totally defied its logic in its radically different mode of hierarchizing (an apple vendor could become a Vizir).[38] French courtiers needed to entertain negative opinions of the Turks in order to demonstrate solidarity and loyalty to their own ruler, and French military were obligated to consider them at all times as the enemy, despite the fact that they also functioned as sometime allies, especially with regard to the Habsburgs. In similar spirit, we remember that, like a trader, Médée was a useful ally whose methods were not questioned as long as she was assisting the Argonauts in obtaining the Golden Fleece; it was only once she accompanied them back to their world and didn't fit in that she became a problem – their problem.

The negative discourse on the Ottomans was almost invariably cast in terms of religion. The depravity the French saw in the Turks was always a consequence of their "barbarity," which amounted to the fact that they were infidels and enemies of Christendom. From behind this powerful screen, the French could cast aspersions on their Mediterranean neighbors, their local others, and maintain their own protective posture of defensive righteousness.

Thus, although intensified and accelerated contact was producing a more realistic view of the Ottomans among the French, strong prejudices still held sway. And the French right, indeed the moral duty to judge the Ottomans, went absolutely unquestioned. So it went with Médée, the "Other."

TRAVEL ON TRIAL

Fundamental to these pronouncements on the Turks were the actual travelers who made them. The Mediterranean basin was populated by travelers of all sorts: they would take up this life of travel in the seventeenth century for different and often complex reasons. They engaged in variously motivated movement – in trading ventures, on government business, in search of objects or souls, out of curiosity, out of need, out of covetousness. In some cases they went because they chose to leave their own communities, in others because they were forced out, and in yet others (in the case of slaves) they had no choice at all, but were moved like chattel.

An example of such mixed motives is the story of the merchant Jean Chardin (1643–1713), whose travel account is quoted above. It is significant that he was the son of a jeweler. The jewelry trade and the whole economy of preciosity is based on rarity and distance. Beauty alone does not determine the value of a stone. If it is common, that is, easily found and acquired, then it is of lesser value. Therefore travel was a key component of a jeweler's stock and trade. The other important feature of Chardin's background is that he was born into a Huguenot family. Taking his cue from his father's business and settling on the profession of merchant, he made his first great voyage, as far as Persia, from 1664 until 1670, traveling under the auspices of the French crown. Upon his return to France, he realized that the climate had become increasingly inhospitable for Protestants, and that as a consequence his personal prospects were not good. He shifted his allegiance to the English crown and his base of operations to London, and made his second great voyage from there. Upon his return, he published his travel journal for both of his voyages. He dedicated the volumes to England's Charles II in recognition and gratitude for the protection his reign had afforded him: "que votre Trône auguste soit toujours l'inviolable Azyle des Oppressez." ["May your august throne always be the inviolate refuge of the oppressed."] Despite the shift of his base of operations to England, the disaffected Chardin remained anchored in his French mother tongue, and so there is an interesting dissonance between his political and his linguistic allegiances, necessitated by his religious orientation, but not troubling his profession in commerce, which adds up to a complicated identity structure:

J'avois trouvé à mon retour en France, que la Religion où j'ay été élevé, m'éloignoit de toutes sortes d'emplois, et qu'il falloit ou en changer ou renoncer à tout ce qu'on appelle honneur et avancement. L'un et l'autre me parossoit rude: on n'est pas libre de croire ce qu'on veut. Je songeay donc aussitost à retourner aux Indes, où sans changer de Religion, ni sans sortir aussy de la condition de Marchand, je ne pouvois manquer de remplir une ambition modérée; parce que le commerce y est un emploi si considérable, que même les Souverains le font tout ouvertement.[39]

[Upon my return to France I found that the religion in which I had been brought up, excluded me from all sorts of occupations, and that it was necessary either to change my religion, or give up hoping for any kind of honors and advancement. Both choices were difficult; one is not free to believe what one wishes. I thus immediately thought of returning to India, where without changing my religion or quitting the profession of merchant, I could not fail to satisfy moderate ambitions; for trade is such a considerable thing there that even sovereigns conduct it quite openly.]

Note that in his homage he expresses concern about the respectability of his profession in commerce, and claims to find confirmation of the legitimacy of his métier not in the example of any European kings, but in the way this merchant identity enjoys a positive valence in the Orient. And he can point this out in his discourse to the English king perhaps more easily than he might have to the French king. Not only was religion a barrier to his social or material advancement in France; so, despite Richelieu's earlier efforts, was his profession in commerce. It appears it was easier for industrious noblemen to shore up their titles through trade than it was for successful merchants to climb the ranks (as we will see in 1670 with Molière's *Bourgeois gentilhomme*).[40] But in what would become known as the Protestant "nation of shopkeepers," where even kings did not disdain to engage in such concerns, he had found a more secure and nurturing home base.[41]

Chardin's travels took him as far as Persia, and this alone made him remarkable. What further distinguished him as a traveler was his route. In the seventeenth century, the Black Sea was closed to foreigners. In order to enter, travelers coming from the Mediterranean were required to obtain a passport from the Ottomans at Constantinople, and these were not readily distributed. Chardin was one of the few Europeans to reproduce the itinerary of the Argonauts, and to actually make his way to Persia across the Black Sea and through Medea's land of Colchis. In so doing, he both reinscribed its value as exotic – far away, seldom seen, and then only with difficulty (the sea was particularly treacherous) – not unlike the jewel; and as negotiable – he made it through the country; and he made it susceptible to narrative, he wrote to tell of it. He dined out on his stories both while on the road and then at home, and capitalized generally on the reputation he had built for himself through his adventures. Thus the activity of travel itself became commodified. Further, as a consequence of his travels, Colchis began to fall from complete mythic exoticism into a more prosaic geography, and the limits of the imagined world shrank as the frontiers of the known world expanded.

Chardin and his fellow-travelers – Thévenot, Tavernier, D'Arvieux, Grelot, Bernier – who plied the Mediterranean and produced judgments such as those cited above, are among the very ones mentioned regularly as the early and unwitting practitioners of the discipline of anthropology. For historians of anthropology looking back, they represented a new breed of seekers, setting the pace of a new form of enquiry, and making way for the formation of the eventual discipline of anthropology. It is to the specific formation of French anthropology in the 1950s that we now turn as we prepare to study Corneille's play in these contexts.

THE TRAVELER-SAVANT – EARLY MODERN ANTHROPOLOGY

Three centuries after the staging of the classical mind-set, after Corneille's invention of the Pollux character – prototypical budding anthropologist – Claude Lévi-Strauss, France's preeminent anthropologist ("the Dean of Structural Anthropology" / "de l'Académie française"),[42] implicitly admits to the hold of the classical ideological model on his imagination. In his meditative and despondent *Tristes Tropiques* of 1955, he found himself out in the field in Brazil, obsessed and casting about for a form for framing his worries: "Il me sembla que les problèmes qui me tourmentaient fournissaient la matière d'une pièce de théâtre."[43] ["It seemed to me that the problems which were tormenting me would furnish material for a play."] Lévi-Strauss attempted to take control of his anxieties by casting himself as the playwright, and specifically a playwright modelled after the cultural icon Corneille: "Ma pièce s'intitulait: 'L'Apothéose d'Auguste,' et se présentait comme une nouvelle version de *Cinna*."[44] ["My play was called: 'The Apotheosis of Augustus', and was presented as a new version of *Cinna*."] Note that in the French edition (unlike in the English translation), Lévi-Strauss has simply named the play, taking it for granted that everyone knows Corneille to be the author; such is the presumed hold of the classical canon on the French-educated.

That Lévi-Strauss should have found himself coping with his alienation in the wilds of Brazil by summoning up familiar memories of Corneille, and thinking his anguish out through the old schooldays paradigm, speaks worlds of his firm rooting in his own French culture despite his life-long project to immerse himself in and to know others. His distinguished career as student, teacher, traveler, cultural diplomat, anthropologist crowned by academic awards at home is rudimentarily prefigured in the character of Corneille's Pollux. Indeed, Lévi-Strauss's orientation is considered by anthropologists to be of a more literary bent than that of his contemporaries: "[*Tristes tropiques*] was philosophical, elegant, and worthy of reflection and rereading, destined to be taught in literature classes as a model of belles-lettres."[45] Corneille and Lévi-Strauss may thus have more in common as French literary figures than in any other regard, but in addition, they each, across the centuries, respectively, anticipated and played out through their writing the trajectories of the many seventeenth-century travelers who began in increasing numbers to mediate culturally and politically between their French homeland and the rest of the world?[46]

Studies of the development of the French collection of human knowledge as it accompanies the rise of the paired phenomena of exoticism and colonialism regularly skip the seventeenth century and also tend to overlook these activities in the more local Mediterranean basin.[47] More often than not, scholars make the leap from the standard springboard of Montaigne's "Des Cannibales" (Brazil) right over into the eighteenth century, lighting on Montesquieu's *Lettres persanes* (Persia), with just an occasional nod to Molière's *Le Bourgeois gentilhomme* (The Ottoman Empire).[48] What is so comforting and perhaps so wrong about this familiar story that we persist in telling ourselves and each other? And what is so disturbing about another paradigm, that could take into account the period of the seventeenth century? What do we gain and what do we lose in this shorthand? I maintain that what we sacrifice is the unwieldy and shifting messiness of a transitional period, but above all the embarrassing spectacle of the colonialist mentality in the making, at its practice stage and close to home. In order to attend to this construction in process, we cannot examine it as a moment in history that happened punctually. After all, had not the Greeks and the Romans, not to mention the Phoenicians, set the pattern of colonizing in this part of the world long before? But we need to investigate the dominant Western European ideological framework regarding entitlement over this period. We need to see how it was conducive to what would become the world-defining and shattering move of colony and then empire building of the early modern period.

It is roughly the period of the sixteenth and seventeenth centuries that the historian of anthropology Margaret Hodgen identifies as witnessing the birth of the "discipline" of anthropology, marked by "the progress from mere curiosity to scientific enquiry, with the development of specific categories of investigation and evolving hypotheses regarding the diversity and similarities of cultures, the sequence of high civilizations, and the course of cultural change."[49] And another historian of anthropology, G. E. Von Grunebaum, concurs, specifically with regard to early modern European travelers in the Ottoman world. He is attentive to their observing, writing, and reporting skills, and traces their emergence as models of what would become known as collectors of human knowledge, to be professionalized in the nineteenth century as anthropologists.[50]

The seventeenth century thus is viewed as a transitional period during which we see the emergence, refining, and proliferation of this new profile. And here, in this more local and immediate Mediterranean world, writing travelers were setting the standards for observation and analysis of the "Other." It is here that we see the clear emergence of anthropology as a vocation.

The literary historian Pierre Martino claims that there was a sudden surge of interest in the Levant among the French as of 1660,[51] although he earlier cites 1670, the date of the founding of the Compagnie du Levant as the inaugural date, and then states that it is the last

Frontispiece portrait of Jean Thévenot from *his Relation d'un voyage fait au Levant dans laquelle il est curieusement traité des Etats Sujets au Grand Seigneur, des Moeurs, Religions, Forces, Gouvernements, Politiques, Langues et Coustumes des Habitans de ce Grand Empire.* Paris: Lovis Bilaine, 1664. The traveler returned home and now local savant.

third of the seventeenth century that witnesses a significant growth in the exoticism industry (p. 173): "il y eut, vers 1660, un accord indéniable des circonstances et des oeuvres qui permit le brusque développement du goût exotique" (p. 356).[52] ["Around 1660, an undeniable combination of circumstances and published works gave rise to the rapid development of a taste for exoticism."] Yet Martino registers contradiction with himself as he proceeds carefully to note the earlier writings of Michel Baudier such as *L'Inventaire de l'histoire générale des Turcs* (1617), *Histoire générale du Sérail et de la Cour du Grand Seigneur* (1624), *Histoire générale de l'histoire de la religion des Turcs avec la naissance et la mort de leur prophète Mahomet* (1625) that indicate there is already a strong early French interest in this exotic culture. And the sixteenth century had witnessed important investigational contacts under the reigns of Francis the First and Soliman the Magnificent.

Labelling and "fetishizing," indeed all attempts at periodizing (merely a retrospective means of managing knowledge) must be viewed with some suspicion, not simply because they are so specific or in contradiction with one another, but also because these dates do not take into account the time lag between the actual travel dates of these many observers and the publication of their writings.[53] Chardin's *Voyages* came out in 1686, but he travelled between 1664 and 1677. D'Arvieux lived between 1635 and 1702; he started documenting his travels in 1653, but his *Mémoires* were not published until 1735. But news of these men's adventures, their own tales, had already circulated, and more information was in demand before the written accounts actually hit the press. We are looking at a transitional phenomenon here that is gently taking hold. We need to be attentive to it as such and less anxious to frame it or claim it with specific dates. Historical change takes place over time, fluidly, and sometimes even imperceptibly. The articulation of "anthropology" and specifically with regard to the "field" of the Levant took place discretely. The invention of the traveler–observer in the figure of Pollux for the theatre season of 1635 is only part of the story of the emergence of this new stock character, not just on the stage, but in the world. And for this reason the story of Medea was an old one, but one worth revisiting and rewriting in seventeenth-century France.

KNOWLEDGE AND GOODS ON THE MOVE

In order to evaluate Pollux and his role in Corneille's *Médée* as a useful early modern model of the anthropologist for the French seventeenth-century theatre audience, we need to examine his primary activities.

As an argonaut, he participates in the expedition to recover the Golden Fleece. As a by-product of this voyage to Médée's Colchis and subsequent travel in Asia, he accumulates and brings back knowledge of that part of the world and its ways. Upon his return he has occasion to offer his knowledge to his part of the world. As Lisa Jardine has elegantly demonstrated, the acquisition of knowledge and the accumulation of goods in Europe from the early Renaissance on, enabled by a significant increase in European capital (itself a consequence of expeditions across the Atlantic) and facilitation of travel, went hand in hand. Manuscripts, books, rare objets d'art, jewels, curios, exquisite fabrics, and worldly travelers flooded Europe shaping tastes, creating collectors and their collections, and profoundly affecting local knowledge.[54]

If Jardine focuses on material proof of this movement, the historian of science Bruno Latour theorizes this same activity in the early modern period.[55] According to him, "knowledge" is defined as "familiarity with events, places, and people seen many times over" (220). Each expedition will build on the knowledge brought home by the prior one. "Bringing home" requires the exotic to be mobile, stable, and combinable (223). A cycle of accumulation "allows a point to become a centre by acting at a distance on many other points" (222). This act, by implication, establishes a periphery as well.

The ancient Greeks, like the later seventeenth-century French, saw themselves as the centre, and other cultures as the periphery (32). Hence knowledge for them would be what they could accumulate in their own space about their periphery. Some of their myths, and notably the Jason and Medea tale, had to do with their earliest stories of collecting and establishing pre-eminence for themselves as center. What was gathered was not simply facts and figures, as Latour points out (225), but things, and in this case, also wardrobes. Collections furnished the stuff of and occasioned knowledge:

Things [were] extracted from their context and taken away during expeditions. Thus the history of science is in large part the history of the mobilization of anything that can be made to move and shipped back home for the universal census. The outcome, however, is that in many instances stability becomes a problem because many of these elements die – like the "happy savages" anthropologists never tire of sending to Europe. (225)

This is roughly the plot line of the "Golden Fleece"[56] and Medea stories together. Along with the restitution of the fleece to its Greek home-land, comes Medea – the volatile imported heroine (the anthropologist's "happy savage"), and with her her poison (which will mark Greek praxis as seen in the later story of Phaedra[57]), her "uncombinable" knowledge of the occult, and notably here, her "unstable" dangerous golden robe. A by-product of the expedition, and of further ones, is that Pollux's understanding of the ways of Médée and her world is significantly advanced. He has done his field work. Goods and knowledge have come home to roost, but, in Corneille's bleak vision here, the knowledge is of no avail and the goods are deadly.

Jason's retrieval of the fleece (a defamiliarized singular item with its own story, and of indisputably high symbolic value[58]) sets the scene for the bloody bartering of brides and murder of children to be staged back home in Greece. With its restitution, Greece can again proclaim itself center and Colchis periphery. However, with that coveted fleece have come the stranger Medea, her exotic patrimony and her fearful magic – more than Jason and his fellow Greeks had ever bargained for. Despite Pollux's cautions, these imports succeed in wreaking havoc with the local order. Along with repatriation will come importation and alienation. This woman, her belongings and her brand of knowledge, removed from their familiar world and introduced into the Greek one, destabilize and explode it. Here the guilt-stricken western imagination spins out its own punishment. If Pollux's travel-honed wisdom appears a possible boon at the crucial moment, we should remember that it has come as a direct spin-off of the earlier ugly tale of the Argonauts, and that it is ineffectual. Here we have the nightmare of the early modern scientist – concerned not so much with the effect of "collecting" on the periphery as on the center – and the bare-bones plot of much of today's science fiction.

Seventeenth-century travel was notable among the French for the windows it afforded on other cultures, windows that lent perspective to their own culture and imparted a form of worldly wisdom. It was also, and often primarily, motivated by a seeking of material goods, not only staple products such as skins, wheat, oil, or cotton, etc., but curios, mementos, manuscripts, medals, objects often of purely symbolic value, and rarities, precious gems, spices, fragrances, etc., of frivolous value. As Jason had brought back the fleece and Medea, so the seventeenth-century French set about in increasingly systematic fashion collecting, plundering, bringing back to Paris and organizing there things and information from the Orient. They extended the Renaissance humanist project, but ventured beyond the usual Greco-Roman terrain, as if that center (those neatly conflated capitals) had already been absorbed.

Despite the misgivings regarding precise dating discussed above, it is important to signal one scholar's belief that the very decade that saw the staging of *Médée* (1635) marks the moment of the intensification and acceleration of the acquisitive Orientalist movement in France to collect goods, hence of active aggression to establish that space as periphery. According to the scholar Henry Laurens, "Le mouvement naît réellement vers 1630–40."[59] ["The movement is truly born around 1630–40"] Laurens cites the archeological missions sent to the Orient by the French monarchy at this time to purchase manuscripts and curios. Cultural commerce thus operated as a form of conquest.

The French project of systematizing the collecting and centering process had already advanced with the establishment of the Royal Library in 1617, and would take further shape in the following decades through the establishment of the great trading companies, such as the Compagnie des Indes Orientales (1664) and the Compagnie du Levant (1670), the Académies (such as the Académie des Inscriptions, 1663), and the academic chairs consecrated to the study of oriental languages in the universities, as well as the Ecole des langues orientales (1669). As this movement became increasingly organized, the king would hire scholars specifically for this sort of task, such as Monsieur Vaillant, whose official title was "Médecin et Antiquaire du Roy." ["Doctor and Antiquarian to the King."] This man's sole mission was to travel through the Orient, to procure objects of value and of interest, and to bring them back to Versailles. Such would also be the case for Antoine Galland, the future translator of *Les Mille et une nuits*, sent by Colbert to buy manuscripts, rare medals, and coins.[60]

In addition, travelers eager to distinguish and ingratiate themselves were constantly on the lookout for rarities to enhance their own status or to offer to the king for that same purpose. These rarities were not always objects or manuscripts.[61] Sometimes they were maps, drawings, stories, bits of news, but the accumulation of this information, its attachments to its purveyors, transformed these persons into experts and, as they gravitated around royal power – attracted by the patronage system – repeatedly confirmed the centrality of the king and the shaping of a useful body of knowledge. As Erica Harth succinctly puts it:

From the 1660s on, voyagers began to constitute a new kind of insider . . . They possessed an expertise that was fast becoming the new basis of glory for the monarchy. They harbored a new scientific truth vital to the economic development of modern France.[62]

Individual savants entertained no illusions of producing knowledge in a vacuum, but were acutely aware of the fact that they were participating in a project larger than any one of them. They were intent to contribute to the development of a body of knowledge, to encourage its accumulation, and they competed in an increasingly informed manner to ensure both that they were not simply repeating one another and that their results would stand out. Up until then, it had been common (if not entirely condoned) practice to incorporate, without attribution, into one's own discourse, textual or otherwise, any and all information gleaned from other sources (consider, for example, the inclusive nature of André Thevet's writings).[63] This was no longer the acceptable case, even if plagiarism abounded. Monsieur du Loir, when he wrote his *Voyages*, specified that he was not recording everything he knew, but only what he knew had not yet been written down by anyone else: "Je me suis étudié particulièrement à ne remarquer que ce qui ne l'avait point encore été, ou qui ne l'avait pas été exactement."[64] ["I particularly applied myself to noting only what had not already been said, or what had not been said precisely."] And the artist Grelot would preface his book with the same claim, signaling its value in the originality of his drawings:

J'observois en toutes les Relations que je lisois, que la plûpart des remarques que j'avois faites estoient presque semblables à ce que tant d'illustres Voyageurs avoient donné au Public devant moy; & qu'à moins de vouloir passer comme beaucoup d'autres, ou pour copiste ou pour Plagiaire; je ne pouvois pas honnestement publier sous mon nom ce que plusieurs s'étoient déja attribuez. Mais enfin voyant que le grand nombre de Relations qui ont paru n'ont toutes ensemble donné pas un seul plan, élévation ou figure fidèle de tout ce qui est décrit dans celle-cy. J'ai resolu pour satisfaire à la curiosité de plusieurs personnes qui me font l'honneur de m'aimer, de faire graver quelques-uns des Plans et des Desseins que j'ay tirez dans le Levant.[65]

[I observed that in all the accounts I was reading, most of the remarks I had made were almost the same as what so many illustrious travelers had offered to the public before me; & unless I wanted to appear, like so many others, as either a copier or a plagiarist, I could not in all honesty publish under my name that which several had already attributed to themselves. But finally, upon seeing that among the great number of accounts which have appeared, none present a single map, sketch or faithful representation of what is described therein, I resolved to satisfy the curiosity of several friends, and to have engravings made of some of the maps and drawings which I did while in the Levant.]

The importing of objects bespeaks a materialistic grasp. It manifests itself early on in Greek civilization and is passed on into the western

mindset through the hallowed medium of the myth. The mentality
and behavior it organizes thus constitutes an unquestioned given of
seventeenth-century travelers. Furthermore, along the same materialistic model, objects, knowledge, and persons are interchangeably equated,
commodified, and marketed. The collusion of artists, scholars, poets,
traders, administrators, and teachers that this economy requires will
proceed to play out on an ever greater scale over the centuries in relations between France and other parts of the world. In the transitional
seventeenth century the mechanisms of French colonialism are just shifting into place. It is thanks to the Golden Fleece that Pollux makes his
first voyage into Asia and has his first-hand experience of Médée, her
world and her ways. Thus it is that an "interested" material quest will
occasion the "disinterested" knowledge that sets his persona as a staged
exemplar of the new breed of anthropologist.

"THE PLAY'S THE THING"

As I have said, Corneille also brought the Orient home. He appropriated
the familiar myth as a vehicle for examining these mechanisms, their
operators, and the consequences. The story of Medea was familiar to
theatre audiences, at least in broad strokes; so it was not in anticipation
of a new story line that they came to see the play, but rather to see
what the playwright had done with the received version to speak to
them of their times. Corneille acknowledges only the two most ancient
and most prestigious sources for his play, Euripides and Seneca, and
thereby strategically aligns himself among the greats. But what is striking
is that he takes a radical departure from both of them with barely any
acknowledgment of his innovation and without indicating any major
reason for it.

POLLUX

In Corneille's version, the new character, Pollux, replaces the traditional
chorus of sympathetic Corinthian women to whom Médée's nurse (in
Euripides) or Médée herself (in Seneca) confides her woes, thereby laying
out the fabric of the plot. Corneille makes few claims for the need to
eliminate the Chorus[66] or for Pollux's particular usefulness, other than
that he has been away, and so needs to be informed by Jason, upon
his arrival, of recent events. While in the earlier versions, the chorus
of women and Médée's old nurse identify readily if uneasily with the

wronged Médée, the new Pollux might be expected to align himself with his friend Jason. Either way, a jury situation is automatically set up by the classical dramatic constraints of form. Corneille puts Pollux in place to hear the case of Jason and Médée:

Pollux est de ces Personnages protatiques qui ne sont introduits que pour écouter la narration du Sujet. Je pense l'avoir déjà dit, et j'ajoute que ces Personnages sont d'ordinaire assez difficiles à imaginer dans la Tragédie, parce que les événements publics et éclatants dont elle est composée sont connus de tout le monde, et que s'il est aisé de trouver des gens qui les sachent pour les raconter, il n'est pas aisé d'en trouver qui les ignorent pour les entendre. C'est ce qui m'a fait avoir recours à cette fiction que Pollux depuis son retour de Colchos avait toujours été en Asie, où il n'avait rien appris de ce qui s'était passé dans la Grèce que la Mer en sépare. ("Examen" of 1660, 538)

[Pollux is one of those protatic characters who are introduced only for the purpose of listening to the narration of the Subject-matter. I believe I have already said so, and I add that these characters are ordinarily quite difficult to incorporate into tragedy, because everyone knows about the public and astonishing events which compose it, and if it is easy to find people familiar with these events and who can talk about them, it is not easy to find those unaware of them and thus disposed to listen. This is why I have recourse to the fiction that since his return from Colchis Pollux had been in Asia, where he had heard nothing of what happened in Greece, since the two are separated by the sea.]

Pollux finds himself in the paradoxical position of being knowledgeable since he has traveled in Asia, but ignorant (and therefore useful to Corneille) with regard to current events at home.

Corneille does not pause before this interesting situation. Indeed, he seems so inattentive to Pollux as to actually blur his character's story: just above he claims that Pollux had remained in Asia after the Golden Fleece expedition, whereas in the play his character Pollux has stated that he had been back in Corinth just before a new trip to Asia (1.1.51–52). This degree of insouciance regarding the activities of a character who is, after all, a significant innovation on the received story rings curiously coming from a playwright who elsewhere takes such pride in his inventiveness.

In his "Trois Discours du poème dramatique," Corneille's concerns are of a purely dramaturgical nature, and therefore it is understandable that he does not focus more closely on Pollux's novel profile; nevertheless, it stands out that, here again, he will not touch on the crucial ideological and moral purpose that his new character serves in the play. Perhaps it was invisible, even to him:

Il passe par Corinthe en allant au mariage de sa soeur, et s'étonne d'y rencontrer Jason qu'il croyait en Thessalie; il apprend de lui sa fortune, et son divorce avec

Médée, pour épouser Creüse, qu'il aide ensuite à sauver des mains d'Egée qui l'avait fait enlever, et raisonne avec le Roi sur la défiance qu'il doit avoir des présents de Médée.[67]

[He goes by Corinth en route to his sister's wedding, and is astonished to find Jason there, believing him to be in Thessaly; he hears what has happened to him, his divorce from Médée in order to marry Creüse, whom he then helps escape from the hands of Egée who had kidnapped her, and he reasons with the King about the suspicions he ought to have concerning Médée's gifts.]

Thus Pollux to all appearances is simply fulfilling a mechanical need to be the unknowing recent arrival in need of and also worthy of elucidation. His arrival allows for the exposition of the facts leading up to the action of the play.

But the corollary disappearance of the women of Corinth leaves Médée more alone than ever. Gone is the chorus that understood her grief, appreciated her predicament, sought to console her, to integrate her in their world. Gone also is her nurse from childhood. Instead of being cared for by the wise old woman and befriended by the women of Corinth, Médée stands alone, and herself takes responsibility for the welfare of her only companion Nerine. She has become a singular creature in every way, less representative of womankind and more similar to the exhibits of "happy savages" being imported from the new world in Corneille's day.[68] She stands out as more of a freak since no other women save her timorous servant Nerine occupy the stage to double her; the king's daughter Creüse only heightens the contrast. Médée here is the absolute alien "barbare."

If this Médée is more isolated, she is also more reasonable, more resourceful than her earlier avatars. It is clear that a lawyer turned playwright is weighing, examining, and pleading her cause. In the "Epître" of 1639 (the play had come out in 1634–35 and was only then being published), Corneille still expresses concern that his play be properly understood, not as an unqualified praise of Médée, but as an example of these "belles imitations d'une action qu'il ne faut pas imiter" (535). ["these beautiful representations of an action that must not be imitated."] That is, he has not advocated behavior, but attitude. However, by the "Examen" of 1660, he will vaunt the apparent success of his plea: "Médée . . . attire si bien de son côté toute la faveur de l'Auditoire qu'on excuse sa vengeance" (540). ["Médée . . . so garners the Audience's entire sympathy that her vengeance is excused."] Although she is staged alone now, her radical isolation permits a stronger and more forceful portrayal of this wronged woman.

What else is gained? Pollux will be billed as "Argonaute, ami de Jason" in the list of the cast of characters (540). His loyalty to his friend is clearly stated; it is the constituent aspect of his role. He demonstrates through his words that he knows Jason well, and he remains loyal to him even if he disapproves of his actions. He has traveled with him in the past, and shared in his adventures. He has taken due note of the fact that each of Jason's amorous liaisons has involved conquests and political gain:

> Hypsipyle à Lemnos, sur le Phase Médée,
> Et Creüse à Corinthe autant vaut possédée
> Font bien voir qu'en tous lieux sans lancer d'autres dards
> Les sceptres sont acquis à ses moindres regards.
>
> (1.1.21–24)

[Hypsipyle in Lemnos, Médée in Phasis / And Creüse soon to be wed in Corinth / All well show that everywhere, with no other weapon / Than the merest of his glances, he gains scepters.]

If Pollux suspends judgment on Jason's behavior, it is out of the loyalty of friendship; he is certainly not blind to his friend's weaknesses, but he is the reliable friend. His own decency of character serves as a foil to point up the inadequacy of Jason's. Jason doesn't deserve such a fine person for a friend, but the playwright may need him to highlight the hero's failings, and this in order to plead Médée's cause more effectively. Pollux's voice, supporting Médée's own defense, not the husband's or the king's, serves as vehicle for the didactic legalistic case that Corneille constructs as he restages the moral trial of Medea.

In fact, Pollux proves to be pivotal: he is the most prescient of the characters, the wisest, and plays an important role throughout the play in making astute observations and offering timely warnings, even if they go unheeded. As friend to Jason, he has spent enough time with him and observed his behavior long enough that he is able to guess his actions and even his motives before they are spelled out for him ("Sans l'entendre nommer je l'avais deviné. / Jason ne fit jamais de communes maîtresses" [1.1.16–17]). ["Without hearing her named, I had guessed it / Jason never had ordinary mistresses."] And he hasn't been completely out of touch with events in Greece. He had been up to date on Jason's and Médée's doings (e.g., the rejuvenation of Jason's father) until called away:

> Ce fut, s'il m'en souvient, ici que je l'appris,
> D'où soudain un voyage en Asie entrepris
> Fait que, nos deux séjours divisés par Neptune,
> Je n'ai point su depuis quelle est votre fortune.
>
> (1.1.51–54)

[It was, if I recall, here that I heard about it, / Then I undertook a sudden trip to Asia, / And thus, since our journeys were divided by the sea, / I have not been able to find out what became of you.]

The suddenness ("soudain") of Pollux's departure suggests both his own importance and the urgency of the situation – he was needed elsewhere, and so stepped away from his own familiar surroundings where news of his friend circulated, and he remained only indirectly in touch. Also, man on the move that he is, and carrier of so much information, Pollux remembers having heard the story of Médée's rejuvenation of Jason's father, but cannot pinpoint exactly where he heard it ("ce fut ici, s'il m'en souvient"). Here is the sketch of a worldly, traveling man with, perhaps, more important things on his mind.

Pollux could be likened to an early model for the anthropologist who travels into another community, becomes absorbed in that local culture, loses contact with his own, and needs to be apprised of what is happening upon his return. His perspective on events at home may indeed be sharpened as a consequence of his absence and experience elsewhere. He remains sufficiently anchored in his own culture that he can notice gaps, differences, infractions against the norms of that culture because those norms have become that much more visible to him in contrast with others which he has had occasion to observe. In fact, his ability to assess, his sensitivity to difference furnishes the core methodology of his new empirical science. Here we see the role of the collector of human knowledge once back on the home horizon.

It is consequential that Pollux should have been away in Asia specifically. For the Greek polis, this alien space was already staked out for colonialist expansion and therefore needed to be brought into local discourse, first subjected to a narrative, as part of that project.[69] Euripides particularly favored and practiced the dramatic staging of such inclusion (116). Asia was the cultural space featured as "Other" at the time of the first versions of Medea. And through Corneille, seventeenth-century France appropriated and repeated the ancient gesture.

But if Corneille's eye was on a mythic Asia, the Ottoman exotic was certainly one potential, handy referent. And on his public's mind. It was neither too close nor too far away – it was a familiar but formidable exotic, a nearby periphery, distant enough in space, if not in time (as with other current theatre subjects such as the revered ancients Alexander and Darius) to be subject to critical analysis. And the immediate exotic – the "Other within" – communities of Jews, Huguenots, Rosicrucians,

Freemasons, etc., within the hexagon, was apparently too threatening to the building of French collective identity and therefore not admissible on the French stage. The French had not yet achieved sufficient critical distance and established sufficient national identity to examine their own complex population. On the other hand, more distant new worlds and peoples (of the Americas, of the Far East) were coming into focus, but they were usually experienced as so alien as to remain for a time beyond the ready possibility of narrative inclusion of the more local and familiar Mediterranean "Other" with whom the French had regularly to contend.[70] And they were not yet admissible on the stage according to the tenets of classical theatre that the French followed and practiced.[71]

The contemporary Ottoman exotic was unlike the Chinese, the Siamese, the Indian, the Persian, the Caribbean, or the North American, in that it was close at hand, and, for purposes of trade and commerce, had to be negotiated by a significant number of French subjects on a daily basis. Locally exotic, as we have discussed in the Introduction, the Mediterranean contact zone was subject to a specific theory and praxis of proxemics, in the service of personal and national enrichment. It behooved both individuals and the state to take into account the particular ways of this culture and to proceed accordingly. Pollux constitutes a handy model for the go-between.[72] Having been outside of his own community, he is better able to see it for what it is once he returns, and, having had contact with this other world, he can attempt to help his own to contend with it. His view of how things should be is firmly grounded in the ethical code mapped out in his own home territory. Even if he is familiar with many cultures, he is the product of a specific one, and he assesses life accordingly.

Pollux furnishes the model of the worldly savant who will negotiate between these varied cultural spaces. As such he plays many roles: ethical adviser, loyal friend, correct guest, effective defender. Jason consults him as his conscience. He seeks his opinion, argues his case before him, and appeals to him for understanding, as if Pollux had some sort of privileged relationship to justice, and can exonerate him from guilt if he will only condone his behavior: "Qu'eussé-je fait, Pollux, en cette extrémité / Qui commettait ma vie avec ma loyauté?" (1.1.127–28). ["In this extremity, Pollux, what could I have done / Without compromising my life and my loyalty?"] Not only loyal, Pollux will prove also to be a shrewd judge of character. He reacts unequivocally to the news Jason shares with him at the outset. When Jason announces that he is about to marry, Pollux's reaction is short and to the point: "Quoi! Médée est donc morte à ce compte?"

(1.1.7). ["What! Médée, then, is dead?"] The only condition under which
he could imagine Jason marrying again is if Médée were to be dead. If
Jason is marrying, then she must be. She is not a wife to be ignored;
she is a powerful woman ("Dieux! et que fera-t-elle?" [1.1.9] ["Great
gods! And what will she do?"] – note that the question is not the given of
"whether she will do something," but, more starkly and to the point, the
ominous "what?").[73] Pollux is immediately sensitive to the greater consequences of Jason's behavior. Quite simply, he sees further than Jason,
and this because he has seen more, repeatedly, or for a longer stretch.

Even worldly Pollux is horrified to learn about Médée's manipulation
of Pelie's daughters. She had slyly promised them that they could reju-
venate their father just as she had done for Jason's father, if they would
follow her instructions. Instead, she led them to kill their father (1.1.89–
92). Despite Pollux's shock at Médée's murderous behavior, he levels his
moral code just as frankly against Jason for abandoning her. This behavior is unworthy (if not atypical) according to the moral code they share
and that should govern Jason's behavior. The act of leaving Médée is
lowly and ungrateful ("Je ne puis toutefois l'approuver qu'à demi. / Sur
quoi que vous fondiez un traitement si rude, / C'est toujours vers Médée
un peu d'ingratitude. / Ce qu'elle a fait pour vous est mal récompensé"
[1.1.140–43]).[74] ["I can, however, hardly approve it. / On whatever you
may choose to base such rude treatment, / It still shows ingratitude to
Médée. / What she did for you is badly recompensed."]

It turns out that Pollux knows Jason's wife better than Jason himself
does. Not only does he find Jason's behavior toward Médée ignoble, he
also recognizes the danger in affronting this woman. Here we have an
idealizing and instructive contrast between the prototype of the knowing
anthropologist and the insensitive adventurer. This man, just returned
from Asia, Médée's land, and not her own husband, appears to know
her best. He alone understands and dreads her powers. Jason can only
tell little stories, recount anecdotes about his travels and make limited
observations, about even his wife. Pollux on the other hand, can see
patterns, contextualize, generalize, theorize, and even predict. He, the
more seasoned traveler, the more knowing man, recognizes the possible
consequences of Jason's opportunism as of the gravest concern. He does
not hesitate to tell his friend that his repudiation of Médée is dangerous
as well as unjust. Along with accrued information, a certain degree of
detachment may be necessary to evaluate the situation with such sang-
froid as this (do we have here a pre-cartesian model of scientific objectivity
and neutrality?) Not only is Pollux not married to Médée or in love with

her, neither is he in love with the king's daughter or throne as is Jason, so he is not blinded by emotions or ambitions. The injustice of the situation may be a personal affair to be argued among the two friends, but the danger is a matter for state concern, and calls for alert at the highest level.

After his reunion with his friend, Pollux will proceed to pay his respects to his official host, the king of Corinth. Thus the more personal contact is followed by the demands of protocol: "Permettez cependant qu'afin de m'acquitter / J'aille trouver le Roi pour l'en féliciter" (1.3.151–52). ["Nonetheless, allow me to do my duty / And go find the King to congratulate him."] Pollux's visit then is not simply an opportunity to catch up with an old friend, but takes on the frame of a state visit. "Un soin officieux" (1.3.155) ["An official concern"] requires that he pay his respects to Creon. And as a responsible citizen / guest, Pollux will sound the warning note to Creon: "Appréhendez pourtant, grand Prince" (4.2.1105). ["Beware, however, great Prince."] Apparently, Pollux feels no conflict between his obligations to ties of friendship with Jason and those to the state with Creon, but behaves neutrally, guided only by his conscience. Both personal and civic duty dictate his behavior upon his return to his native culture, and immediately upon acquitting his personal duty, he must act in relation to the state.

When Aegée attempts to kidnap Creon's daughter, it is Pollux who comes to the rescue. He, and not Jason the high-profile hero, restores order. He returns Creüse to her father, and by the same coup returns Jason's betrothed to him; he destroys Aegée's best soldiers and puts him into prison (4.2.1069–76). Creon sings his praises ("Invincible héros . . . "[4.2.1071]). Of course Pollux diplomatically returns the compliment, and credits the king and Jason with the victory over this insurrection ("Grand Roi, l'heureux succès de cette délivrance / Vous est beaucoup mieux dû qu'à mon peu de vaillance" [1077–78]). ["Great King, the happy outcome of this rescue / Is much more due to you than to my little valor."] Courteous, courageous, sensitive, self-effacing, attentive to personal and to civic duties, here is how the ideal traveler-savant returned home behaves. If Pollux is too good to be true, that is precisely the point. Let us not lose sight of his role as very paragon for the new wave of travelers. He immediately puts his skills and knowledge at the service of his society. He enters into the unspoken laws of hospitality, not as they obligate the host, but as they dictate the guest's behavior. They are the laws of the land.

Pollux is neither a total guest – he belongs to this Greek society generally; nor is he a total insider – he is not a Corinthian (he will leave before the dénouement to attend his sister's wedding to Menelaus in another region). Thus, he is at once detached and engaged; but his general fealty is to this Western part of the world. Creon feels the state is safe as long as Pollux is on hand to look out for it ("Qu'avons-nous plus à craindre et quel destin jaloux / Tant que nous vous aurons s'osera prendre à nous?" [4.2.1103–04]). ["What more have we to fear, and what jealous Fate / Will dare attack us as long as we have you?"] Pollux has demonstrated his own courage and strength of character – which should guarantee that his warning about Médée be taken seriously. But, though Creon values Pollux, he is lulled into complacency by the false illusion of control, blinded by the local cultural values of authority and honor. Pollux's warnings will fall on deaf ears.

It is not simply Pollux's military strength that renders him valuable to the state; it is his superior cultural knowledge – if Creon would only listen. Creon thinks he has the situation in hand since he has ordered that Médée must leave Corinth within twenty-four hours. But Pollux, who knows Médée's cultural Scythian self well, appreciates precisely that Médée is not bound to local authority and local relations.[75] Further, her magic is not constrained by time ("C'est peu pour une femme, et beaucoup pour son art" [4.2.1120]). ["That is little time for a woman, and a great deal for her craft."] Pollux attempts to convey to the king the danger he sees ahead: "Si vous ne craignez rien, que je vous trouve à plaindre." (4.3.1142). ["If you fear nothing, then I think you are to be pitied."]

He specifically warns Creon against the gift of the robe that Médée has agreed to offer to Creüse (4.3.1144–46), invoking a general maxim of suspicion, and cites as evidence his own personal knowledge of Médée's power: "Je connais de Médée et l'esprit et les charmes." ["I am familiar with both Médée's mind and her spells."] (4.3.1146), and is willing to wager his own life that this gift is a deathtrap.[76] From experience, he has gleaned a general maxim, based on simple cost-benefit analysis, to govern desire in perilous circumstances: "Où le péril égale, et passe le plaisir, / Il faut se faire force, et vaincre son désir." ["Where danger equals, and surpasses pleasure / You must hold back, and conquer your desire."] (4.3.1159–60). He offers this wisdom to Creon, but it will go unheeded by the obstinate king ("Ma parole est donnée et je la veux garder" [4.2.1120]). ["My word is given and I intend to keep it."]

Through sensitivity developed and tested in foreign parts, Pollux divines the future and accurately predicts that Médée will wreak her vengeance on Jason through their children. He knows her mind, and can imagine just how she will react to Jason's perfidy. He foretells her revenge: "Peut-être que contre eux s'étend sa trahison, / Qu'elle ne les prend plus que pour ceux de Jason, / Et qu'elle s'imagine . . ." (4.3.1151–53). ["Maybe her betrayal will extend to them / Taking them to be merely Jason's children / And she may imagine . . ."] He hypothesizes correctly what the stranger in their midst will say and do. Able to enter into Médée's logic without once encountering her in the course of the play, Pollux functions like a premonitory shadow. His general knowledge and his specific warnings alert the spectator to side with no one character, but to remain disengaged in the observer position like the one he models. If Creon does not avail himself of such prudent and knowledgeable counsel, it is not for Pollux's lack of trying. Here at home, and within the play, the traveler-savant becomes the voice in the wilderness – a local Cassandra – proclaiming the self-evident, what no one else can see. Or wants to see.[77] Except of course the privileged spectator who stands in a position to assess the general situation and is guided by the wisdom of Pollux.

Creon, blinded by paternal desire to satisfy his daughter's eagerness for Médée's robe, proceeds in what he considers a sufficiently prudent manner, but his daughter's materialistic ways, his son-in-law-to-be's political maneuvering, and his own lack of wisdom bring down the conflagration upon them all. Pollux's knowledge has fallen on deaf ears and gone unheeded. The insight and advice of the anthropologist at the service of the state do not save that state, but make its downfall appear all the more foolish – and tragic.

Thus, despite Corneille's claims for the mere convenience of Pollux's presence as the newly arrived figure who must be brought up with current events, a situation that allows for educating the audience as well, Pollux enjoys great stature and plays a key role in the play. No one takes advantage of the superior knowledge and insight he tries repeatedly to share; no one heeds his warnings. The consequences are disastrous for all. He never meets with Médée in the course of the play, or shares the stage with her and Jason together, or with her and Creon. For the audience, experientially, this fact of non-contact enhances his scientific stature. He knows her best, not because he has had personal dealings with her, but because he knows Asia, the place of the "Other," where she's coming from.

For her part, how does Médée see Pollux? She sees him simply as one of the many young men ("tous vos Argonautes") ["All your Argonauts"] that she rescued when they had intruded on and sought to plunder her homeland:[78]

> Je ne me repens point d'avoir par mon adresse
> Sauvé le sang des Dieux, et la fleur de la Grèce,
> Zéthès, et Calaïs, et Pollux et Castor,
> Et le charmant Orphée, et le sage Nestor,
> Tous vos héros enfin tiennent de moi la vie.
>
> (2.2.433–37)

[I do not repent of having used my abilities / To save those in whose veins flows the blood of gods, the flower of Greece, / Zéthès , and Calaïs, and Pollux and Castor, / And the charming Orpheus, and the wise Nestor, / All your heros, in the end, owe me their life.]

Here Pollux is paired with his twin brother, and grouped with a band of adventurers led by Jason, one of many, a discreet profile that allows him to blend anonymously in with the others. There is nothing about him to draw attention to himself, and as such his powers of observation are not affected by a particular role, an unusual heroics. He can see without being seen, observe from the sidelines and take in the full picture. If he were to be singled out and caught up in particular action, his observational powers would be compromised, and his perceptions more suspect. Médée is unaware of Pollux's good fix on her, and her ignorance of this is important to Pollux's freedom to share his knowledge of her with impunity.

Corneille's invention of Pollux corresponds to the emerging profile of the traveler/observer/participant who remains tied to his own native culture, whose ultimate destination and tie to his homeland is family. He travels abroad on unspecified missions, brings his acquired knowledge home, and attempts to offer it to the service of friends and the state.[79] We see in this new staged profile a discreet reflection of a new breed of person that was becoming increasingly common in the seventeenth century, that called for attention, to which Corneille responded in his apparently unwitting construction of this new character. Pollux is a precursor of the subject who gathers knowledge of other cultures, other ways, and offers his new empirical and not bookish wisdom to the use of the state – the explorer/adventurer/diplomat . . . anthropologist – whose words go unheeded. Significantly, the state will increasingly incorporate this "innocent" knowledge into its own apparatus, using it to establish, expand, and protect its interests abroad, in other climates. Today's more wary anthropologist must take into account who ultimately stands to profit from work done in the field. In the history of the discipline, the anthropologist has been both the instrument of the state and the sub-versive critic. Pollux prefigures both roles.[80] This Corneillian invention finally, in a larger sense, summons up the entwined mythological and astronomical roles of the twin stars, Castor and Pollux – orienting stars for navigators, saviors in distant lands, and above all protectors at sea – in short, guiding lights for travelers.

TRAVEL

As for Médée, she remains per force the volatile import. All human spaces are closed to her since she has cast her lot with Jason. She who has traveled so widely and who knows so much, because she has subordinated herself in this relationship to Jason's ambitions, and in so doing has transgressed moral code after moral code (including her native one), finds herself without home and without refuge:[81]

> Irai-je sur le Phase où j'ai trahi mon père
> Apaiser de mon sang les Mânes de mon frère?
> Irai-je en Thessalie où le meurtre d'un Roi
> Pour victime aujourd'hui ne demande que moi?
> Il n'est pas de climat dont mon amour fatale
> N'ait acquis à mon nom la haine générale,
> Et ce qu'ont fait pour vous mon savoir et ma main
> M'a fait un ennemi de tout le genre humain.
>
> (3.3.789–96)

[Will I go to Phasis where I betrayed my father / To appease my brother's shades with my blood? / Will I go to Thessaly where the murder of a King Now requires only me for a victim? / There is no country where my fatal love / Has not added general hatred to my name, / And what my knowledge and my hands have done for you / Has made me an enemy of all humankind.]

We know that, grateful for the intervention of her magic, Aegée has offered her safe haven in Athens, and his hand.[82] But whether she takes him up on his offer is not within the scope of Corneille's play. If, in the end, she takes flight in her chariot, soaring into the air, this solution is the effect of her magic, not of her relations with people. She circulates without lighting. "Climat" here refers not merely to geographic place, but, more generally, to human climate, general opinion, social acceptance.[83] For Médée there is no longer a place in society, any society. She stands apart as a complete outcast, but her presence still hovers over the world she has left behind. Indeed, her perceived absence constitutes that world's very limits and sense of itself. Her absent presence confirms the meaning of the term "foreign." She is the "barbare," the freak, the outsider who reassures all others of their normalcy – their insider status.[84]

Médée circulates freely in the Western imagination, enjoying access to landscapes unknown to others. When she has finished preparing the poisonous potion that will permeate the robe and destroy her rival and her enemy (Creüse and Creon), she describes its quintessentially exotic composition to her servant Nerine in incantatory tones, invoking the far reaches of a complex world from which she has drawn her materials – snakes from Africa, the tongue of a harpy, the blood of the Hydra, etc., all speculative space for the imaginary. But she also alludes to another mysterious landscape:

> Ces herbes ne sont pas d'une vertu commune,
> Moi-même en les cueillant je fis pâlir la lune,
> Quand, les cheveux flottants, le bras et le pied nu,
> J'en dépouillais jadis un climat inconnu.
>
> (4.1.993–96)

[These herbs have no common powers / I myself made the moon turn pale when I gathered them / With flowing hair, with bare arms and feet, / I gathered them in an unknown land.]

To find her magic herbs, Médée has traveled where no one else has been. Here "climat" suggests less a society and less a place, a strange geography beyond the margins of even the exotic world, beyond even her native Colchis. But this place is not necessarily located to the east of Colchis, further into Asia. It floats, as does her hair, somewhere under the sign of the moon, and there are no clues for getting there. This is the climate of the occult, more a mood than a place or a people, the imagined space of the radical and irrecuperable "Other."[85]

Stripped first of her marital status and then having sundered her maternal identity which had tied her, however precariously, into the fabric of Greek society, Médée comments sarcastically on the sentence of banishment pronounced on her, which condemns her once again to travel, but this time alone, unhinged, and without purpose except such as she might choose to assign to it:

> On ne m'a que bannie! ô bonté souveraine!
> C'est donc une faveur et non pas une peine!
> Je reçois une grâce au lieu d'un châtiment!
> Et mon exil encor doit un remerciement!
>
> (3.3.845–48)

[I've only been banished! O sovereign goodness! / It's a favor then, and not a punishment! / I receive grace instead of condemnation! / And my exile again means I owe thanks!]

In an ironic turn of justice, Jason, from adventurer and plunderer, from presumed heir to the crown of Corinth, also finds himself plunged back – in the aftermath of Médée's crime – into the uncertainty of nomadism, this time without the useful protection of Médée's magic. In this precolonial era, nomadism has not yet been celebrated as a desirable state. Bereft of family, of place, of direction, reduced to the very state he had willed upon his spurned wife, he proceeds to interrogate himself feebly on how to proceed to avenge the deaths of Creüse and the children:

> Creüse, enfants, Médée, amour, haine, vengeance,
> Où dois-je désormais chercher quelque allégeance,
> Où suivre l'inhumaine, et dessous quels climats
> Porter les châtiments de tant d'assassinats?
>
> (5.5.1617–20)

[Creüse, children, Médée, love, hatred, vengeance, / Where can I henceforth find some allegiance, / Where can I follow this inhuman woman, and in what countries / Can I execute the punishment of so many assassinations?]

"Climats" here suggests a bewildering multiplicity of travel directions for Jason to pursue as he would attempt to catch up with Médée. But his thought remains a question, one to which there is no answer. His own punishment consists precisely in living out this vain pursuit. He faces ceaseless travel to far-flung places for naught, hopeless wandering, vagabondage. Significantly, this had been Médée's angry wish for him, her curse:

> Qu'il coure vagabond de Province en Province,
> Qu'il fasse lâchement la Cour à chaque Prince,
> Banni de tous côtés, sans biens, et sans appui.
>
> (1.3.217–19)

[May he run like a vagabond from province to province / May he basely court the favor of every prince, / Banished from all sides, without possessions, and without aid.]

This life of exile, of nomadism, of banishment, of flight, of perpetual motion, is precisely the one she and Jason had known together. As a couple, they had been able to negotiate such peripatetics together, but their fragile union come to cross-purposes could not withstand the pressures of either of their native cultures. To a Dante-like punishment and to a search for revenge doomed to failure from the start, Jason will prefer death by his own hand (5.5.1651–53).

Médée's own state of abandonment in Corinth represents a moment of alienated stasis for her, but also a precise mirroring of the situation in which Jason finds himself by the end of the play:

> Jason m'a fait trahir mon pays et mon père,
> Et me laisse au milieu d'une terre étrangère,
> Sans support, sans amis, sans retraite, sans bien,
> La fable de son peuple et la haine du mien.
>
> (1.4.293–96)

[Jason caused me to betray my country and my father / And he leaves me in the midst of a foreign land, / Without help, without friends, without a home, without possessions / The talk of his people and hated by my own.]

Fatherland, family, friends, spouse, safety, and a material base – these are the mainstays of identity and the source of well-being. They are totally missing both to Médée and to Jason by the end of the tragedy. They are also the cornerstones of the idea of nationhood, premised on a sense of belonging which is fostered by webbings of the above-mentioned ties, and it is this idea that Médée – seduced into betrayal and consequent loss of honor – has made impossible. In breaking with her family to help and flee with Jason, she had broken with her own country; and in breaking with his, Jason has reproduced the same alienation. They have broken with the social contract. The two are no longer grounded – they are reduced to the status of adventurers, depending on the kindness of others, but ultimately on their own wits, and here Médée has the obvious advantage over Jason.

Médée, without a country and without a partner, falls back on her only resource: "Moi, / Moi, dis-je, et c'est assez" (1.4.316–17). ["Me, / Me, I say, and that is enough."] She believes her ego to be her sole but sufficient hope. Médée must both protect and avenge herself in her moment of abandonment; she is reduced to pure ego, but a tried and strong one.[86] In her predicament, she has only herself to fall back on, but this self is a real resource. However, precisely what Médée will lack and which all her ego cannot avail, without which her "moi" is for naught, is context, place, situation.

For his part, Jason expresses no regret at leaving his homeland, just as he has no regret for loves that have outlived their usefulness. He simply moves on and seeks to attach himself to the next love, the next country. Thus his final harangue invoking noble reasons of state rings hollow, argued as it is from his personal, contingent interest. Jason is all context,

Médée all ego. With regard to questions of the state, his womanizing and self-serving opportunism have proven as destabilizing and anarchic as Médée's magic and vengefulness. Their mutual recriminations come from radically different positions despite their shared history.

Jason first departed on a quest, then returned to his homeland. For her part, Médée accompanied Jason and in so doing fled her own country. They escaped from Thessaly and found refuge in Corinth. Although they both traveled together, Jason and Medea were not thereby always engaging in the same act. Their relations to space were fundamentally distinct. These different nuances of movement suggest the complicated motivations that color the act of travel. To these are added yet two other significant ones: banishment and wandering. Both of these are presented as negative, because they bespeak a lack of purpose – the person is not useful to the state, is indeed harmful, therefore must be expelled. Likewise, wandering is without aim or goal. Because it does not organize itself in terms of a movement away from and then back towards a centre, it is without value. For travel to be of value, it must be in the service of materially or symbolically gainful, or somehow negotiable pursuit, whether that be in the form of things, people or knowledge, and the value depends on bringing it home. It is instead to valueless travel – alienating banishment and pointless wandering – that Médée and Jason condemn each other.

The above examples illustrate the importance of the motif of travel in the play, and point to the interest of problematizing this activity for an increasingly mobile seventeenth-century theatre audience.[87] Only Pollux is wise, because he has ventured abroad and returned in a purposeful manner; he arrives at the right time and he also knows when to leave, taking his departure just before Médée's revenge begins. He does what he can while there, renewing his friendship with Jason, assisting his host Creon against Aégée, sharing his worldly wisdom with both his friend Jason and his liege Creon. Nor does he appear surprised when his admonitions are not heeded. All of this Pollux knows and does because he has spent time in the Orient, in Asia. He has been there not once but twice. His knowledge of the "Other" sets his wise purposefulness, and constitutes the value of his presence in the play.

MÉDÉE'S GOLDEN ROBE

Although Pollux is the wisest, the most stable gatherer, a gatherer of wisdom, Médée, the stranger, also imports – in a more material sense. In Corneille's play, Médée's robe, as in the earlier classical versions, plays a key role in the story of the couple's undoing in Corinth.[88] This is the sole object Médée had brought with her as she fled from her homeland of Colchis, and it is all that remains of her patrimony, a patrimony which, significantly, is itself the result of her father's local plundering:

> Des trésors dont son père épuise la Scythie
> C'est tout ce qu'elle a pris quand elle en est sortie.
>
> (2.4.573–74)

[Of the treasures her father depleted from Scythia / It was all that she took when she left.]

Now that Médée is disgraced and about to be banished, she must also be despoiled. Jason's bargaining logic casts the robe as only an encumbrance that can be exchanged against a more useful currency, when he persuades Nerine to intervene and ask for the garment on the part of Creüse:

> Sa robe dont l'éclat sied mal à sa fortune,
> Et n'est à son exil qu'une charge importune,
> Lui gagnerait le coeur d'un Prince libéral,
> Et de tous ses trésors l'abandon général.
> Elle peut aisément d'une chose inutile
> Semer pour sa retraite une terre fertile.
>
> (3.1.773–78)

[Her robe, whose splendour ill suits her fortune / And burdens her exile, Could win her the heart of a generous Prince / And easy access to all his treasures. / She can easily give up a useless thing / To provide abundantly for her retreat.]

In all fairness to Jason, we must keep in mind that it is Creüse's desire and not his own that he is representing, but so intent is he on securing his position as her consort, that her desire becomes as his. Curiously, and unlike his illustrious predecessors, Corneille does not stage the moment of direct negotiation for the robe – between Nerine on her errand for Jason and her mistress Médée. Nor does he show the actual transfer of the robe first to Nerine, then to the children, and finally to Creüse herself. This is a well-known story, and the audience can easily supply what is only alluded to. Nevertheless, such discretion is worth pondering. Is there something inherently unseemly about the transfer of goods? Along with the murder scene of the children, would bartering also have been considered too lowly to show on the stage? Is it a question of conscience or a question of class? Had Richelieu's new laws not taken cultural hold? How, in either or in any case (and certainly unlike England's Shakespeare in the case of his Shylock), does this reticence translate into an aesthetic choice, a matter of bienséance?[89]

Through the act of descriptive narrative – or of covetous rapture – the materialistic nature of the Greek culture, with resonance for the French, surfaces. Creüse waxes eloquent in her desirous praise of the robe:

> Qu'elle a fait un beau choix! jamais éclat pareil
> Ne sema dans la nuit les clartés du Soleil;
> Les perles avec l'or confusément mêlées,
> Mille pierres de prix sur les bords étalées
> D'un mélange divin éblouissent les yeux,
> Jamais rien d'approchant ne se fit en ces lieux;
> Pour moi tout aussitôt que je l'en vis parée
> Je ne fis plus d'état de la toison dorée,
> Et dussiez-vous vous-même en être un peu jaloux,
> J'en eus presques envie aussitôt que de vous.
>
> (2.4.575–84)

[What a superb choice she made! Never did similar splendour / Sow the Sun's brightness in the night; / Pearls carelessly mixed with gold, / A thousand precious gems spread along the edges, / This divine combination blinds me, Never was anything like this seen here; / For myself, as soon as I saw her wearing this, / I stopped caring about the Golden Fleece / And at the risk of making you jealous, / I wanted the robe almost as much as I did you.]

Creüse contends that the robe is desirable because, aside from its beauty, it is so unusual, never before seen in this part of the world. Its value is clearly tied to the fact that it is an import, not readily available and probably unique. The exoticism of the robe in Corinth ("jamais rien d'approchant ne se fit en ces lieux") accounts significantly for its perceived beauty. And yet the fact that Creüse can describe it in detail attests to her familiarity with the elements of which it is composed – pearls, gold, precious gems. Value already attaches to these in the local currency. Although the robe is unusual in its overall design and effect, it is made up of these identifiable materials; hence it is appreciably familiar. It is desirable because it translates easily into a Corinth fashion lexicon; it is locally exotic, at once replicable and extraordinary. By this new standard of comparison, even the hard-won and sacred Golden Fleece already diminishes in value ("Je ne fis plus d'état de la toison dorée"). The new arrival eclipses and relegates to the wings what now becomes the old. Or, the value of the symbolic object is superseded by the value of the material one. And so the import market drives itself, feeding on the desires of the elite for novel goods.

According to the staged paradigm, the imperious young princess is just that. She is only daughter to a king, with no mother in sight; her sole social function must be to secure a mate who will then be her father's successor. She is scripted for material desire. She is a woman of privilege brought up in a world of male-defined values, trained to develop desires for ornamentation that will signify her male-assigned worth, which display will serve tautologically as justification to advance the male activity of plunder. And so, in Corneille's vision, women enter actively and complicitously into the accumulation cycle.

In the earlier versions, it is a vengeful "barbarian" Medea's idea to offer the robe to Creüse as a wedding gift, but here, importantly, the idea comes from the covetous Greek princess Creüse who sees the robe, and promptly enters into negotiations, bartering it against children with Jason in order to have it ("Je ne veux rien pour rien" [1.3.191]). ["I do not want something for nothing."] A minor corollary suggests that since Creüse wants what is properly Médée's – her dress (already having won her husband Jason), Médée has at least a minor case against her, which may not legitimate the turning of the garment into a killer-robe, but does at least offer an extenuating circumstance. Creüse claims not only that the robe is just as impressive as the Golden Fleece, but that she is almost as desirous of it as she is of Jason ("J'en eus presques envie aussitôt que de vous" [2.4.584]). The objectification of the person of Jason through the expression of comparable desire, the attractiveness of a man weighing in against the merits of a garment, translates the man into merely another barter item, and thus hints at the extreme consequence of thinking in such terms – the fundamental equation of persons and things: the flesh trade.

The importation of items such as this robe, from Asia into the West, bargaining for them – and for men as part of the deal – constitute the troubling subtext of the story. For Creüse, even children are not exempted as negotiable currency, and their valuation is directly correlative to her desire:

> J'avais déjà pitié de leur tendre innocence,
> Et vous y servirai de toute ma puissance,
> Pourvu qu'à votre tour vous m'accordiez un point
> Que jusques à tantôt je ne vous dirai point. [. . .]
> Si je puis sur mon père obtenir quelque chose
> Vous le saurez après, je ne veux rien pour rien.
>
> (1.3.185–91)

[I already took pity on their tender innocence, / And I will do all in my power to help you there, / Provided that in your turn you grant me something / Which I won't tell you until later. [. . .] / If I can gain something from my father / You will know afterwards, I do not want something for nothing.]

This complicates the above equation, now suggesting that children are equal in value to a dress which in turn is equal (almost) in value to a man. The moment that the act of exchange or barter of people for things, based on the notion of their equivalency, enters into the discourse, the way is ideologically paved for the colonialist enterprise – a necessary step in the formation of a capitalist economy.[90]

The assignment of covetous vanity to Western woman operates both as a cover and alibi for Western man's will to dominate and a perilous handicap for Western woman's will to be. Creüse must adorn herself with the pearls and the gold off another woman's back, the back of a woman from the East, in order to acquire and signify value. Without this fashion accent, or any accent, she is merely Creuse – an empty vessel.[91] Corneille's Médée may be vengeful and murderous when wronged, and deserving of banishment, but another danger resides in the character of Creüse, a social danger, grounded in Western greed. This is the insightful story Corneille recycled from the Greeks and Romans and staged for the French as they launched into ever more intense phases of trading, exploration and colonization beyond the confines of Europe.

CONCLUSION

Corneille touched on current issues rising to the fore of French consciousness in the early decades of the seventeenth century, just before they became justified and taken for granted in the name of "progress" with Colbert's comprehensive program for establishing French hegemony. His play offered to French theatre audiences the opportunity to reflect on state-stimulated activities of "Other"ing, on a mercantile economy hitched to maritime travel, and on the acquisition of foreign knowledge and goods. Médée was the outsider woman, and as such the double victim, with whom marginalized women would empathize over the centuries; but how many women would recognize in themselves Creüse, the complicit insider woman, consumer of exotic commodities? Almost as an antidote to the nascent rampant materialism and exploitation Corneille detected taking hold, he traced out and idealized a new character, the traveler-savant, who would disinterestedly but usefully bring home knowledge of foreign people and offer it to local purposes, but who would at the same time cast a critical eye on his own society. He thus sketched out in the rough and put into question the elements of colonialist mentality shortly before it developed into state policy. That his vision was invisible even to him illustrates how the narration of history precedes the actualizing of that history, how story precedes history. Here is the critique the Cassandra/Pollux/poet – the seer Corneille – offered to and performed on his own society.

CHAPTER 2

Staging politics: Le Cid

SUMMARY

Corneille's Le Cid *(1637)*

The play is set in Seville, where king Fernand has settled his court for the past ten years in order to keep a watch out for Moorish sails. Despite Chimène's misgivings, which she confides to her governess Elvire, it seems that she and Rodrigue are about to realize their love dream come true when their fathers, Don Gomès and Don Diègue, fall out over the king Fernand's favoring of Rodrigue's father, Don Diègue. The angry Don Gomès insults Don Diègue, and Don Diègue, too old to defend his own honor, beseeches his son Rodrigue to avenge him. Rodrigue agonizes over the dilemma this request presents: to choose Chimène and accept the offense to his father's honor, or to defend his father and lose Chimène.

Don Gomès refuses to apologize, despite the king's command. Chimène is in despair, and the Infanta comforts her, despite the fact that she, the king's daughter, is in love with Rodrigue and wishes he could attain the equivalent of her high station and thereby become a suitor worthy of her. The king meanwhile has learned that the Moors are at the mouth of the river and waiting for the night tide to sail into Seville and attack the city. Rodrigue kills Chimène's father in a forbidden duel, and both the wronged daughter and the avenged father seek out the king, the one to demand justice, the other to beg for mercy. Rodrigue must be either punished or forgiven.

Rodrigue comes to Chimène, but finds her governess Elvire, and when Chimène arrives, is hidden by Elvire behind a door. Thus he is privy to Chimène's refusal to allow another suitor, Don Sanche, to step in to avenge her father's death. And he also overhears Chimène admit to Elvire (who draws her out) that despite the course dictated by family honor, she is still in love with Rodrigue. Whereupon Rodrigue springs from hiding, and the two lovers renew their love vows despite Rodrigue's crime and Chimène's continued commitment to seek justice for her father's death. Immediately after, Don Diègue finds his son and shares the news that the Moors are about to come up the river and attack Seville. This is the moment for Rodrigue to prove himself a hero and earn his king's forgiveness.

Rodrigue is victorious over the Moors, recounts the bloody battle that has transformed him into Le Cid, and the king is in his debt for saving Seville. The Infanta advises Chimène to drop her case against the new state hero. The king tricks Chimène into showing her love for Rodrigue by first reporting his death to her; but when the truth comes out, Chimène recovers composure and persists in demanding justice. The king allows one duel to decide the case, and Chimène accepts Don Sanche's offer to champion her cause.

The two lovers share a final moment. Rodrigue has decided to let himself be killed by Don Sanche, but Chimène begs him to live. The Infanta sees that the love of this couple is so great that she must resign herself and give up hope of Rodrigue's love, despite his demonstrated worthiness. When Don Sanche returns from the duel alive with sword in hand, Chimène assumes Rodrigue has died and once again betrays her love publicly. The king reassures her that Rodrigue is still alive. He orders Chimène to rest and Rodrigue to go off and do further great battle against the Moors. He recommends that the couple leave their fate up to his wisdom and to time's healing.

Questions to ponder

(1) Why does Corneille trouble to reset this Spanish play in Seville instead of retaining the original setting of Burgos? Why does he need an up-tide river to make his vision of the plot work?

(2) What exactly was the nature of relations between the Moors and the French when Corneille was recasting the play as compared to between the Moors and the Castilians when the epic was originally conceived? How does Corneille take history into account? Or does he?

(3) Does the king distinguish between his tactics for dealing with the Moors and with Chimène?

There has never been a document of culture which was not at one and the same time a document of barbarism. (Walter Benjamin, "Theses on the Philosophy of History," VII)

Along the Mediterranean coasts of Europe today, Saracen towers, or their vestiges, crop up with regularity, poised within strategic hailing distance of one another and the communities they were designed to alert. They hark back to an earlier but not yet forgotten era of piracy, pillaging, and slavery. Today they no longer signal warnings to each other, but remind us of the real danger of attack to the coastal towns and seafaring people of Mediterranean Europe in earlier times. These towers also stand as territorial stakes marking frontiers through an epoch of frequently shifting borders and allegiances from approximately the ninth through the eighteenth century. Most eloquently, they attest to the tradition of Christian–Muslim hostility that played out under their watch, and that can hardly be said to have altogether disappeared even today. It is in the figurative and still real shadow of these towers that this study of *Le Cid*[1] takes its shape.

This chapter investigates the political subtext of this perhaps most "canonical" of Corneille's plays. If we are looking for a coherent ideological agenda in this playwright's works, we will be disappointed, for the political agenda that can be read into his earlier *Médée* of 1635 and what we can extrapolate from *Le Cid* of 1637 are radically different programs. Where in the first play, Corneille appears to espouse the cause of the wronged "outsider" and to argue her case tenaciously, in this second one, his major concern is with domestic politics.[2] However, here again, the "outsider" plays a prominent role, and has a vital function in the galvanizing of the polis. In *Le Cid*, in the process of exploring the workings of power within a structured community, Corneille offers important insights on the role of the threatening "outsider" in coalescing and producing the bonding of that community. And so the focus of this play casts the "outsider" in both a different role and a different light.[3]

Those Saracen towers that dot the Mediterranean landscape along coasts that we recognize today as "European" stand as witnesses to a heritage of real everyday fear. Ever since the "Chanson de Roland," the French rallied literately around their terror of the Moor, the infidel, the Muslim, the Saracen – their local "Other." If the "Chanson de Roland" claims pride of place as the great founding French epic, then the cultural construction of France is indeed highly dependent on the Moor for a sense of its identity. The seventeenth century was no exception to the elaboration of this bonding fear. Corneille may have borrowed his play from the Spanish, but he did not have to import the sentiment that gave it life and meaning for the French. That had been there since the ninth century. In the seventeenth century, these local "Others" practiced a politics of aggression, but the French, sheltered by their Ottoman ties, also harbored their own hegemonic agenda. Both sides (along with other European contenders in the Mediterranean) engaged in such repetitive and consistent behaviors toward one another that, from a distance, they appear uncannily well orchestrated and choreographed.

Accordingly, it is fitting to read *Le Cid* not against the coincidence of specific events, but against a socio-historical map in the Mediterranean biogeographic region of the more "longue durée."[4] Fernand Braudel's mapping features the tides, the currents, the winds, and takes into account sheltered coves versus open seas – all of these factors determined

the range of human events possible and even likely around the basin.
His concept of history offers a useful framework for considering together
ongoing hostile behaviors between communities of Mediterranean people and a play that captured the French collective imagination for over
a good part of the seventeenth century, one that continues to loom large
there still today, enjoying its own success of "durée."

And this analysis is dependent, for its coherence, on subscription to the
concept of "durée;" for many of the texts that will be cited in examining
Le Cid here date from years subsequent to its first stagings. This can only
be justified by pointing to Corneille's visionary talent for capturing in
the present what will be increasingly documented in the future, for his
extraordinary insight into political issues that might have seemed remote
from his experience (After seeing *Sertorius*, did not the great military
leader Condé ask 'Où M. Corneille a-t-il appris l'art de la guerre?'), or
by appealing to Homi Bhabha's contention that the narrative of story
precedes that of history.

Corneille demonstrates his sensitivity to the very kinds of geopolitical
concerns that Braudel would elaborate in deciding to reset *Le Cid* on the
Guadalquivir river of Seville. For, in seventeenth-century France, if the
people feared surprise attack, it was surprise attack from the sea, not by
land, and this is, after all, the crux of the plot. Accordingly, Corneille
takes pains to remove the action of *Le Cid* from the traditional land-bound
town of Burgos and to set it in Seville, where an up-river tide permits him
to stage precisely the trauma of invasion from the sea.[5] He specifically
explains in his "Examen" (704) that a surprise attack could never come
by land and hence his need for water, for Seville.[6] His concern here is not
for historical accuracy but for seventeenth-century French plausibility.[7]
This change brings the *Cid* story closer to the geopolitics of the time as the
French contended with piracy along their Mediterranean coastline, and
significantly rewrites the Guillén de Castro version which was Corneille's
source.[8] In inventing this incursion up the Guadalquivir river, Corneille
was harnessing the story to represent current tensions between his French
audience and their marauders from the sea.[9] The version he wanted to
give was of an "outsider" sea-borne menace enabling (within the requisite
twenty-four hours) the solution of "insider" land-anchored problems.

But what exactly was the reach of this land? We are confronted with
an inconsistent territorial picture in the play; this may be because a
seventeenth-century French view of the contemporary Iberian political
situation is mapped onto a twelfth-century Castilian epic. In the in-
tervening time – between the twelfth and the seventeenth centuries,

boundaries have shifted; the Moors have already been driven from Andalusia – they were expelled in 1492, two centuries after the epic first surfaced. Corneille's geopolitical map clearly bears the mark of his time.

The original epic of *Le Cid* (1140) dates from well before the establishment of the Ottoman Empire (Osman, the Empire's founder, lived *c.* 1281–1324); but by 1618, in Castro's retelling, he has the vanquished enemy actually surrendering an Ottoman flag. Corneille will continue in the spirit of Castro's new fiction; however, instead of mentioning the flag, he will stress instead association of the invaders with the African continent – hence the Barbary Republics. These two signals combined, "la devise ottomane" (the Ottoman standard from Castro) and "l'Afrique" (from Corneille) suggest, once again, that the immediate interest of this story for the early seventeenth century turns more on its functioning as a reminder of current Mediterranean tensions than as a faithful mirror of the past. Corneille's "Mores" correspond more likely to the combined populations of the indigenous Moors and displaced Moriscos of seventeenth-century North Africa than to the earlier rebellious Moriscos who remained on the Iberian peninsula after the mass expulsion until they too were forced out, or to the Andalusian Moors of the early epic poem.

But Corneille will not be consistent: in his same play, the Infanta will envision Rodrigue occupying the throne of Granada – with adoring Moors at his knees (2.5.538–39). Andalusian Moors, or Moriscos, or Moors from the Barbary Republics, sailing under the Ottoman flag? Corneille's inaccuracies and inconsistencies point up above all that he does not much care. For his story he seeks to establish only three facts: (1) the enemy comes by sea; (2) the enemy is Moorish; (3) the enemy is associated with Africa. With regard to the first fact, he goes to great length to arrange this in the play and then to defend it in his "Examen." With regard to the second and third, he relies on the spectators to fill in. For them, "More" connoted fierce, fearful, infidel, barbary – real and present danger; this was what mattered, and for this Corneille could count on his audience. This is the story Corneille chose to tell. Then, the question becomes "why"?

The coastline enemy of Corneille's era was the Ottoman enemy, and all those Muslim communities subsumed under the Ottoman rule of empire. The Ottomans controlled the Levant, Egypt, and their power extended around the entire southern coast of the Mediterranean. The Barbary Republics that rimmed the sea (Libya, Tunis, Algiers) were under the jurisdiction of Constantinople, and their rulers answered to the Vizir, ultimately to the Sultan.[10] International agreements ostensibly binding the republics were negotiated at the Sublime Porte, the seat of government for the Ottoman sultan at Constantinople. So when the French had cause to complain about the dangers of the high seas, about marauders along their coasts, it was not only to the local "days" (rulers) of these republics that they brought their complaints, but to the Sublime Porte.

Trade agreements and assurances of safe passage were of great concern to the French. Francis the First and Soliman the Magnificent had first instituted formal understandings (the "Capitulations") in the sixteenth century that were to benefit commerce and ensure safety for all. But by the seventeenth century, when Richelieu and then Colbert were intent on building French maritime mercantilism, these conventions had lost their hold; the seas were unruly.[11] Piracy, raiding, and slavery were of immediate concern to French travelers, traders, coastline dwellers, and all who had any ties to the Mediterranean. The threat was at the back of everyone's minds, and a spirit of Cold War vigilance reigned. Such was the mood of the times when *Le Cid* was first staged. It was not until 1673 that the "Capitulations" were formally renewed.

During these years of guerilla seafaring, numerous attempts would be made to protect the French and to establish peace with the enemy. But the enemy was formidable: not simply the Ottomans out of Constantinople, but especially the corsairs of Tunis, Tripoli, and Algiers continued to strike. And they were not alone. "Christian" pirates abounded as well. It is in the context of these general facts that we must consider Corneille's borrowing of *Le Cid*. Although seventeenth-century French theatregoers did not comment on the similarity between the real danger of maritime attacks and this major theme in the play, they (like all theatre audiences) understood the plot, borrowed and reworked from the past, to be speaking to and about their present, playing on their general sensibilities. Piracy was an immediate as well as an abiding concern.

In setting the scene for this politico-piratico-mosaico reconsideration of the French cultural icon, *Le Cid*, I will begin by mapping out the kinds of contacts the French and the Ottomans and their allies engaged in at sea and along the French coastline during the seventeenth century – the activities of piracy that prevailed and that are, however discreetly, echoed in the play – as they spell out the terms of the metonymy.[12] This reading relies then on the suggestive cobbling of bits and pieces of history and story, and on the reader's participation in imagining a sea-stressed context for a traditionally love-, honor-, and land-bound play, and thereby reconsidering the play as part and parcel of a more generalized and only retrospectively coherent cultural production.

STAGING POLITICS: SETTING THE SCENE

La flotte qu'on craignait dans ce grand fleuve entrée
Vient surprendre la ville et piller la contrée,
Les Mores vont descendre et le flux et la nuit
Dans une heure à nos murs les amène sans bruit,
La Cour est en désordre et le peuple en alarmes,
On n'entend que des cris, on ne voit que des larmes...

Le Cid 3.6.1083–88

[The fleet we feared is in the river, plans
To fall upon the town and pillage it.
Within an hour, the floodtide and the night
Up to our walls will bring them [the Moors] soundlessly.
The court's in disarray, the people fear.
All that one hears are cries and sees are tears...][13]

The pirate alarm was sounded even on the Paris stage, and did not surprise but only confirmed the audience in their anxiety. In his *Mémoires*, the chevalier D'Arvieux, accomplished linguist, traveler, diplomat, and at one point "envoyé extraordinaire" to Tunis, would recount regularly the frequent raids, the skirmishes, the near brushes, the attacks, the pleas by slaves, the constant vigilance that set the tone for life on and around the sea.

One consequence of this regular hostility was that many Frenchmen – captured by the Barbary pirates, or North Africans (historically related to the Moors and, plausibly, for our purposes, in the French collective imaginary, to the Moors of the play in question) – were scattered and enslaved throughout the Mediterranean.[14] As early as 1626, approximately 8,000 French sailors were held slaves at Algiers and Tunis.[15] French officials were constantly tripping over their compatriots taken slaves, as well as other Europeans.[16] These captives constituted almost a form of currency. Depending on the current politics of the local markets, their features (age, strength, beauty, family wealth, political importance, etc.) and their national fealties, they commanded or did not command exchange value.[17] They could end up as cooks, gardeners, concubines, field laborers, galley slaves, household help, confidantes, even ministers.[18] They were given, sold, ransomed, substituted, and could even, on occasion, earn their own freedom.

Seemingly endless negotiations went on in attempts to protect French subjects from such humiliation and hardship. D'Arvieux even entertained the notion that the remedy to this vexing situation was for the "Christians" to finance a great fighting fleet to rid the seas once and for all of this scourge. He concluded this would be less expensive than France's frequent chore of ransoming back compatriots.[19] However, at the same time, the French king's galleys themselves were manned in great part by infidels taken captive, and the king was loathe to part with his own labor force through exchange negotiations.[20] This generalized practice suggests a mentality about slavery, indeed about human life, which was a shared Mediterranean feature, and that dated from medieval – indeed, even earlier – times.

Robert Mantran, Ottoman Empire scholar, underscores the operative Christian/Muslim distinction that set the inhabitants of the South of the Mediterranean Basin and those of the North against one another, drawing a clear line between the "European" population and the "Ottoman/Barbary" one. As he tells it, the Ottomans and their protectorates were clearly the aggressors.[21] However, such neat parceling is perhaps more the mark of retrospective research than an accurate representation of the times. On-site witnesses to this world of conflict admitted to a more complex reality.

Robert de Dreux, the French almoner and traveler we have already mentioned, writing in 1665, was not as ready to accuse the Ottoman pirates. He acknowledged that the Ottomans were guilty of ferocious sea behavior, but he reminded his French readers that they were hardly innocent themselves, that their own king's galley ships were manned by Ottoman slaves, and that they themselves engaged regularly in the trade of human flesh, making special mention of the important Livorno and Malta markets.[22] When the Sultan's envoy, Soliman Ferraca, made an official visit to France in 1669, one of the great concerns around that visit was to ensure that his itinerary took him nowhere near the sprawling slave colonies on the French Mediterranean coast, where his mood might be soured by the sight of so many of his compatriots and subjects held captive.

The renowned story spinner, Antoine Galland, translator of *The 1001 Nights*, claims to transcribe as he first heard it the story of a merchant, Jean Bonnet, from the little sea town of Cassis, next to Marseilles, who was taken prisoner and made a slave, but who managed to negotiate his way back to freedom, and finally to escape home to Cassis. This he did by feigning conversion to Islam and ignorance of his mother tongue as necessary, and not, of course, without surviving numerous near-death adventures.[23] Then, after a few months of peaceful family life, he headed once again to sea to avenge his captivity, and spent the rest of his life trading and pirating around Cyprus. If his tale merits mention, it is not for its exceptionality, but because it is simply one of the most complete accounts of a quite common experience of those days. One has but to peruse the journals of Grelot, Chardin, Tavernier, Thévenot, Guilleragues, or any number of sea travelers from this general period to capture the flavor of the common incidence of piracy and slavery, of alternate experiences of aggression and of victimizing.

This swashbuckling way of life was probably more understandable to the people of Marseilles, "La Porte de l'Orient," than to the Parisians. The city of Marseilles, with its fleets of galley ships, its vast slave quarters, and its bustling contact with all points of the Mediterranean, was already exotic to the French of the North. At the same time, it was real, in that goods from the East, when they did not come overland from Venice, most often made their way to Paris from Marseilles. When Mme de Sévigné came down to stay with her daughter in Provence, one of her regular desires was to visit this city that held her fascination.[24] In January of 1673, she made her first trip from Grignan, where she was visiting her daughter, down to Marseilles with her son-in-law, and the ambiance of the city surpassed the fantasy she had already concocted. She had a full tourist experience that exceeded even her most fanciful expectations:

Je suis charmée de la beauté singulière de cette ville. Hier le temps fut divin, et l'endroit d'où je découvris la mer, les bastides, les montagnes et la ville est une chose étonnante . . . La foule des chevaliers qui vinrent hier voir M. de Grignan; des aventuriers, des épées, des chapeaux du bel air, des gens faits à peindre, une idée de guerre, de roman, d'embarquement, d'aventures, de chaînes, de fers, d'esclaves, de servitude, de captivité: moi qui aime les romans, tout cela me ravit, et j'en suis transportée.[25]

[I find the city's singular beauty charming. Yesterday the weather was divine, and the spot from which I saw the sea, the outcroppings, the mountains and the city, is an astonishing thing . . . The crowd of gentlemen that came to see M. de Grignan yesterday; adventurers, swords, handsome hats, people who looked as if they belonged in a painting, an idea of war, of a novel, of undertaking a journey, adventures, chains, irons, slaves, servitude, captivity: I who love novels, all this delights me, and I am transported by it.

But other aristocratic Parisians who could not make the trip South were also avid consumers of the events and flavor of the Mediterranean world, and reporters played especially on the "frisson" evoked in them by the leveling notion of slavery. Guilleragues, author of *Les Lettres portugaises*, served as French ambassador to the Porte from 1679 to 1685, in which capacity he also cultivated his flair for the epistolary genre. He would attempt to satisfy his Paris-bound friends' curiosity with his lively letters and then with his *Mémoires*. He offered to the elite generous accounts of the "bagne" (or slave colony) in Constantinople in order to give a sense of the particular quality of the slaves' living conditions: "D'ailleurs on peut dire que le bagne est moins une prison qu'une ville. Les prisonniers y travaillent, et l'argent qu'ils gagnent tourne à leur profit. Plusieurs d'entre eux tiennent cabaret, et quelques-uns même y ont fait bâtir des maisons qui sont fort agréables, et très bien meublées."[26] ["Moreover, it can be said that the slave colony is less a prison than a city. The prisoners work there, and the money they earn is theirs to keep. Several of them run cabarets, and some even have houses, which are quite pleasant, and very well furnished."]

And another reporter, the French traveler-artist Guillaume Joseph Grelot, mentioned earlier, in his book dedicated to the king, sketched out a rather positive picture of the same Turkish slave colony life: "Les esclaves des Turcs ne sont pas si mal-traittez que l'on se l'imagine, ils sont bien souvent les seconds maîtres du logis, et j'en aye connu même qui se trouvent si bien de leurs Agas, qu'après en avoir obtenu la liberté, et s'en estre revenus en Europe (où ils n'avaient pas trouvé ce qu'ils espéraient) s'en sont retournés en Turquie pour se remettre volontairement dans des chaînes dont la pesanteur leur avait semblé insupportable."[27] ["The Turks' slaves are not as badly treated as one might imagine, they are often the second-in-command of the house, and I have known some who found themselves in such a good situation with their Agas, that after having gained their freedom and returned to Europe (where they did not find what they hoped) they returned to Turkey, to voluntarily put themselves back in the chains whose weight had formerly seemed unbearable."]

Since anyone venturing to sea or living on the coasts could be taken slave and end up in these places, their conditions were a matter of concern to all classes alike. After all, it was merely a matter of chance, and the odds were not good. We recall the story from Dreux, cited in the "Orientation," of "un jeune gentilhomme des meilleures familles de Paris" ["a young gentleman from one of the best families in Paris"] who in tourist fashion had traveled "voir le siège de Candie" ["to see the siege of Candia"] and his fate: "le vaisseau où il était fut pris et lui-même fut vendu à un Turc vanier."[28] ["the vessel on which he sailed was captured and he himself was sold to a Turkish basket-maker."] Thus it is that the first mention of the threat of pirates in *Le Cid* comes from the king Fernand himself. Not only were any and all equally susceptible to the danger of being taken slave and hence stripped of social difference; the elite were especially so, since on the market they could command handsome ransoms for their takers. Corneille's play underscores this specifically aristocratic fear.

Very disparate people bonded as a consequence of finding themselves in the same predicament; they had to make their way carefully, but could often count on one another for cover and assistance. The French who were taken slaves negotiated for themselves within the constraints of their situations, and worked at shaping their own destinies under these difficult conditions. There was usually an extraordinary mix of loyalties and nationalities among a crew of slaves. And the slaves would often discover that even their captors were fellow patriots turned renegade. Frequently the captives survived and escaped not only as a consequence of good will and solidarity among themselves, but even with their guards.[29]

It was crucial to know how to play roles in order to survive in these complex milieux, for identity mattered, but was not always what it appeared; it was assumed and shed as necessary and as possible. The ability to disguise one's identity could mean the difference between life and death. Obviously, such markers as religion and language could be neutralized more easily than that of physical appearance. Circumcision often featured as a key proof of being Muslim or at least non-European, as did accent or dialect. Fluency in the enemy's language was most useful, and conversion could serve as a practical expedient to survival; but apostasy did not sit well: popular wisdom held that a bad Christian would make just as bad a Muslim.[30] For there stood this absolute categorical difference between Europeans and Ottomans (and their subjects of North Africa): you were either Christian or Muslim, and everything hinged on that.

Ruthless Christian pirates of various nationalities, free agents, along with the Barbaries and the Ottomans, also roamed the Mediterranean. Their allegiances were unclear but they were useful to Venice and to other western states in their readiness to wreak havoc on the Turks without implicating these nations in complications that would be prejudicial to their diplomatic standing as friends to the Ottomans. Pirates of French provenance, for example, frequently sailed out of Malta, masqueraded under that flag, and served primarily their own, but occasionally French interests in their marauding. The European powers quietly protected these Christian pirates, using diversionary tactics, warning them of the approach of Turkish and Barbary ships.[31] It was contended that these corsairs were at least as, if not more, ferocious than the Barbary ones.[32] But since they could be useful in protecting European trade routes, their fearsome ways were more readily tolerated by the French. Thus absolute righteousness in condemning piracy was not an option; as with Corneille's king Fernand, a practice of "Realpolitik" prevailed. It was just as legitimate to set traps for marauders from the sea as to make any attempt at above-board negotiation.

The disruptive influence of the Barbaries on the seas provoked misunderstandings and hostilities between the French and the Sultan, who was supposed to have control over his lieges. The Parisian *Gazette*, from its inception in 1631, followed Mediterranean events with lively interest.[33] The hostilities would continue on through the eighteenth century, and even, in more isolated instances, into the nineteenth century. This is not a story of discrete events but of deeply ingrained patterns of behavior. Piracy was newsworthy in Paris, but all too real to French coastline dwellers and seafarers.

In 1620, a brutal massacre of forty-eight Turks took place right in the city of Marseilles. Barbary pirates at large off the French coast had struck too close to "home," seizing a French ship just out of port; all sailors save two had been killed or drowned. The two who lived to tell the tale brought it to Marseilles. The outraged population took its revenge not against the perpetrators themselves but against the Turks at hand. The affair sounded the alarm, reminding all of France of the enmity between the Turks and the French. The indignant French took the offensive, and in justifying their vicious retaliation, accused the Turks.[34] They generalized their anger and condemned in sweeping terms all that this other culture represented:

Il n'y a nation que ceste maudite Secte n'ait attaquée, Royaume qu'elle n'ait tasché d'envahir, ny Province qui n'ait senty les efforts de ses atteintes: et ce qui est le pire, . . . ils se vengent sur les particuliers, ruinent les familles, emmeinent hômes, femmes, enfants, et tout ce qu'ils peuvent rencontrer, et les réduisent à une misérable captivité, pire mille fois que la mort, qui ne peut affliger qu'une seule fois, et ne tourmente plus, . . . Quelle mort plus cruelle et sensible, que de se voir une chaisne au col, aux pieds, aux bras, et souvent au gros du corps.[35]

[There is no nation that this cursed sect has not attacked, no kingdom it has not tried to invade, no province that has not felt the effects of its reach: and the worst part . . . is that they avenge themselves on private individuals, they ruin families, they carry off men, women, children, and all that they meet with, and reduce them to a miserable captivity, a thousand times worse than death, which only strikes once and is felt no more . . . What death is more cruel and more painful, than to see a chain around your neck, your feet, your arms, and often most of your body.]

Here was the kind of risk that faced Don Fernand's kingdom as the Moorish ships approached the harbor and planned their surprise attack. But his liege, the young Rodrigue would ensure that if bloodbath there was, only enemy blood would be shed. If Corneille's character ascended so rapidly and securely to the status of national hero for the French, it should be remembered that it was against the backdrop of real scarifying events such as the above that he did.

In time, Colbert would attempt to systematize security on the seas: he would institute the practice of organizing merchant ships and French naval vessels in convoys with the idea that traveling together would ensure safer passage. But this solution proved harmful to trade, since French vessels would arrive together at trading ports. They would seek to sell their cargo all at the same time, and thereby glut the market and reduce profit for themselves. Rodrigue's individualistic heroism was only a piece of the greater state story of maritime mercantilism in the making.

In the "Capitulations" (or trade treaties) finally agreed upon and signed by the French and the Ottomans in 1673, the main concern would still be to curb the piracy of the corsairs and to offer some assurance of protection to French subjects. Accordingly, a sweeping statement engineered by the ambassador to the Porte, Nointel, reminded the Republics of Tunis, Algiers, and Tripoli, as well as the Turks, of their subservience to their masters, the ruling Ottomans, and brought them to explicit account under a clause that would have them report all French slaves to the Porte for adjudication: "Et s'il se trouve par nostre Empire des Esclaves Français, estant reconnus pour tels de l'Ambassadeur ou Consuls, ceux au pouvoir de qui ils se trouveront faisant refus de les livrer, soient obligez de les envoyer à nostre Porte, afin d'estre jugé à qui ils appartiendront."[36] ["And if in our Empire French slaves are found, and recognized as such by the Ambassador or the Consuls, those in whose power they are found refusing to give them up, will be obliged to send them to our Porte, so that it may be judged to whom they belong."] These attempts at controlling relations in and around the Mediterranean basin

throughout the seventeenth century confirm to what extent the situation
was deeply vexed for the French. They needed heroes like Rodrigue.

POLITICS AT STAKE, POLITICAL STAKES

Such clearly territorial and socioeconomic clashes were glossed at the
time by the more ideologically palatable and conventional difference of
religious belief. Religion was regularly inscribed as lying at the heart
of all conflicts in seventeenth-century East–West relations. The East–
West distinction itself (often enough of a rather North–South tilt, as
Mantran suggests earlier), around the Mediterranean basin at least, appeared to be premised on tensions between Christians and Muslims.
This understanding was not groundless. Indeed, it is to be noted that
eleven religious crusades, seven of them French, were undertaken just
between 1600 and 1620.[37] The Roman Catholic Church continued to
encourage such crusading enterprises, and specific lay groups, such as
the Knights of Saint John, dedicated themselves to such causes.[38] At
the same time, the Church took full advantage of the religious hostilities, and maintained its own bustling slave trade, centered on the
island of Malta, justifying the imprisoning of infidels as appropriate
to Christian tenets.[39] This important example certainly contributed
to dissipate any possible moral scruples on the part of Christian slave
dealers.

On the seas, despite differences of national interests, and despite internal conflicts of clustered groupings, the participants were perceived as
polarizing neatly into rifts pitting Christians and Muslims against each
other. Jean Chardin, as a French protestant sailing under the flag of the
English Crown, was particularly sensitive to this irony in 1666: "Les
Chrétiens apprennent dans l'Orient à conserver la paix entr'eux, et à
demeurer en bonne intelligence, malgré la diversité de leurs sentiments.
Il y a mille sectes, et cependant on n'y connaît que deux Créances, la
Chrétienne, et la Mahométane."[40] ["Christians in the Orient learn to
keep the peace among themselves, and to maintain a good understanding with each other, in spite of the diversity of their sentiments. There
are a thousand sects, and nonetheless only two Faiths are known, the
Christian and the Mahometan."] Findings in the French press confirm
that even through the "enlightened" eighteenth century all news relating to conflicts in the Mediterranean was occulted under the banner of
religion – tattered of course, but still capable of rallying the troops:
"Tout tend dans la *Gazette* à faire croire que les guerres poursuivies par

les Turcs n'ont que le but de convertir les Chrétiens à l'Islam . . . "[41] ["Everything in the *Gazette* leads one to believe that the wars the Turks pursue have no other goal than to convert Christians to Islam."]

However, in Corneille's *Le Cid*, first staged in 1637, despite the fact that the plot features hostilities between the Castilians (Christians) and the Moors (Muslims), no mention at all is made of religious conflict.[42] The Moors are referred to strictly as Moors; the Castilians as Castilians. The palpable outside tension that occupies the stage and that sharpens the ambiance for the seventeenth-century French theatregoing public, that strikes chords in the collective imaginary, is the familiar one: fear of Muslims from the sea. This everyday fear dates, as we have seen, from long before the production of the drama, and spans the years of the play's immediate success throughout the century, but does not explicitly harness religion. On the stage, this fear requires no ideological justification; it is self-evident. The discourse of religious difference, so apparent in the journalistic register of regular reporting, gives way in the dramatic register of entertainment to a rhetoric of more pervasive secular cultural persuasion, one which, in the place of religion harbors its own subtext, as we shall see – of racial superiority.

The secular staged ritual of the play, organized around the "Otherness" of the Moors, is couched in a celebratory rhetoric of the Castilian obsession with "race," and subscribes unself-consciously to a program of aggression. Like most phenomena grounded in prejudice, it goes without saying. The story of *Le Cid* represents and repeats at each performance the occasion for a collective celebration of superiority of one "imagined community" over another, tautologically justifying the socioeconomic and territorial claims of the Castilians over their enemy.[43]

In Corneille's historically if imprecisely inspired play, the threat of attack from the Moors diffuses the internal crisis at Don Fernand's court and occasions the transformative heroism of the protagonist Rodrigue. The display of competing strategies and comparable nobilities, and this representation of the infidels as the alien yet essential coalescing force in mediating domestic politics demonstrates the political usefulness of the "Other" / enemy in the organizing of the state. Again, religion plays no role in the staged articulation of the tensions between Castilians and Moors. Rather, alterity appears to operate in its place.

Also, and again, the only aspect of the play which appears to require no explanation is the threat of the Moors. This may be partly because the subject is derived from the twelfth-century epic version of an eleventh-century story based on a seminal event (hardly recognizable in these later permutations), understood as "historical," confirmed as such by the scholar Mariana, and then recirculated in 1621 by Guillén de Castro (*Las Mocedades del Cid*),[44] from whom Corneille borrows the device.

Thus naturalized, the story has a life of its own, and the Moors are merely a feature of the familiar plot. However, it is important to keep in mind, as we have insisted, that in "real" life the French continued to view the Moors in the seventeenth century just as they did in the early middle ages (the thirteenth-century saracens of *Aucassin et Nicolette* for example), as a threat to their sea trade and coastline settlements.[45] The play, *Le Cid*, then, gestures to the long-standing enmity recounted above, an enmity that had played out over the centuries along the Mediterranean and which would still be of paramount concern in the trade negotiations – the "Capitulations" between the Porte and Versailles in 1673, almost four full decades after the production of *Le Cid*.

The traditional contextualizing criticism seems only partially adequate to account for the production and success of the play.[46] It has insisted on the fact that Spain and France were waging war with each other at the time the play was produced, and on the consequent prestige that Spanish culture enjoyed at the time. But even that fact of Spanish–French enemy attraction does not fully explain the appeal of the plot.[47] It is certainly true that displays of cultural interest in the enemy and its ways are not altogether unusual: as recently as the Vietnam War we have been witness to marked fascination with the "Other," in such films as *Apocalypse Now* and many others of its ilk.[48] I would argue however that the fascination is displaced here, and does not invoke merely the acknowledged surface tensions between the French and the Spanish in 1637, but, even more pertinently, if also more discreetly and circuitously, those between the French and the Ottomans' subjects, specifically the pirating Moors of North Africa, indeed those same tensions documented in the memoirs and trade agreements cited earlier.

Just as religious difference plays no explicit role in this play setting Christians against Muslims, there is also another notable absence, another feature that stands out in this French version of *Le Cid*: the Moors are at once essential to and missing from the play as staged. This is significantly different from Guillén de Castro's earlier play, Corneille's supposed model. In Castro's version, the Moors are represented by four kings who are very much present: they enter on the stage, whereupon one of them reports directly Rodrigue's victory to Don Fernand. In so doing, the spokesman identifies himself and his comrades specifically as Moorish

Ottomans in search of booty – that is to say, Barbary pirates. This script and these details allow for an anchoring of the characters visibly on the stage and concretely in History. One of the Moorish kings summarizes:

> Quitónos el español
> nuestra opinión en un día,
> y *una presa* que valía
> más oro que engendra el sol.
> Y en su mano vencedora
> nuestra divisa *otomana*
> sin venir lanza cristiana
> sin une cabeza *mora.* (emphasis mine)[49]

[My translation: The Spaniard obliged us to abandon / In just one day the scheme / And the booty which was worth / More gold than all that the Sun produces. / And in his conquering hand falls / Our Ottoman banner / And no Christian lance appears / devoid of a Moorish head.]

But in Corneille's play, the number of his in any case invisible kings is reduced to two, their role is diminished, and their discourse is appropriated. It is Rodrigue himself who reports his own victory. Further, in Castro's version, it is one of the four kings who names Rodrigue their "Cid" and he does so directly onstage. But for Corneille it is his Don Fernand who will be the one to designate Rodrigue "Le Cid" as he reports and echoes the exchanges of the two kings. In Corneille's play, then, the Moorish presence is occulted and absorbed in the dominant discourse, emptied of its political content, to occupy a much vaster interpretive space.

Nevertheless, despite this seeming obfuscation, the immediate threat and then the actual attack of the Moors are essential to the playing out of the politics within Seville. The technical reproach made to their introduction to the plot by seventeenth-century critics was that they came from without and thereby produced a *Deus ex machina* effect on the characters and events already in play. Corneille, however, claims this effect to be a virtue. Against criticism of the suspicious coincidence of the unexpected death of the count and the punctual arrival of the Moors, he observes that the Moorish attack is necessarily a surprise and therefore a plausible event.[50] But just as importantly, from within the text, it is suggested that they and the threat they represent have always been part of the picture.

Indeed, the king claims to have established the site of the capital of Castille at Seville ten years before for the very purpose of keeping an eye on the coast and out for Moorish sails (2.6.623–26). Accordingly, when their proximity or presence is announced, it comes as no surprise, but rather features as simply the latest episode in that old and ongoing story, the one that in this particular avatar pits Castilians and Moors against each other. Corneille's seventeenth-century French version repeats and appropriates for present times the earlier Castilian gesture of state consolidation through the staging of this shared and continuing antagonism. In spirit, it contends with the same hostilities as those of the twelfth century, and even earlier; the weight of the burden of an ongoing problem extends outside of the story line back into the past and forward into contemporary history.

The story and the story line thus call for closer scrutiny. There are two distinct histories that need to be taken into account: the one is of the inherited story represented in the play – the versions handed down from the twelfth century on, the borrowings, etc. – the other is the history of the text of Corneille's own play. The history of the story does not concern us here except to the extent that we have already roughly traced it. However, the textual history of Corneille's play does, not in all of its detail, but insofar as certain ideological shifts germane to this investigation of the role of the outsider in the bonding and shaping of the state mark the text and add weight to our argument. Corneille reworked his play several times, responding to the many criticisms of Scudéry and the Académie française as they subjected not only the content but every verse to rigorous scrutiny. It is not my aim here to study the famous Quarrel of *Le Cid*, but to focus on some of the relevant changes introduced in particular verses, and the bearing of these changes on the message of the play.

ELOQUENT VARIANTS

Corneille first published the script of the play in 1637, the year of its premiere (p. 1477).[51] A definitive author-approved edition, containing many revisions, appeared in 1660, succeeding several interim editions.[52] Take, for example, the following verses. In 1637, King Fernand speaks:

> N'en parlons plus. Au reste on nous menace fort:
> Sur un avis reçu, je crains une surprise.
>
> (a 2.6.610–11)

> [Let's talk no more of this. We are faced with a serious threat:
> Because of word I've received, I fear a surprise.]

But, by 1660, he will assert the following:

> N'en parlons plus. Au reste, on a vu dix vaisseaux
> De nos vieux ennemis arborer les drapeaux;
> Vers la bouche du fleuve ils ont osé paraître.
>
> (b 2.6.607–9)
>
> [Let's talk no more of this. Ten vessels tall
> Of our old enemies have hoist their flag,
> Daring to sail up the river's mouth.]53

In the original version, the king is weak. He has no specific information, but relies on quasi anonymous rumor; he is threatened but does not appear to know even by what; he experiences fear, and is susceptible to surprise. By 1660, Fernand has the same situation much better in hand, and speaks from a position of knowledgeable command. Here he knows the imminent danger is coming from the sea; he knows precisely how many ships, to whom they belong, which standard they bear, and exactly where they are located. Fernand is more kingly by 1660 than he was in 1637.

The corollary to that greater kingly presence is a more insistent demonizing of the enemy. Here again, the variants bear this out. In 1637, the Infanta fantasizes that the renown of Rodrigue's valor will carry him as far as Africa to be celebrated even there:

> Porter delà les mers ses hautes destinées,
> Au milieu de l'Afrique arborer ses lauriers.
>
> (a 2.6.544–45)
>
> [Beyond the seas swelling his destinies,
> Planting his laurels in the midst of Africa.]

But by 1660 the same lines have become bloodthirsty. The victor's laurels are smeared with enemy blood:

> Porter delà les mers ses hautes destinées,
> Du sang des Africains arroser ses lauriers.
>
> (b 2.5.542–43)
>
> [Beyond the seas swelling his destinies,
> His laurels red with blood of Africans.]54

It is no longer sufficient that Rodrigue should simply celebrate his greatness in Africa; now he must needs celebrate his greatness by spilling African blood. A strong king and vanquished enemies are recipes and necessary conditions the one for the other, and this is clear to the French theatrical sensibility in no uncertain terms, by 1660.

That this Moorish/African blood should be related to Barbary blood is borne out by the important role of the sea in the play. We must keep in mind that it is the playwright Corneille, not the king, Don Fernand, who chose the site of Seville to enable the device of a threat of attack from the sea, claiming that any attack by land could never come as a surprise (704). And it is the element of surprise and unpreparedness that occasions Rodrigue's heroism, the necessary feature of the story. Given that the French were constantly contending with Barbary pirates at sea and along their coast, it stands to reason that even unconsciously the seafaring Moors of the play would be associated in the French collective imagination with this clear and present, but unpredictable danger.

The king and Don Arias discuss the latest surprise attack that appears to be in the offing:

> Les Mores contre vous font-ils quelque entreprise?
> S'osent-ils préparer *à des efforts nouveaux*?
> > (a 2.6.612–13; emphasis mine)[55]
>
> [Do the Moors undertake some new enterprise against you?
> Do they dare prepare for new attempts?]

Here the integration of the Moorish element is introduced and at the same time firmly established in the structure of the play by insistence on the repeated and ongoing nature of the hostilities between the Castilians, who have conquered and now rule over the former Moorish Andalusia/ Granada, and the Moors, who persist in attempting to reclaim their last foothold on the peninsula (a 2.6.619–22). Indeed, Rodrigue acknowledges, if only discreetly, that the Moors have been just as much a part of Spain as other groups, and among the most distinguished, listing them together. They enjoy the dubious status of insider outsiders:

> Est-il quelque ennemi qu'à présent je ne dompte?
> Paraissez, Navarrais, *Mores* et Castillans,
> Et tout ce que l'Espagne a nourri de vaillants
> > (a 5.1.1568–70; emphasis mine).[56]
>
> [There is no foe I cannot now subdue.
> Come, Navarrese and Moors, Castilians, come,
> And all the valiant men that Spain has bred,][57]

By the end of the play, the king will encourage Rodrigue to attack the Moors in what is now their allotted space, which, given that he now rules Andalusia, can only be Africa, thus escalating from a defensive position to one of outright attack and veritable territorial expansion.[58] The king has resumed control of the situation and turned a quasi-embarrassing defeat into grounds for a glorious offensive. Now that Rodrigue has conquered the Moors locally, and successfully defended the immediate frontier, the shores of Seville ("nos bords") (a 5.7.1 849), he is ordered to wreak havoc on them in their "own" land, implicitly, Africa:

> Va jusqu'en *leur pays* leur reporter la guerre,
> Commander mon armée et ravager leur terre.
> (a 5.7.1 851–52, my emphasis)

> [Go, carry war back into Africa,
> Command my army, devastate their fields;][59]

But it is precisely the question of just what is their land that makes of these Moors such a floating, numinous enemy. Here the tendency toward grandiose abstraction in the lexicon of seventeenth-century theatre serves well to inspire and convey terror, but does not serve as well the generic expectations of factuality and clarity for history. Andalusia appears to be no longer under Moorish rule, but does that mean the Moors have already been expelled? Or are they still there but simply subjects of the Crown of Castille? The seventeenth-century theatre audience knew that the Moors were not expelled from Spain until 1 492. But fiction here has the upper hand over fact. Onomastically, the Moors have already been relocated. In both the 1 637 and the 1 660 versions, Don Diègue assures his son that his band of followers

> Se tremperont bien mieux au sang des *Africains*
> [Would find in Moorish [African] blood a better prize.][60]
> (a 4.1.1 095/b 3.6.1 084 [my emphasis]).

Just as the staging of the nation anticipates its establishment, so the naming of the Moors as Africans pushes them off the peninsula and makes them African. Saying it so makes it so.

Finally then, in this scanning, it bears repeating that the Moors at no time appear on the stage; they are featured only as threats, in the reports of battle and in the Castilian discourse that recognizes in them a means to glory.[61] From the dramatist's point of view, their absence serves to ensure that, despite their worthiness as enemies, they will not gain the sympathy of the audience and thus complicate public sentiment toward the main – that is, visible – characters.[62] This absence further invites the audience to project their own multifarious phantasms of the Moors onto the stage and to participate thereby in the collective shaping of the imagined French enemy.

It is also interesting that the first invocation of the Moors in the play comes from the Infanta, as she tries to imagine a sufficiently glorious conquest that would elevate Rodrigue to a heroic status worthy of the love she already bears him, thereby transforming him into an eligible marriage partner. Through the act of naming, she seeks to make her fantasy real. The exotic presence of the Moors is required in order to stage the apotheosis, and their spectacular defeat is necessary in order to accomplish it:

> J'ose m'imaginer qu'à ses moindres exploits
> Les Royaumes entiers tomberont sous ses lois,
> Et mon amour flatteur déjà me persuade
> Que je le vois assis au trône de Grenade,
> Les Mores subjugués trembler en l'adorant,
> L'Aragon recevoir ce nouveau conquérant,
> Le Portugal se rendre, et ses nobles journées
> Porter delà les mers ses hautes destinées,
> Au milieu de l'Afrique arborer ses lauriers.
>
> (a 2.5.537–45).[63]
>
> [In thought I see that, at his least exploits,
> Whole realms will fall and pass beneath his sway,
> And my fond love already pictures him
> Seated upon Granada's mighty throne,
> The Moors, subdued, trembling, adoring him,
> Aragon hailing this new conqueror,
> Portugal yielding, and his noble feats
> Beyond the seas swelling his destines
> Planting his laurels in the midst of Africa.][64]

The image of conquest invoked by the Infanta is a territorial one for the most part. In the abstraction, Portugal and Aragon will cede to the imagined *conquistador* with dignity. In the case of Granada (Andalusia), however, more is required; not only will Rodrigue occupy the throne, but he will bring the conquered people – the Moors – to their knees. Here again, Corneille's historical mapping is inconsistent. By this telling, the Moors are still on the peninsula; it is their throne in Granada that Rodrigue will occupy. Yet in this same fantasy, in 1637 Rodrigue will continue on to Africa for what by 1660 will be his definitive victory. Meanwhile Rodrigue's father, both in 1637 and in 1660, will refer to Moorish blood as African blood. As far as the Frenchified Castilians are concerned, if the Moors have not yet been physically expelled from Granada, they are well on their way. The issue thus is not historical accuracy (whether the Moors are or aren't still on the Iberian peninsula), but the political symbolic (the shoving of the Moors off onto the African continent). The Infanta's wishful thinking renders foremost a tableau of humiliation for the Moors and of apotheosis for Rodrigue. The Moors then are very much present on the margins and in the collective imagination, if not on the scene of Castille, just as they are graven in its memory.

As we have seen, the 1637 Infanta has introduced the image of Rodrigue crossing over the sea, staging his apotheosis and enjoying his laurels there. But by 1660 she will more aggressively have him perform a bloody victory dance over the displaced Moors, now to be squarely called "Africains." "Porter delà les mers ses hautes destinées, / Du sang des Africains arroser ses lauriers" ["Beyond the seas swelling his destinies, / His laurels red with the blood of Africans."][65] (b 2.5.542–43). The king's concluding royal order (cited above) merely echoes the Infanta's wishful and increasingly bloodthirsty prediction. Her strong desire has made of her a gifted visionary. Rodrigue's glorious future is geographically contingent on the only territory arrogated henceforth to the Moors, and depends there not merely on his victory but on their total defeat.

Structurally then, and from the collective imaginary point of view, the Moors are at the heart of Castille. The Infanta's wishful thinking does not have the precise uptake she would want (her own royal "race" cannot mingle with Rodrigue's), but her predictive words map out with sharp accuracy the course for Rodrigue's meteoric career in the space of the play. From the moment of the Infanta's voiced imaginings in the play, it is clear that Rodrigue must not fail to meet her image of him. The task has been set. Rodrigue must coincide with this fantastical dream of himself. And so must the Moors prove to be worthy enemies.

By the time Rodrigue is reporting on the battle he has won, he has become the hero of everyone's expectations and comports himself as such. In an important and classic test of heroic character – the ability to recount his own greatness without alienating his audience through too great a display of hubris – he magnanimously shows appropriate respect for his enemy, particularly the leaders (a 4.3.1319–21).[66] As he tells it, the Moorish kings enjoy a status vastly superior to that of their subjects. But at the same time, being two, they are neither numerous nor unique; the fact that there are two of them makes them doubles one of the other – which diminishes reciprocally their individual status, and makes both of them less kingly than the sole Monarch of Castille.

And their soldiers, who should have supported them in the moment of adversity, just as in that of glory, are depicted as vanquished dead or as cowards in flight, having abandoned their leaders at the crucial juncture (a 4.3.1320–27).[67] In Rodrigue's speech, it should be noted that the plural "les Mores" slips and becomes the singular "le More" ("Le More vit sa perte et perdit le courage" [a 4.3.1320])[68] ["The Moor saw that he was defeated, and lost his courage"], a generic label that allows assignment of cowardice and unfaithfulness to an entire people suddenly conveniently knowable as one – all alike, interchangeable, indistinguishable one from the other – and underscores the exceptionality of the two, but therefore, unexceptional kings. In this way, the audience is entitled to have split feelings for the enemy – contempt for the common Moor, and terror and respect (but not too much) for the doubled and invisible kings. This splitting is necessary to the function of the Moors within the economy of the play. They must be worthy enemies, but enemies nonetheless. Only a formidable opponent could render the title "Le Cid" meaningful and lend it some weight in Rodrigue's own society.

This title however is bestowed on the stage not by the two captive Moorish kings, but by Rodrigue's king, who reports their words rather than let them speak for themselves. Fernand alone is authorized to honor and entitle his subjects. He assigns an unthreatening, official translation to the title, one with which he, as sole king, can be comfortable. What slips away in the king's translation is the possessive adjective ("leur") as the Moors would claim him as their leader, to be replaced by a more potentially loyal or at the least neutral article ("le"). Fernand strips the title of its subversive ring:

> Ils [les Mores] t'ont nommé tous deux leur Cid en ma présence,
> Puisque Cid en leur langue est autant que Seigneur,
> Je ne t'envierai pas ce beau titre d'honneur.
> Sois désormais le Cid . . .
>
> (a 4.3.1232–35)[69]
>
> [They've named you both in front of me their Cid.
> Since in their tongue Cid is as much as lord,
> I'll not begrudge you this fair title. Be
> Henceforth the Cid.][70]

By the end of the play, when it is in Don Fernand's interest to invoke the power of the title "Le Cid," now linguistically appropriated and harnessed to his interest, he will be able to order his coveted leader to head up his military offensive, and only then will he acknowledge the real power of the title:

> A ce seul nom de Cid ils trembleront d'effroi,
> Ils [les Mores] t'ont nommé seigneur, et te voudront pour Roi.
> (a 5.7.1853–54)[71]

> [At the sole name of Cid, they'll quake with fear.
> They've named you lord. They'll want you as their king.][72]

"Seigneur" and "Roi" prove too threatening to the king's preeminence, and so the term "Le Cid" appears to resist translation. The accolade ultimately defies assimilation with Castilian hierarchical nomenclature.

Here, though, is Rodrigue's dilemma: it is due to his enemy's respect that he commands the respect of the Castilian king, but the Moors' respect will be short-circuited and used against them. It at once bestows much and counts for little. In which case, what is the negotiable value of Rodrigue's newly won title? Don Fernand will now order Rodrigue to pursue and attack the Moors on what is assigned them as their own territory. The power of his title "Le Cid" will be his most powerful weapon, states the king. Yet ironically, this honorific weapon has been assigned to Rodrigue by the very same enemy, the Moors, he is now under order to attack. The continent to which the Moors are relegated, named but only vaguely – by inference, from a distance, separate, theirs ("leur pays" [their country]) – is now designated as a place to be conquered. If Castille already rules over Granada, this place can only be Africa. Rodrigue is ordered by his king to cycle his prestige into royal service, to betray and attack the very Moors who have just honored him, to head up the king's army (not, we note, his own) in a campaign of slash-and-burn destruction. Thus the king of Castille takes the first step towards transforming a successful defense into a project of territorial expansion:

> Après avoir vaincu les Mores sur nos bords,
> Renversé leurs desseins, repoussé leurs efforts,
> Va jusqu'en leur pays leur reporter la guerre,
> Commander mon armée et ravager leur terre . . .

But this with a caveat:

> Mais parmi tes hauts faits sois-*lui* toujours fidèle.
> (a 5.7.1849–53, 1855; emphasis mine)[73]

> [After, on our own shores, routing the Moors,
> Thwarting their plans, repulsing their assaults,
> Go, carry war back into Africa,
> Command my army, devastate their fields . . .

[but with this caveat:]

> Be faithful *to her*, though, in all your deeds.][74]

Lest Rodrigue proceed too autonomously in search of glory, the king reminds his subject of his allegiance by waving in front of him the promise of the prize: "sois-lui toujours fidèle." Here through adroit psychological slippage, the king seeks to secure his loyalty. The "lui" in question, Chimène, the king's other subject in this struggle for justice, serves as a lure to keep Rodrigue from allying with the smitten enemy and putting his new-found glory to his own profit. His love for Chimène can be counted on to keep him loyal, that is subordinate, to the king.

And the king needs to shore up his sovereignty when confronted with a hero such as Rodrigue. By his admission that it is beyond his power to adequately compensate Rodrigue for defending Seville except through the legitimation (without translation) of the title "Le Cid," he is addressing a real problem, the limits of that power:[75]

> Pour te récompenser ma force est trop petite,
> Et j'ai moins de pouvoir que tu n'as de mérite.
>> (a 4.3.1223–24)[76]
>
> [I cannot fittingly reward your deeds,
> And I've less power than you have excellence.][77]

The interdependence that characterizes the relationship between the king and his people poses a constant danger to the king's standing.[78] If Rodrigue is now "Le Cid," what can his relation to his king be, and what, perhaps most importantly, is the king's relation to him?[79] Luckily for the king, there is Africa, and there is Chimène.[80] This distribution and balancing of power – territorial, racial, and now gendered as well, – resonates and informs the politico-cultural message of the play.

CHIMENE AND THE MOORS: MANAGING THE MARGINS

The relationship between Chimène and power, that is her ties to Rodrigue and to the king, mirrors the dynamic between the Moors on the one hand, and Rodrigue, the king, and the Castilians, on the other. Rodrigue, traitorously hidden by Chimène's confidante Elvire in Chimène's own home space, is there made privy to Chimène's innermost feelings as she is interrogated and drawn out by Elvire within earshot. When Rodrigue springs from his hiding place, Chimène is justifiably horrified. She has been emotionally ambushed. Her words have been drawn out of her and delivered to the wrong, or perhaps to the right, but certainly not to the intended ears. Chimène will be duped two other times in the same way. The next time, by the king who, in a highly unworthy fashion, will put her feelings for Rodrigue to the test by announcing false news of his death; then by herself when she misinterprets Don Sanche's return to the court from his duel with Rodrigue as a sign that her lover is dead.

What is important to note here is that a similar dynamic applies in the battle between the Castilians and the Moors. The Castilians have seen the Moors coming, know the attack is nigh, and, led by Rodrigue, make their plans for a surprise ambush attack accordingly:

> La flotte qu'on craignait dans ce grand fleuve entrée
> Vient surprendre la ville et piller la contrée,
> Les Mores vont descendre et le flux et la nuit
> Dans une heure à nos murs les amène sans bruit.
> (a 3.6.1083–86)[81]

> [The fleet we feared is in the river, plans
> To fall upon the town and pillage it.
> Within an hour, the floodtide and the night
> Up to our walls will bring them [The Moors] soundlessly.][82]

The Moors, like Rodrigue at Chimène's and later in his counter-ambush, had planned to keep their presence secret until the appropriate moment, and, like Chimène in confiding only to her confidante, had hoped to keep their innermost thoughts to themselves as they proceeded. But, in the act of executing their plan, they, like Chimène, and unlike Rodrigue, are discovered, trapped, and attacked. They have certainly contributed to their own demise by coming there in the first place, but this is a territory which not long ago was theirs as rightfully, or indeed, as arbitrarily, as it is currently the Castilians'. If the Moors are enemies of the Castilians, it is because, in their time, they have been aggressed upon themselves.[83]

At once similarly and profoundly differently, Chimène persists in claiming her place on the side of the law, only to come up again and again against the king, unreliable dispenser of the law. For the law itself is unreliable, unjust; it does not apply in the case of Chimène and of the Moors. They are *outside* the Law. It is a system of justice that applies only to the king's male subjects, and only when they agree not to take it into their own hands. The king *is* the law, and he *is* the law as long as he *is* king. Despite the fact that he has outlawed duels, he can authorize them as well, as necessary, absolute but responsive to the community he

governs (a 4.5.1435–42).[84] Thus, in the end, Chimène and the Moors
are the outlaws – the one is ordered to rest, the others must retreat and
be vanquished; while Rodrigue, the male subject who has in fact broken
the law, remains in the king's good graces. In fact, Rodrigue is *above* the
law; he has established himself as a military hero necessary to the state,
and hence untouchable. The rules of the game have been flouted in all
three cases, but then the game only admits certain players.

Or perhaps the rules have simply been exposed and the lesson brought
home: the exigencies of the public domain will always prevail over the
cause of the particular. And rules on stage surface primarily for two purposes: to be made and to be broken; only rarely, and then uninterestingly,
to be obeyed. While Chimène's grievance is a personal one, Rodrigue's
heroism has catapulted him into the public domain – a space that traditionally excludes women and that, in order to maintain itself, all too
readily identifies groups as friends or foes. This may be the lesson of the
play, but it also becomes evident that the distinction between public and
private is a specious one of convenience, as the personal politics of family
rivalry and individual love have featured so prominently in the playing
out of public affairs – even war. Ultimately, the out-laws Chimène and
the Moors cancel each other out in Rodrigue's favor. The crime committed by Rodrigue against Chimène's father, and for which she is seeking
redress, is conveniently reassigned to the Moors, the guilt is dispatched
and "justice" is dispensed in one short line: "Les Mores en fuyant ont
emporté son crime" (a 4.5.1424).[85] ["The Moors in flight have carried
off his crime."][86] Thus their usefulness on the local level.

Just as conveniently, for their purposes, the Corneillian Castilians have
two names for their enemy: the one, "les Mores" or "le More" is the name
that attaches them to their history on the Iberian peninsula. The other
appellation "Africains" ("Tu les as prévenus; mais leurs vaillantes mains /
Se tremperont bien mieux au sang des Africains" [a 3.6.1093–94]),[87]
["You had forestalled them, but your valiant hands/Would find in
Moorish [African] blood a better prize."][88] relegates them to another
continent and authorizes the Castilians to view them as invaders to be re-
pulsed, indeed to be punitively attacked. The label "Africain" effaces their
status as sharers of the Iberian peninsula, evacuates them completely
from their last foothold there, and casts them henceforth as outsiders.
With all bonds of prior claims or familiarity denied, this people thus
named becomes a fair target for bloodshed and the continent to which
they are assigned is confirmed as a legitimate and even opportune space

for conquest – a foreign terrain ideal for the exporting and regulating of domestic problems, such as the threat to the king's sovereignty represented in Rodrigue's new heroic status.

OPEN CONCLUSION

Working toward conclusion, let us reflect on the comments from and concerning the seventeenth century, cited earlier, which gloss all conflict between the French and the Ottomans and their protectorates, the Barbary republics, as being of a religious order. Juxtaposed to them, on the stage, from roughly the same period, we are witness to the representation of a conflict, invented certainly, but plausible, drawn from a prior historical and dramatized model, playing on the same tensions reported in the news of the day, and based on a simplistic binary political view. Religion plays no explicit part in it, but is rather suppressed in favor of a more powerful and more diffused vehicle, that is: secular culture. On the seventeenth-century stage, it is not under the aegis of crusade or jihad that tension between the Christians and the Muslims finds its legitimating expression. Rather, Corneille's theatre here absorbs from the community and reflects back to it, magnified for possible edification and contemplation, subtle messages of racism, territorial aggression, socio-economic ambition, and, as we have seen with Chimène, psychological warfare. However, these discourses, in their aesthetic setting, are dangerously exalted to the status of noble truth. They will operate henceforth hand-in-glove with that older one of religion.

The community from which the theatre draws the messages it will recast is often an interested one: the elite. The theatre is the space where the aristocracy of France participate in the activity of nation-building. Although the theatre audience was mixed early on, and other segments of the population (attendants, domestics) had access to privileged space, the tone was set by the patronizing nobility.[89] This group fell in line with royal taste and the playwright sought to please. So high culture and high social status collaborated in the shaping of a vision of "Frenchness," and if "race" features as an important element in this theatrical vision of state-making, it is no accident. The nation is staged first, then created, but by a select group, bound by a shared vested interest in the primacy of "race."[90] And one of the foremost levers for the legitimation of the state would be that of regulation through biocultural identity. In order to stage this point, the raw material of many French early modern plays would necessarily include outsider "others." In *Le Cid*, the lack of control represented by the threat of the Moors and the vulnerability of Fernand's kingdom to this menace would serve to justify the construction of a strong state. Rodrigue would thus embody a form of patriotism which would become increasingly the norm as the idea of statism took hold in the seventeenth century. In which case, the threat of piracy and the staged celebration of victory that is *Le Cid* mutually implicate one another.

French literate society then becomes saturated with textual / theatricalized attitudes discreetly embodied in literary works, that have their roots deep in their own naturalized history. These attitudes in time become readers' or spectators' assumptions. And eventually, these assumptions, unquestioned, play a legitimating role in transforming their own accumulation into what can only be called prejudice. The role of these textual attitudes, thus, will be an important one, as in the example of *Le Cid*, with its links to an authenticating and authorizing past (Guillén de Castro), its steady reverberations in a seventeenth-century French present, and, from there, its links to an impressive anchored future (in its capacity as a "classic" in our time) which ensures the uninterrupted transmission of prejudice through generations of the culturally literate in France and in French literature classrooms throughout the world. Unless interrogated.

On that one (conservative) hand, we have the cultural monument of Gérard Philippe's performance of *Le Cid* at the 1951 Avignon Theatre Festival. So impressive and moving was his performance as Rodrigue that he was actually buried in his costume when he suffered a youthful (and therefore heroic) death, and his own personal legend further contributed to immortalizing the "longue durée" of the conventional story of *Le Cid* for our times. This is a chapter from France's official story.

On the other (oppositional) hand, the Anglo-Irish director Declan Donnellan has recently radically interrogated that official story. In the summer of 1998, he ventured intrepidly into the heart of the French canon and challenged the received story. It was clear that he had taken on a sacred text; as Alan Riding, an American critic, reviewing Donnellan's production, put it:

Le Cid has become a central pillar of the French canon, its most famous speeches learned by heart by generations of high school students, a task facilitated by both the predictable rhythm and limited vocabulary of its verse. Many French adults can also remember seeing one or another production of the play as children. And if, as likely, it was at the Comédie Française, they would have seen it interpreted as an epic tragedy. In tackling *Le Cid* then, Mr. Donnellan was also taking on French memories.[91]

It is precisely the healthy interrogation called for above that Donnellan initiated in his casting for his production of *Le Cid*: "His first surprise was to cast a young black French actor, William Nadylam, as Rodrigue."[92] Such a move reveals to the audience and challenges them on their own operative but tacit assumptions about the place of race, the casting of roles, in the play and beyond.

But, in the future, would it not also be useful to introduce readings or performances of this canonical play with a moment of reflection on the title? *Le Cid*. This Arabic term, "sidi," was formally "assimilated" into the French language only recently, in the twentieth century. The *Petit Robert* offers the following definition:

Sidi–n. m. (déb. XXe; <<monsieur, seigneur>>, 1847; mot arabe). *Péj*. Indigène nord-africain établi en France. <<Ceux qui traitent les Nord-Africains de bicots ou de sidis>> (E T I E M B L E).[93]

Sidi: Masculine noun (early 20th century; «sir, my lord» 1847; Arabic word. Pejorative Native North African settled in France. «Those who call North Africans bicots or sidis» (Etiemble).

From the nobiliary nomenclature of exotic <<seigneur>> all the way to the pejorative local connotation, the devaluation of this term and the problematic of assimilation which vexes French society today, had already been announced in Corneille's staging of *Le Cid*, and finds its troubling encapsulation here in this terse acknowledgment that fixes it in the current French lexicon. Meanwhile, in the very shadow of Paris's Sacré Coeur, in the "Goutte d'or" neighborhood, numerous tea stalls and small restaurants abound, bearing the names of their respected owners, "*Sidi* Hassan," etc. The honorific title still resists translation, but the resistance now comes from the other direction, and, at the same time, from close to "home."

Finally, the weight of this great classic is beginning to lighten. From within France, not only is Donnellan producing a new staged version of *Le Cid*, but someone is actually "writing back" to Corneille. Henri-Frédéric Blanc's *Sidi, Tragédie bouffe en cinq actes* (1997) takes on the timely if not overdue task of spoofing Corneille's venerated "tragédie comique." With all deliberation, Blanc positions himself *vis-à-vis* Corneille's generic hybrid with his pointed epigraph: "La farce

périra par la farce." ["Farce will perish through farce."] The setting
is a North African neighborhood in Marseilles, two competing bars,
Corsican gangsters headed up by – who else? Fernand! Sidi is an outsider,
a Beur, in love with Chimène, whose father owns the Bar de l'Univers.
Sidi celebrates not the enmity of two rival factions – the Corsican and
the Beur – or their outsider status on French soil, but, wishfully, their
ability to enjoy one another, and together to contribute to the linguistic
and cultural enrichment of, not the Paris-standardized French language
and ethos (manifestations of the strong state), but the Marseillais dialect
and way of local life.[94] Here is celebrated a new local politics, a new
local language, a new local culture, but only fully appreciable against
the backdrop of that old statist story, that classic, *Le Cid*. Isn't this what
classics are good for?

Lest such a project appear too idealistic, consider that it is grounded in
the very real demographics of today's Marseilles. The concluding envoi,
the final word of the latter-day Fernand, is no longer a stately gesture
toward empty time, austere virtue, and kingly authority ("Laisse faire
le temps, ta vaillance et ton roi" (a 1637: 5.7.1866; b 1660: 5.7.1840).
["Leave it to time, your valiance and your king."][95] but warm praise
and recommendation for another solution altogether: for that timeless,
fabulous, imposing knob of flavor that respects no frontiers – individual,
territorial, racial, psychological, or socioeconomic – and certainly has
little to do with religion, but which signals an enthusiastic shared taste
that effectively and enduringly bonds the Mediterranean world: garlic!
"Allons, enfants de la patrie, que l'ail c'est bon pour le coeur!" (129)
["Onwards, children of the fatherland! How good garlic is for the heart!"]
In the meanwhile, those Saracen towers still stand watch, but appear
increasingly mysterious as their purpose slips into oblivion.

CHAPTER 3

Acculturating the audience: Le Bourgeois gentilhomme[1]

SUMMARY

Molière's Le Bourgeois gentilhomme *(1670)*

Louis XIV commissioned Molière to work with the chevalier d'Arvieux and the court musician Lulli to produce a comedy featuring some "turqueries" following the trying visit of the Ottoman grand vizir's envoy, Soliman Ferraca to the French court. The result was this play.

Monsieur Jourdain is a wealthy man, son of a successful merchant, who wants to be a nobleman. He hires a tailor, a music teacher, a dancing teacher, a fencing teacher, and a philosopher tutor in order to acquire the trappings of nobility. His efforts are comically fruitless. He has one noble friend, an impoverished cad Dorante, supposedly his entree to Court. Dorante borrows money from his wealthy friend incessantly. The fact that Monsieur Jourdain is infatuated with Dorante and his gilded promises does not get in the way of his keeping an accurate tally of Dorante's accumulating debt to him.

Dorante sets up a situation whereby he assists Monsieur Jourdain in trying to woo a wealthy widowed marquise who, in fact, is his own lady love. In acting as the go-between, Dorante is able to claim credit for all the gifts and attentions Monsieur Jourdain lavishes on her, and thereby succeeds in winning her hand for himself.

Meanwhile, Monsieur Jourdain's nobiliary aspirations wreak havoc with his family. He refuses to allow his daughter to marry Cléonte, the man she loves, because he decides that Cléonte is not noble enough for his taste.

Cléonte's valet, Covielle, comes up with a scheme to make the marriage possible. He gets everyone (except Monsieur Jourdain and family) in on it. Disguised as a long-absent merchant, friend of Monsieur Jourdain's father, he acts as go-between to announce that the son of the Grand Turk (Cléonte in disguise) wants to marry Monsieur Jourdain's daughter, but that in order for the match to be possible Monsieur Jourdain must first be elevated to an appropriate rank of nobility (a fictitious "mamamouchi") in the Turkish order.

Monsieur Jourdain is thrilled with the prospect of this social advancement, and the elaborate, hilarious ceremony of induction into "turquerie" takes place. After much entertainment, Cléonte and Monsieur Jourdain's daughter are united,

and Monsieur Jourdain attains and remains in a state of ignorant bliss.
The comedy concludes with the Ballet des Quatre Nations.
Questions to ponder
(1) What are Turks doing in this play about French class relations?
(2) Why, in a French play addressed to a French-speaking audience, do the
players use so many other languages? Are they incomprehensible to the spectators?
(3) Why does the play conclude with the "ballet des quatre nations" when
it appears to have so little to do with the plot?

Il (l'ambassadeur Nointel) fit sa harangue, qui dura près d'un quart d'heure. Elle ne servait de guère, car l'Interprete n'en expliqua que le sens au Vizir, et en peu de paroles, et le Vizir le dit *en deux mots* au Grand Seigneur. [emphasis mine](Jean Chardin, *Journal du voyage du chevalier Chardin*)

[He [the ambassador Nointel] delivered his harangue, which lasted nearly a quarter of an hour. It hardly served its purpose, for the Translator only explained the meaning to the Vizier, and in few words, and the Vizier told it to the Grand Lord *in two words*.]

(M. Jourdain: Tant de choses *en deux mots*? [emphasis mine])

[So many things *in two words*?] (Molière, *Le Bourgeois gentilhomme*)

Mention of Molière's comedy, *Le Bourgeois gentilhomme*, more often than not evokes the knowing riposte: "ah, le grand mamamouchi"! ["Ah, the great mamamouchi!"] The play functions as a standard marker in the story of French exoticism. Molière's plot resolution depends totally on a cross-cultural contrivance – Frenchmen disguised as Turks – dressing like them, behaving like them, speaking like them, and on cultural markers such as rugs, dervishes, even the Koran reduced to the status of props. While the credulous lead star, Monsieur Jourdain, will believe his eyes and fall for the visuals of the ruse, even he will have trouble believing his ears: "Tant de choses en deux mots?"[2] ["So many things in two words?"] He, son of a merchant, knows how to count, and misapplies the skills of his family trade to assess translation. While this is a moment of high comedy, it is also a reminder that language and commerce are intimately related through the process of exchange they both represent. Such serious spoofing suggests that we look at the linguistic and commercial, and, by implication, diplomatic and cultural relations that obtained between the French and the Ottomans in and around 1670, when the play was first staged.

The seventeenth-century relationship between Paris and Constantinople required linguistic competence. For the French, as they moved in on the Levant to trade, dictionary knowledge of Ottoman was not sufficient; fluency in the spoken language as well as the ability to negotiate formal treaties was necessary. This implied a performative seamlessness not simply between the Ottoman and the French languages, but also between the two cultures. In his blissfully ignorant wisdom, Monsieur Jourdain has put his finger on a crucial problem – the cultural abyss that separated the two worlds, which business and diplomatic interests were endeavoring to bridge. *Le Bourgeois gentilhomme* demonstrates the complexity of issues around translation, and invites us to investigate how the French handled the language barrier in their various negotiations with the Ottomans at the time of the production of the play. The play also stands as ample evidence of fraught cross-class relations between French bourgeois and aristocrats, and intense rivalry of the French with the Turks. These tensions call for reflection.

OUR FOUR HEROES: D'ARVIEUX, MONSIEUR ROBOLY, MONSIEUR JOURDAIN, COVIELLE

The pages that follow focus on and weave together, in speculative fashion, the stories of two real people who attained a certain textual and hence historical importance, and of two dramatic characters who, because the comédie-ballet they star in was put to paper, also enjoy textual reality. These four figures – a traveler/linguist/diplomat, a merchant/ambassador, a would-be gentleman, and a valet/dramatic improvisor – when considered together, offer commentary on one another, and also on the greater issues of French class attitudes and French–Ottoman relations.

The major character in this story is the chevalier Laurent D'Arvieux (whom we met briefly in chapter 1 with regard to his career choice, and who surfaces regularly in chapter 2 because of his knowledge of the pirating situation). D'Arvieux, linguist and eventual "envoyé extraordinaire" for Louis XIV, was an ambitious Marseilles merchant (Arviou) of modest background with claims to noble parentage (he became "D'Arvieux" only once in Paris), well traveled and fluent in several languages (Ottoman and Arabic foremost among them).[3] His *Mémoires* register not only his adventures abroad, but also his successes and failures as he insinuated himself into French court life, and made himself useful to the king and to royal envoys, becoming one of these himself in the due course of his career. D'Arvieux made his mark in the annals of literary history that recount the genesis of Molière's *Le Bourgeois gentilhomme* as indispensable consultant-informant to the playwright.[4] He was an undisputed expert in matters of exotica. However, upon his arrival at court, he was actually engaged in the same task of mastering the aristocratic master code as that to be tackled by our comical hero Monsieur Jourdain on the stage. This world was more foreign and inscrutable to him than the Ottoman one.

Initially, D'Arvieux's exotic travels allowed him to ingratiate himself with the leisured members of the court who thirsted for novelty. They were fascinated with all that he could communicate to them of this other culture, down to the clothing of the people: "Je fus obligé de faire venir de Marseille mes habits Turcs et Arabes, afin de paraître dans ces habits devant le Prince" (4:98). ["I had to send to Marseille for my Turkish and Arab dress, in order to wear it before the Prince."] In exchange for his stories, they promised him protection and advancement. D'Arvieux's unusual store of knowledge was such that he soon enjoyed great popularity at the French court, but he despaired when this was not translating into material gain or a position of honor:

Je fus bientôt connu de tous les Grands de la Cour: Ils prenoient plaisir à me questionner sur les moeurs des differens Peuples que j'avois vûs. Tous me promettoient leur protection, et pas un ne songeoit à me procurer la moindre grace, ni le moindre poste où je pusse servir le Roi et avancer ma fortune. J'étais si neuf dans le métier de Courtisan, et si peu accoutumé au langage de la Cour, que je me nourrissois d'esperance, et me desesperois quand cela manquoit" (4:101).

[I was soon acquainted with all the important people at Court. They took pleasure in questioning me about the customs of the different people I had seen. All promised me their protection, but not a single one of them thought of obtaining me the smallest favor, or the least position in which I could serve the King and advance my fortune. I was so new to the trade of a Courtier, and so little accustomed to the language of the Court, that I fed on hope, and despaired when it was lacking.]

He finally found a more solid welcome with the learned uncle of a fellow traveler-savant, Melchisedech Thévenot, a great traveler and linguist like his better known nephew, Jean Thévenot. D'Arvieux agreed to collaborate with him on a geography book in return for his hospitality. In Thévenot's household, he was able to do some work on a Turkish grammar and dictionary as well. When Pierre Vattier, the Royal Professor of Arabic at the Collège de France, died in 1667, D'Arvieux hoped the chair would be his. But when it turned out to be destined to another more academically credentialed and well-connected candidate, he claimed to be just as happy without it, for reasons of class: "[Il] n'était nullement de mon goût; parce qu'il m'aurait fallu endosser une robe de pédant avec un bonnet quarré, équipage qui ne quadrait point avec mon épée et ma

Croix de Chevalier" (4:106). ["It was in no way to my taste; because I would have had to wear a pedant's robe along with a square cap, a get-up which did not square at all with my sword and my Knight's Cross."]

D'Arvieux did end up enjoying a distinguished and rewarding career in the king's service as a consequence of his linguistic talents. But he consistently set himself apart from other courtesans, and maintained a posture of outsider and underdog in the world of the court and the academy. He was of a new breed that did not yet have a clear niche in the social fabric of his day. He was not "merely" a merchant, but neither was he "quite" a scholar; furthermore, as we shall see, he failed to secure for himself the coveted title of ambassador. We can think of him as an example of one of the first high-profile French career consultant-types, serving occasionally as diplomats-at-large, a sort of Pollux, as opposed to the diplomatic political appointments represented by the succession of official and, not incidentally, distinctly aristocratic ambassadors to the Porte: de Césy, de la Haye, de la Haye fils, de Nointel, de Guilleragues.

The words that most reassured D'Arvieux, lovingly inscribed in his *Mémoires*, were those addressed to him by the king himself, He earned them with his linguistic talent, and all of his hopes for an illustrious future hung on this skill: "N'oubliez pas vos langues Orientales, car je pourrai vous employer pour mon Service dans *ces Païs-là*" (4:110). ["Do not forget your Oriental languages, for I will be able to engage you in my Service in *those countries*."] In Molière's play, we find an echo of these cherished words. When Cléonte's valet, Covielle, concocts the play within the play that will serve his master's interest (to secure the hand of the would-be gentleman's daughter), he sets himself up as translator and cultural informant. At a certain moment, in response to Monsieur Jourdain's naïve but too probing questions, his at once expert and vague explanation will allude just as nonchalantly as the king's words to that same amorphous zone of exotica that falls outside the care of close scrutiny, and is at the same time easily contained in the sweeping vagueness: "Ce sont façons de parler obligeantes de *ces pays-là*" (4.4.768).

As both the king and Covielle refer to the Levant, the "là" in the expression "ces pays-là" firmly sets a dissociative distance between their world and this other. Perhaps Covielle, Molière's creature, is performing a mockery of D'Arvieux's most cherished words, and "ces pays-là" not only gestures dismissively to a part of the world that eludes French domination, but also loops back to allude just as readily to the world of the French court where the king caresses his subjects with flattering words ("façons de parler obligeantes") that bind them in service to him, notably the expert consultant D'Arvieux himself. After all, he was assigned as Moliere's collaborator to ensure local color and veracity in the play's representation of the Ottomans. What kind of relationship did D'Arvieux and Molière enjoy? Was Molière spoofing D'Arvieux? This was not a spontaneous voluntary collaboration but a royally imposed one. We do know from D'Arvieux's *Mémoires* that D'Arvieux does not get the plot of the play right; and it is not difficult to read passages of Molière's play as sly digs at him. With his keen eye for human foibles, Molière never missed a trick. And we also have seen that D'Arvieux was sensitive to slights. Did these two have difficulty working together? This, unfortunately, is a piece of the story about which we can only speculate.

The fictitious Monsieur Jourdain, socially ambitious like Laurent D'Arvieux, also aspired to entry into the world of the court, of "les gens de qualité" ["people of quality"] (1.2. 714). Of course, he could not succeed and still remain a comical character; but in Constantinople, a common merchant, a Monsieur Roboly, did in fact combine the social background of Monsieur Jourdain and the linguistic skills of D'Arvieux, and actually was prevailed upon during a stretch of tense relations (1661 through 1665, when the French ambassador had been recalled but not yet replaced) to serve as the official French representative at the Porte. This put entirely into question the need for aristocratic representation of the crown as well as for the specialized skills of a government consultant such as D'Arvieux, thereby threatening to suggest that the nobility and the burgeoning civil service were superfluous altogether. Monsieur Jourdain then was condescendingly constructed as an endearing object of ridicule on the Paris stage because his real counterpart, Monsieur Roboly, was so successful in Constantinople. In the play, semantically glossed in positive valence as considerate, important, knowledgeable, busy, generous, Monsieur Jourdain père (and by implication his son, our hero) is at the same time clearly pegged as a member of the bourgeois merchant class:[5] "Tout ce qu'il [le père de M. Jourdain] faisait, c'est qu'il était fort obligeant, fort officieux; et comme il se connaissait fort bien en étoffes, il en allait choisir de tous les côtés, les faisait apporter chez lui, et en donnait à ses amis pour de l'argent" ["In everything he [Monsieur Jourdain Sr.] did, he was quite obliging, quite zealous; and as he knew a great deal about fabric, he went about everywhere to get it, had it delivered to his house, and gave it to his friends in exchange for a sum."] (4.3.766).

The père and fils Jourdain and Monsieur Roboly were clearly cut from the same cloth.

These four characters, Monsieur Jourdain, Covielle, Laurent D'Arvieux, and Monsieur Roboly – all four would-be gentlemen, each in his own way – incarnate not merely the tensions of individuals in society but those of entire communities. For just as Paris was increasingly becoming the elitist center of the French kingdom and the hub of the French state, so Marseilles epitomized the bourgeois heart of France's commercial life on the Mediterranean, while Constantinople represented a lucrative market, but also a bizarre, exotic and therefore almost silly world. As Dorante stands in for a decadent and opportunistic Paris aristocracy, so all of Marseilles is in a way lampooned in the figure of Monsieur Jourdain. As heir to a bourgeois fortune, built on commerce, this character epitomizes all that Marseilles represents to the privileged capital of Paris. Jourdain, not so benightedly (but to the discomfort of the traditional aristocracy), believes he can buy distinction and so accede to the class of the elite. At the same time, in the strange but real world of Constantinople, Monsieur Roboly is successfully acquitting himself as French businessman and diplomat. And in this parade of truth-bearing topsi-turviness, it is the lowliest of the low, Cléonte's valet Covielle, who invents and runs the show within the show, himself playing the crucial role of the "truchement"/diplomat which was to be in fact D'Arvieux's ticket to fame and success. This ambiguity concerning entitlement and identity produces collective anxiety at the court. On the stage, it results in the conflation of the domestic competitor class (the rising bourgeoisie) and the Ottoman "Other," eventuating in this dramatized statement of French national identity – its marked class-consciousness and elitism honed against the foil of the "Other."

THE SITUATION

While Molière's play can be viewed as an even-handed swipe at the Turks, at the rising merchant class, at the indebted and consequently devious aristocratic class, concern for the advancement of the collective enterprise that is France informs the spoofing. Paris and Constantinople were nominally political allies, especially against the Habsburgs, but Paris also competed with Constantinople as a power center and this implied financial as well as military might. Colbert's commitment to advancing commercial interests and his goal of increasing the wealth of the nation caused stirrings throughout the French kingdom and wherever the French did business. Along with the rest of Europe, France felt the economic effects of its enrichment, a direct result of its exploitation of the New World, the influx of silver in particular, and was looking for investment opportunities. The Ottomans were eager to buy this silver and to exchange raw materials (including fibers for textiles, wood, ashes, oil, coffee, wheat, drugs, perfumes, spices, as well as curiosities) for French finished products (especially cloth, but also including paper, tooled leather, hardware, glass, wax, spirits, pins, needles, refined sugar, lead bullets, clockworks), and to facilitate the trading of goods in their domains for the tax advantages that thereby accrued to them.[6]

The Ottoman Empire mattered to the French economy, not just as a vast commercial crossroads – a space through and in which caravans and ships traveled and traded goods transported from afar – but as a partner, albeit an unequal one, to whom the French sold their new metal at a profit. In addition, along with other European powers, the French underhandedly dumped bad coins (often alloyed, sometimes plainly counterfeited) on the Ottoman market.[7] Their other primary trading good, cloth from Languedoc, proved to be so inferior in quality that they eventually could no longer compete with England and Holland, who showed more respect for Turkish standards and discernment.[8]

The French vied with other European powers for favored nation status as a trading partner in the Ottoman Empire, but were more eager to enjoy preferred treatment than the Turks were to bestow it, and therefore they negotiated at a disadvantage. Further, not only did French merchants compete with traders from other European countries; they competed with their own official representatives – state-appointed consuls, even ambassadors – who viewed their positions in the Orient more as opportunities to shore up their own personal fortunes than as responsibilities of trust and representation. French official envoys were seriously compromising the merchants' interests, with expectations of bribes for routine services; thus diplomacy became the most lucrative of commercial enterprises in the Levant, at the expense of the French merchants.[9] In this same spirit, Molière's well-connected Dorante would take complete advantage of Monsieur Jourdain in the play – promising the right words to the right ears in exchange for cash loans:

MONSIEUR JOURDAIN   Voilà deux cents louis bien comptés.
DORANTE   Je vous assure, Monsieur Jourdain, que je suis tout à vous, et que
   je brûle de vous rendre service à la cour. (3.6. 744)

[MONSIEUR JOURDAIN   Here are exactly two hundred gold louis.
DORANTE   I assure you, Monsieur Jourdain, that I am at your service, and that
   I am extremely eager to be of use to you at Court.]

But the French merchants created problems for themselves as well by
lacking in cross-cultural sensitivity, in courtesy, failing to pay the necessary
tributes and homage to the local powers with whom they wanted to
do business. In this way, they compared unfavorably with and thus fell
behind their rivals: they would cheat the Turks as often as they could get
away with it, whereas the English and the Dutch gained their confidence
by treating them honestly (204). In contrast, Monsieur Jourdain would
want to be assured that he was getting his money's worth, though he
would be repeatedly hoodwinked; but he always behaved honestly, and
even obsequiously, with his purveyors. If he is lampooned by Molière for
his pretensions, he remains nonetheless a model businessman.

   The consequence of the failure of concerted representation on the part
of French officials and merchants alike was alienation from one another,
among themselves, and with the Turks:

"Les Français non seulement n'étaient plus des privilégiés, les seuls alliés
des Turcs, mais au contraire ils étaient terriblement maltraités par ces
derniers . . . [Notre commerce du Levant] portait en lui-même des germes de
désorganisation et de décadence: abus d'autorité, avarice, concussions et mauvaise conduite des ambassadeurs et des consuls de France; manque d'une autorité suprême capable de réprimer tous les abus. Cet état de choses contrastait
singulièrement avec la parfaite organisation du commerce des Anglais et des
Hollandais, qui nous firent dès lors une concurrence redoutable."(212)

[The French not only were no longer the privileged, the only allies of the Turks,
but on the contrary they were terribly mistreated by them . . . [Our trade in
the Levant] carried within itself the seeds of disorganization and corruption:
abuse of authority, avarice, embezzlement and inappropriate conduct on the
part of France's ambassadors and consuls; lack of a supreme authority capable
of stamping out all these abuses. This state of affairs formed a singular contrast
with the perfect organization of trade among the English and the Dutch, who
then became stiff competition for us.]

It is clear that French–Ottoman relations were in need of repair, and
the French infra-structure around the Mediterranean – both diplomatic
and commercial – was in need of revision. This general breakdown
in internal and foreign relations abroad finds resonance not so much
with the "turqueries" as with the tensions in domestic class and familial
relations represented throughout the play.

LANGUAGE LESSONS

A succession of failed deals and misunderstandings made it increasingly clear to the entire French community that the Ottoman language would be required for official trade negotiations regarding taxes, rights, permissions, etc., and it was evident that the Turks automatically warmed to those who bothered to learn their language. As D'Arvieux put it: "Le langage acquiert aisément l'amitié des Turcs; cette facilité de s'exprimer en leur manière fait mieux connaître les intentions, et attire une certaine confiance avec laquelle un Agent peut éviter bien de méchantes affaires" (4:228–29). ["Knowledge of their language is an easy means to acquiring the Turks' friendship; this ease of expression in their manner makes one's intentions better known, and inspires a certain confidence through which an agent can avoid alot of bad deals."] And so the challenge for the French, in order to maneuver successfully, was to master the language of the "Other."

If the French felt a pressing need to communicate with the Ottomans in the seventeenth century, this was not mutual. Not only did the Ottomans not need the West; by many accounts, they were indifferent to the West.[10] At this time, and throughout their reign, the Ottomans were, as the sociologist Karen Barkey puts it: "far more interested in the military aspects of state building and ignored the economic aspects that would have led them to protect their merchants and offer them incentives."[11] Not only were the Ottomans not interested in developing their own trade, they held the French in contempt for showing concern for such unworthy pursuits. The Ottoman rulers considered business affairs to be beneath their own dignity, and when official representatives of the French king pressed too hard for trading advantages, the vizir responded disdainfully: "Se peut-il faire qu'un empereur aussi grand que vous dites qu'est le vôtre, ait si fort à coeur une affaire de marchands?" ["Can it be that an emperor as great as you claim yours to be should be concerned about a mere transaction of merchants?"][12] While this may have been a strategic rhetorical stance in a given situation, the aptness of the quip is borne out in histories of the period. In the Turks' disdain for the trading profession, they echoed French aristocratic sentiment, which, despite Richelieu's and Colbert's efforts, remained contemptuous of mercantile pursuits.

If it is clear that the French were motivated to pursue linguistic knowledge of the Ottoman world in continuance of the renaissance humanist project and in keeping with the general value placed on erudition, it is even more apparent that they were urgently spurred on by purposes of commerce. They needed to be able to travel safely around the Ottoman-controlled Mediterranean and across the lands of the Empire, and to manage their trading posts ("échelles" or "nations") in Ottoman-ruled territories. Therefore it was the French who moved first to find the words. Initially, however, neither the French nor the Ottomans troubled to learn the other's language. They relied instead on third parties, the "truche-ments" or "drogmans." This term designates a person who speaks specif-ically Turkish (Ottoman at the time), Arabic, or Persian, and at least one European language, and who translates for others. In the seventeenth century, both the Turks and the French drew primarily from the same minority group in Constantinople to translate; these were the Ottoman Greeks, the Phanariots (so called because they lived in the Phanar district of Constantinople).

One of the common ways that the Phanariots had learned European languages was through study abroad. Many went to Italy (to Padua in particular, then a great center of learning) to study medicine or law, and returned not only professionally trained but fluent in European languages. This learning was often the key to great influence and promi-nence for them as official "truchements." According to the historian Peter Sugar, the Phanariots became indispensable to the Ottomans be-cause of their linguistic and cultural competency, for at this time, despite their preferred isolationism, the Ottomans needed to enter increasingly into diplomatic negotiations, with the result that "in 1669 the office of grand translator was created, and the holder of this position became, for all intents and purposes, the foreign minister of the Ottoman Empire."[13]

Such was the case for two outstanding members of the Phanariot com-munity. The historian Robert Mantran charts their career trajectories: first, Panayotis Nicousias, having studied medicine in Padua, became the grand vizir Mehmed Köprülü's personal physician. Köprülü then named him "first translator" because of his fluency in foreign languages. This was a key position since wars and treaties were being waged and negoti-ated at that time. Then Alexandre Mavrocordato followed the same route to prominence. Having also studied medicine at Padua, Mavrocordato became physician to the grand vizir Fazïl Ahmed Köprülü as well as to the French ambassador to the Porte, the marquis de Nointel; and from this position was appointed "first translator," and counselor of the *reis ul-küttâb* (Minister for Foreign Affairs).[14]

The French held their own strong opinions concerning the Grand Vizir's linguistic helpmates. D'Arvieux, Panayotis's aspiring counterpart in France, had this to say about the Greek translator:

Il avoit beaucoup d'esprit, étoit rusé, fin et fourbe autant qu'un Grec le peut être; c'est tout dire. Il étoit extrêmement attaché aux interêts de son Maître, ennemi déclaré des Catholiques Romains, autant et plus qu'aucun de sa Communion, et ennemi particulier des François, parce qu'il n'en tiroit aucun profit, pendant qu'il recevoit des pensions considerables des representans des autres Nations. Il étoit particulierement dans les interêts de la Maison d'Autriche, dont il étoit comme le premier Drogman; et comme il connoissoit les inclinations du Grand Vizir, il affecta une aversion extraordinaire contre nous.[15]

[He was quite intelligent, as sharp, quick, and sneaky as a Greek can be; that says it all. He was quite attached to his Master's interests, the open enemy of Roman Catholics, as much as and more than any of his faith, and the particular enemy of the French, because he got no profit from them, while he gained considerable sums from the representatives of other Nations. He was particularly engaged in the interests of the Habsburgs, where he was the highest-ranking interpreter; and as he knew the Grand Vizier's inclinations, he affected an extraordinary aversion to us.]

Of course, it was in D'Arvieux's interest, in describing Panayotis, to suggest by contrast the uniqueness of his own combined talent of fluency in the language of the "Other" and his absolute loyalty to his French ruler. But the traveler-merchant Jean Chardin's less self-promoting opinion of the same Panayotis was similar:

C'est un Grec, homme de grand esprit, et qui sait plusieurs langues de l'Europe, entr'autre la Latine, et l'Italienne, dont il se sert avec beaucoup de lumière, et de force, tant à écrire, qu'à parler. Ce Grec a une parfaite fidelité pour le Grand Vizir, et l'on voit bien, qu'il a un attachement tout entier aux interêts de la Porte, au prejudice des Chrêtiens.[16]

[He is a Greek, a man of great intelligence, and who knows several European languages, among them Latin and Italian, which he uses with great learning and ability, as much in writing as in speaking. This Greek is perfectly faithful to the Grand Vizier, and one can well see, that he is entirely devoted to the Porte's interests, at the expense of the Christians.]

The French also drew on this same Phanariot pool to act as linguistic intermediaries, and relied upon such minority "drogmans," with an occasional Armenian, ex-slave or former prisoner thrown in.[17] The French diplomats followed the example and even the will of the more experienced French merchants with regard to translators, when they were not exploiting them, since the diplomatic corps at that time was still in the process of taking shape and organizing into an arm of the state.[18] Consuls and ambassadors were dependent on the Compagnie de Commerce de Marseille for their appointments and for guidance, since it was only in the course of the seventeenth century that French envoys would become salaried agents of the state.[19] Hence Marseilles had a certain purchase over Paris at this time with regard to Mediterranean affairs, and French diplomats looked to Marseilles merchants for guidance in identifying capable and trustworthy translators.

And so it was that, in Molière's era, Turkish officials, French merchants, and, at their example, French diplomats all relied on "truchements" recruited from minority groups to communicate. The problem this posed is obvious: these minority groups looked out for themselves and their own. It was in their interest to maximize economic and political advantages for themselves, and to insinuate themselves into the bureaucracy. Thus, neither the French nor the Ottomans could be assured that messages were not being significantly distorted, blocked, or even leaked as they made their way through this outsider community. After all, these subjects of the Sultan did not enjoy diplomatic immunity and had every reason to fear the vengeance of the pachas and the vizirs if, in the heated discussions in which these powerful men engaged with foreign ambassadors or consuls, they translated unwelcome words too faithfully. In the midst of such an interview, more than one translator found himself insulted, beaten, and even imprisoned.[20] The translators, then, were in a vulnerable position; they had every reason to look out for their own interests, and no incentive not to.

The ironic consequence for the truchements was that neither the Ottomans nor the French trusted them. Their employers complained equally that they were "unreliable, indiscreet, and disloyal." Eighteenth-century consular reports attest to the fact that the French in particular directed a good deal of venom towards all minority groups (Jewish, Greek, Armenian), whereas the Ottomans were more tolerant, if also more demanding. At the same time, in their roles as truchements, these minority people occupied the position and wielded the power of knowing subjects over their dependent and hence suspicious masters. Both the French and the Turks were at their mercy, though the French, as outsider outsiders, suffered the greater disadvantage. D'Arvieux, himself a gifted linguist, recognized the problem posed in relying on these insider outsiders. Of course, as we have already seen, he played the card of his fluency and loyalty, so he may have somewhat overstated the case. Nevertheless, he describes a real conflict:

Une des principales causes de l'engagement et des méchantes affaires qui arrivent au commerce, est l'infidelité de quelques truchemans du Païs, Sujets du Grand Seigneur, desquels il faut necessairement se servir...Ils sont toujours du côté des Turcs, pour lesquels ils ont des complaisances et des souplesses que les Français n'auroient pas . . . Leur attachement à ceux qu'ils servent est foible . . . Ils sont tous parens et alliés avec ceux des autres Nations. Ils se revelent les secrets et se maintiennent tous les uns avec les autres, aux dépens des interêts de leurs Maitres. Ils se taisent quand il faudrait parler dans les Audiences. Ils biaisent les sentiments des Magistrats, quand ils craignent de déplaire aux Turcs . . . Ils tournent les demandes et les réponses comme il leur plaît . . . Enfin on est misérable lorsqu'on ne les entend pas. On a beau se plaindre de leurs voleries, leur interêt, leur lâcheté, et la crainte du bâton leur fait tout entreprendre, et l'on ne sçauroit rien faire sans le secours de leur ministère.[21]

[One of the principal causes of the complicated and mean-spirited affairs which occur in trade, is the infidelity of some interpreters in the Country, Subjects of the Grand Lord, upon whom one is necessarily forced to depend . . . They are always on the side of the Turks, whom they flatter and cater to in a way the French would not . . . Their attachment to those they serve is weak . . . They are all related to and allied with those of other Nations. They reveal secrets to each other and all maintain contact with each other at the expense of their Masters' interests. They keep silent when they should speak during Audiences. They alter the Magistrates' feelings when they are afraid of displeasing the Turks . . . They modify questions and answers as they like . . . To sum up, one is in a tight spot when one does not understand them. Complain as much as you want about their thieving; their self-interest, their cowardliness, and their fear of beatings makes them try anything, and you cannot do anything without their help.]

Lest the translating issue be seen as a problem that only the French encountered, it should be noted that other European groups were subject to the same communication conditions. For example, the English ambassador Paget would express particular frustration with the language barrier even at the end of the century (1693–1703): "Not speaking the language, and so, not being able to treat with some who I perceive are reasonable men, so fully and freely as I could, without an interpreter, I find my selfe unable to press the business committed to me, as I would, for want of an understanding Druggerman."[22]

Nevertheless, it should be noted that translators served an important function in that they saved face for the two negotiating parties. As long as business was conducted through a third person, neither the French king's direct representative – his ambassador – nor the Sultan's voice piece – his vizir – could be subject to direct insult, and differences between the two parties could always be neutralized through the translating medium. This, of course, was underscored by the vizir's self-interested translator

Panayotis, as Chardin recounts it, but his point was not altogether without merit:

Panaioti ajouta, comme pour confirmer l'opinion du Vizir, qu'en Turquie les affaires ne se faisoient jamais bien que par un tiers, que le Vizir, et l'Ambassadeur ayant reciproquement à conserver la gloire, et les interêts de deux grands Empires, nul des deux ne voudroit commencer a se relâcher de ses prétentions: qu'il étoit fort facile qu'une Negociation en personne aigrit l'esprit du Vizir, & celuy de l'Ambassadeur; mais qu'une Negociation conduite par leurs interprétes, ne pouvoit si facilement produire de mauvaises dispositions dans l'un, ni dans l'autre.[23]

[Panaioti added, as if to confirm the Vizier's opinion, that in Turkey things never went so well as with a third party present, that the Vizier and the Ambassador both needing to preserve their dignity, and the interests of two great Empires, neither of the two would want to start to give up his claims: that it was quite easy for a Negotiation in person to irritate the Vizier and the Ambassador; but that a Negotiation carried out by their interpreters, could not as easily produce negative inclinations in the one or the other.]

If we are to consider Molière's play in this light, before even examining the conspicuous staging of the "truchement" in the go-between antics of Covielle, we can conjecture that Cléonte's bid for Monsieur Jourdain's daughter's hand might have been successful, and the need for "turqueries" avoided altogether had Cléonte arranged for a relative or distinguished friend, as was often the case at the time – a judicious translator – to speak for him, and not have spouted off himself vaingloriously about his own "noble" but untitled honesty. Instead, the direct negotiation between the suitor and the father resulted in an unequivocal negative: "Touchez là, Monsieur. Ma fille n'est pas pour vous" (3.12.755). ["Let's shake hands then, Monsieur. / My daughter is not for you."] At the same time, we might note the ways in which Dorante, as Monsieur Jourdain's go-between (translator) in his courtship of the marquise Dorimène, consistently worked the situation to his personal advantage and actually concluded a successful wooing of the marquise for himself as he supposedly represented his "friend"/creditor's suit. Thus Molière offers in his play a good deal of indirect commentary both on the needs for translators, and on their sometime wily ways.

While the need for translation posed significant problems for the diplomats, it was not as much an issue for the merchants, because the Ottomans were less suspicious of them. Although the Ottomans were not bent on developing their own commerce, they viewed merchants from elsewhere as harmless people going about business that was useful and profitable to all. So observed M. Ricaut:

Encore qu'ils [les Ottomans] perdent ordinairement le respect pour les Ambassadeurs, dans les Occasions de rupture, ils ne touchent jamais au bien des Marchands qui sont sujets au Prince avec qui ils ne sont pas bien; parce qu'ils considèrent les Marchands, comme des gens qui font mieux leurs affaires dans la paix que dans la guerre, et qui ressemblent, pour me servir de leur propre comparaison, aux Abeilles laborieuses, innocentes, ingénieuses, et utiles, qui apportent du miel dans la ruche, et qui méritent qu'on en ait pitié, et qu'on les protège, ce qui est bien considérable parmi les barbares.[24]

[While they [the Ottomans] typically lose respect for Ambassadors, in moments of disagreement, they never lay hand on the goods of the Merchants who are subjects of the Prince with whom they are on bad terms; because they consider Merchants as people who do their work better during peacetime than during war, and who resemble, to use their own terms, worker bees, innocent, clever, and useful, who bring honey to the hive, and who deserve pity and protection, which is quite a considerable thing among barbarians.]

Indeed, the Ottomans had every reason to encourage and protect the merchant community, since they significantly benefited from their industry. They controlled this vital crossroads space uniting the continents of Europe and Asia; they levied the various customs, import, docking and anchoring, and access taxes that helped keep their coffers full; and they were, as I have mentioned, also avid consumers in this relationship; hence they supported the foreign merchants.

Such respect and tolerance for the merchant class, however patronizing, may have been the case, but it was also true that the merchants were not as totally dependent on local translators for their day-to-day dealings. Direct trading required less linguistic competence on the part of the French merchants. In addition, the minorities made up much of the Istanbul trader population, since the Ottomans disdained such activity; and as a group, the minorities spoke more French than did the Turks. Moreover, the pan-Mediterranean language of "sabir," a lingua franca made up of elements of Arabic, Spanish, Italian, and French, would remain the practical mode of communication that sailors, slaves, and merchants used in their hands-on business among themselves.[25] *Le Bourgeois gentilhomme* showcases this easy esperanto and even its very name in the elaborate conversion ritual imposed by the false Turks on Monsieur Jourdain, where the term itself, "sabir," self-evidently translates as "savoir," "sapere":

> Se te sabir
> Ti respondir;
> Se non sabir,
> Tazir, tazir.
> etc.
>   (4.4.573)
> [If you to know
> You to answer
> If you not know
> Keep quiet, keep quiet]

Although long-time merchants had generally developed fluency, more recent arrivals and those engaged in complicated negotiations did need translators for formalities such as contracts and letters of agreement, and then, more often than not, they expected their local French representatives (consuls, ambassadors, and the like) to furnish them.

While on-site translating conditions for the French were unsatisfactory, they were no better at home. In France, scholars deciphered manuscripts and studied a bookish Ottoman which had little to do with the spoken language. Petis de la Croix (another nephew of the above mentioned Melchisedech Thévenot) and members of his family served as the king's official translators, but when it came to the actual Paris visitation from an Ottoman delegation in 1669 – the one that would provide inspiration for *Le Bourgeois gentilhomme* – their skills proved woefully inadequate to the task. Instead, this was the occasion when the linguistically gifted D'Arvieux became the crucial player, secured a place in the royal limelight, and from a position of relative obscurity rose to prominence, eventually becoming "envoyé extraordinaire," serving as diplomat-at-large, in Arabic- and Ottoman-speaking countries, for the king.

And so we see that, both in Constantinople and Paris, fluency in the language of the "Other" opened the way to positions of prominence and even power for individuals equipped with this skill. But eventually, it became clear in both capitals that these arrangements were insecure at best. The two cultures proceeded to address their need for reliable translating systems in distinct styles.

The Ottomans decided to make important concessions in order to secure the services of the Phanariots, and this group was eager to cooperate. Without requiring their conversion to Islam, the Ottomans sold to them administrative offices in two Romanian principalities around the Danube, Moldavia, and Wallachia; they thereby bound them through a shared political interest, and secured their general fealty.[26] The Phanariots thus bought their way in. This process of incorporation bears a striking resemblance to the rise of the French bourgeoisie in the seventeenth century as they increasingly challenged the hereditary prerogatives of the aristocracy and as the venality of office became a common practice for feeding the royal coffers. But the Ottomans' religious tolerance for the Christian Phanariots is in equally striking contrast to the policies and behaviors regarding the protestants and other minorities in seventeenth-century France. And even within Constantinople, the Ottomans showed greater tolerance for the various minorities than the French, who, while they used these groups as needed, made scathing remarks about them in the consular reports they sent home.

For their part, it became increasingly clear to the French that they could not continue to draw on the Phanariots with any assurance of their disinterestedness. And so they borrowed from the model the Venetians had adopted long before during the heyday of their own trading relations with Constantinople: "i giovani di lingua."[27] In so doing, they also anticipated the system the British would attempt to establish (unsuccessfully) in later years.[28]

On November 17, 1669, Louis XIV decreed the establishment of a language school for the "jeunes de langues" [language-youth]; the Marseilles Chamber of Commerce legislated; and the following year, on October 31, 1670, Colbert implemented the plan for the school, which involved on-site training in the sheltering space of Catholic monasteries located in the country of the target language.[29] Six French boys would be sent every three years to the Capuchins of Constantinople and Smyrna to learn Oriental languages and become interpreters in the Echelles of the Levant and Barbary. The new decree from the Chamber of Commerce spelled out the terms:

Afin qu'à l'avenir on puisse être assuré de la fidélité desdits drogmans et interprètes, il sera envoyé aux dites échelles de Constantinople et de Smyrna, de 3 en 3 ans, six garçons de l'age de 9 à 10 ans, qui voudront y aller volontairement, lesquels seront remis dans les couvents des capucins, des dits lieux, pour y être élevés et instruits à la religion catholique, apostolique et romaine et à la connaissance des langues, en sorte que l'on puisse s'en servir avec le temps pour interprètes.[30]

[So that in the future we may be assured of the fidelity of said drogmans, every three years six boys aged between nine and ten years who so desire, will be sent to the said trading posts of Constantinople and Smyrna, and will be placed in

Capuchin monasteries, to be brought up and instructed in the Roman Catholic and Apostolic religion and in the knowledge of languages, so that in time they may be used as interpreters.]

Once enough young French boys had been educated through "l'école des jeunes" ["the school for youth"] and the French outposts staffed with an adequate number of translators, this group would repatriate to Paris a sufficient amount of expertise to make a school there viable. Known today as the "Ecole nationale des langues orientales vivantes" ["National School for Living Oriental Languages"] or "Langues O," this institution was originally organized as a professional school, clearly distinct from the more rarefied academic milieu. Its sole mission was to provide good linguistic help for the Crown.[31]

In the development of the Ottoman and the French translator cadres, the role of religion played out in two distinct ways. As we have seen, the Ottomans did not require conversion of the wealthy Greeks (who were Orthodox Christians), but secured their loyalty and effected their incorporation by selling them a share of administration and control in the empire. They made them Ottoman but not Muslim. Thus despite their fundamental difference of religion, the way was smoothed between the Ottoman translator and the speaker. This is quite unlike Molière's spin on Ottoman orthodoxy, with the requirement of Monsieur Jourdain's conversion rite to Islam in order that he might become "mamamouchi." Molière's mufti will interrogate him: "Star bon Turca Giourdina?" ["Are you a good Turk, Jourdain?"] And the staged Turks will answer in the affirmative for him: "hi valla" (4.5.770). ["God willing"] "Turqueries" these may be, but they have a distinctly French and slightly coercive flavor.

In sharp contrast, and more consonant with Molière's vision, religion loomed large for the French in their conception and implementation of language schooling. They appeared fearful that the word might be taken for The Word. Thus the choice of the Capuchin monastery as a safe haven for the young French students. There they were to study not only the target language, but to further their knowledge of their own native religion, as if this would anchor them against any temptation to conversion that might seep in through their language acquisition. This was hardly a neutral space. In fact, it was a harsh and austere, a highly Roman Catholic place. Although it could spell social advancement, and families clamored to have their sons accepted for the program (just as some Ottoman-ruled families sent their sons to the Janissaries), it was not to the liking of all the adolescents.

Laurent D'Arvieux recounts the story of one renegade child in particular, to whom he refers as "le petit garçon qui s'était fait turc" ["the little boy who became Turkish"]:

Le 22 un de ces enfants envoyés pour apprendre les Langues âgé de 13 à 14 ans, s'étant enivré le soir d'auparavant, et craignant d'être châtié par les Capucins qui sont chargés de leur conduite, s'enfuit du Couvent dès que la porte fut ouverte, et s'en alla chez le Cady de Galata, auquel il déclara qu'il voulait se faire Mahometan, et demanda d'être circoncis; on le lui accorda sur le champ, après quoi on le conduisit chez le Caïmacan. M. l'Ambassadeur envoya le demander dès qu'il en fut averti, mais il n'était plus temps; et comme il savait déjà assez la langue Turque pour s'expliquer, on ne pût pas dire qu'il avait été trompé.[32]

[On the 22nd, one of these children sent to learn Languages, aged between 13 and 14 years old, having gotten drunk the night before and afraid of being punished by the Capuchins who are in charge of their education, fled from the Monastery as soon as the door was opened, and went off to the Cady of Galata to whom he declared that he wanted to become a Muslim, and asked to be circumcized; his request was immediately granted, after which he was brought to the Caimacan. Monsieur the Ambassador sent for him as soon as he heard of this, but it was too late; and as the child already knew enough Turkish to speak for himself, it could not be said that he had been tricked.]

This scandalous child transgressed the boundary between "speaking like" and "going native." It was in the interest of the French that the young boys achieve fluency without losing their French identity, which in this instance was localized in a religiously freighted foreskin. For the French, in contrast to the Phanariots, there was no way for these young go-betweens to become Ottoman without becoming Muslim. French meant Catholic. Therefore, to become Turkish for the French meant to convert to Islam. Religious and national identity were of a piece in their thinking.

The solution this child sought to his predicament was extreme in comparison with the one the Ottomans and their Phanariot translators were able to negotiate. The intolerance the child realistically expected from the Capuchins and thus anticipated from the Turks had he not converted was more likely than anything else a projected imagining of French domestic policy, which allowed little tolerance for those not of the Catholic faith, despite the Edict of Nantes, which was shortly to be revoked.

Like Monsieur Jourdain, this French child seeks a solution in a conversion experience, in his case one that will remove him from the authority of the monastery and protect him from punishment. That he is prepared to accept circumcision as a more palatable alternative to a Catholic "bastonnade" indicates the strictness of life with the Capuchins. He is motivated by a desire to escape, whereas M. Jourdain is eager to join. And this child can control his future because of his linguistic competence, whereas all M. Jourdain can do is enthusiastically agree to an ordeal that makes little sense to him, but that holds out promise of social advancement, albeit in a foreign order. He will blindly submit to the "bastonnade" initiation, whereas the child will knowingly seek the circumcision.

And finally, the greatest advantage this child enjoys is his youth; learning at his tender age has yielded the fluency necessary to enable him to escape. His youth also protects him from the bad light in which apostasy was viewed by the Ottomans. By contrast, all M. Jourdain can do is regret not having studied earlier – "Ah! que n'ai-je étudié plus tôt, pour savoir tout cela!" ["Ah! Why didn't I take up my studies earlier, in order to know all that!"] (2.4.729), and rail against his parents for not having seen to his education when he was still educable – "J'ai toutes les envies du monde d'être savant; et j'enrage que mon père et ma mère ne m'aient pas fait bien étudier dans toutes les sciences, quand j'étais jeune" ["I have every desire to be learned; and I am furious that my father and mother didn't have me educated in all the different branches of knowledge when I was younger."] (2.4.726). He wishes precisely for the experience the child seeks to escape: "Plût à Dieu l'avoir tout à l'heure, le fouet, devant tout le monde, et savoir ce qu'on apprend au collège!" ["Would to God that I had been whipped in front of everyone, and know what is taught at school!"] (3.3.737). Monsieur Jourdain, for all of his foolishness, has at least the sense to realize that he has missed out on the advantage of youth for the formative experience of a proper education. It is this very advantage – youth – that would be tapped as a national resource in the institution of the "jeunes de langues."

THE GAFFE

Diplomacy calls for a high degree of "savoir-faire." Although this term has been disseminated into the greater Anglo-European lexicon in its French dispensation, and therefore presumably is practiced with superior elegance by the French themselves, the French have not in fact always distinguished themselves with polished manners in international affairs, and the term "gaffe" also has made its way around. The mid-seventeenth century was one of these periods. Two anecdotes will illustrate French diplomatic "gauche"-ness, and not incidentally help explain how it was that in Paris the king, the public, and the playwright might conspire in coming up with as culturally problematic a play as *Le Bourgeois gentil-homme.* If the French recognized that they needed to develop linguistic fluency in order better to represent themselves and their interests in the Ottoman world, it is also true that they needed to work on their manners.

Relations between the French and the Ottomans were tense at the time of the appointment of Küprülü Mehmet Pacha as Grand Vizir in 1650: there had been a string of Grand Vizirs in rapid succession, and the Ottoman government was unstable. This was largely because the Sultan Mahomet IV, having come to the throne in 1648 at the age of seven, was in his minority. The Porte was in chaos as Mahomet's mother Turhan and grandmother Kösem vied for regency status, until finally the grandmother was assassinated. This period has gone down in history as the "Sultanate of the Women."[33] The French ambassador to the Sublime Porte, Jean de la Haye (from 1638 until 1659), taking note of the turmoil and of the constant turnover, decided to sit back rather than pay his respects and offer the requisite present to each new Grand Vizir who came along. In 1650, Küprülü Mehmet Pacha became Grand Vizir, and as with the others, the French ambassador bided his time, assuming that Küprülü's tenure would be of short duration. All of the representatives from the other countries went and paid their gift-inflected respects; only the French held out. By the time the arrogant de la Haye realized Küprülü's staying power (Küprülü held the position until his death in 1662) and decided to pay his official visit, it was too late:

Voiant enfin, que Cupirly s'établissoit à la Cour sur la ruine de plusieurs Grands, & que selon toutes les apparences, il seroit quelque tems Grand Vizir: il l'alla voir, & luy fit son present. Ce fut là veritablement une visite, et un present perdus; car le Vizir indigné de la negligence, et du peu de consideration qu'il avoit témoigné pour luy en cette importante rencontre, avoit formé le dessein de s'en vanger sur luy, et même sur toute la Nation Françoise.[34]

[Seeing at last that Küprülü was establishing himself at Court through the ruin of several people of importance, and that according to all appearances, he would be Grand Vizier for some time: he went to see him, and paid his respects. The visit and the respects were truly a lost cause, for the Vizier was indignant at the negligence and lack of consideration that [the ambassador] demonstrated in this important meeting, and he had formed the design of taking revenge on him and even on the entire French Nation.]

The Grand Vizir had taken mortal offense, and never forgave the ambassador, nor his successors – his son (1666–71) who succeeded him, or M. de Nointel (1671–78) who followed the son as ambassador – with the net result that because of this "chagrin personnel" brought on by this "faux pas" of the first order, French–Ottoman official and trading relations were disastrous for the following twenty years.

But this was not de la Haye's only "faux pas." In addition, the Parisian Donneau De Visé (cited earlier in the "Orientation") recounts a particular story that illustrates the French ambassador's signal failure in tact and diplomacy. Granted, the reporter De Visé was a notorious rumor monger, a muckraker always eager to publish titillating bits of sensational scandal, and an overnight Orientalist with an active imagination when he realized the popularity of news from the exotic Levant – but this story is also reported in the archives of the French Ministry of Foreign Affairs where the correspondences of official envoys from that time are kept, as well as by Jean Chardin, also cited below.[35]

As the story goes, the Grand Vizir Küprülü Mehmet Pacha was an Ottoman parvenu with a success tale that must have especially offended the sensibilities of this French entitled elitist. Küprülü was of an undistinguished background; he had come up through the ranks, beginning as a simple apple vendor with a stall near the seraglio. He attracted the attention of the then Vizir, and began to perform small tasks for him as requested. From there he was promoted to responsibility for the ritual of preparing the Vizir's coffee. He thereby earned a place in the constant presence of the Vizir where he gained his total confidence, such that he succeeded him as the next Vizir. De Visé offers a thumbnail sketch of him. He was, from the French vantage, an unforgiving type: "Il était fier, obstiné, vindicatif, insolent, et avait toutes les qualités d'un méchant homme."[36] ["He was proud, obstinate, vindictive, insolent, and had all the attributes of a mean-spirited man."]

De Visé, in his gleeful tabloid style, elaborated the news from Constantinople, and recounted in his local scandal sheet how the Vizir learned of de la Haye's insolent attitude concerning his career trajectory:

Il [le Vizir] sut qu'un ambassadeur, dont il n'est pas nécessaire de dire le nom, avait fort recommandé la civilité à tous ses domestiques, et de n'être pas avares de saluts en passant dans les rues de Constantinople, et surtout de n'oublier pas à saluer les vendeurs de pommes, parce qu'il leur était impossible de savoir s'ils n'en auraient pas un jour besoin, puisqu'il pourrait arriver que quelqu'un d'entre eux devint Grand Vizir.[37]

[He [the Vizier] found out that an ambassador, who shall remain nameless, had strongly encouraged all his servants to be polite, and not to be stingy with greetings when passing through the streets of Constantinople, and especially not to forget to greet apple-sellers, because they couldn't be sure that one day they wouldn't need them, since it might happen that one of them became Grand Vizier.]

This story made its way, as gossip is wont to do, to the Vizir himself, and the snobbish French ambassador was never pardoned for this gaffe. De la Haye was treated as persona non grata in Constantinople, and the entire French community suffered as a consequence of his cultural insensitivity for the duration of his tenure and this Vizir's rule.

It is not here then that the French earned their reputation as gifted diplomats; they behaved badly. These stories, beyond encapsulating diplomatic boorishness, illustrate seventeenth-century French anxiety with the social mobility of the Ottoman world, a fluidity the French found incomprehensible and disquieting – at once different from their own system and resembling the direction theirs was beginning to take as Colbert's meritocracy supplanted the tradition of the aristocracy.[38]

Even as late as 1672, the ambassador Nointel was not finding favor with the Sultan's ear, and audiences were lost endeavors:

C'est là au vrai la source et l'origine de la mauvaise correspondance qu'il y a eu entre la France et la Turquie durant tout le Ministère de ce Vizir, qui a été de douze années, et depuis même sous le Ministère de son fils qui lui succéda. De manière que la dureté de la Porte envers les trois derniers ambassadeurs de France, Monsieur de la Haye le Père, Monsieur de la Haye le fils, et Monsieur de Nointel, et les diverses avanies qui ont été faites aux François pendant vingt ans, se doivent raporter à un chagrin personnel... [39]

[Here is the real source and origin of the ill feeling which existed between France and Turkey during the tenure of this Vizier, which lasted twelve years, and even continued under the tenure of his son who succeeded him. In this way, the severity of the Porte towards the last three French ambassadors, Monsieur de la Haye *père*, Monsieur de la Haye *fils*, and Monsieur de Nointel, as well as the various humiliations [penalty fees] inflicted on the French for twenty years, has to be attributed to a personal chagrin.]

This period of diplomatic failure lasted until 1679 when Guilleragues succeeded Nointel as ambassador and was able to ease relations with a new cast of characters, but the rough patch he smoothed over was the one Molière had by then immortalized.

This information is important to an appreciation of *Le Bourgeois gentil-homme* since it is against this tense diplomatic background that the idea of such a play took hold in the French imaginary. It is also important to keep in mind that, during this stretch, the only remotely successful French official representation at the Porte was conducted, not by an ambassador, but by the common merchant, Monsieur Roboly, during an interim period of 1662–65. Both de la Haye, père and his successor de la Haye, fils were personae non-gratae in Constantinople during these years. They had succeeded in alienating not only the Ottomans, but the entire merchant community of Marseilles, who felt their interests had not been well represented and that business was going poorly for them because of the ineptness of the ambassadors.

There was bad blood between these two groups: the ambassadors had developed the habit of running up enormous debts in Constantinople and then obliging the merchants to pay them off if they were to represent their interests. Further, when the ambassadors incurred penalty fees ("avanies") as a result of "incidents" with the Turks, again the merchants were expected to bail them out.[40] The city of Marseilles, the seat of French commerce in the Levant, felt doubly cheated when its merchants were required to remedy situations in Constantinople since it already paid a hefty tax specifically dedicated to covering ambassadorial expenses in Constantinople.[41] When the French Foreign Affairs minister, Monsieur de Lionne, needed to appoint a replacement for de la Haye fils, Laurent D'Arvieux was a serious contender for the honor.

SELF-PROMOTION

D'Arvieux wrote a detailed memoir to the king ("Mémoire presenté au Roi sur les affaires de Constantinople et sur le Commerce") in which he argued at length in favor of a French resident representative for the Crown who would not hold the status of ambassador.[42] This advice was all but a job description that only the chevalier himself matched. He argued first that it was inappropriate to send an ambassador to Constantinople since the Sultan did not send comparable representation to France; after all, the French wanted simply to be on an equal footing with the Turks. He drew up a balance sheet. In his list, he did not hesitate to point out the legitimate grievances of the Ottomans against the French (selling them false currency, attacking them at sea under borrowed standards, openly supporting the war against the Turks in Crete, the defeat of the Turks at Saint Gotthard, etc.). On the other hand, he cited the aggressions of the Ottomans against the French (the insults accumulated against the French ambassador, the attacks at sea by the Ottomans and their Barbary subjects, their more favorable treaties with other European powers, the increases in import and customs taxes for French goods, etc.).

D'Arvieux then enumerated the mutual needs of the two nations for each other. He pointed out that, since representation at the ambassadorial level had been withdrawn, and the French had been represented simply by a local French merchant, Monsieur Roboly, relations had been smooth, and the French commercial community had been well treated by the Porte. However, he also insinuated that Monsieur Roboly was not himself the ideal representative for French interests because of his possibly compromising familial ties; after all, he had married in Constantinople, with his children registered as subjects of the Sultan (220), and hence his allegiance was unsure should push come to shove.

At the same time, D'Arvieux went to great lengths to argue that ambassadorial representation was inappropriate – the concerns of commercial relations were beneath such dignity; if the ambassador was offended, the king himself was, and such insults could not be ignored or papered over as they could be in the case of a lesser subject, etc. D'Arvieux went so far as to argue that ultimately French commercial and diplomatic interests would always be at fundamental cross-purposes (223). The rest of his argument is basically a description of his own stellar qualifications for the position of official resident, lacking only his name as prime candidate.

The king would have been perfectly disposed to name D'Arvieux to the position, but the Marseilles Chamber of Commerce was up in arms. This group was frustrated by years of incompetent diplomatic representation at the Porte, and determined to improve a situation on which all of Provence's economic wellbeing was so dependent. The Chamber blocked the appointment, claiming that it needed more prestigious and efficacious representation in Constantinople than that which could be furnished by a linguistically gifted but otherwise undistinguished person, such as the chevalier. Hence, Monsieur de Nointel. But the king, in a letter addressed to Nointel from Paris on December 16, 1670 (shortly after the premiere of *Le Bourgeois gentilhomme*), warned Nointel that he was to do nothing that would jeopardize the business of the French merchants in Constantinople, and that he was to consult with them in all matters that would affect trade.[43]

And so it is important to see both that there were real conflicts regarding French–Ottoman relations between the Paris aristocracy as represented by ambassadorial appointments and the Marseilles merchant community, and that these merchants played an active role in

determining foreign policy. This adds some depth to the tensions between these two groups so perceptible in Molière's comedy. The least
distinguished but entrepreneurial Covielle, Cléonte's valet, invents the
farce of the "mamamouchi," and performs the ingenious role in the play
within the play (all supposedly of his invention) both of "ambassador" and
interpreter for the Sultan's son. He thereby stages a social promotion for
himself. Again, was D'Arvieux being mocked through this casting even
as he collaborated in the play?

DIPLOMATS, THE CONSUMMATE ACTORS

For their part, the Ottomans preferred dealing with merchants and considered ambassadors a nuisance. They mistrusted the French generally
("Les françois sont nos amis, mais nous les trouvons par tout avec nos
ennemis") ["The French are our friends, but we find them everywhere
with our enemies."][44] But they specifically suspected ambassadors of
spying – identifying their strengths and weaknesses, and reporting all
information they gathered to their sovereign. In this they were not mistaken. As the historian Lucien Bély summarizes, this was precisely their
task:

Ils [les ambassadeurs] s'efforçaient de connaître le pays dans lequel ils vivaient,
en étudiant la personnalité du souverain, le jeu des institutions nationales, les
principaux ministres, les forces politiques, les cabales de cour, les partis lorsqu'ils
existaient . . . , les forces sociales, les ressources financières, les forces militaires.
Il s'agissait d'informer le souverain lointain, mais il fallait être aussi prudent car
l'ambassadeur ne devait pas être soupçonné d'espionnage.[45]

[They [the ambassadors] made an effort to know the country in which they lived,
by studying the sovereign's personality, the workings of national institutions, the
principal ministries, the political forces, the Court intrigues, the factions that
existed . . . the social forces, the financial resources, the military strength. They
did all this in view of informing their distant sovereign, but they also needed to
be prudent, for an ambassador must not be suspected of espionage.]

It is no wonder that a play should be the site of critiquing French–
Ottoman and aristocrat–bourgeois relations. The art of diplomacy is an
art of representation, of acting in the place of. An individual is vested with
authority to speak and act for the government of his/her country. It is a
trust and an honor. Above all, it is a role. The diplomatic function rests on
the convention that the host country will distinguish between the person
of the ambassador and the ambassador as official representative, just as
we distinguish between actors and the roles they play. The most successful

diplomat would know "l'art de cacher son interieur, et de decouvrir celuy d'autruy" ["The art of hiding one's inner self, and uncovering that of the other person."] (Chardin 1:45).

The historian W. J. Roosen associates the purpose of mid-seventeenth-century French diplomacy specifically with preparation for, conduct of, and recovery from war.[46] And he suggests that the Porte was well aware of this dark side to official representation, pointing out that "the Sultan at Constantinople was willing to receive permanent embassies at his own court, but he himself maintained none abroad until the end of the eighteenth century" (10). The Sultan's "willingness" was only a tolerance for this perhaps hypocritical ceremonial European practice. Given the fact that diplomacy in residence implied not working relations but tense ones, and, as pointed out by both Bély and Roosen, that the function of diplomats in residence was to gather information, it is quite understandable that the Sultan should have preferred a Monsieur Roboly to an official spy.

THE LANGUAGE OF DIPLOMACY

From the lessons above, we can conclude that diplomats needed not only to represent their own countries but to blend in unobtrusively with local mores, as appropriate.[47] They also needed to be able to read the signals and codes of the cultures of the countries to which they were assigned. Thus language entailed much more than mere linguistic competence.

In the same way, Monsieur Jourdain embarks on a broader project than simply learning to speak like a noble. He must in every regard transform himself. From the outset of the play, the bourgeois is engaged in mastering another language, that of "les gens de qualité" (1.2.714) ["people of quality"]. It includes a manner of dress, of carriage, of comportment, of expression, of taste, and, not least, a body of knowledge to none of which he is born but which he must make his if he is to pass. Hence his many "maîtres" – of music, of dance, of arms, of philosophy, of fashion, and the assistance of his informant/translator Dorante.

Whereas M. Jourdain was able to hire his teachers – these purveyors of culture – the eventual "envoyé extraordinaire" D'Arvieux had to rely on his own powers of observation and his given skills to absorb and reproduce as he could the behavior around him both where he traveled and at the court of his king. Jourdain would remain hopelessly mired in the land of "wannabe" while D'Arvieux, with his exceptional survival skills, would plunge into successful imitation. But, for all of D'Arvieux's success abroad, he would not succeed in breaking the barrier into the French Parisian aristocracy and garnering for himself the title of ambassador he so coveted. If he secured for himself the exceptional assignment of "envoyé extraordinaire," the root "ordinaire" still grounded and limited the scope of this distinction.

The language of diplomacy, not surprisingly, did and still does revolve around literal entitlement. Pecking order is established and acknowledged by titles, and therefore official recognition of preeminence, dominance, is all summed up in the mode of address. Consider the following passage from Jean Chardin's *Journal* where he recounts a series of exchanges between the Grand Vizir and the ambassador de Nointel, where the game of titles is actively deployed as the two representatives parry regarding the status of the French king:

Il [le Grand Vizir] lui mandoit, que le terme de six mois, qu'il avoit pris pour faire venir une lettre du *Roy son Maître*, étant expiré; il desiroit savoir si elle étoit venuë, ce qu'elle contenoit, & quels ordres il avoit de *Sa Majesté*. L'Ambassadeur répondit de bouche à celuy qui lui rendit cette Lettre, Que la réponce de *l'Empereur de France* n'étoit point encore venue, que c'étoit tout ce qu'il pouvoit mander alors au Grand Vizir; *n'étant pas resolu de faire réponce à une Lettre, qui ne donnoit pas à son Maître les titres qui appartiennent à Sa Majesté Imperialle.* Monsieur de Nointel en usa ainsi, *parce que le Vizir ne donnoit au Roy dans sa Lettre, & sur le dessus, que le titre de Craul, qui est moins grand chez les Turcs que celuy de Padcha, quoy que tous les deux signifient un Souverain.* Ils se servent du dernier terme pour nommer le Grand Seigneur, et ils s'en sont toujours servis aussi pour nommer le Roy de France. (italics in original)[48]

[He [the Grand Vizier] sent word to him, that the term of six months he had used to request a letter from the King his Master, having expired; he desired to know if it had arrived, what it contained, & what orders he had received from His Majesty. The Ambassador answered the person who had given him the letter from the Grand Vizier, that the answer from The Emperor of France had not yet arrived, and that was all he could say to the Grand Vizier for the moment; not being resolved to answer a Letter which did not give his Master the titles which belonged to His Imperial Majesty. Monsieur de Nointel acted thus, because the Vizier in his letter & on the envelope gave the King only the title of Craul, which is less important among the Turks than that of Pasha, although both refer to a Sovereign. They use this last term to refer to the Sultan, and they have also always used it to refer to the King of France.]

Eventually, Nointel got his way: the Grand Vizir "mit sur le dessus de la Lettre, selon les anciennes coûtumes, *à l'ambassadeur de l'Empereur de France*, au lieu qu'à la precedente il avoit mis, *à l'Ambassadeur du Roy de France*"

(32–33; italics in original). ["wrote on the envelope, according to the old custom, *to the ambassador of the Emperor of France*, where previously he had written, *to the Ambassador of the King of France.*"]

Despite much speculation as to its possible meaning and significance, the title "mamamouchi" in Molière's play may not have any analogue to help us understand it; precisely it needs none. It is clearly a title, a floating one – a signifier that carries meaning itself as signifier and otherwise is empty. In this way it draws attention to itself precisely for its value as pure title. As Chardin attests above, Monsieur Jourdain's infatuation with the prestige of a title is not exceptional, but indeed reflects an important feature of everyday diplomatic negotiations. Nor does Monsieur Jourdain's seduction by the idea of becoming a "mamamouchi" spring from nowhere. Titles are already important markers in the world to which he aspires, and Molière has prepared us and his hero for this high moment in his bourgeois career in the earlier scene (2.5.733) with the chorus of calculatingly sycophantic tailor apprentices. Each time they address Monsieur Jourdain with a more prestigious title, they receive a more generous tip from the flattered client. Through their verbal graces he graduates from "Mon gentilhomme" to "Monseigneur" to "Votre Grandeur." ["Sir/ My Lord/ Your Greatness"] This comical sketch pokes fun not only at bourgeois pretensions, but just as sharply at the politics of obsequiousness that are part and parcel of the language of diplomacy, and exposes the financial underpinnings of the rhetoric.

LINGUISTICS AND CULTURAL COLONIZING: "MIMICRY, MOCKERY, MENACE"

Following the thread of language concerns, let us look at how Molière spells out the terms of the problem in his representation of his hero and in his plot. Note that Monsieur Jourdain's first encounter with a foreign language comes not in a conventionally exotic context, but earlier, in what for him is just as exotic (thus underscoring the relativity of "exoticism"), in his lesson with his Maître de philosophie:

MAÎTRE DE PHILOSOPHIE   Ce sentiment est raisonnable: *Nam sine doctrina vita est quasi mortis imago*. Vous entendez cela, et vous savez le latin sans doute?
MONSIEUR JOURDAIN   Oui, mais faites comme si je ne le savais pas. Expliquez-moi ce que cela veut dire.
MAÎTRE DE PHILOSOPHIE   Cela veut dire que Sans la science, la vie est presque une image de la mort.
MONSIEUR JOURDAIN   Ce latin-là a raison.

(2.4.726)

[PHILOSOPHY MASTER   Your feelings are understandable: *Nam sine doctrina vita est quasi mortis imago.* You understand that, and doubtless you know Latin?

MONSIEUR JOURDAIN   Yes, but act as if I didn't. Explain to me what it means.

PHILOSOPHY MASTER   It means that *Without knowledge, life is almost an image of death.*

MONSIEUR JOURDAIN   That Latin guy is right on the mark.]

Latin is not simply a foreign language, it is a heavily freighted language. Not only does it connote learning, but it denotes erudition, as in the citation above. The initiated are the bearers and makers of high culture; it is they who assign meaning and value in the world (although Molière insinuates here that they do so for base cash). However, to appreciate even this, Monsieur Jourdain would need to be already inducted into the history and values of the class to which he aspires. And of course this is forever impossible since, as Molière has put it in his oft-cited adage: "les gens de qualité savent tout sans avoir jamais rien appris."[49] ["People of quality know everything without ever having learnt anything."] What M. Jourdain seeks he can never learn, since he is not "to the manor born." And so, he misses the point. But he has his own method for making his own sense, maniacal as that may be.

He seizes knowledge and makes it his like the servant Martine in *Les Femmes savantes* (2.6.1 009) who familiarizes "grammaire" as "grand-mère."[50] ["grammar" as "grandma"] He doesn't know enough to realize that "Latin" is another language, but takes it instead for a person: "Ce latin-là a raison" (2.4.528). He has gotten himself into this situation by pretending to know what the maître is talking about: "Oui, mais faites comme si je ne le savais pas" – by acting. And he seeks to negotiate the situation by requiring that his interlocutor act ("faites comme si") as well.

His lack of education is such that he is unable to conceive that language might serve as the medium for an exchange of philosophical ideas (as Latin continued to function in his time) rather than for down-to-earth negotiation between people in bargaining positions. Or is his cagey detour around Latin simply a pragmatic desire to take shortcuts and dispense with unnecessary knowledge? "Latin" for him is conflated with the person who speaks this way and says these things – certainly not another language, since he doesn't even know yet that languages other than the one he speaks exist. This is how, centuries later, it will be seen that the colonized spout back words and expressions of the colonizer without a clue as to their meaning, and with only a desire for intended effect. This is languaging.[51] Monsieur Jourdain's imaginary has been colonized by the hegemonic discourse of the aristocratic ethos. At the same time, this would-be-gentleman may have more in common with the aristocrats to whose company he aspires than may be immediately evident, since, like them, and despite his desire to be learned, he has little use for pedantry.

Monsieur Jourdain's first lesson of substance will build on the little of the veneer he already and unwittingly knows: how to make the sounds of his native tongue. But the lesson will present this not-so-new knowledge in a fresh authoritative frame – that of the science of phonetics. In this lesson, he learns not how to make sounds, but how it is that he does make the sounds he has made his entire life. In following the instructions of his "maître de philosophie," he takes the vowel sounds, practices them, and learns the system of their production. He thereby learns some elementary theory and has a heady taste of the master discourse. The process of defamiliarization convinces him he has arrived, whereas what he is spouting back is the code of the local savant.

In contrast to Monsieur Jourdain's exhilarating lessons in the language he already knows, we will see Covielle invent a convincing Turkish persona by stringing together the meaningless and yet accurate sounds of a language he does not know. The sounds he produces (e.g., "Acciam croc soler ouch alla moustaph gidelum amanahem varachini oussere carbulath" [4.3.767]) make no more sense to him than to anyone else. But they sound authentic, and, since he is also the translator of these sounds, he enjoys complete control over the communication situation (not inconceivably unlike his possible model, D'Arvieux). He achieves credibility by pure imitation, or mimesis. The sounds come from a fixed Ottoman/Arabic phonetic repertoire as opposed to the French one, and are laced with an occasional genuine Ottoman word (such as "mustaph" or "salamalequi") that lends, through its "effet du réel" ["reality-effect"], credibility to the rest, which is simply Ottomanish-sounding gibberish. In producing these sounds, disguised as a Turk (4.3.768), Covielle introduces and serves as a bridge for the son of the Grand Turk (Cléonte in Turkish costume) and his entourage of six Turks, accompanied by Turkish musicians, four dervishes, and the Mufti (played by Lulli at the time). What follows will be a performance of reverse mimicry. The French culture will take on the coloration of the Ottoman one, not in admiring imitation, but more in a spirit of mockery.

The "Turkish" ceremony of initiation serves the purpose of resolving the internal conflict of the play. It eases the social tensions by projecting Monsieur Jourdain's ambitions outward, into an exotic and therefore unproblematic space of fantasy, but the specificity of that exotic space, carefully articulated, also produces a ridiculing commentary on that space. The goal appears to be not so much a performance of successful passing, as a playful but unmistakable expression of contempt.

Here, despite the improbability of the pairing, I am leaning heavily on *post*-colonialist theory to consider how reverse mimicry might have operated in this early modern stand-off. Plays as literary productions (and of course the desires they stage) can have a role in articulating antagonistic politics. The post-colonialist theorist Homi Bhabha invokes Said's observation: "The work of Edward Said will not let us forget that the 'ethnocentric and erratic will to power from which texts can spring' is itself a theatre of war."[52] Bhabha describes the demeanor of the colonized *vis-à-vis* that of the people who have colonized them, and the effect of that demeanor on their colonizers. However, in the case of *Le Bourgeois gentilhomme*, we are not at all analyzing a colonialist situation: the French and the Ottomans were both powerful states at the time, and the French had no real ascendancy over their Turkish sometime allies. And we invoke Bhabha with a cautionary note, since his colonial paradigm is drawn from British–Indian relations, markedly different from the French–Ottoman impasse, or even Said's closely related later Levantine model.

Let me propose, though, that what we witness in Molière are pre- colonial "turqueries." In examining this play, I am reviewing the antics of a people ridiculing by imitation the people they did not, and would not (but would no doubt have liked to) colonize. Obviously, the two situations (the one all too real, the other hypothetical and only sketchily true) are radically different. And yet, they bear an uncanny resemblance to each other. It is important to recognize the French cultural offensive as a reaction, as a defense. The Turks, it would appear, had already and unwittingly, through no real effort on their part, colonized the French imaginary, and the only way the French could manage and contain this phantasm was by staging a representation of the Turks that at once demonstrated their mastery of the Turkish lexicon (in the full sense of the term) and their disdain for it. But this same display of bravado, in this comedy, betrayed their uneasiness with, even their fear of, this formidable "Other."[53]

Early colonial "turqueries"? I say even pre-colonial because, although the French, through their tireless "mission civilisatrice," ["civilizing mission"] did succeed over time in imposing certain cultural standards of "accomplishment" in the Ottoman part of the world, and did eventually take over parts of the empire, such as the Barbary Republics – Tunisia and Algeria, Egypt – in varying degrees, they never succeeded in colonizing the Ottomans per se. The Ottoman dynasty persisted, albeit diminished, until 1923, when it was overthrown and the Republic of Turkey proclaimed. What we see staged in Molière's comedy is an arrogant, anticipatory, and, as history bears out, only wishful and never realized French act of domination over the Ottomans. Instead it was the seventeenth-century French imaginary that had come to be colonized by the very culture of the empire the French state sought to dominate. What we also see, in Ottoman drag, is a staging of the tensions that marked French class relations in the early modern period, especially during the ascendancy of the bourgeoisie encouraged by Louis XIV's minister, Colbert, with the aristocrats cast as would-be-colonizers, and the bourgeois as eager-to-be-colonized.

Bhabha defines what he calls the colonial mimicry that he sees the colonizer striving to produce in the colonized as the measurable marker of the degree of the colonizer's effect on the colonized: "the desire for a reformed, recognizable Other, as *a subject of difference that is almost the same, but not quite*."[54] In Molière's play, the French actors play the roles of both the colonizers and the colonized. By analyzing the performance of mimicry, mockery, and menace within the context of the would-be colonizer's real life theatre, we can consider the ways in which the colonialist mentality manifests in the identity of the would-be colonizer as well as in that of the putative colonized, at least in terms of farce.

In the situation Bhabha is analyzing, the colonized would have absorbed the signs and practices of the colonizers' culture, but only as layered over and interlaced with their own. While the colonizers would want to make the greatest imprint possible on the colonized, they would also want the reassurance of fundamental difference between themselves and the colonized, and therefore would seek to see "an almost same but not quite" image of themselves reflected back to them in these others. Their sense of superiority would be confirmed both by their power to mark the colonized significantly and, at the same time, by the reassuring failure of the colonized to become identical to them. Here, then, we see the ways in which the colonialist mentality marks foremost the identity of the would-be-colonizer.

Molière's "turqueries" render a virtual performance that parallels the act of colonial desire described by Bhabha: "A desire that, through the repetition of partial presence, which is the basis of mimicry, articulates those disturbances of cultural, racial, and historical difference that menace the narcissistic demand of colonial authority. It is a desire that reverses 'in part' the colonial appropriation by now producing a partial vision of the colonizer's presence" (88). However, here we see it is the French, the would-be colonizers themselves, or their actors, their "representatives," staging "a partial vision" of the Turks they prefer to consider as colonized. We have Frenchmen transparently disguised as Turks, but the humor of the comedy depends entirely on these characters not being mistaken for one moment for the Turks they are playing. We see a willfully skewed and maliciously humorous vision of the Ottoman world. But, in this instance, the French are reduced to mirroring both themselves and the people they would have mirror them. It is a closed-circuit situation, which demonstrates foremost the strong hold the Turks have on them!

While spoofing the Turks, the French establish their mastery of this other culture by enacting scenes that betoken at least a surface familiarity with it (reduction of such features as dervishes, muftis, carpets, etc. to the status of props). The play degrades the Turkish religion by parading it, and specifically the Koran, on stage; it pokes fun at the Ottoman way of dress by treating it as costume; it makes nonsensical travesty of Ottoman rhetorical etiquette: "Je vous souhaite la force des serpents et la prudence des lions" ["I wish you the strength of serpents and the prudence of lions"] (5.3.774). The dressed-up Frenchmen speak a gibberish that, although it bears a strong resemblance to the Ottoman language, and even has an occasional recognizable word thrown in, does not for a moment want to be taken for the real thing.

In mimicking the Turks, then, Covielle and his troupe are emptying their language of meaning and at the same time demonstrating that they control the signals of these people. Mimicry here passes to mockery. They are not merely imitating, they are making fun of this other linguistic community and culture. It is the double vision of the Frenchman disguised as Turk, playing, miming the Turk, but still clearly visible as French that produces not only humor, but vicious humor – mockery. And from mockery, it is not far to "menace."

This illustrates Bhabha's remark to the effect that "mimicry is at once resemblance and menace."[55] According to Bhabha, colonized people mimic out of insecurity, from behind which can be detected mockery; here, inversely, the mimicry is performed out of arrogance and disdain by the Turkifying French, but belies a greater fear underneath. Conflict is played out and even explicitly celebrated on the stage, with the ritual "bastonnade" ["beating"] that brings our presumptuous and ever-so-handy would-be gentleman / would-be-mamamouchi, the local threat and the interchangeable scapegoat, to his knees, and finally, with the exclusionary "Ballet des Nations."

Molière's staging anticipates closely the scenario of the colonial situation and produces the same effect of "ambivalence" as that analyzed by Bhabha: "In order to be effective, mimicry must continually produce its slippage, its excess, its difference . . . Mimicry is thus the sign of a double articulation; a complex strategy of reform, regulation and discipline, which 'appropriates' the Other as it visualizes power" (86). In this way, the French make use of the Turks, foreign objects of their desire and fear, to regulate the domestic issue of bourgeois ascendancy; but in so doing, they betray their own fixation on their foil. Here it is evident that it is the French imaginary that has been colonized. The actors are not only playing their French class-marked characters and displacing domestic conflict onto French–Ottoman tensions; they are playing Turks because the real ones are out of reach, but not out of mind. Theirs is a wishful but, as it turns out, not a prophetic fantasy.

In this not-so-upside-down comedy, mimicry of the Turks is conflated with the happily incorrigible Monsieur Jourdain's mimicry behavior. His bourgeois imaginary also is colonized, by a fantasy of the world of the French élite to which he aspires. He seeks to take on the trappings of the aristocracy, but out of naïve desire to become one of them. There would appear to be only this one difference between himself and the French Turks: his desire is sincere, he truly wants to become an aristocrat; whereas the French feign to be "almost" Turks simply in order to mock them, and to have their way with Monsieur Jourdain. But both postures are in the end comparable to ones to be found among colonized and colonizers. The colonized might say, like Monsieur Jourdain: "I truly want to be just like you" / The colonizer: "I want you to be just like me (but I know you can't)" / and yet the other colonized, the Turkifying French: "I will pretend to be just like you, but only in order to have a good laugh at your expense." As Monsieur Jourdain acts out his desire, and is led along, he falls gullibly into the elaborate snare, enticed by the star role of "mamamouchi" offered him. He is punished by ridicule and put in his place, even though, reassuringly, he remains blissfully oblivious. In like manner, the Turks have been ridiculed, but in absentia. In this way, both domestic and foreign stress points in the construction of French identity are exposed and played out. The French push off against both the bourgeois and the infidel as they negotiate who they will be. Although swipes will be made at members of all classes, it appears that it is primarily the aristocrats (only mildly lampooned in the figure of Dorante) who have the last word on what constitutes "Frenchness."

The final whoop-la, "Le ballet des nations," resembles as much the rehearsal of a war dance as any courtly dance. The allied tribes are gathered on the eve of attack. This odd assemblage, with its fragmented and only vaguely coherent casting, poses squarely the question of the basis for French identity: "un homme du bel air," " une femme du bel air," "un Gascon," "un autre Gascon," "le Suisse," "un vieux bourgeois babillard," "une vieille bourgeoise babillarde," ["an attractive man / an attractive woman / a Gascon / another Gascon / the Swiss / a talkative old bourgeois / a talkative old bourgeoise"], setting up tensions of gender, dialect, mercenary affiliation, class, intelligence, age and regional concentration. How do you tell "one Gascon" from "another Gascon"? Was Molière, with these doubled Gascons, underscoring the conundrum of identity? Or was he critiquing a particular French concept of identity? If he was pointedly indicating two valets, then perhaps the latter. After all, these servants often bore merely the names of their regions of provenance, and did not enjoy the status of any more specific identity. Identity then was a class-restricted commodity. At the same time, the final dance sorts out, legitimates and promotes through acknowledgment and inclusion three distinct nationalities: "trois Espagnols," "Italiens," "Français." ["three Spaniards/ Italians/ Frenchmen."] With this political gesture of naming, the final scene winnows out and excludes, eliminates, the very group – the Turks – the play has so pointedly staged, mimicked and mocked. If the French aren't quite set on who they are, they are stridently clear on who they are not!

The idea of French national identity is planted in this play, through a double gesture – first, a carefully orchestrated performance of mimicry, mockery, and menace, and second, through a choreographed dance of exclusion. If we do not have colonialism here, we have all the markers of the will to colonize. As Bhabha puts it: "The epic intention of the civilizing mission ... often produces a text rich in the traditions of *trompe-l'oeil*, irony, mimicry and repetition ... In this comic turn ... mimicry emerges as one of the most elusive and effective strategies of colonial power and knowledge" (85).

Conclusion

Molière's play was not simply a comedy with a few "turqueries," but a compensatory exercise in which the French indulged to console themselves for their inability to manage the Ottomans to their advantage and to keep the French nouveaux riches in their place. What they couldn't control in the world, they would control on the stage. If Louis XIV and his court were seeking to get the upper hand and have the last word on a situation that threatened to elude them, the evidence is, to the contrary, that the situation had already gotten the best of them. That they had to stage this play for themselves suggests to what extent the Ottoman world (with no deliberate intent), as well as the local bourgeois (with considerably more), had actually succeeded in colonizing the French aristocratic imagination. And that Monsieur Jourdain, despite his foolishness and the ridicule to which he is subjected, remains so endearing reminds us that Molière's sympathies were a great deal more complex than his king's.

Over time, the French would attain an ascendancy of great influence in the Ottoman Levant; they would maintain religious and commercial footholds throughout the Empire, and they would increasingly set the cultural tone in the circles of the Turkish elite. Concomitantly, the Turks would maintain their posture of disinterestedness and superiority *vis-à-vis* France and the West, even while taking in what trimmings they chose of their culture. And within France, the same would obtain between the bourgeois of Monsieur Jourdain's world and the aristocracy's. The aristocrats (like Dorante) would borrow only what they materially needed from the bourgeois, while the bourgeois (messieurs Jourdain) would persist in seeking out their company and imitating their ways.

Hence, we can see *Le Bourgeois gentilhomme* as a complex site of cultural articulation where discourses concerning language, commerce, custom, religion, class, and nationhood come together, producing echoes and tensions, each strand tugging at itself and at the others, contending, competing, vying for the honor of enjoying preeminent explicatory value of this phenomenon called France.

CHAPTER 4

Orienting the world: organizing competition and gendering geography in Tite et Bérénice and Bérénice

Tite et Bérénice *(Corneille, November 28, 1670)*

The play is set in Rome, where Domitie loves Domitian. But, as daughter of a prominent Roman statesman, she is slated to marry Domitian's brother Tite now that he is becoming emperor upon his father's death. Her ambitious pride dictates that she must sacrifice her love for Domitian and have this marriage, but her worry is that Tite is still in love with the flame of his youth, Bérénice, queen of a part of Judea. When Domitian, unsuccessful in persuading her of the wrongness of her decision, shares his unhappiness with Albin, his conniving confidant, Albin discloses that he has arranged for Bérénice to return to Rome and speculates that this may distract Tite from his duty to marry Domitie.

But Tite, although still in love with Bérénice, is prepared to marry Domitie. When his brother Domitian confronts him, Tite insists on setting the example and urges his brother to sacrifice his love for Domitie as he must his for Bérénice. Domitie enters and Tite orders her to declare her heart before the two brothers together, but she says only that this is a matter of duty, not of heart. Bérénice arrives to render homage to the new emperor, her erstwhile lover, and Tite's resolve is shaken. Domitie now is also upset, worried that her marriage with Tite may not take place.

Domitian out of spite proposes marriage to his brother's love Bérénice, and Bérénice reports this to her rival Domitie. The three lovers realize that their real enemy is the state which dictates Tite's decision and prevents the two couples from uniting. Tite and Bérénice argue, and Tite resigns himself to stepping down and going off into exile in order to be with her; but she insists he hold on to both her and the empire, knowing he can never leave the throne except by death, and Tite reassures her of his love, vowing that at least he will never marry Domitie.

Bérénice's confidant Philon advises her to give up hope of winning back Tite, but Bérénice tries to gain local support and Domitian encourages her to think there is still hope. Domitie asks Domitian to avenge her if Tite goes against the will of the Senate, the tradition of Rome, and marries Bérénice; Domitian insists that he himself will marry either her or Bérénice. The Senate meanwhile is dealing with another crisis: the volcano Vesuvius has erupted. Tite and Domitian continue to blackmail each other regarding their respective loves.

Tite vacillates. He asks Domitie's understanding for his unresolved love, but she feels he should be able to sacrifice his love for the State as she has hers. Tite asks Bérénice for counsel; she answers with the request that he, not his Senate, be responsible for deciding her future. Directly after, Domitian brings the news that the Senate has adopted Bérénice as a Roman in order to be able to approve Tite's marriage to her. Bérénice is moved and grateful, but also suspicious that such generosity cannot last, and proposes instead that they immortalize their love in the form of example to the universe. Triumphant in Tite's heart and in the Senate, Bérénice is now content to leave, and even to bless Tite's marriage to Domitie. Now generous, Tite gives Domitie to Domitian, and pledges himself to his memory of the now departing Bérénice, swearing he will never marry another.

Bérénice *(Racine, November 21, 1670)*

Antiochus, king of Commagene, having loved and trailed for five years after Bérénice, queen of Palestine, and Titus's consort, has finally decided to declare his love and leave, now that Titus's father has died and Titus is about to succeed him as Roman Emperor. This he does, and Bérénice pardons his frankness, regrets his departure since she has imagined them good friends all this time. She would have liked him present for what she imagines is about to be the glorious moment of her official union with Titus, but she does not dissuade him from taking his leave. In the meanwhile though, she frets that she hasn't herself seen Titus in over a week, past the official mourning time, and wonders if this is a portentous sign.

Indeed, now Emperor, Titus has decided against marrying Bérénice, and plans to confide her to their friend Antiochus for her return trip to Palestine. He cannot risk alienating his people by marrying a foreign queen against the Roman tradition. But when he and Bérénice finally meet, he does not have the courage to tell her of his decision. Something is clearly wrong though, and Bérénice's worst fears appear justified.

Titus seeks out Antiochus and charges him to break the news to Bérénice, and Antiochus regains hope for his own suit. When he tells Bérénice of Titus's decision, she assumes that he is lying out of jealousy. The distraught Antiochus, rather than leave immediately as he would prefer, defers his departure to reassure himself of Bérénice's welfare.

Bérénice anxiously awaits to see Titus. Titus enters and is torn between his love and his duty as sovereign. When the two finally are united, Titus this second time finds the courage to speak his decision, and Bérénice, mad with grief, threatens to kill herself. Titus is now distraught. Antiochus begs Titus to show mercy for Bérénice. The Roman people call for Titus, and he goes to them.

Once again, Antiochus takes hope upon learning that Bérénice has written to take her leave. But he then yet again despairs upon seeing Titus so miserable, and decides to kill himself. Titus has read what turns out to be her suicide note, and threatens to kill himself as well if she persists in not understanding the necessity of his decision. Persuaded by Titus, Bérénice resigns herself to leaving, and finds in her love the strength to depart, but without Antiochus. Titus and Bérénice take consolation in immortalizing their love as exemplum. The three lovers separate, Antiochus now more alone than ever.

   Questions to ponder
   (1) Why this subject in 1670? Why two plays by the rivals Corneille and Racine on the same subject within a week of each other?
   (2) Why the insistence in the Corneille version on a volcano eruption; why, in Racine's, on the introduction of another character from the East?
   (3) Why this representation of East–West rivalry in the setting up of Judea/Palestine/Commagene tensions with Rome?

Après de si grands avantages, et qui luy sont si particuliers, il ne faut pas s'étonner de ce que le Grand Constantin quitta si facilement les délices de la ville de Rome pour transporter à Bysance le siège de son Empire, et luy donner son nom. Aussi n'y a-t-il point de ville plus propre qu'elle à commander tout l'Univers; elle en voit d'une seule oeillade les deux plus belles parties, & peut en moins d'un quart d'heure faire passer ses ordres de l'Europe où elle est située, jusque dans l'Asie, qui semble ne s'approcher d'elle que pour venir se soumettre à ses loix. Ainsi quand l'art & la nature se seroient accordez ensemble pour former un lieu où la beauté & l'abondance fussent égales, ils n'auroient jamais pu mieux réussir qu'en faisant ce qui est à Constantinople.

[Seeing that it has such great advantages, and those peculiar to itself, we need not wonder that Constantine the Great, so easily quitted the delights of Rome, and Transported the Seat of his Empire to Byzantium, and that he call'd it by his own name; nor indeed is there any other City so proper to command the Universe. With one glance of her eye she beholds the two most lovely parts of the whole, and in less than a quarter of an hour can send her orders from one part of the World where she is seated, to the other. Which therefore seems to make so near an approach to her lofty Towers on purpose to receive her Commands and submit to her Obedience. So that had Art and Nature consulted together, to form a Place where Beauty and Plenty should equally contend, they never could have been more successful, than in the adornment of that where Constantinople stands.] (Guillaume Joseph Grelot, *Relation nouvelle d'un voyage de Constantinople* (1680) *A Late Voyage to Constantinople* (1683))

The year 1670, date of the production for three of the plays under consideration in this book, marks the high point of the Orientalist obsession in French classical theatre. The tense diplomatic relations between France and the Ottoman Porte described in the previous chapter; the Turkish invasion of Austria, the titular home of Louis XIV's mother, Anne of Austria, in 1663; the war over Crete between the Ottoman Empire and

France from 1667 to 1669; the failed visit of an official delegation from Constantinople to the French Court in 1669 do much to explain this apparent obsession. This series of events spawned a heightened interest, or Ottomania, and an intensified jockeying for national preeminence characterized this collective focus. In particular, Constantinople and Rome would be compared, and the Ottoman threat would be brandished, especially by Habsburg allies (as we saw earlier with Leibniz) as they attempted to channel Rome-emulating French aggressions away from their own borders.

The prime models setting the competitive pace were Louis XIV and the Sultan. As we have seen in the diplomatic parlance discussed in chapter 3, the rulers' representatives vied with each other as to who was the more powerful ruler. For example, when the Ottoman envoy Aga Soliman Ferraca visited Paris, the initial discussion between him and the king's translator D'Arvieux turned on why the Sultan had sent only an envoy to the French court rather than an ambassador. Although ostensibly merely settling preliminary matters of protocol, significant energy went into determining relative rank and appropriate address, and did not augur well for the visit. D'Arvieux and Soliman each waged heated verbal battle for his master. Since Soliman's discourse is translated and reported by D'Arvieux, it cannot be assumed that it is accurately represented. Hence perhaps its failure to be as long or as strong as D'Arvieux's, who portrays himself and his king as the victors in this antagonistic exchange:

Il[Soliman] m'interrompit pour me dire que le Grand Seigneur son Maître étoit le plus grand Roi de tout le monde, et qu'il ne fait cette ceremonie qu'à l'égard de l'Empereur de l'Allemagne, qui est le chef de tous les Rois de la Chrétienté, & qu'il n'a jamais envoyé en France ni ailleurs des Ministres d'une qualité plus relevée que lui. Je lui dis, que si l'Empereur son Maître étoit un très-grand Seigneur, ce n'étoit que dans la partie du monde qui lui est soumise en partie, qui est l'Asie Mineure: mais qu'il ne connoissoit pas assez bien l'Europe & les autres parties du monde pour juger de la puissance de l'Empereur de France; qu'il devoit savoir qu'il étoit le plus grand Roi de la Chrétienté, etc.[1]

[He[Soliman] interrupted me to tell me that his Master the Grand Lord was the greatest King in the world, and that he stood upon such ceremony only for the Emperor of Germany, who is the head of all the Kings of Christendom, & that he never sent Ministers of a higher quality than [himself, Soliman] to France or anywhere else. I told him, that if the Emperor his Master was a very grand Lord, it was only in the part of the world which is in part under his control, namely Asia Minor: but that he was not familiar enough with Europe and other

parts of the world to judge the power of the Emperor of France; that he ought
to know that he was the greatest King in Christendom, etc.]

At every level, from the king down, the tone was set for rivalry. The
marked increase in the French presence around the Mediterranean
during these years dictated more than mere circulation of money, goods,
and labor; prestige counted, and this needed to be clearly marked in
language.

Competition of the French *vis-à-vis* the Ottomans is evident in their
discourse – not only as they weighed in with their respective rulers, but
as they considered the history of the relative standings of the capitals
Rome/Paris and Constantinople over time.[2] The cognoscenti appreciated in the contemporary Ottoman city a political marvel that rivaled
even that of Rome:

La pluspart des Peuples de l'Europe regardent les Turcs comme une Nation
barbare et mal-disciplinée; ce qui fait qu'il y a peu de Personnes qui s'adonnent
à la lecture de leur histoire; Mais les plus sages et les plus éclairés en jugent
tout autrement; et voyant que *les Ottomans ont plus fait en trois cents ans que les
Romains en huit cents*, ils infèrrent de là avec beaucoup de justice, que la Politique des Turcs n'est pas si méchante que le vulgaire se l'imagine, et que
leur Gouvernement est fondé sur de bonnes maximes, puisqu'elles réussissent
si bien.[3]

[The majority of European peoples consider the Turks as a barbarian, ill-
disciplined nation; with the result that there are few people who take an interest
in their history; But the wisest and most enlightened judge otherwise; and seeing
that *the Ottomans have done more in three hundred years than the Romans in eight hundred*,
they infer from this, quite accurately, that Turkish politics are not as corrupt
as the common people think, and that their Government is founded on good
maxims, since they succeed so well.]

This same discourse of rivalry characterizes the production of two
plays on the same subject by two contemporary playwrights; competition seeps onto the stage and into the very plots. In Corneille's version, the Roman Domitie will compete with the Oriental Bérénice for
the right to Tite. In the Racine version, Rome itself – the Senate and
the traditions of the city – will compete with the seductive Bérénice
for sway over Titus. And the total East, as staged in Paris – even the
masculine – in the person of Antiochus, will be brought to knee before
mighty Rome. Thus, competition is the guiding principle for all of these
relations. The over-arching tension is between West and East, with the
ultimate consequence that the East and the feminine are elided and, in
this state of conflation must submit, first, on stage, to Rome, and then,

by extension, to "the new Rome" – Paris. How to understand these relations?

In the seventeenth-century Mediterranean world, Marseilles, Genoa, and Venice were only a few of the cities, but some of the major ones, vying for the international spotlight. However Paris and Constantinople were tied through their claims to a Roman heritage into a particular dynamic of competition. These two cities would take on magnified roles in the East–West agon of the West's invention. In order to appreciate Paris and Constantinople in their seventeenth-century valences, we must briefly revisit a few key facts: Rome once ruled what was considered "the world" – the *imperium mundi*. In the Christian era, an important shift surfaced when *Byzantium* (which had gone by many names: *Chryfoceras*, *Acropolis*, *Lygos*, and which briefly, even after it became Byzantium, was renamed *Antonina*, and then even *Anthusa*) was designated the Christian capital for the Roman Empire. In 324 AD, the Roman Emperor Constantine converted to Christianity, and actually moved the capital of the Roman Empire to Byzantium, which he willed the "New Rome," called initially *Constantinian New Rome*, and then named squarely after himself, *Constantinople*. Over one thousand years of empire, until 1453, the city kept this name.[4]

At this time the Ottomans, under Mehmed II, took possession of Constantinople and the city became *Istanbul* (which in Ottoman roughly means "going toward the city"). This brings us, *grosso modo*, to the seventeenth century. Paris then fancied and willed itself the "new" Rome – the new "imperium romanum" with Louis XIV "le Grand" casting himself as Caesar Augustus.[5] The heyday of Louis's reign would be celebrated and commemorated as the "classical" period. Thus each city – Constantinople and Paris – claimed a founding story in Rome – the one historical, the other cultural, and they vied as logical competitors for preeminence. The Ottoman capital was a vital hub of commerce, culture, and military might; and as such seriously challenged French ambition. In France's grand design, the Ottomans could be useful allies together against their common enemy the Habsburgs, but otherwise needed to be contained, humored, and ultimately subjugated. The Ottoman seat of power was also the strongest local expression of Islamic might, and so the obvious challenge to Christian dominance.

In keeping with this contestatory relationship, French visitors to Constantinople persisted in using the Christian name for the city, and only occasionally mentioned that the natives called their city by that other name – Istanbul: "Quoy-qu'il en soit, ce dernier nom [Constantinople] est toujours depuis demeuré à Bysance, & sur tout parmy les Latins & autres Chrétiens d'Europe, car pour les Turcs & autres peuples de l'Asie, de l'Afrique, & de l'Europe, ils l'appellent tous aujourd'huy Stambol."[6] ["Be that as it may, this last name [Constantinople] has always since stuck to Byzantium, and especially among the Latins and other Christians of Europe, whereas for the Turks and other peoples of Asia, Africa, and Europe, today they all call it Stambol."] The preferred name for the city divided clearly along East (Istanbul)/West (Constantinople) lines. The Europeans (and here specifically the French) performed a mini-conquest over the city each time they used her Christian name and ignored her Ottoman one. They thereby closed their eyes to both her ancient and her recent history. So subject to change, depending on current conquerors and influences, answering to so many names, the city appeared fickle and manipulable – she had been had, she could be had. The city was a woman – desirable and contested. In the French mindset, Constantinople was ripe for the taking.[7]

In keeping with France's expansionist view, an appropriation of Ottoman culture also took place. Emissaries were sent out to Constantinople by Louis XIV and his minister Colbert on errands to find and buy as many manuscripts, jewels, and rarities as possible for the Royal library, for Royal adornment, and for Royal prestige. Monsieur Vaillant was the French king's designated "antiquaire," but many travelers would participate in the activity of collecting capital for the capital. As Colbert would phrase it, in his instructions to Antoine Galland regarding the judicious purchasing of manuscripts: "ce seroit orner nostre France des dépouilles de l'Orient."[8] ["This would be to ornament our France with the spoils of the Orient."] France's ambition was to strip the Orient of its jewels in order better to adorn its own self.

How then to think about places, theatre, and competition together? Let us first consider Corneille's *Tite et Bérénice* and Racine's *Bérénice*, both written and performed in Paris, in rival theatres, within a week of each other in 1670 – Racine's on November 21, Corneille's on the 28th. Needless to say, the two plays were produced and staged in a spirit of intense competition between the two playwrights – the one on the wane, the other on the rise.[9] While Corneille dedicated his play to no one when he published it, Racine more savvily dedicated his to Colbert. This was most fitting, since his play (like Corneille's) featured an East–West rivalry, and the powerful minister in that same year had established the Compagnie du Levant which was intended to facilitate and regularize trade relations for France with the world of the eastern Mediterranean – especially between the major centers of Paris and Constantinople. It is also worth remembering that the two vying plays dominated the stage of 1670 alongside *Le Bourgeois gentilhomme*, with its frivolously purposeful mocking fascination for "turqueries." Indeed, the three stagings cast a general East–West shade over the Paris theatre-going experience for that year as a whole.

Although the Bérénice plays bear the distinct marks of their respective authors, and the same well-known story becomes quite different in the two tellings, there is an important commonality: this is the essentialized representation of West and East.[10] These two plays illustrate how gender aligned along geographical terms and signified for Paris audiences. The operative constant throughout both plays is that the West coincides symbolically with the masculine, the responsible Titus, and the seat of power, Rome; while the East elides with the feminine and seductive Bérénice, who puts her love of Titus before all sense of responsibility for her eastern kingdoms, and therefore, by implication, is not fit to rule. Both plays are set in the mighty center of Rome, where Titus is at home and Bérénice is a foreigner. Within the plots of both plays, if the affective tension is between the man and the woman, the rivalry is set up between the public domain, the seat of empire, Rome (the city; the concept; the righteous people in need of an emperor) – and the private domain (the unruly East; the charming queen Bérénice, merely a woman in need of her lover). Titus himself is above all of this, but implicated since he must choose between Rome and Bérénice, public duty and private happiness.

In their competing versions of the same love story, Corneille and Racine produce a recycling of the Anthony and Cleopatra and the Dido and Aeneas tales, keystone paradigms that persistently feature the rivaling spaces of West (Rome) and East (the rest). Such romances function like politically expedient origin myths; they are invented long after the fact, and are a good deal less messy than the events they purport to represent. For example, the Trojans – the future Romans after all – are Easterners from Phrygia; and Cleopatra's dynasty was actually Greek in origin. Be that as it may, these familiar stories cycle beliefs of Western dominance dear to Western hearts. The fundamental trope to which the two competing playwrights and their audiences subscribe without question throughout this active polarizing is the consistently gendered political geography: the man – the West shall rule, and the woman – the East shall be ruled. We can think back to Corneille's *Médée*, discussed earlier, where this assumption was both put forth and frustrated. Essentializing the Orient in classical France was not the ideological faux pas it has become in our time.[11] While varying perspectives on the East proliferated in the seventeenth century, none questioned the French right – indeed moral obligation – to generalize, and from there to conclude.

The seventeenth-century French process of constructing on stage a self-identity in opposition to an Oriental "Other" consistently involves this highly gendered rhetoric: the French self is projected as the normative masculine self, while the Oriental "Other" is by connotation feminine.[12] This distinction, a cumulative effect of symbolic language on the spectator, becomes especially palpable through side-by-side readings of *Tite et Bérénice* and *Bérénice.*[13] A subtle effect of this rhetoric, despite the undisputed record of female prominence and accomplishment during this same period,[14] is tacitly to exclude the female population from the patriotic community that is in the process of inventing itself in the theatre. An important consequence of this omission will be the eventual alienation of women as potential citizens. Their role is restricted to that of behind-the-scene enablers and facilitators. The two plays offer eloquent examples of this dynamic of displacement, conflation, and exclusion.

The Titus and Bérénice story was already well known to the seventeenth-century audience through Coëffeteau's *Histoire romaine,* through Le Moyne's *Peintures morales* and through Scudéry's *Les femmes illustres,* as well as another play, *Tite,* by Magnon, and an unfinished novel of Segrais, *Bérénice.* Erudite readers knew as well versions of the history by Suetonius, Tacitus, Flavius Josephus, and Juvenal. Thus, the general Roman representation of the Orient held the French reading and theatre-going public captive during this century of important mercantile expansionism. They sought inspiration and guidance from the classics, and not only borrowed from their textual history but at the same time from their store of "idées reçues" ["received ideas"] inherited from the Roman repertoire. The relations the French might cultivate with the East were already well fixed by the example of their chosen models.

The dilemma as rehearsed on the Paris stage turned on the timely question of marriage between a Western man and an Eastern woman. The dramatized liaison between the Western conqueror and the Eastern subject represented, writ large, a common if less momentous dilemma at the time. What was a Western man to do for female companionship while off in the far reaches serving the will of the imperium? Seventeenth-century merchants faced the same problem. For the most part, these merchants were young men of modest means hoping to make their fortunes outside of France. The Marseilles Chamber of Commerce saw it as a potential disadvantage to their own profit-making enterprise to have families accompany their representatives and associates to these outposts. Families might be taken by pirates, women might be widowed, children might be orphaned in these remote places, and then their recovery and welfare would become the responsibility of the Chamber of Commerce. And so, the organization outlawed the travel of families to the Levant in 1658. French women and children would not be allowed to follow their family men to the Orient until this law was undone by the "Ordonnance" of March 17, 1716.[15] At the same time, it was in the interest of the French to settle its trading colonies, and therefore to encourage stabilizing ties of domesticity. The young bachelor merchants were faced with the question of the relations they might hope to have with women in the East, and the conditions that would govern those relations.

The Chamber came up with an accommodating solution, based on a local practice already in place: "Il est toutefois licite pour un étranger de prendre une épouse locale à titre temporaire en passant une sorte de contrat devant le Kadi: c'est ce qu'on appelle le 'mariage à Kabin' (kébine) qui a connu un grand succès dans toutes les échelles du Levant."[16] ["It is permitted, however, for a foreigner to take a local wife on a temporary basis, in submitting a kind of contract to the Cadi: this is what is called 'Marriage à la Kabin', which enjoyed great success in all the trading posts of the Levant."] The chronicler Paul Ricaut, who had accompanied the English ambassador to Constantinople, spelled out the terms of the arrangement, lacing his text with commentary on the ways of European men in the Levant:

Les Turcs ont aussi parmi eux une espece de demi mariage, qu'ils appellent *Kabin*. C'est quand un homme prend une femme pour un mois, pour deux mois, ou pour quelque autre temps fixe et limité, dont les parties ayant convenu, ils s'accommodent du prix en la presence du *Cadis*. Les etrangers, qui n'ont pas le don de continence, et qui veulent avoir des femmes par tout, se servent fort de cette sorte de mariage.[17]

[The Turks also have among themselves a sort of half-marriage, which they call *Kabin*. This is when a man takes a wife for a month, for two months, or for some other fixed and limited time, agreed to by both parties, they settle the price in the presence of the *Cadi*. Foreigners, who do not have the capacity for self-control and want above all else to have wives, make great use of this kind of marriage.]

While the "Kabin" was apparently a necessary and a popular arrangement, and many French merchants would go this route, others tended to gravitate toward Greek or Armenian women in these trading posts; in this case, a wedding before a Catholic (emphatically not Orthodox) priest was required. Otherwise the groom was sent back to France forthwith. Eventually, this resulted in the stabilization of the resident expatriate population of these "échelles," since the Greek and Armenian wives were not inclined to want to return to a France they didn't know, but preferred to remain in the familiar communities of the trading colonies.[18] Such policies and accommodations formed a discreet echo chamber for the two Bérénice plays, a background context for two very different stories about the marriage that could not be.

TITE ET BÉRÉNICE

In Corneille's version, two women, Domitie and Bérénice, are pitted against each other and the contrast between them shapes the play. Domitie, daughter of a great general, product and emblem of the Western tradition of ambition and glory-seeking – quintessentially Roman – prefers to overcome her love for Tite's brother Domitian and rise to her honorable responsibility to marry Tite. In her stoical way, she views "tendresse" as "faiblesse" ["tenderness" as "weakness"] (1.1.131–32), and thus portrays a noble but unfashionably tough (for seventeenth-century taste) woman. She may be included in Scudéry's *Femmes illustres* as well, but it is clear that here, in Corneille's version, she does not stand as paragon of "woman." The very man who loves her accuses her of ambition, of coldness, and even the final resolution of the play uniting her with this man whom she supposedly loves does not remove the taint of unnaturalness from her profile. If she is a good Roman, she is not a good "woman" because she does not acknowledge the importance of feelings: "Et je n'ai point une âme à se laisser charmer / Du ridicule honneur de savoir bien aimer" (1.3.221–22). ["And I in no way have a soul easily charmed / By the ridiculous honor of knowing how to love well."] She comes across as above all proud and manly, determined to marry the emperor Tite – the man she does not love – and not to marry Domitian – the one she does love – in order to live up to her father's glorious past and to ensure for her family continued claim to the leadership of Rome. As Tite puts it to his brother: "Vous voyez dans l'orgueil Domitie obstinée: / Quand pour moi cet orgueil ose vous dédaigner" ["You see Domitie obstinate in her pride / When this pride dares disdain you for me"] (4.5.1368–69).

Her lover Domitian sees even further. Despite his attachment to this principled woman, this "femme forte," he does not hesitate to name her "colère" ["anger"] (4.5.1375). However, for all of Domitie's strength of character, she has no voice or even place in the final outcome of the play. She has disappeared long before the dénouement. After first being subjected to her love Domitian's bullying manner and blackmailing approach to the dilemma (he is determined to marry either Domitie or Bérénice), she is subjected to his brother Tite's imperial will as he assigns her to Domitian with the paltry consolation for her that at least he, Tite, will not marry her rival Bérénice. But Domitie herself has no final word, and if she does not speak, it is because her words have no dramatic interest at this point. She has served her function as foil, and is relegated to the past of the plot. Domitie is both an unnatural woman and an unnatural Roman, because, in the economy of this play she is a Roman woman, that impossible creature – a *Western* woman.

Bérénice, on the other hand, epitomizes for the West the idea of woman. A passionate temptress, she hails from the East, where her affair with Tite first flared. She had held the young man's heart captive as long as he had no responsibilities; she had even aided and abetted him in his conquests of her world, but she needed to be dismissed once his adult life began. Tite's dilemma then is how to put behind the follies of youth once they are no longer useful or harmless.

Tite, however, had done what would be frowned on by the Marseilles Chamber of Commerce: he had brought his Bérénice back to Rome with him, installed her in his father's (to be his) palace, and divorced his Roman wife for her (1.1.113–18). As Médée had been a dangerous "import," so also was Bérénice. Her presence in the capital was a threat not only to Roman Law – to all that the Senate, the people, the "res publica" upheld – but to local Roman women and their claims on their men. It was a threat to "Roman-ness," as mixed marriages in the seventeenth century would have been considered a danger to "French-ness" (with the exception of the necessary political alliances formed by certain noble and royal marriages, but even these were negotiated always and only within the boundaries of Europe).

Emblem of the threat to marital conventions, Bérénice also aligns subtly alongside the other crisis with which the Senate must contend at the same time, the erupting volcano of Vesuvius (2.1.463–65). The volcano figures as a double for Bérénice, a natural, unpredictable, volatile force, capable of reducing civilization to ruins. Thought to be at a safe distance – already sent away – it turns out that Bérénice is suddenly back in Rome, at the underhanded Albin's behest:

> Et si je vous disais que déjà Bérénice
> Est dans Rome, inconnue, et par mon artifice?
> Qu'elle surprendra Tite, et qu'elle y vient exprès,
> Pour de ce grand Hymen renverser les apprêts?
>
> (1.3.343–46)

[And what if I told you that Bérénice
Is already in Rome, unsuspected, and by my doing?
That she will surprise Tite, and that she specifically comes
To undo the preparations for this great wedding?]

Bérénice is not merely a threat; she is an imminent reality, a disruptive force present and about to be unleashed on Tite and Rome. Tite's reason fails him in the face of his desire: "Ma raison s'en veut faire en vain un sacrifice, / Tout me ramène ici, tout m'offre Bérénice" (2.1.451–52). ["My reason in vain wants to sacrifice itself / Everything brings me back here, everything makes me see Bérénice."] But the Law stands between him and Bérénice, the Law of the Father now to be internalized by the son as he steps into his place: "Je m'impose à mon tour les lois qu'il m'imposait, / Et me dis après lui tout ce qu'il me disait" ["I in my turn impose on myself the laws he set me, /And following his example, I say to myself all he said"] (2.2.493–94). Bérénice represents unruliness – anathema to him who would rule the Universe – and her presence can only be countered by rejection. Now governing all else, the emperor faces the greatest challenge, according to the Western mindset, that of self-mastery. He must rule over himself in order to be worthy of ruling.

Bérénice's surprise arrival stages the return of the repressed. Her claim to want to offer her homage to Tite before the kings arrive to offer theirs is impulsive, characteristically unruly – out of line, un-Western. This is a woman who does not know her "queenly" place. She wants to be first, and proclaims her impatience. She is indeed a symbol before she is a character. Tite exclaims: "O Dieux! est-ce, Madame, aux Reines de surprendre?" ["O Gods! Madam, is it fitting for Queens to cause surprises?"] (2.5.619).

Bérénice knows she does not fit in, not only because she is a foreigner, but because she is a queen, of part of Judea or of Palestine, depending on the version. And in the political economy evolved out of the history of

Rome, the Romans after Tarquinius abhorred anything associated with monarchical rule. Emperors and queens can't mix – they are systemic and hierarchical contradictions in terms – the one dominates and cancels out the other.[19] But she also knows the power Tite possesses to make her fit in if he so chooses, that is, if he cedes to the temptation to live above the law. Of this she sarcastically reminds his brother Domitian:

> Pour moi qui n'eus jamais l'honneur d'être Romaine,
> Et qu'un destin jaloux n'a fait naître que Reine,
> Sans qu'un de vous descende au rang que je remplis,
> Ce me doit être assez d'un de vos Affranchis,
> Et si votre Empereur suit les traces des autres,
> Il suffit d'un tel sort pour relever les nôtres.
>
> (3.1.727–32)
>
> [I never had the honor of being a Roman,
> Jealous destiny had me born as a mere queen,
> Without one of you stooping to the rank I uphold,
> To be one of your freedmen should suffice for me,
> And if your Emperor follows in the footsteps of others,
> Such a fortune suffices to raise ours.]

In the process of reminding her rival Domitie of her devotion to Tite, and therefore to all things Roman, and, as a consequence, of Tite's – of Rome's – debt to her, Bérénice instead illustrates all too vividly her ineptness as ruler herself:

> Il peut se souvenir dans ce grade sublime
> Qu'il soumit votre Rome en détruisant Solyme,
> Qu'en ce siège pour lui je hasardais mon rang,
> Prodiguai mes trésors, et mes peuples leur sang,
> Et que s'il me fait part de sa toute-puissance
> Ce sera moins un don qu'une reconnaissance.
>
> (3.3.859–64)
>
> [He may remember, in this sublime dignity,
> That in destroying Solyme he made your Rome submit,
> That in this siege, I risked my position for him,
> I exhausted my wealth and my people their blood,
> And that if he has me share in his great power
> It will be less a gift than an acknowledgment.]

She lists systematically that she risked her sovereignty, her country's wealth, and even sacrificed her own people for Tite's greater glory. This is not the portrait of a committed leader, but of an irresponsible traitress driven by her passion. Later, she will assert that Tite's victory and glory are due largely to her support (3.5.1015–20), and wish she had been less supportive of him in Judea so that he might be still merely a marriageable general as opposed to the unapproachable emperor he is fast becoming. Tite succumbs reluctantly to her plea, to the temptation of this woman from the East who suggests that he renounce responsibility, power, and glory, for her, as she has for him – that he follow her example. Is he gambling that Bérénice will see the folly of such an idea once articulated – stressing it through a *reductio ad absurdum*? Or is he seriously, if only momentarily, considering abdication? His "Et bien" suggests only a grudging will, and certainly no enthusiasm:

> Et bien, Madame, il faut renoncer á ce titre
> Qui de toute la Terre en vain me fait l'arbitre;
> Allons dans vos Etats m'en donner un plus doux,
> Ma gloire la plus haute est celle d'être à vous.
>
> (3.5.1027–31)
>
> [Well, Madam, I must give up this title
> Which all the earth vainly bestows on me;
> Let us go to your lands and find me a sweeter one,
> My greatest glory is belonging to you.]

Bérénice has a destabilizing effect not only on Tite but on Rome altogether. In 4.1, Philon reports to her that Rome is most grateful to her and eager to demonstrate its gratitude, but firm in the conviction that she needs to marry elsewhere and not look to Tite as a possible husband. However, by the end of the play, the contagion of Bérénice's persuasiveness has spread, as Rome has reversed its decision and stands ready to receive her among them: "D'une commune voix Rome adopte la Reine" ["With one voice Rome adopts the Queen"] (5.5.1672).

Like the destructive volcano, Bérénice's passion for Tite has destroyed all in its path: "Si j'ai vu sans douleur mon pays désolé, / C'est à Tite, à lui seul que j'ai tout immolé" ["If I felt no pain in seeing my country devastated / It is for Tite, for him alone that I sacrificed everything"] (4.1.1084–86). Just as Rome wishes that the river of Vesuvius's lava would reverse direction and be swallowed back up into the pit of the volatile mountain, Domitie would like nothing so much as that the foreigner go home, back where she belongs: "Qu'elle n'ait repassé les rives du Jourdain" ["Would that she had not crossed Jordan's banks"] (4.4.1278). Unfortunately, like the eruption of Vesuvius, a simple reversal is not so simple. The laws of nature do not respect banks, shores, boundaries, frontiers. The project of Empire-building does not find an ally in this woman's capricious and this volcano's inexorable ways.

Like lava cooling over its field of destruction, Bérénice requests to linger, to stay near Tite, and to die there: "Laissez-moi la douceur de languir en ces lieux, / De soupirer pour vous, d'y mourir à vos yeux" ["Let me have the sweetness of languishing in this place / Of sighing for you, of dying here under your gaze"] (5.5.1617–22). The temptress very nearly succeeds; indeed, the smitten Tite is ready to abandon Rome and follow her back to Judea (5.5.1640). In the end, the Senate handles the two natural disasters: it deals not only with the volcano, but also with this other crisis, submitting everything and bringing everyone to Reason. Bérénice has obtained what she wanted – assurance of love, acclaim, and the right to stay – and so can now leave with her head held high. But it is Tite who resolves the basic conflict – between Bérénice and Domitie – in willing Domitie to Domitian. Tite will remain emperor, pledged unmarried to his love for Bérénice; and he will be great, sustained by her love. The women's rivalry, which only he could settle, has become moot, and the related Domitie/Domitian subplot, which might have threatened his reign, is resolved. The great love story is transformed into an exemplum – an "illustre souvenir," ["an illustrious memory"] (5.5.1758) as it will also, with Racine, become an "exemple à l'univers" ["example to the universe"] (5.7.1502), and the extent of its fame will coincide not only with the span of the entire empire (which includes, ironically, Bérénice's own still devastated country), but also with the duration of the memory of that empire:[20]

> Du Levant au Couchant, du More jusqu'au Scythe
> Les Peuples vanteront, et Bérénice, et Tite,
> Et l'histoire à l'envi forcera l'avenir
> D'en garder à jamais l'illustre souvenir.
>   (5.5.1755–58)
> [From the rising to the setting of the sun, from the Moor to the Scythian,
> People everywhere will proclaim both Bérénice and Tite
> And history will vie with the future
> To forever preserve their illustrious memory.]

Just as the exemplum carries the love story into the future, it also serves as vehicle for the idea of empire. If the seventeenth century was attached to the Tite and Bérénice story for its portrayal of sacrifice of personal passion to the greater cause of state, it also found inspiration in the image of the grandeur of that state.

Bérénice has been portrayed as the woman from the East – the foreigner, and hence, in Corneille's dispensation, as woman par excellence, in contrast to her Western female counterpart Domitie. Her seductive charms have been effective not only on the emperor but on the entire Senate. Her capriciousness in arriving unannounced, her eruption onto the stage (manipulated nonetheless by the behind-the-scenes Albin) at the moment of Tite's marriage is matched only by its contagious effect on the Senate, witnessed by its change of mind concerning Bérénice's acceptable status in the Roman dispensation, a change that could again reverse itself, as Bérénice herself well knows. Her leadership qualities are illustrated as inappropriate, since in supporting Tite she has brought upon her own people deprivation and death.

In short, Corneille's Bérénice is the misogynistic portrait of the perfect woman. She has acted according to gendered expectations of her, putting affairs of the heart before affairs of state, and has tempted Tite to succumb to her example. In the subtext of the play, it is not only because she is from Judea and a queen that she is dangerous to Rome, but because she is a woman. And "woman" already implies "foreigner." But it is only by casting her as from the East that this danger can be articulated. She can only fully represent "woman" by virtue of coming out of a different space from the West. For Rome is the phallic center of the play, and Tite the male figurehead. Domitie and Bérénice are to be evaluated, assimilated, resisted in accordance with their harmony with that center. Domitie, Western woman, can be disregarded and dispensed with (like Lavinia, Aeneas's wife in the *Aeneid*, she is merely a political match), but Bérénice, Oriental temptress, must be contended with and ultimately dominated. Corneille's play, with its cumbersome plot, enjoyed only a moderate success, and Racine's streamlined version triumphed over it, but as we will see, they both operate along the same principles of gendered geography.

BÉRÉNICE

Where Corneille's play focuses on the rivalry between the two women Domitie and Bérénice (and only secondarily on that between the two brothers), the competitive tension in Racine's is between Bérénice and all of Rome – one Eastern woman against the mighty power of the seat of Empire. And as if to underscore the total incommensurability of East and West, Bérénice is accompanied by a man from the Orient, Antiochus, who does not measure up as a man. This Racinian invention of a male character from the East does not disrupt the gendered pattern of the East–West geography set forth by Corneille, but, rather, simply advances it further by putting also into question the very masculinity of the Eastern male. Just as Corneille's Domitie cannot be a true woman because she is a Western woman, but even more radically, Racine's Antiochus cannot be a real man because he is an Eastern man. In this way, the West is thoroughly phallic, and the East is thoroughly castrated. However, the drama here is the risk of Titus's vitiation by his feminizing attachment to the East in the persons both of Bérénice and Antiochus. Does he not, like Antiochus, weep for Bérénice and sigh his way like Antiochus through the play in un-Roman manner? This is the real danger. Gender here is not merely a cultural, but also a sexualized, category, and Titus is at risk.

Political geography here is not only ideologically gendered, but, with regard to the East, it is also factually casual. In Racine's play, Bérénice is from the geographical area of Palestine, whereas in Corneille's she is from the more specific Roman province of Judea. Racine's seeming lack of concern for historical accuracy is mirrored in the way Levant kingdoms are handed out, given away, redistributed by Racine's Roman Emperor as rewards for supportive behavior and as consolation prizes. The identity, integrity, and autonomy of these subordinated countries pale in the face of empire. Titus bestows on Bérénice the consolation prize of numerous kingdoms before sending her back to Palestine, and he offers to Antiochus from Commagene (to the Northwest of Palestine) the kingdom of Cilicia (between Commagene and Palestine) so that he and Bérénice will be neighbors. This insouciant distributing of countries and arranging of borders along friendship lines is the gesture only an emperor can make. It is in keeping with Titus's new role: perhaps such magnanimity is particularly characteristic of the inaugural moments of an imperial reign. But the attitude toward the Levant expressed by such largesse is one of contempt for its local arrangements and history. The East is a space of inconsequential identity that has been divided and conquered, down to its very leaders who are loyal not to their people but to the emperor. She is a Woman.

This vision was perhaps a comfort to the French theatre-going audience, for whom the galling truth was just the opposite. Let us not forget that at the time of the production of this play, it was the Ottoman Empire that represented territorial greatness, no longer the Roman Empire, not quite the Habsburg Empire, and certainly not France: "By the death of Sulleiman the Ottoman Empire covered the area now occupied on the map by all or parts of Hungary, Yugoslavia, Albania, Greece, Bulgaria, Rumania, the Ukraine, the Crimea, Turkey, Iran, Iraq, Syria, Lebanon, Jordan, Israel, Saudi Arabia, Yemen, Egypt, Libya, Tunisia, Algeria, and other lands as well."[21] Ultimately, the choice of Palestine over Judea as Bérénice's place of provenance may amount to no more than arbitrary concerns for rhyme schemes by the two playwrights, and the histories consulted by them were likely viewed as mere repositories for Orientalist material that might yield engaging stage stories, material to borrow and use freely, to enact certain tensions – particularly to stress the greatness of the Roman Empire and its would-be successor France in the face of the formidable Ottoman "Other." In any case, the plays are both firmly set in the western center of world desire, in Rome, and the feeble Levant profile ("La Judée en pâlit" ["Judea paled because of it"] [1.4.197]) is consistently cast and invoked as a pathetic outsider foil to the powerful Western one, as if they were both full-fledged characters.[22]

Racine's play opens at the moment of decision.[23] The day has finally come when Titus will speak and begin his reign as emperor. For five years Antiochus had held his peace; he finally made his way to Rome and here he has waited passively for a flicker of change, an opportunity to declare himself to Bérénice. For the past eight days, all of Rome has been in a state of paralysis, in mourning for the death of Titus's father. But this state has also been one of suspense; everyone is waiting – some in anticipation, some in dread – : Bérénice to see Titus; Titus to begin his reign; and Antiochus finally to speak his piece and leave. This slow motion passivity represents not so much the mourning of the death of the father as it suggests the subversive stasis of the depressed and depressing Orient, the Eden of Titus's youth – the site of absolute nostalgia, toward the former place and the former relations – youth, love, innocence, that lock the three characters together in a mirroring syndrome and prevent them from proceeding to invent their lives anew in their changed circumstances.[24] The death of the Father heralds the call to adult duty and the end to a more idyllic past.

The typology of the Orient as elaborated in and by the West is epitomized clearly in the female character Bérénice, but even more strikingly in the male Antiochus. After all, in contemporary European accounts of the Orient, Ottoman women were depicted as having a profound influence on their consorts, and it was this affective climate of the seraglio that was the ready French reference for the East. Bérénice simply fit the general description and satisfied French expectations: "La Cour des Princes Ottomans est sujette, autant que pas une autre, aux cabales et aux factions. Quelque fois la Reine mère y gouverne; quelquefois le Kuflir Aga y commande, et assez *souvent quelque belle femme y est maîtresse du pouvoir, aussi bien que de l'affection du Sultan*" ["The Court of Ottoman Princes is subject like no other to cabals and factions. Sometimes the Queen Mother governs it; sometimes it is the Kuflir Aga who is in command, and *rather often some beautiful woman is mistress of power as well as of the Sultan's affection.*"] (emphasis mine).[25] Concomitantly, the subjugated king from the East, Antiochus, appears castrated by the situation in which he finds himself; this too is a typing, which will be more explicitly elaborated in Racine's next play, *Bajazet*, analyzed below (see chapter 5). Silenced for five years, pained witness to a love that is not for him, Antiochus is on the verge of speaking and leaving, and can emit only a deep and contagious sigh: "Hélas!" (1.1.61).[26] His decision to leave, coming just at the moment when Antiochus's benefactor and friend Titus should be about to show his gratitude, surprises his confidant Arsace; but that Antiochus has tarried as long as he has equally surprises him: "Quoi depuis si longtemps la Reine Bérénice / Vous arrache, Seigneur, du sein de vos Etats; / Depuis trois ans dans Rome elle arrête vos pas." ["What! For such a long time the queen Bérénice / Has torn you, my lord, from the bosom of your lands / For three years she has restricted your footsteps to Rome."] (1.3.80–82).

Antiochus has been seduced, emasculated, lured away from his responsibilities as king, not by Rome, but by a woman, another royal subject from the Levant, who herself is captive to the charms of the West in the person of Titus. Arsace tries to break the hold of this woman on Antiochus and restore him to his senses by recalling to him his feats of bravery, his acts of glory, and all Titus owes him:

> Un Prince [Titus] qui jadis, témoin de vos combats
> Vous vit chercher la gloire et la mort sur ses pas,
> Et de qui la valeur, par vos soins secondée,
> Mit enfin sous le joug la rebelle Judée.
> . . .
> Vous seul, Seigneur, vous seul, une échelle à la main,
> Vous portâtes la mort jusque sur leurs murailles.
>
> (1.3.101–11)

> [A prince [Titus] who, in former times, witness to your combats,
> Saw you seek glory and death in his footsteps,
> And whose valor, supported by your efforts,
> Finally put rebellious Judea under the yoke.
> . . .
> You alone, my lord, you alone, a ladder in hand,
> You brought death to their very walls.]

Significantly, Antiochus alone enabled the successful outcome of the Roman siege of Jerusalem, unlike Corneille's version where it is Bérénice herself who enables Tite's victory. However, Judea was an enemy not of Commagene but of Rome, and the "local" Antiochus had simply thrown in his lot with that of the empire, and risked his very life for this "greater" cause. His heroism is tainted by his questionable allegiance, but this same heroism also bears witness to the friendship between him and Titus. Arsace will attempt to remind Antiochus of his good fortune in being loved by Titus: "Le ciel mit sur le Trône un Prince qui vous aime." (1.3.100) ["Heaven placed on the throne a prince who loves you."] And Bérénice will remind Antiochus of demonstrations of Titus's love for him "Titus vous embrassa mourant entre mes bras." (1.3.113) ["Titus embraced you as you were dying in my arms."] But her discourse also registers an important nuance of difference in the feelings of the two men for each other: "Titus vous chérissait, vous admiriez Titus" (1.5.270) ["Titus cherished you, you admired Titus"]; to the point where a note of ambiguity leaves us to wonder if Titus confided to his friend Antiochus his love for Bérénice, or rather his love for Antiochus himself: "Vous m'avez, malgré moi, confié l'un et l'autre, / La Reine son amour, et vous Seigneur, le vôtre." (5.7.1448–49) ["In spite of myself, you both confided in me, the queen her love, and you my lord, yours."] Were Titus's feelings for Bérénice inextricably bound up with his feelings for Antiochus, or vice-versa? If this cannot be clear, Racine's text categorically states that in this relationship the one man demonstratively loved whereas the other merely admired. Without dwelling on the articulated homosociality and its resonance for the French who were struck by the open displays of affection among Ottoman men, we can postulate more generally that relations of power among men determine and play out in all aspects of their dealings, even their love for each other. The weaker ally's feelings of love cannot but be compromised because he is not in a position to choose his love object freely; he can only admire abjectly. Whereas Titus, the conqueror, enjoys license to love the necessarily lesser Antiochus. Did he? Racine leaves us wondering.

While Antiochus might well expect rewards for his efforts from the distant Rome and his friend, has he not compromised the integrity of his own immediate vicinity, and violated pacts of neighborliness in assaulting the empire's enemies as if they were his own? On the one hand, it should be remembered that the Romans were simply the latest in a long line of conquerors in the Eastern Mediterranean, all of whom modified the arrangements and history of that area. On the other hand, the binary lesson of the play suggests that only a Roman citizen could be unquestioningly loyal to Rome. Any other person of integrity would necessarily have to grapple with a conflict of loyalties between the local and the Empire. The Empire tramples and absorbs not only territories but psyches.

Further, it is Bérénice who has succeeded in enlisting her suitor Antiochus in the service of his rival. He has advanced the dubious cause of his beloved Bérénice, making captives and victims of her own people. If he is praised as a hero, his victory is not his own but, performed for her, belongs to Titus. Bérénice recognizes her debt to him:

> Je n'ai pas oublié, Prince, que ma victoire
> Devait à vos exploits la moitié de sa gloire,
> Que Rome vit passer au nombre des Vaincus
> Plus d'un Captif chargé des fers d'Antiochus,
> Que dans le Capitole elle voit attachées
> Les dépouilles des Juifs par vos mains arrachées.
> (3.1.689–92)

[I have not forgotten, prince, that my victory
Owed half its glory to your exploits,
That Rome saw among the number of conquered men
More than one captive bearing Antiochus' chains;
That it sees the Jewish spoils torn away by your hands
Placed in the Capitol.]

Antiochus's position is more compromised and complex than Bérénice's because as a "man" he has actively participated in abetting the Roman cause and has neglected his own local interests. He has shown poor judgment, a failing to be expected perhaps of a woman, but inadmissible in a man. He has allowed himself to be guided by his impossible love for Bérénice and his tortured fascination with Titus's power greater than his own, so that he has contributed to sow destruction in the very part of the world that would have been his to minister and protect. Expectations for a man are greater than for a woman, but a man from this part of the world, it is clear, is hardly a man by Western standards. Not only his hopeless love for Bérénice, but his compromised status as a man, make of him doubly a woman, and as such a strong signifier of the East for the West.

As Racine represents the political stakes, the Empire wreaks havoc not only with discreet psyches and mapped territories but with local communities as well, profoundly disturbing the status quo. In acknowledgment of the queen's loyalty to Rome, but spurred by a more personally motivated, guilt-fed generosity, as he sends Bérénice away, Titus arranges her takeover of several countries:

> Là, de la Palestine il étend la frontière,
> Il y joint l'Arabie, et la Syrie entière [. . .]
> Il va sur tant d'Etats couronner Bérénice.
>
> (1.4.171–72, 175)
>
> [There, he extends Palestine's frontier;
> He adds all of Arabia and Syria to it [. . .]
> From so many states he will make a crown for Bérénice.]

This imperialist gesture, oblivious of the local political landscape, performs shifts and changes that only a mega-power could make. If the French envied the Ottoman expanse, it was through a remembrance and claiming of Roman power that they could imagine such ambitions for themselves.

In Antiochus's desperate attempt to break out from under the spell of greater power, to reclaim Bérénice and take her home, he reminds her that their first encounter was decisive for him. He summarizes their story:

> Madame, il vous souvient que mon coeur en ces lieux
> Reçut le premier trait qui partit de vos yeux.
> J'aimai, j'obtins l'aveu d'Agrippa votre frère.
> Il vous parla pour moi. Peut-être sans colère
> Alliez-vous de mon coeur recevoir le tribut;
> Titus, pour mon malheur, vint, vous vit, et vous plut.
>
> (1.4.189–93)
>
> [Madam, you may remember that in this place
> Your gaze first pierced my heart:
> I fell in love. I obtained the approval of your brother Agrippa;
> He spoke to you for me. Perhaps, not displeased,
> You were going to receive my heart's tribute;
> To my despair, Titus came, saw you, and was pleasing to you.]

Antiochus hearkens back to an earlier idyllic time when things went as they were supposed to in his world: Bérénice's initial captivating glance resulting in Antiochus's immediate love for her; permission from a male relative to stake a claim; and the promise of love requited. All of this was then disrupted by the arrival of Titus. The tributes of the heart that Antiochus would have bestowed on Bérénice suddenly paled in the face of a new suitor. But there is another more important distinction suggested in this courtship summary. In the first instance, Antiochus is seen by Bérénice, and falls victim to her seductive gaze; in the second,

Titus sees Bérénice. The one male is passive and the other male active. The act of the conqueror – veni, vidi, vici – operates as love metaphor. The laurels go to the Western ocular aggressor.

Passivity marks Antiochus throughout the entire play, despite and against the recounting of his heroics at the siege of Jerusalem. Although he has resolved to speak and to leave, and has articulated this from the beginning of the play, he accedes to the one only with great difficulty, and at his rival's insistence, and for his rival's cause, and does not manage to leave at all, except under orders from Titus and from Bérénice. Tears and sighs characterize his discourse throughout the play; again and again Bérénice rebuffs him and Titus silences him. He is a piteous figure. However, tears and sighs also dangerously characterize Titus, who in the past was aggressive in the East, but is currently passive and speechless, as he cannot yet see beyond his past into his present.

Antiochus recounts the desolation he experienced when first abandoned by Bérénice:[27]

> Rome vous vit, Madame, arriver avec lui.
> Dans l'Orient désert quel devint mon ennui!
> Je demeurai longtemps errant dans Césarée,
> Lieux charmants, où mon coeur vous avait adorée.
> Je vous redemandais à vos tristes Etats,
> Je cherchais en pleurant les traces de vos pas.
> Mais enfin, succombant à ma mélancolie,
> Mon désespoir tourna mes pas vers l'Italie . . .
>
> (1.4.233–40)
>
> [Madame, Rome saw you arrive with him.
> In the deserted Orient how great was my sorrow!
> I remained a long time wandering in Caesaria,
> In the delightful spots where my heart had adored you.
> I asked and asked after you in your mournful lands;
> Weeping, I looked for the traces of your footsteps.
> But finally, succumbing to my melancholy,
> My despair bent my steps towards Italy.]

The eastern lands thus depicted suggest a psychic scenery of desertion, of sterility, of sadness, of abandonment, of nostalgia, of stasis, of ennui. This representation of a bleak mental landscape echoes a more contemporary and politically motivated one, yet another flourish in Leibniz's 1672 plea to the French king to intervene against the Turks (see the "Orientation" and ch. 1). In order to persuade Louis, the philosopher must paint these people as benighted: "Il fait nuit dans leurs âmes serviles; sortis de leurs déserts, ignorant le monde, ils vivent, pour ainsi dire, au jour le jour: . . . Nul souci de posterité ou d'immortalité; ni générosité, ni ent-housiasme; point de commerce, d'industrie, de science nautique; tel est le tableau de l'empire et le secret de sa faiblesse."[28] ["It is dark in their servile souls; having emerged from their desert, ignorant of the world, they live, so to speak, from day to day . . . No thought of posterity or of immortality; no generosity, no enthusiasm; no commerce to speak of, nor industry or nautical science; such is the picture of the empire and the se-cret of its weakness."] The moral landscape without the beloved person becomes an emptiness that echoes the emptiness within. In Leibniz's text, the missing "beloved" would narcissistically be the West, in this strategic case, Louis.

The sense of hollowness represented in the character of Antiochus and claimed by Leibniz for the Ottoman Empire corresponded, iron-ically, to a hollowness that was actually experienced by French envoys to Constantinople, who left behind them their beloved King and his world. They missed their active social lives, their daily contact with friends and persons of importance at Versailles, and the frenzy of cur-rying for favor that set the tone of the court. Buoyed by the prestige of a noble mission (as well as the possibility of enriching themselves abroad), diplomats eagerly took on assignments for Louis XIV only to find themselves alone, in the provinces, out of touch with their own world.

Thus would Guilleragues (French ambassador to the Sublime Porte, 1679–85), recently arrived in Constantinople, express his forlornness in a letter to the influential minister Seignelay in 1680: "Il n'y a rien au monde qui puisse m'être plus douloureux que votre oubli, je meurs de peur d'être tombé dans ce malheur que je n'ai pas craint, et que je n'ai pas mérité; je suis privé de vos ordres, de vos avis, des nouvelles de votre santé et de tous les détails qui vous touchent. En vérité, sans faire l'affectueux, cet état est bien triste pour un homme qui est avec un attachement sensible et respectueux plus que jamais personne ne pût être, Monsieur, votre très humble, etc. . . ."[29] ["There is nothing in the world more painful to me than being forgotten by you, I am deathly frightened of having fallen into that misfortune which I did not fear, and did not deserve; I am deprived of your orders, your advice, news of your health and all details concerning you. In truth, without playing the lover, this state of things is quite sad for a man who is, with an attachment more sensitive and respectful than anyone's could ever be,

Monsieur, your very humble, etc. . . . "] Guilleragues here mobilizes more a heavy rhetoric of flattery than a realistic psychological account of his state; nevertheless, it is constructed around the now familiar trope of emptiness, as if his condition too has been contaminated by his Oriental surroundings. However, the key difference is that Antiochus is from the Orient, but because of his love, even for a woman from the Orient herself, his own home has become a place of exile.

Just as Guilleragues in Constantinople bemoaned his isolation from the French court world, afraid as he was of falling out of favor, so, in the play, this condition of dejection is articulated through the discourse of the Oriental character. Antiochus is unable to tolerate his loneliness, and instead of continuing his kingly functions in Commagene, goes trailing off after Bérénice, and sits at her feet for three years in Rome, serving there not only as a witness but as accomplice to her affair with Titus. On the Western stage, this lovesickness suggests a flaw of character – a lack of center, the embracing of the role of loser. It comes across not as the quirk of a particular individual, but, magnified, as typical of all males from Antiochus's part of the world, indeed as typical of the East. The entire Levant is characterized as melancholic, aimless, empty, defeated. And so it is up to the West to fill it up, give it life and purpose. So goes Imperialist reasoning. As Titus had activated local energies in his conquest of Jerusalem, so he will relay them back from Rome as he redistributes lands, according to his whims, and rewards his faithful local subjects Antiochus and Bérénice.

While Titus bestows new lands on Bérénice, Paulin comments on the Palestinian queen's increased power: "L'Orient presque entier va fléchir sous sa loi" ["Almost all of the Orient will bend to her rule"] (2.1.339). Not only Antiochus, but the entire Orient appears then as a feminized character, completely under the rule of a Bérénice empowered by Rome; this whole part of the world will become subject to her will. By contrast, Titus not only can reconfigure the map of the East according to the dictates of his heart, but master even these feelings. Antiochus then, more than Titus, represents here the dangers of encounter with too strong a woman – the woman from the East. Only a Western man is able to resist her charms. The East left to its own devices, Antiochus and Bérénice to each other, spells impotence.

Paulin appeals to the competitive in Titus when he recalls to him the reasons behind the law forbidding emperors to consort with queens. To do so, he summons up various history lessons. He reminds the Emperor that three of his antecedents – Caesar, Caligula, and Nero – whatever else they might have done, respected this one law, and that Cleopatra, another Oriental temptress, was the downfall of Anthony. As if all of this were not reason enough, he further reminds Titus that in Bérénice's family tree there is a former Roman slave who was freed, and that this taint poses a further obstacle just as serious to a marriage between them as does her status as queen (2.2.381–412). Marriage was an act implicating "le sang," ["blood"] – hence the possibility of contamination, to be envisaged always with an eye to posterity. Titus needed to emulate his ancestral models and respect Roman law if he were to be a glorious Emperor.

The sorts of values Titus needed to embrace made sense and mattered to the French even if they did not correlate exactly with their own. At the same time, they puzzled at the more fluid class and political system of their ever handy referent for the Orient – the Turks – in comparison with their own more predictably regulated hierarchy. Both systems, albeit absolutist, fostered political competition, but encouraged quite different values and rewarded different behaviors. The Porte, the seat of Ottoman government, was dismissed as a slave galley: "C'est proprement une prison pleine d'esclaves, qui ne diffère de celle des Galeriens que par la proprete du lieu, et par la richesse des chaines." ["It is properly called a prison full of slaves, which only differs from the galleys by the cleanliness of the place and the richness of the chains."][30] Yet the French nobility recognized Versailles at some level in the mirror of the Porte, and also feared the fluidity in the Ottoman model that fast threatened to become a feature of their own government as they lost purchase on the bourgeoisie in key appointments to positions of real power and influence (see chapter 3). They claimed to be horrified at the incomprehensibility and seeming chaos of the Ottoman system. The chronicler Sir Paul Ricaut would lament the lack of a discernible sense of order at the Porte: "Comme il n'y a point de honte parmi eux de déchoir de la grandeur, aussi ne sont-ils pas surpris de voir des gens de néant croître comme des champignons, et s'élever par la faveur du prince, aux plus hautes dignités de l'empire."[31] ["As it is no shame among them to fall from greatness, thus they are not surprised to see insignificant people spring like mushrooms, and elevate themselves through the Prince's favor, to the highest dignities of the empire."] And it echoes almost verbatim Leibniz's ravings about "cette prison d'esclaves gouvernée par un fils d'esclave,"[32] ["This prison of slaves governed by the son of a slave"] as he decries "De quelle manière les hommes y sont élevés tout d'un coup par la flatterie, par le

hasard et par la seule faveur du Sultan, aux plus grandes, aux plus impor-
tantes, aux plus honorables charges de l'empire, sans avoir ni naissance,
ni mérite, ni aucune expérience dans les affaires."[33] ["In what manner
men there are suddenly elevated by flattery, by chance and by the Sultan's
favor alone, to the greatest, most important, most honorable positions in
the empire, without being highborn, without having merit or experience
in official matters."] Ironically, much of the same criticism Ricaut and
Leibniz leveled against the Ottomans might just as well have been directed toward Louis's government. In fact, their distress rings much like
the well-known malcontent Saint-Simon's complaints about the irregu-
larities at Versailles, including the king's too great reliance on women's
opinions.[34]

A striking example of the sort of appointment that baffled French
sensibilities and threatened French propriety was one reported by the
traveler Laurent D'Arvieux, to the effect that the son of a Marseilles
butcher, a French subject, passed into the Turkish world, and became the
Sultan's High Admiral of the Ottoman Fleet in D'Arvieux's time.[35] This
appointment scandalized the French. From this exotic instance, people
in Marseilles might get ideas about their own local prospects. The West
could find itself contaminated by such unruliness, just as Titus risked
emasculation through keeping company with the likes of Bérénice and
Antiochus. If the French could compete for rather than inherit privilege,
where would this lead?

Constantinople appears to the French as a topsy-turvy world, where
Western values don't obtain, where familiar protocols don't apply, where
the known grid doesn't work. Instead, in their uncomprehending eyes,
unruliness and depravity characterize this capital, marked by profound
cultural difference. The experience of the Orient for the French is concentrated in the staged representation of this part of the world through
Racine's figures of the wayward Bérénice and Antiochus, and countered
by the more familiar admonitions to an affectively besieged Titus to
honor his ancestry and Roman precedence. In contrast with Racine's
systematic construction of insidious and threatening East–West cultural
difference, Corneille's Bérénice appears more a singular freak of nature,
and hence, less threatening.

Akin to Corneille's Bérénice, but more radically, Racine's does not enjoy the stature of a queen by Western standards. Like the other Bérénice,
she is not fit to rule; she, too, is emphatically not interested in affairs
except of the heart. She knows that in coming to Rome with Titus, she
has abdicated all power except whatever she might have over her lover,

now become emperor: "Depuis quand croyez-vous que ma grandeur me touche? / Un soupir, un regard, un mot de votre bouche, / Voilà l'ambition d'un coeur comme le mien" ["Since when do you think that my grandeur moves me? / A sigh, a look, a word from you, / There you have the ambition of a heart like mine."] (2.4.575–77). Her position and abjection are more clear and in the end less interesting than Antiochus's. She is a woman and behaves like a Woman. This role has included showing Titus the path to glory; he owes to her his triumph. Like Antiochus, who conquered Jerusalem really to advance Bérénice's love interest, Titus also conquered out of love for her. But he further succeeded in winning her very self. However, in the interest of his greater glory, she must become dispensable. Bérénice is the lure, the war trophy, the muse, and the mere tool, all in one: "quintessential woman."

The queen's lament as she awaits another interview with Titus characterizes not only her personal demeanor but sums up the driftless nature of the Orient as a whole, as Racine poeticizes it: "Je m'agite, je cours, languissante, abattue, / La force m'abandonne, et le repos me tue" ["I'm agitated, I run, languishing, worn out; / Strength abandons me, and rest kills me"] (4.1.955–56). Her dejection echoes Antiochus's earlier plaint after his abandonment in Caesarea by Bérénice, when she had followed Titus to Rome: "Dans l'Orient désert quel devint mon ennui! / Je demeurai longtemps errant dans Césarée" ["In the deserted Orient how great was my sorrow! / I remained a long time wandering in Caesaria"] (1.4.233–34). His purposeless movement, as with Jason and Médée, signals Antiochus as worthless, since no value can be assigned to or gleaned from his activity. Together, Bérénice's and Antiochus's despondency sum up the inadequacy of the Orient.

Like Rome, the Orient throughout the play is as much a person ("Que l'Orient vous voie arriver à sa suite" ["Let the Orient see you follow her"] [3.2.759]) as a specific place or a particular character, and suffers from a condition brought on by the desertion of the caretaker, the woman, the mother. Entire states have been reduced to mourning by Bérénice's absence, and life drags on in these forlorn regions in a state of perpetual nostalgia for the past, for the plenitude of the mother's presence. Antiochus names his state "melancolie" (1.4.239), but Bérénice combats the same dis-ease. She is missing to herself. Both are seeking that mirage of plenitude to be had only with the other – Antiochus with Bérénice, Bérénice with Titus. Both, moreover, are thwarted in their quests. Thus is the Orient portrayed as insufficient to itself and needy, as if to justify the West's expansionist project.

Titus steels himself to combat Bérénice's seductive power in their final interview; the two will compete against each other, and ironically Titus will summon to his aid the very quality traditionally ascribed to her world: "Car enfin au combat qui pour toi se prépare, / C'est peu d'être constant, il faut être barbare" ["For in the end, in the combat awaiting you / Being constant matters little; you must be barbaric"] (4.4.991–92). Here the term "barbare" no longer means simply "foreign" but, as with the eventual connotation of the mere name "Médée" for the French, cruel and ruthless. Now if Antiochus and Bérénice are themselves "barbares," they need to be countered as such. But they cannot be counted as such. Their lands have been absorbed into the empire. Like Médée, they have betrayed their own people in cleaving to the Romans; and now Titus must sunder with them as they did in their pacts with their own peoples. The term "barbare," then, no longer designates simply an outsider. It circulates, absorbed in the West, like the Eastern lands, but persists in assigning the stigma of "un-civilized," that is "un-Western," behavior: it is permanently imputed to the compromised and dominated East. Indeed, here Titus recognizes that in order to be Western (fulfill his political duty), he has to be cruel, "barbare." Hence "barbare," domesticated, has become key to Western rule.

In the final scene, Bérénice yields to the will of Rome her arch-rival, assumes the position of Titus over her, and uses it over Antiochus. The man of the Orient is crushed by the woman from the Orient who subscribes to the Occidental model. Antiochus is emasculated in his relations both to Titus and to Bérénice. The abjection of the abandoned lover and the empty Orient are collapsed into this conflagrational scene of renunciation. All of the characters exit into melancholy despite the rhetoric of glorious exemplum with which they console themselves. And the audience is left with the sensation of the very "désert" that has been so regularly evoked. This theatrical experience legitimates public thinking about the Orient not as an ensemble of cultures and peoples, but as a void appealing to the West for an assignation of meaning. At the same time it lays the gauntlet for the other playwright, Corneille. Where Corneille prides himself outdatedly in a complex plot, Racine demonstrates that he can make something even out of nothing.

Thus did Corneille and Racine do battle on the stage. In so doing, they tapped into the great West/East competition, as staged by the West for closed circuit consumption, and fed the flames. In appropriating and recycling in double feature this story of Roman triumph (moral strength

and military might) over the charms and temptations of the East on the
Paris stages, France flexes, aligns with, and implicitly claims to be, the new
Rome. With this claim comes a built-in attitude toward the East. France,
the West, must dominate. The project of construction of a powerful
Western national identity in France proceeds by celebrating a tradition
which features opposition to and triumph over an Oriental "Other". In
keeping with this competitive spirit, and as claimed from the outset here,
the relationship also is encoded in a highly gendered rhetoric: the French
self is projected as the normative masculine triumphant self (however
reluctantly and elegiacally in Racine, however relentlessly and nobly in
Corneille), while the Oriental "Other" is by connotation feminine – in
thrall, at once capricious and submissive.[36] This distinction played out
on the stage in 1670, and contributed to the organizing, consolidating,
and articulating of French identity.

CONCLUSION

The seventeenth-century artistic world flourished on relations of rivalry
as writers and artists vied for royal and public favor. In their attempts
to speak to the mood of the day, they subscribed unquestioningly to the
greater geopolitical competition their country was engaged in. Drama-
tists such as Corneille and Racine staging the Orient in Paris were
only a few of the vast French artistic contingent engaging in personal
competition and at the same time representing the king's greater vision
of dominion. Together they fed into and competed in the same immense
cultural project: they fostered the illusion of "Frenchness." In shaping
their preferred versions of their story about themselves, the French had
recourse not only to the Roman model, but also to the borrowed convenient foil of the exotic "Other" as well, updated in the form of the
Ottomans. And, in so doing, as significantly, they drew on and elaborated their even more local, pervasive, and time-honored fears of their
own women. Their mode of conceptualizing the "Other" as "woman"
nurtured a gender-based culture that depended for its articulation on
sexual innuendo. As developed on the stage, women of the West were
unnatural creatures, to be dispatched with and dismissed: the West was
male, and by Western logic meant to rule. The woman of the East was by
turn, a disruptive, naturally volatile seductress; a conquered and abject
slave to passion; or a feminized, emasculated, dominated man: the East
was a woman, good for the having. On the French classical stage, artistic

acts such as Corneille's, Racine's, examined, appropriated, depicted, rescripted, and set the role of this "Other." In the French classical imaginary, the "Other" was manifestly woman. In the name of and through the use of "High Culture," but nourished by gritty tales, always subject to the stimulus of competition (with its ever implied ubiquitous "Other"), and ever in gendered terms, France became France.

CHAPTER 5

The staging of France: Bajazet, Mithridate, communication and the detour

SUMMARIES

Racine's Bajazet *(1672)*

The play takes place in the seraglio of Constantinople. Acomat, the Grand Vizir, has fallen from favor with Amurat, the Sultan. Demoted, he has been assigned to duty at the seraglio instead of accompanying Amurat on his military campaign. He plots a palace coup to avenge himself. He has decided to back the Sultan's brother, Bajazet, who is confined to the seraglio so as not to pose a threat to the Sultan's supremacy. The Sultan has delegated Roxane, his favorite concubine, to govern the seraglio in his absence, but she, in love with Bajazet, supports Acomat's design, and the two seek to persuade Bajazet to head the coup.

Although Bajazet remains faithful to his long-standing love Atalide, she, Atalide, recognizes that if Bajazet is to survive, he must placate Roxane, and so she plays the intermediary between them, better representing Bajazet's courtship than he would himself. Bajazet is weak and undecided about the course of action he should take, but his pride is offended at the idea of being constrained by Roxane; despite her current power, her status is that of lowly slave. At the same time, he realizes that this coup may be his only chance at survival. The long-standing bachelor Acomat and Roxane have struck a deal whereby Roxane will marry Bajazet and he, Acomat, will marry Atalide — both of them of noble Ottoman blood, and thereby advance and secure their own positions.

The time has come to stage the coup, but Roxane insists that first Bajazet must agree to marry her. He refuses, and she has him arrested. Acomat tries to persuade him that he must agree to this condition, even if only temporarily and in false faith, and Atalide, concerned for his survival, also insists that he must accept to marry Roxane, despite her love for him, and now even her insecure doubts concerning his love for her. She threatens to kill herself if Bajazet refuses to cooperate and is put to death, and yielding to the pressure of these two characters, Bajazet accepts to at least see Roxane again.

But Atalide, despite her support for this plan, is jealous, and, learning from Acomat of the apparent success of Bajazet's interview with Roxane, accuses Bajazet unjustly of infidelity. As a consequence, Bajazet is cold in his next interview with Roxane, and she, noting the difference between Bajazet's direct contact with her and Atalide's warmer representation of Bajazet's feelings for her, begins to suspect the ploy.

At this moment Orcan, the Sultan's fearsome envoy suddenly arrives with the written order to execute Bajazet (Amurat had sent another envoy earlier, but he, along with his message, had been intercepted and silenced.) Atalide and Bajazet have exchanged letters assuring each other of their love – Atalide be-seeching Bajazet to submit to Roxane's will for love for her, Bajazet vowing his undying love for Atalide come what may. Roxane tests Atalide's true feelings by showing her the death-order message Orcan has brought. Atalide faints and Roxane's suspicions are confirmed. Further, her servants find Bajazet's letter on Atalide's body, and now Roxane cannot deny the material evidence, but decides to confront him with it before acting on it. In the meanwhile, Acomat is still deter-mined to stage the coup and bring Bajazet to power, despite the delay caused by Roxane.

Now, Roxane, on the verge of executing the Sultan's orders, sees Bajazet once more, shows him the letter and accuses him of duplicity to which he confesses and which he attempts to explain. She gives him one last chance: to agree to her condi-tions and to be witness to the execution of Atalide. He is horrified at the idea, and so she sends him to his own death. Roxane next sees Atalide who also confesses, but Roxane is interrupted by the news that the coup is taking place, and goes off to take charge. As Atalide seeks to escape, Acomat arrives, only for both of them to learn that Orcan, following the Sultan's further (and unwritten) order, has also executed Roxane. More news comes to them: Orcan in turn has been killed by Acomat's supporters, but the condemned Bajazet has not survived the bloodbath either. Acomat attempts to persuade Atalide to flee with him, but she, blaming her doubting love for the failure of the coup, kills herself.

Racine's Mithridate *(1673)*

The play is set in Nympheum, a seaport on what is known today as the Crimean peninsula, along the Cimmerian Bosphorus, the strait off the Northeast corner of the Black Sea. Here Pharnace and Xipharès, the sons of Mithridate VI, have come, each independently, and here their father's betrothed, Monime, has been confined during his absence at war. The mighty king, Mithridate, a living legend who has successfully resisted the Romans over many years, has been defeated and is now believed dead. Both sons are in love with their father's Monime and have come for this reason, each to press his suit. But Xipharès remains loyal to his father's determination to keep Asia free of the Romans whereas Pharnace wants to treat with the enemy. Monime, secretly in love with Xipharès, comes to him requesting protection from his brother Pharnace, and Xipharès proclaims his love for her, legitimate now that his father is dead. But it turns out that the news of Mithridate's death was a false rumor, planted by the king himself to help cover his escape, and he is arriving back in Nympheum. The two brothers are now in a bind; nevertheless Xipharès refuses to follow Pharnace's lead and prepares to fall back in line with his father's orders.

Monime is unable to face Mithridate, and the suspicious king, having consulted with his confidant Arbate about goings-on in his absence, and having been assured of Xipharès's innocence and Pharnace's guilt, orders Xipharès to guard Monime. Monime confesses her love to Xipharès, but nobly insists she will remain loyal to the king, and orders her beloved Xipharès to avoid her henceforth.

Mithridate refuses to accept his defeat and reveals to his sons his great plan to march on the Romans and attack Rome itself. Xipharès approves of his father's plan whereas Pharnace attempts to dissuade him. However, his father, suspicious of Pharnace's attachment to Monime, orders him to depart to marry the daughter of the king of Parthia, off to the south-east, away from the Romans. Pharnace believes he has been betrayed by Xipharès and denounces the reciprocal love of his brother and Monime. The uncertain and jealous king tests the truth of Pharnace's words by ordering Monime to marry Xipharès. After much protestation and resistance, Monime is drawn into the trap and admits her love for Xipharès. Alone, Mithridate plots his revenge: he will isolate Xipharès from any troops that are loyal to him, and kill him.

Xipharès comes to warn Monime of Mithridate's furor. She sees that she was duped. Righteously angry to have been the victim of Mithridate's cunning and to have betrayed Xipharès, she stands up to Mithridate and refuses to marry the king. He is bewildered by her stand, but distracted from his meditation on this turn of events upon learning that the Romans have attacked Nympheum, assisted by Pharnace, and perhaps, he thinks, also by Xipharès.

Convinced that Xipharès has died in battle, Monime attempts unsuccessfully to hang herself, and is relieved upon receiving the order, delivered by Mithridate's servant, to poison herself. However Arbate arrives with the news that Mithridate is dying and that Xipharès has ousted the Romans. Expiring by his own sword rather than risking death from the enemy, Mithridate, who had thought himself vanquished by the Romans and his collaborator son Pharnace, has just time to unite Monime and his faithful Xipharès, who has proven his filial worthiness, and to give to his now apparent successor advice for continuing to resist the Romans.

Questions to ponder

(1) Why turn to such a recent and then to such a distant past in these two plays?
(2) Why showcase problems of communication – letters, truths, lies, deviousness?
(3) Why the double standard?

Racine, *Bajazet*, 1672 [emphasis mine]:

> Après tant d'injustes *détours*
> Faut-il qu'à feindre encore votre amour me convie?[1]
>
> [After so many unjust detours
> Must your love still ask me to dissemble?]
>
> (4.1.1135–36)

From Bajazet's message to Atalide, which she will read and then hide, but which will be discovered on her body and reread by her rival Roxane

Nourri dans le sérail, j'en connais les *détours*.

[Brought up in the seraglio, I know its hidden ways.] (4.7.1428)
Acomat to his confidant Osmin

Racine, *Mithridate,*1673 [emphasis mine]:

> Le Roi, toujours fertile en dangereux *détours*
> S'armera contre nous de nos moindres discours.
>
> [The King, always full of dangerous ruses
> Will arm himself against us with the least of our words]
> (1.5.369–70)

Pharnace to Xipharès

> Ma foi ni mon amour
> Ne seront point le prix d'un si cruel *détour*.
>
> [Neither my faith nor my love
> Will in any way be the price of such a cruel feint.]
> (4.4.1369–70)

Monime to Mithridate

> Un grand Roi descend-il jusqu'à cet artifice?
> A prendre ce *détour* qui l'aurait pu forcer?
>
> [Does a great King stoop to this ruse?
> Who could have forced him to use this feint?]
> (4.1.1148–49)

Phoedime to Monime

Vos *détours* l'ont surpris, et m'en ont convaincue.

[Your ruses have caught [my love] by surprise and convinced me [of its strength]]
(4.4.1344)
Monime to Mithridate, having been caught in his trap

As the Turks and legendary Black Sea heroes of *Bajazet* and *Mithridate* were featured as characters on the Paris stage, French actors cross-dressed for these roles. And as these supposed Turks and enemies of the West expressed themselves in exquisitely versed French, mirroring actually moved toward merging. Via the detour of the stage, and via the further staged detour through the "Other," French ethnographic information about far reaches of the Mediterranean world and French attitudes towards its populations was organized and disseminated. Articulating these relations in costume, plot, and language, "Frenchness" took shape

and imposed itself as the controlling norm. In setting itself as standard, "Frenchness" circuitously developed the mentality that would
prepare the nation for colonial practice and empire building. If these
far reaches and other cultures could be represented and controlled
on the French stage, then they could be controlled by the French in
the world. Thus the detour of the stage was crucial to the shaping of
France.

Although all of the plays we have examined thus far could be analyzed
similarly, the two plays, *Bajazet* and *Mithridate*, are especially fitting as
models of the way the detour operates on multiple levels. In both of
these plays the detour plays not only a functional, but a thematically and
semantically prominent role. In both instances, the Orientalist imaginary is crucial not merely as a provider of disguises, but as a fiction
which establishes and unites the representation of "East" and "West"
and in that process defines both of the worlds within a French dispensation. Distancing, in time or space – the displacement allowed in the
world of theatre – is crucial for the possibility of the contemplation, the
interpretation, and the resolution of contemporary domestic issues. At
the same time, the daily and local reality of this "Other" world – the
Ottoman "East" – added a dimension of useful necessity to the particular stories. Through engagement with this immediate "otherness,"
the French could practice flexing their colonial muscle and work on
appropriate colonial attitudes. The staged current-day seraglio and the
historical Eastern sea kingdom were not merely a touch of entertaining
exotica, but working laboratories.

In *Bajazet*, detours of misinformation and failed or infelicitous communication converge in context to produce the final effect, a bloody
conflagration. Similarly, in *Mithridate*, detours of misinformation and
attack work their way toward the all too inevitable magisterial suicide.
In both instances, the enemies from the East die, but not before having
imparted many useful lessons as to who and how they are, and hence
who and how the French are. Ultimately, it is the detour of the complex
stories, not the predictable death-endings that matters. In the two plots,
linguistic and military behavior are formalized as one and the same, and
play strategic roles in shaping the plots. In the same way, then, staging
and the development of collective colonial identity work hand-in-glove
toward nation-building. My readings of these two plays analyze the dramatic strategy whereby the Orient is used as a "distant mirror" in which
to practice the enacting of France.

BAJAZET À LA LETTRE[2]

J'ai rendu votre lettre, et j'ai pris sa réponse.
[I returned your letter and I took his answer] (*Zaïre to Atalide*)

Ah! cachons cette lettre.
[Ah! Let's hide this letter] (*Atalide to Zaïre*)

Madame, j'ai reçu des lettres de l'armée.
. . .
Voyez: lisez vous-même,
Vous connaissez, Madame, et la lettre et le seing.

[Madam, I have received letters from the army.
. . .
Look: read it for yourself
You are familiar, Madam, with both the letter and the seal.] (*Roxane to Atalide*)

J'ai trouvé ce billet enfermé dans son sein:
Du prince votre amant j'ai reconnu la lettre,
Et j'ai cru qu'en vos mains je devais la remettre.

[I found this note enclosed in her bosom
I recognized the writing of your lover the Prince
And I thought I should turn it over to you.]
Roxane's servant Zatime to Roxane

The issue of communication was a highly charged one for the French in the seventeenth century, notably for long-distance official representation. Letters were crucial to the establishment and maintenance of the presence of the French crown in the trading outposts that were to bring wealth and glory to the kingdom. Missives between Versailles and Constantinople could take as little as three weeks, as long as six months, or not arrive at all, depending on the vagaries of the sea-crossing as elaborated in chapter 2. A perusal of minister Colbert's administrative correspondence with the various ambassadors, consuls, major trading houses, and the Marseille Chamber of Commerce over the years reveals the extent to which the king was intent on governing his adventuring subjects from afar. Typically, in 1670, Colbert addressed a dispatch to all of the French consuls in the Levant, taking them to task for sloppy office practices, and asserting the royal system's control over their local trade activities:

Entre tous les désordres qui se sont glisséz dans le commerce du Levant, et qui l'ont réduit dans le languissant estat où il est a présent, le roy n'en a point trouvé de plus considérable et qui demande un plus prompt remède que celuy qui s'est introduit dans la convocation des assemblées de la nation, dont les délibérations n'ont pas été ordinairement ni signées par tous les marchands qui y ont assisté, ni en mesme temps registrées aux chancelleries de tous les consulats où elles ont esté prises. C'est par cette raison que S.M. a fait rendre en son conseil royal de commerce l'arrest dont vous trouverez cy-joinct une copie, et qu'elle m'a ordonné de vous dire que son intention est que vous le fassiez, non seulement enregistrer dans vostre chancellerie, mais mesmes que vous teniez soigneusement la main à son entière exécution, en envoyant tous les trois mois, les délibérations qui seront conceues en la forme qui y est prescrite, tant au greffe de l'admirauté de Marseille qu'aux députés du commerce de ladite ville. A quoy je ne doute pas que vous ne conformiez avec toute l'exactitude nécessaire, et que, par ce moyen, S.M. n'ayt lieu de se louer de votre conduite.[3]

[Amidst all the disorder which has insinuated itself into commerce in the Levant, and which has reduced it to its present languishing state, the king has found nothing more considerable and which requires a prompter remedy than that introduced in the convocation of the nation's assemblies, whose deliberations have not usually been signed by all the participating merchants, nor at the same time registered with the chancelleries of the consulates where they were held. It is for this reason that His Majesty had his royal commerce council render the decree which you will find attached, and that he ordered me to tell you that his intention is that you not only have this decree registered in your chancellery, but also that you carefully follow all it requires, in sending every three months an account of all deliberations, in the proper form, both to the clerk of the admiralty of Marseille and to the deputies of commerce of said city. I have no doubt that you will carry this request out with every exactitude, and that in this way His Majesty will have every reason to be satisfied with your conduct.]

Like Amurat, the Sultan in *Bajazet,* but from the center as opposed to the front, Louis through the intermediary of Colbert forcefully reminded his subjects of his concern for detail and his abiding power over them, however removed from Paris they might be.[4] The bureaucracy that developed during the latter half of the seventeenth century extended beyond the hexagon, and encompassed all reaches of French enterprise. In order for the king's voice to carry, and to ensure compliance with the royal will, correspondence developed as a key feature of French presence overseas.

In keeping with this general goal of sustaining the royal voice abroad, and to ensure strategic privacy, elaborate encoding systems were set in place earlier in the century to protect diplomatic missives of envoys and travelers to Constantinople, both official and confidential.[5] These encrypted texts set up tensions of included versus excluded, and tantalized those who were specifically intended not to be privy to the messages.

Jean Chardin, the professional traveler and merchant, tells the story of the ambassador M. de la Haye Ventelay,[7] who used local customs to rid himself of an impoverished, hence potentially renegade, French decoder, Quiclet. In 1659, through an act of treachery, coded letters for the French ambassador passed into the hands of the Vizir:

Un français Vertament fut chargé d'un gros pacquet de Lettres pour l'Ambassadeur de France. Le Français qui n'avait d'autre dessin que de se faire Turc, se présenta au Caimacan de Constantinople, luy dit qu'il avoit quitté le champ des Chrétiens, parce qu'il vouloit abjurer leur Religion pour embrasser le Mahometisme, au reste qu'il avait un pacquet de Lettres de grande importance à mettre entre les mains du Grand Vizir.[8]

[A Frenchman was hastily given a large packet of letters for the French Ambassador. The Frenchman, who had no design other than to become Turkish, went to see the [Caimacan] of Constantinople, told him that he had left the fold of Christians, because he wanted to abjure their religion and embrace Islam, and moreover, he had a packet of letters of great importance to give to the Grand Vizier.]

Thus was the discovery made of a potentially compromising "commerce caché" ["secret correspondence"] (16) between the French and the Venetians. The Vizir was anxious to know the contents of the letters. In need of money, the decoder Quiclet's wife threatened that if the ambassador was not forthcoming, her husband would offer his expertise to the Vizir and decode the letters for him. De la Haye acted decisively:

Monsieur de la Haye, qui savait la grande envie qu'avoit Cuperli d'apprendre ce que contenoient les lettres interceptées, qui apprehendait qu'il n'y eut des choses qui le perdissent, et tous les Français du Levant, et qui savait la pauvreté du déchiffreur français; l'envoya quérir, le mena sur une terrasse du Palais qui regarde le jardin, et apres luy avoir fait quelques tours, l'entretenant de discours qu'on n'a point sçeus; il fit signe à des gens apostés qui lui firent sauter la terrasse; d'autres gens postés aussi à l'endroit où il tomba, voyant qu'il n'étoit pas mort de sa chute, l'achevèrent, et l'ensevelirent secrettement.[9]

[Monsieur de la Haye, who knew how desirous Cuperli was to learn what the intercepted letters contained, who feared that they might contain information which would cause his downfall along with that of all the French in the Levant, and who knew how poor the French decoder was; sent for him, led him to one of the terraces in the Palace overlooking the garden, and after walking with him for a little, discussing things which no one discovered; he gave a signal to men stationed nearby who pushed him off the terrace; other men stationed at the spot where he fell, seeing that he was not dead from his fall, finished him off, and buried him in secret.]

A page from the correspondence of Philippe Harlay, comte de Césy, (French ambassador to the Porte 1634–39)[6] in code and in ciphers, from the *Etat numérique des fonds de la correspondance politique de l'origine à 1871. Archives du ministère des affaires étrangères.* Paris: Imprimerie nationale, 1936, CP p. 394, microfilm p. 2.13, no. 442.

This incident spelled the end of the undiplomatic de la Haye's disastrous tenure as ambassador to the Porte. However, de la Haye's swift action, without the luxury of a Versailles consultation, was effective, and consonant with Racine's staged message to French delegates abroad. De la Haye did what Roxane should have done as soon as she realized she had no hold on Bajazet; he promptly put an end to an unsure situation that could only have further deteriorated French–Ottoman relations. As executor of the King's reach, he played Orcan to France's Amurat.

De la Haye was not alone in his concern for confidentiality. On a more frivolous note, another French gentleman, Monsieur du Loir, explained to his correspondent, Monsieur Charpentier, why he hesitated to write letters from Constantinople:

Je vous apprendrais des aventures d'amour que vous ne seriez pas fâché de savoir, si j'osais fier ici à l'écriture des mystères que la discretion m'ordonne de réserver à un entretien de vive voix. Une lettre, comme vous savez, peut être interceptée, et nous ne sommes pas ici tant de français qu'on ne put découvrir l'auteur. Et outre que ces secrets sont de la dernière importance entre des Chrétiens et des Turcs, ce serait dommage après tout, qu'une lettre de cette nature vînt à périr sur mer.[10]

[I would tell you about some love intrigues to which you would not be indifferent, if I dared confide to my pen mysteries which discretion orders me to save for a spoken conversation. A letter, as you know, can be intercepted, and we are not so many Frenchmen here that the writer couldn't be detected. And leaving aside the fact that these secrets are of the greatest importance among certain Christians and Turks, it would be too bad, after all, if a letter of this kind were to be lost at sea.]

This concern for security and preoccupation with censorship of the written word was not restricted to travelers and diplomats in Constantinople: within France itself there was Louis XIV's "Cabinet Noir."[11] Surveillance was a given condition of seventeenth-century correspondence. Codes were established, elaborated, and changed regularly in order to disguise meanings of messages to third parties; letters were addressed to fictitious people in order not to attract attention, or they were sent by means other than the conventional channels.[12] Letters were misplaced in fiction, as in Mme de Lafayette's *La Princesse de Clèves*; they were stolen and then published (Mlle de Montpensier);[13] they were invented and then passed off as real (*Les lettres portugaises* by Guilleragues). And the unfortunate Mme de Villedieu saw her personal correspondence published by her own husband. Any number of variations bore witness to the fact that letters were a genre to treat with care, precisely because of their status as truth documents. At the same time, France as a nation was becoming increasingly dependent on letters to extend its will to the reaches of its trading posts in the Levant (the "échelles"), and to its more distant colonies during this first wave of colonialism. There was genuine concern regarding long-distance communication, since a colonial project was inconceivable without securing lines of contact.

Accordingly, in *Bajazet* the conveyance of messages is the focus of a rigorous staged analysis that dramatizes the problematic of communication.[14] From the very beginning of the play, a confidential directive ("Un esclave chargé de quelque ordre secret" ["A slave assigned some secret order"] [1.1.70–71]) that would have drastically altered the direction of events has been intercepted, countered by another ("Un ordre . . . l'a fait précipiter dans le fond de l'Euxin" ["He was ordered to be thrown into the depths of the Euxine"] [1.1.79–80]), and the material movement of information along with the conditions for, and consequences of, its felicitous or infelicitous arrival at destination is announced as the crux of the tragedy. Racine's examination of the communicatory circuit contributed to a greater conversation that engaged society both in theory and in practice.[15]

From first preface to final act, *Bajazet* relays the problem of communication like a parlor game through different registers, into regressive infinity, deferring and ultimately defying resolution, ending abruptly yet inexorably where communication stops, at death's door as a minor character, the maid Zaïre, strains to follow her mistress Atalide across that threshold. The issue of communication in *Bajazet* is articulated in specific thematic declensions: the issue of honesty – truthful message or misinformation; of efficacy – the transmission or failure of the message; of the medium of the message – voice, body, or letter; and finally, of the reception of the message – skepticism, belief, credulity – all of these subject to interception and interpretation. Thus, even communication in all of its stages and valences would answer to that stronger power of contingency – context.[16]

This play treats not so much the more obvious "détours" of the seraglio as it does the "détours" of language, those of the spoken word as well as of the material written one. With *Mithridate*, Racine will elaborate the more formalized "détours" of militaristic strategizing and of tactical family management; but here first, in the guise of a highly particularized setting, he explores the realms of linguistic, interpersonal, and material contingency. In his examination of communication, even body language – the slightest twitch – can be considered only in light of the detour of context, so that all communication is ultimately reduced to interpretation. The only certainty then is uncertainty. Life is guess-work.

The exotic framing of *Bajazet* itself is a "détour," one that in the guise of distant Constantinople politics allows as well for close scrutiny of the dynamics of "entregent" ["civility, savoir-faire"] in Paris.[17] Corneille, Racine's rival and hardly a neutral expert, will both correctly and mis-guidedly insist on the emptiness of his rival's portrayal of the Oriental "Other": "Il n'y a pas un seul personnage qui ait les sentiments qu'il doit avoir et que l'on a à Constantinople; ils ont sous un habit turc, le senti-ment qu'on a au milieu de la France."[18] ["There is not a single character who has the feelings he ought to have and that one has in Constantinople; clothed in Turkish garb, they have the feelings one has in the heart of France."] Corneille's insistence on the inadequacy of the representation at once willfully misses the point and makes it. He disregards the more profound subject of the play – communication, critiquing instead the history/literature, fact/fiction surface tension.

The issues of communication raised in *Bajazet* are just as readily per-tinent to any closely watched and controlled grouping, be it the classical court society or the more distant colony. Racine suggests as much in his second preface as he justifies his choice of intensifying locale, casting communication concerns as love concerns:

En effet, y a-t-il une cour au monde où la jalousie et l'amour doivent être si bien connues que dans un lieu où tant de rivales sont enfermées ensemble, et où toutes ces femmes n'ont point d'autre étude, dans une éternelle oisiveté, que d'apprendre à plaire et à se faire aimer? (Seconde Préface).

[In fact, is there any court in the world where jealousy and love can be so well known, as in a place where so many lady rivals are locked up together, and where all these women have no other occupation, in endless idleness, than to learn how to please and how to make themselves admired?]

The seraglio furnishes an exaggerated model – a hothouse to use as a vehicle for commentary on communication generally. While there might be a degree of self-recognition by the seventeenth-century French audience in the characters and the intrigue, it was mitigated by the distancing and distracting afforded by the exotic setting.[19] The French court audience resisted recognizing itself in Racine's oblique critique and at the same time succumbed to the attraction of the staged mirror, much as audiences respond today to staged critiques of contemporary society.[20] But the exotic model spoke more directly perhaps to those French administrators engaged in managing French representation and interests abroad.

The theme of communication is first announced to the reader in the prefaces to the play, those after-the-fact texts (1672, 1676) that purport to contextualize and justify the workings of the plot. Here Racine claims that the story he stages is one he heard from the Chevalier de Nantouillet, who heard it from the ambassador de Césy, who was told the story since he was in residence in Constantinople at the time of the reported event.[21] Racine also alleges to have consulted another ambassador, the by now familiar de la Haye. Thus, while the play might, given such diplomatic input, constitute something of an "official story," it is also at best a third-hand account of an event, no doubt modified and embellished through these several tellings, perhaps closer to gossip. One must view then with some suspicion Racine's insistance on the "très véritable" ["very truthful"] (Première Préface) nature of his subject. Further, Racine professes to have authenticated his play through consultations of written histories of the Ottomans. But these too are second-hand accounts, produced by European outsiders (of course "insider" history likewise would have its own bias). Would on-site reports – "official stories" from the colonies – not all be similarly unreliable constructions? (1.5.354).

The play reduces complex events to a composite and imaginative rendering, using the few known facts merely as a point of departure, and Racine's truth claim must be reviewed beyond the stresses of fact and fiction, in the conditions of their mutual possibility. Indeed, that is the essence of classical tragedy as "historical" genre. But, to further complicate the truth claim, what interests us here is the construction of the complementary double standard (the truth for some; lies for others, as the occasion dictates), hardly a seventeenth-century invention, but a discourse that would be increasingly characteristic of colonial positioning.

The core story from which *Bajazet* is concocted is that during de Césy's tenure as ambassador to the Porte (1634–39), Mourad IV had two of his brothers strangled, one of whom was the popular Bajazet, and the city was in consternation. Indeed, by his own admission, the closest the on-site witness de Césy ever got to Bajazet was a glimpse from the sea of him up on a seraglio parapet. What is gained and what is lost in the communicative circuit cannot be determined, but claims for veracity in the prefaces can certainly be viewed with some skepticism.[22] Or these claims can be counted as the first "détours" staged by Racine himself in his dramatization of the problematic of communication.[23]

Racine's play reached beyond the stage, and spoke to the concerns of the new seventeenth-century press. There again, the accuracy of Racine's portrayal of Ottoman society was contested, just as it was by Corneille. In the first issue of *Le Mercure Galant* (January 9, 1672), Donneau de Visé, our muckraker (see "Orientation" and chapter 3) and also a Corneille partisan, displayed his quickly acquired expertise and denounced the "docu-drama" for its inauthenticity. When *Mithridate* was first staged the following year, this critic would repeat his gripe about *Bajazet*, and add to it more objections: "Il ne lui est pas moins permis de changer la vérité des histoires anciennes pour faire un ouvrage agréable, qu'il lui a été d'habiller à la turque nos amants et nos amantes."[24] ["He is no more allowed to change the truth of ancient history in order to produce an agreeable piece, than he was allowed to dress our lovers in Turkish clothes."] Still beside the point, but more titillatingly for his tabloid, de Visé located the worth of the play in its faithful representation of the gallant Turkish character. He cited, as confirmation of this trait, the evidence of a letter from the same Monsieur du Loir cited earlier:

La galanterie et l'honnêteté des Turcs n'est pas une chose sans exemples, et nous en avons une histoire très agréable dans une lettre de Monsieur du Loir écrite à Monsieur Charpentier en 1641 que vous serez peut-être bien aise que je vous rapporte.[25]

[The gallantry and integrity of the Turks does not lack for examples, and we have a very agreeable story on that score in a letter from Monsieur du Loir, written to Monsieur Charpentier in 1641, and which you may perhaps like to hear.]

Just as in the play itself – missives from Amurat to Roxane, Bajazet's letter to Atalide – the letter is privileged here as a reliable truth source. Cited in the frame of a newspaper piece, du Loir's letter enjoys further enhanced status as a proof document. In the domains both of fiction and fact, the letter stands apart as sure truth text. Indeed, de Visé exploited this common conviction: in 1672, his own nascent journalistic enterprise, *Le Mercure galant* itself, was framed as a weekly letter from a Parisian to a lady of the provinces. But the authority that the letter enjoys in minds such as de Visé's forecloses on "the purpose of playing" allowed in the speculative space of the stage, and leaves little room for exploring the letter's all-important context.[26]

Casting fact as fiction, and treating fiction as fact, made possible the conveyance not so much of either as of editorial positioning – is opinion not the contrary of speculation? The French were moving in with increasing purpose on their more indifferent Ottoman trading partner in the Levant. They sent home information already framed in attitude regarding this part of the world – sometimes accurate and appropriate, sometimes not. The recent newspaper genre, feeding off data gleaned from letters, combined information and commentary on French foreign affairs, setting a stage for journalistic realism while dramatizing and rhetoricizing the world. Moreover, in its beginning, it engaged in literary critique. De Visé's review of Racine's *Bajazet* in *Le Mercure Galant* confounded the distinctions between rapportage and review. Was the seventeenth-century reader to understand his "Discours sur Bajazet, tragédie du Sieur Racine" as international news or as local cultural commentary? The contemporaneity of the event and de Visé's supposed expertise regarding Ottoman ways interfered with appreciation of the play per se. Here the blur between fact and fiction was instantiated.

In his analysis of "imagined communities," Benedict Anderson highlights the status of the newspaper as stage itself. Anderson links the newspaper with notions of theatricality and a consumer market, a reading audience eager to take in and evaluate a staged world-view in print, which is precisely what the newspaper provides – an invented plot and a fixed duration for its unfolding: "If we now turn to the newspaper as a cultural product, we will be struck by its profound fictiveness . . . a juxtaposition of events, actors . . . The arbitrariness of their inclusion and juxtaposition shows that the linkage between them is imagined . . . This imagined linkage derives from two obliquely related sources. The first is simply calendrical coincidence. The date at the top of the newspaper, the single most important emblem on it, provides the essential connection – the steady onward clocking of homogenous, empty time. Within that time, 'the world' ambles steadily ahead. . . . The second source of imagined linkage lies in the relationship between the newspaper, as a form of book, and the market."[27] These were the generic characteristics that were just beginning to unfold in de Visé's pages; despite the similarities, the newsprint stage and the actual theatre would have importantly different missions – the one would convey fact and opinion, the other fiction and speculation. In this spirit, then, de Visé's inaugural attempts at newspaper production resembled more performance than rapportage.

If Anderson's insights afford a contemporary perspective on de Visé's docu-review, they do not tell us how to read Racine's prefaces – these bridge texts.[28] The prefaces provide tips from Racine himself on how to appreciate the play, almost as if he were encroaching here on newspaper territory. In order to justify treating the contemporary and newsworthy story of Bajazet on the classical stage, Racine insisted here on the strangeness, the "Otherness" of the culture he was dramatizing. His argument is based on the proposition that physical distance and cultural difference seem commensurable with distance in time:

L'éloignement des pays répare en quelque sorte la trop grande proximité des temps, car le peuple ne met guère de différence entre ce qui est, si j'ose ainsi parler, à mille ans de lui, et ce qui en est à mille lieues. C'est ce qui fait, par exemple, que les personnages turcs, quelques modernes qu'ils soient, ont de la dignité sur notre théâtre. On les regarde de bonne heure comme anciens. (Seconde Préface)

[In a way, the great distance between the two countries makes up for the too great proximity in time, for the people hardly see any difference between what is, if I may venture, a thousand years away from them, and what is a thousand miles away. This, for example, is what gives Turkish characters dignity on our stage, as modern as they are. They are viewed from the start in the same way as the ancients.]

Racine's reasoning for the theatre here is in direct contradiction with the development of the idea of "simultaneity," of "conceiving of things happening in different places at the same time," which Anderson sees as at the heart of the evolution of the press.[29] Racine attempts to play down precisely what Anderson plays up. To justify writing a play about the contemporary Ottomans, he had to suggest that they were as if out of time past, and hence worthy subjects for the stage.

Racine's position, however, is inconsistent: at the same time, in these prefaces, flaunting the daring of his argument, he underscores the recency of the event, its current relevance, and its as yet undigested status. In 1672, he boastfully opens his first preface: "Quoique le sujet de cette tragédie ne soit encore dans aucune histoire imprimée," ["Although the subject of this tragedy is not yet in any history in print"] and he insists again: "C'est une aventure arrivée dans le sérail, il n'y a pas plus de trente ans." ["It is an adventure which took place in the seraglio, no more than thirty years ago."] In 1676, Racine updates and insistently repeats himself: "Les particularités de la mort de Bajazet ne sont encore dans aucune histoire imprimée" ["The particulars of Bajazet's death are not yet in any history in print"] (Seconde Préface). The subject matter is at once too close and too far away, as is any truth – a fact that the play will demonstrate.[30] Taking pains to highlight the currency of the story rather than passing it off more discreetly as "history," he ties it genealogically to the present: "Le Sultan Mahomet, qui règne aujourd'hui, est fils de cet Ibrahim et par conséquent neveu de Bajazet" ["The Sultan Mahomet, who reigns today, is the son of this Ibrahim and consequently Bajazet's nephew"] (Seconde Préface). Racine's narrativizing here appears to be competing explicitly with the newspaper as an alternative, even a more fitting forum for current affairs. Good stretches of his two prefaces concern themselves with problems of communicating in the present about the near present, problems that also will be addressed in the play itself.

By 1676, Racine appears to acknowledge a change in his audience/readership from 1672. His first preface (1672) introduced only the first edition of the play. The second preface (1676) accompanied the second, third, and fourth editions, and Racine suppressed its last paragraph after 1687. In this second preface, not only must he incorporate his responses to early criticisms of the play; this current readership apparently needs more information, needs to be told the story of Bajazet. Whereas in 1672 Racine merely mentions in passing the Ricaut history of the Ottomans, presuming audience familiarity with current gossip, which allows him to move more readily into his play, by 1676 he is reminding his public that books ("il ne faut que lire l'histoire des Turcs" (Seconde Préface) ["One has only to read the history of the Turks"] support the tenor of his play. But this is from the paragraph that will be suppressed by 1678, so perhaps Racine had realized by then that he was in contradiction with himself.

While the Corneille partisans had earlier critiqued the play and found it wanting in plausibility, thereby explaining Racine's defensive remarks, it is equally true that the play itself, first produced in 1672, was slowly slipping into "history" (albeit contemporary), even for Racine himself, by 1676. Pedagogical as well as defensive, the second preface acts as a supplement to shore up the gaps of communication left by the play. The fact that two of them are needed attests to the inadequacy not of the first, the second, or even both, but to the inefficacy of any preface and ultimately of the play itself as a series of communication acts – indeed, of any attempt at communication.[31] This is not an encouraging message for a nation increasingly reliant precisely on long-distance communication.

DETOUR INTO THE PLAY

The communication motif is flagged and highlighted by the frequent use of the term "détour" throughout the play. From the beginning, Bajazet objects to the "détour" of prevarication when he protests against Atalide's plea that he pretend better to love Roxane so as to assure his own life:

> Et j'irais l'abuser d'une fausse promesse?
> Je me parjurerais? Et, par cette bassesse . . .
> Ah! loin de m'ordonner cet indigne détour,
> Si votre coeur était moins plein de son amour,
> Je vous verrais, sans doute en rougir la première.

> [And I would trick her with a false promise!
> I would perjure myself! And by this base act . . .
> Ah! Far from ordering me to proceed with this unworthy ruse,
> If your heart were less full of love,
> I would doubtless see you the first to blush at it.]

> (2.5.753–57)

He sets himself and Atalide apart as belonging to a class ("sang," "rang") of which honor is the mark, which admits of no falsehood. To make a false promise is to act out of rank, beneath one's dignity. Thus, circulation of truth would be group-restricted. The "détour" is a problem for Bajazet insofar as he considers himself a member of the ruling Ottoman dynasty that would locate itself above the pragmatism of its vizir servant Acomat. Witness this exchange between them: Acomat: "Promettez. Affranchi du péril qui vous presse, / Vous verrez de quel poids sera votre promesse." Bajazet: "Moi!" Acomat: "Ne rougissez point. Le sang des Ottomans / Ne doit point en Esclave obéir aux serments." [Acomat: "Promise: freed of the danger pressing on you / You will see what weight your promise holds." Bajazet: "Me!" Acomat: "Do not blush: The blood of Ottomans / Should not slavishly obey oaths."] (2.3.641–44). Whereas Acomat is a product of and consummate player in palace politics ("Nourri dans le sérail j'en connais les détours." ["Brought up in the seraglio, I know its hidden ways/detours"] [4.7.1428]), Bajazet will appeal more naïvely to the ethic of sovereignty – legitimacy versus manipulation, "foi" versus "perfidie" ["honesty" versus "perfidy."] As a consequence, he will perish. Here is a cautionary tale highlighting the vital necessity to lie, to deploy the double standard, in certain circumstances.

Although Bajazet's righteous and nobiliary attachment to honesty sounds like a group ethic, he is in fact the only character to invoke it. After all, Amurat, his elder brother the Sultan himself, sends secret orders and behaves underhandedly; and even Bajazet's beloved Atalide misrepresents and lies on a daily basis in order to protect him – thus underscoring that probity is no longer so much rank-related as context-dependent in the current dispensation. And we have seen the Vizir's pragmatic advice to lie highlighted above. Bajazet may object to being in a situation where he must negotiate with Roxane, a mere slave (however currently exalted in the Sultan's favor), unburdened with his same noble scruples, or so he believes. But it is his own perhaps obsolete class-hobbled and impractical honor code that gets in the way of his empowerment and instead marks him as victim. This was the retraining lesson the French elite would need to take away from this play if they were to become successful administrators, managers, ruling class bureaucrats in the new colonial situation. "L'honnêteté," [integrity] the standard touted as marking the French gentleman, could apply only among themselves. It could be lethal if they clung to it when dealing with "outsiders" as well.[32] They needed to master cynicism, ruthlessness, and the double standard instead.[33]

Despite Bajazet's elitist qualms, he does obey Atalide, and proceeds, but only passively (as far as we can tell), to mislead Roxane. He will protest repeatedly against the demeaning behavior to which he has been reduced by his attachment to her, disregarding in a whining tone the more crucial fact that it is his own reluctant and indecisive attitude that has gotten in his way. Here it is apparent that although the "détours" appear necessitated by a cross-class situation, they are mandated by Bajazet's impractical attitude. He clearly (and naïvely) subscribes to Atalide's assumption that, because legitimated by maternal authorization, their union should prevail without question.[34]

The lesson comes home when cross-class relations and oral communication enter into written relations and tell-tale communication. The letter that Bajazet finally sends Atalide passes through a "détour" which will be their undoing. The document, fallen into Roxane's hands, confirms for her the bond she had suspected but preferred to ignore. Up until the moment when Roxane is confronted with the material evidence, she can willfully dismiss what she only too rightly suspects. Once the written word – hard data – surfaces, she must concede to the facts. On the one hand, this moment is pivotal: from here on, she must accept Bajazet's faithfulness to his own kind – to Atalide – and steel herself to seal his fate. On the other, the savvier "absolute ruler" Amurat has already, from his distanced position, determined everyone's destiny, Roxane's included; but we do not know that until after the fact. The incident of the letter turns out to be of minor importance in the greater scheme of things after all, and the issue of communication is subjected to that even greater force: context.

The "détour" of Bajazet's letter will boomerang back to him in a devastating way, through the voice of Roxane. She, the very person whose lowly but powerful self occasioned the need to prevaricate, expresses contemptuous shock at the noble Bajazet's own debased behavior:

> Mais je m'étonne enfin, que pour reconnaissance
> D'un amour appuyé sur tant de confiance,
> Vous ayez si longtemps, par des détours si bas,
> Feint un amour, pour moi, que vous ne sentiez pas.
>
> [But I am astonished finally, that as gratefulness
> For a love founded on so much confidence,
> You have for so long, and with such base ruses,
> Feigned a love for me that you did not feel.]
>
> (5.4.1481–84)

Thus the differences of class are challenged. Bajazet is gallingly reminded that even he is subject to the moral judgment of someone he considers his inferior, and that this person, by invoking his principles, claims to share them. Both Atalide and Bajazet have been blinded to the dangers of trying to dupe Roxane by their firm belief in her class-marked tendency to credulity as well as by the success until that point of their misinformation campaign.

Here enters yet another condition of communication – the reception of messages. The characteristic of credulity (also understood as "believing" in more trusting circumstances) is introduced and assigned early on in the play, in a passage treating the people: "Je sais combien crédule en sa dévotion / Le peuple suit le frein de la religion." (1.2.235–36) ["I know how credulous in their devotion, / The people submit to the yoke of religion."] Shortly following, Roxane is linked to this tendency: "De ses moindres respects Roxane satisfaite / Nous engagea tous deux, par sa facilité, / A la laisser jouir de sa crédulité." (1.4.374–76).[35] ["Roxane, satisfied by the least mark of respect, / Easily led us both / To let her enjoy her credulity."] Credulity here is not merely convenient to the plot, but echoes observations of French travelers to the Ottoman world.

Chardin, for one, assigns this quality generally to the Turks as he analyzes European dealings with them: "Il n'y a pas de gens au monde plus aisés à tromper, et qui aient été plus trompez que les Turcs. Ils sont naturellement tres simples, et assez épais, gens à qui on en fait aisément à croire."[36] ["There are no people in the world so easy to deceive, and who have been more deceived than the Turks. They are by nature a very simple, thick-headed people, whom one can easily lead on."] Now, how would one know that the people are gullible and easy to fool, if not through experience? Apparently, the merchants had already honed the skills of deception necessary to yield profit in their trade (let us not forget the floating of counterfeit coins mentioned in chapter 3). And they could even reassure their compatriots that they could bank on duping the Ottomans right up through their ranks. If the people are condescendingly cast by Chardin as credulous, so also are the elite: "Le Caprice des femmes et des Eunuques, qui gouvernoient durant le bas âge de Mahamed quatrième, le fit Grand Vizir [Cupruli] . . . Il commença par le Serrail, où il fit étrangler plusieurs Eunuques, et [se rendit] Maître en peu de temps de la credulité, et des affections de son jeune Prince . . ."[37] ["The caprice of women and eunuchs, who governed during Mahomet IV's childhood, made [Cupruli] Grand Vizier . . . He began with the Seraglio, where he had several eunuchs strangled, and in short order [made himself] master of the credulity and affections of his young Prince."]

The French would frequently dupe the Turks, disguising themselves and gaining entry into off-limit spaces; they prided themselves in having mastered the local code and in "passing" as the occasion required. Their general belief in the Ottomans' credulity colored their perceptions, and therefore this feature of the play was not at all idiosyncratic, but merely confirmed on stage what was circulating more generally in the thoughts of the spectators. They were taking in an encouraging and confirming performance of their own mind-set, further fixing their view of the "Other" as dupable and of themselves as in control.

As for Roxane, like the people, not only is she characterized as credulous; she is cast as the agent responsible for Atalide's and Bajazet's unworthy behavior, thereby exonerating them in their own eyes. Bajazet will chafe against the dupery to which he is reduced in order to survive: "Je ne puis plus tromper une amante crédule." (2.5.742) ["I can no longer dupe a credulous lover."] Moreover, he will express feelings of guilt for leading her on: "Moi-même rougissant de sa crédulité / . . . / Je me trouvais barbare, injuste, criminel." (3.4.991, 995) ["Myself, blushing for her credulity / . . . / I found myself barbarous, unjust, criminal."] Nevertheless, he persists in the direction of duplicity, encouraged by Atalide, until found out. For her part, in the end, Atalide will assume complete responsibility for the final disaster (5.12.1729–32), imputing none to Roxane or Amurat. While this may appear noble on her part, it is also a means of claiming (even if only after the fact) total ultimate control ("Moi seule j'ai tissu le lien malheureux." (5.12.1739) ["I alone, I wove the fatal link."]) – she wants and has the last word. The two lovers are quite a pair: to want at once to be both innocent and in control – was this not the ideal of the colonialist?

But Racine here also stages the cautionary lesson against believing one can dupe the "Other" indefinitely with impunity. For Roxane is not as credulous as one might be led to believe by Atalide and Bajazet. Several times she has reflected on the nature of Bajazet's attachment to her, and has expressed doubts. She questions the difference between Bajazet's mode of addressing her, and Atalide's when she speaks in his place. Atalide's representation of Bajazet's love is more convincing than his own, and Roxane does not fail to note the difference: "Pourquoi faut-il au moins que pour me consoler / L'ingrat ne parle pas comme on le fait parler?" (1.3.275–76) ["In order to console me, why at least / Does the ingrate not talk in the way he is said to?"]. At regular intervals, she interrogates her own perceptions, having detected signs of the couple's love for each other: "De tout ce que je vois que faut-il que je pense? / Tous deux à me tromper sont-ils d'intelligence?" (3.7.1065–66). ["What am I to make of all I see? / Are they both in league to deceive me?"]

If Roxane does not leap to conclusions, it is not because she is credulous, but because she intelligently doubts her own perception, and believes too close and too prompt a scrutiny can be just as misleading as too distanced and too considered a one (precisely the lesson drawn from the prefaces). Roxane vacillates between what she sees and what she wants to see, visions that do not coincide, and seeks to accommodate them both: "Mais peut-être qu'aussi trop prompte à m'affliger, / J'observe de trop près un chagrin passager." (3.7.1075–76) ["But perhaps as well, too quick to grieve / I make too much of a fleeting chagrin."] This statement is the reluctant thinking of a clear-sighted strategist, not of a woman blinded by love. Roxane's ruminations on Atalide and Bajazet's behavior, her attempt to scope them out, will be like those of the colonized reading for clues of the colonizer. The colonizer arrogantly tends to forget that he/she is object of the gaze as well as subject. Here was a timely reminder that the intelligence of the "Other" was not to be underestimated.

Having confirmed to her (dis)satisfaction Atalide's love for Bajazet, Roxane must decide how to proceed. Her initial decision is to choose deliberately not to know. She lucidly opts for blindness: "Il faut prendre parti, l'on m'attend. Faisons mieux. / Sur tout ce que j'ai vu fermons plutôt les yeux." (4.4.1235–36) ["It is time to decide, I am expected. Even better:/ Instead, I'll close my eyes to all I've seen."] She concludes her meditation on what she now knows with a resolution: "Je veux tout ignorer." (4.4.1250) ["I want to be ignorant of everything."] This position is hardly that of a credulous person. It is rather a position assumed in the face of unpleasant facts. But, confronted with letter proof of Bajazet's love for Atalide, Roxane finally must submit to the data and accuse her own self of credulity: "Avec quelle insolence, et quelle cruauté, / Ils se jouaient tous deux de ma crédulité!" (4.5.1295–96). ["With what insolence and what cruelty/ They both took pleasure in my credulity!"] She recognizes that she has been duped. Her own love for Bajazet and her desire to believe that he loved her had blinded her to the truth even as she saw it.

But what would Roxane have seen otherwise? Reserve, coldness, indifference, inability to speak the language of love? It is unclear, beyond Bajazet's well-argued refusal to marry and his failure to pronounce the love vow, whether he was actively leading Roxane to believe in his love for her, or whether she protected herself from the hurtful truth with wishful, willful interpretation. After all, how is one to know, beyond the claims of the immediately concerned, Bajazet and Roxane, what is really happening between them during their tête-à-tête? What is it that the outside on-site witness, Acomat, claims to have seen (and what did de Césy actually see?)?:

> J'ai longtemps immobile, observé leur maintien.
> Enfin avec des yeux qui découvraient son âme,
> L'une a tendu la main pour gage de sa flamme,
> L'autre, avec des regards éloquents, pleins d'amour,
> L'a de ses feux, Madame, assurée à son tour.

> [Motionless, I long observed their behavior.
> At last, with a look that revealed her soul,
> One extended her hand as proof of her ardent feelings;
> The other, with eloquent looks, full of love,
> In his turn, Madam, assured her of his passion.]
>
> (3.2.884–88)

Roxane's belief in Bajazet's love for her could well be justified, if one is to believe Acomat's witnessing. After all, is Acomat ("nourri dans le sérail" ["brought up in the seraglio"]) not the very character who claims to know how to know? He has underscored repeatedly and knowingly the importance of body language as a more reliable message medium than speech (4.6.1342–43). So far, so good. But then he is also the old warrior who himself has earlier acknowledged that he knows nothing of love: "Voudrais-tu qu'à mon âge / Je fisse de l'amour le vil appren-tissage?" (1.1.177–80) ["Would you, at my age, have me do of love the lowly apprenticeship?"], so how would he know to read its signs? Is his interpretation of what he sees here not influenced by what he wants to see? Here are marked out the distances between observation, theory, and practice. Acomat's credentials as truth purveyor are uncertain in this instance. This too is a lesson for the colonialist.

In the end, if Roxane acknowledges her own credulity (4.5.1296–97), it is not so much that she has behaved credulously throughout the play. Rather, she has been duped by others, not by herself, and strung along too long; her keen vision sets her apart from the credulous. She herself has been sensitive throughout to the slightest nuances in Bajazet's demeanor: "Quel est ce sombre accueil, et ce discours glacé / Qui semble révoquer tout ce qui s'est passé?" (3.6.1035–36) ["What is this somber welcome, and this cold speech / Which seems to deny all that has happened?"] In any case, the timing of her coming to face with the facts has been too slow to outwit the inexorable action that has been set in motion from outside the Seraglio, at the right time, from the right distance, by Amurat. He knows how to read the failure of communication and how to use silence to his own advantage, and he understands the importance of timing; hence his power.

Is Racine merely cautioning the audience against credulity in his ver-sified version of the facts? Does he understand that, despite the "reliable" sources from which he has gleaned the stuff of the plot, nothing is sure? This would be a key message for an audience/nation beginning to de-velop long-distance colonial power. Little cross-checking can be done, and one person's word may end up carrying too much or too little weight. But also, decisiveness in colonial delegates (as in de la Haye's ruthless dispatching with the renegade decoder) is essential. Credulity surfaces in the play one final time in a conversation between Acomat and his con-fidant Osmin. Osmin misinterprets Acomat's motive for lingering when all is lost, and flight is the only hope for survival. Acomat insists he does not want to stay in order to be witness to Bajazet's death after the ill-fated letter has jinxed their plans for the coup: "Que veux-tu dire? Es-tu toi-même si crédule, / Que de me soupçonner d'un courroux ridicule?"

(4.7.1373–74). ["What do you mean? Are you yourself so credulous / That you suspect me of ridiculous anger?"] Now credulity circulates: not only has Roxane been cast as credulous, Osmin as well might be. From its assignment to "le peuple" to its imputation to Roxane, and here to Osmin, credulity moves contagiously to the inner and upper circles until finally no one is exempt. No one is sure who or what to believe; thus everything appears plausible. In typical Racinian tragic fashion, in the end, no one is more credulous than Bajazet and Atalide themselves, who thought that they could stage such a coup against Roxane just because she was not of their class and in love, and who imagined they could survive their own dupery. They have been blinded, the two of them, each in his or her own way, by a class bias that led them to believe in their moral superiority and in the gullible nature of the people. If they were to have been successful, they would have needed instead to take a better measure of their enemy.

Communication is depicted at its most egregiously feigned and impossible between Bajazet and Roxane. Not only is Roxane a woman (so, after all, is Atalide); she is a slave – favored slave, but slave nonetheless. The peculiar balance of power between herself and Bajazet (Bajazet – a noble man held captive and subject to Roxane's will; Roxane – an enslaved woman ruling over the Seraglio, but subject to surveillance from afar) dooms any attempt at candor. The figure of such a woman at once repelled and fascinated Europeans; less threatening perhaps in an exotic setting than in powerful women closer to home, although or perhaps precisely because they did abound at the time, as in the case of the recent regent queens, the salonnières, and even such figures as Ninon de Lenclos, and eventually, Madame de Maintenon. But if Roxane was an invention of Racine's, and even had her counterparts in Paris, she was not without models in Ottoman history.

Consider this description of Mulki Kadin, a contemporary of the French *frondeuses*, from Sir Paul Ricaut's history:

Nous avons vu un terrible exemple de cela au commencement du règne de Sultan Mahomet. Il y avait dans le Serrail une jeune femme, hardie et entreprenante, qui s'appelloit Mulki Kadin, entre les mains de laquelle estoit tout le gouvernement de l'Empire, par l'amour et par la faveur extraordinaire que la Reine mère luy portoit. Les Vizirs et les Bachas ne donnoient point d'ordres qu'elle ne les eut approuvez. Les Eunuques noirs donnoient la loy à tout le monde, et les Conseils secrets se tenoient dans l'appartement des femmes. C'est là où se faisoient les proscriptions; c'est là qu'on cassoit les

Officiers les plus considérables, et que l'on remplissoit leur place de gens qui estoient plus propres qu'eux à maintenir ce gouvernement de femmes.[38]

[We saw a terrible example of this at the beginning of the Sultan Mahomet's reign. In the Seraglio there was a young woman named Mulki Kadin, bold and enterprising, who held the government of the Empire in her hands, thanks to the love and extraordinary favor the Queen Mother accorded her. The Vizirs and the pachas could not give any orders without her approval. The black Eunuchs set the laws for everyone, and the secret councils were held in the women's apartments. That was where banishings were decided; that was where the most considerable officers were ruined, and in their place were put people more fitting than they were to tolerate this government of women.]

Civil rebellion where women played a prominent role had broken out not only in France during the Fronde and Louis XIV's minority then, but had arisen also during the same decades in Constantinople.[39] Because it had taken place in two such different cultures, it was more than doubly threatening, both from within and without the kingdom. With regard to foreign affairs, the shape of local power in the trading world would not perfectly match the French system, and the French would need to nimbly adapt their approaches and learn new management styles accordingly, without losing sight of their own internal social organization and purpose. It is these kinds of unfamiliar political constructs and events precisely with which colonialism would have to contend.

Roxane's status as Amurat's Sultane is strictly honorific; she has not performed the requisite task of producing a male heir in order to merit the title. Her status, therefore, is precarious and strictly at Amurat's pleasure.[41] Furthermore, her origins are unclear in the play: she comes from an undetermined but subjected place, and hence in a sense represents all of them:[42] "Quoi Roxane, Seigneur, qu'Amurat a choisie / Entre tant de beautés dont l'Europe et l'Asie / Dépeuplent leurs Etats et remplissent sa cour?" (1.1.97–99) ["What! Roxane, my lord, whom Amurat chose / From among so many beauties, of which Europe and Asia / divest their countries and fill his court."] If Orcan is another of Amurat's privileged slaves, he at least has a more precise identity ("Né sous le Ciel brûlant des plus noirs Africains" ["Born under the burning sun of the blackest Africans"] [3.8.1104]).

The failure to assign Roxane a place of origin places her squarely in the amorphous zone of the exotic, and so in this French play she exemplifies the exotic framed within the exotic – the quintessentially Exotic. She has no precise history. The historian Ricaut describes the harem that

186 Histoire des Turcs,

MEHEMET III. DV NOM,
VINGT-TROISIESME EMPEREVR
DES TVRCS.

SVLTAN ECHMET EMPEREVR DES
Turcs Aagè de 30 Ans.

B. Moncornet excudit. 1655.

Mes Baſſas reuoltez, mes troupes mutinées,
Les factions de Cour dans ma minorité
Ont à la fin fait place à mon auctorité;
J'attends pour l'auenir la loy des deſtinées.

Portrait of Mehmet III (1595–1603),[40] from François de Mézeray, *Histoire des Turcs.*
Second Tome. Contenant ce qui s'est passé dans cet empire depuis l'an 1612 jusqu'à l'anneé présente
1649. Avec l'histoire de Chalcondyle par Blaise de Vigenere. Les descriptions et figures des habits des
officiers et autres personnes de l'Empire Turc et les Tableaux prophétiques sur la ruine du même empire.
Paris: Cramoisy, 1663, 186.

Roxane was to emblematize:

Le Lecteur sçaura que cette assemblee de belles, car il n'y en a point d'autres
dans le Serrail, est composée des prises qui se font sur la mer et sur la terre,
et que ces Dames sont amenées - là d'aussi loin que s'étend la domination du
Turc, ou que peuvent aller les courses vagabondes des Tartares. Qu'il y en
a presque de tous les païs, et de toutes les nations du monde; et qu'aucune
n'est jugée digne de cet honneur, qui ne soit tres belle, et veritablement
vierge.[43]

[The reader will find out that this assembly of beautiful women, for there is no
other kind in the Seraglio, is made up of captures made at sea and on land,
and that these ladies are brought there from as far as the reach of Turkish rule
extends, or as far as the Tartars' vagabond courses run. That there are some
from almost every land and nation in the world; and that none is judged worthy
of this honor unless she be very beautiful and a true virgin.]

Plucked out of her world of origin, Roxane has become simply the
"Other," and as such enjoys only the status that is assigned to her. If,
as a strategist, she is intent on marrying Bajazet to protect her future
(she implores him imperiously: "Montrez à l'univers, en m'attachant à
vous / Que, quand je vous servais, je servais mon époux" (2.1.447–48)
["Show the world, in uniting me to you/ That, when I served you, I
was serving my future husband"]), as a constructed character, she may
also be importing French cultural expectations into the Seraglio setting,
seeking to shed her "Other"ness. At the heart of the clash between herself and Bajazet we see the gap of conflicting traditions. Thus she ("qui
n'aspirais qu'à cette seule gloire" [1.3.305] ["who aspired only to this
one glory"]) fails to appreciate Bajazet's objections to marriage. While
she acknowledges a set position against the act among the Ottomans,
she cites as a preferable model the sole exceptional example of Soliman
II, who did marry his slave.

   Bajazet's two arguments against the aptness of that example are constructed diplomatically; to Roxane he will point out humbly the difference in power positions between himself and Soliman (2.1.473–84).
Soliman could do as he pleased without concern for public opinion, so
powerful was he.[44] Thus the play explores not simply an inter-personal
and cross-class tension, but, more broadly, a cross-cultural and cross-
time gap. Bajazet and Roxane argue from such different positions that
neither of them can hope for a level playing field. But, secondly, when
Bajazet later reviews his exchange with Acomat, he vents his anger and
voices his more profound and personal objection: here, it is not he who
would choose a slave as a concubine, instead a slave is forcing on him a

choice between marriage and death. This ignoble situation is intolerable to him. What Bajazet cannot accept is the power relations between himself and Roxane. She is not of his class, and the world is topsy-turvy (particularly as the class-stratified French would see it) when a slave can set such conditions over a member of the royal family (2.5.718–19).[45]

Bajazet also refuses as unworthy of him Acomat's base and calculating suggestion that he make of the marriage an empty gesture, a speech-act without follow-through, and right matters once power has been wrested from Amurat. This is his fatal mistake, and a lesson for the audience to take home. Once again, Bajazet is restricted by the tenets of his class-honed identity. He is not well served by his sense of honor. Meanwhile, Roxane's only protection, if she is to abandon Amurat definitively and support Bajazet, is marriage; this can be the only solution for her to a life-or-death situation, a zero-sum-total game (5.4.1535–40).

Atalide is equally sensitive to her lineage, and appeals to Roxane for understanding for herself and Bajazet on the basis of class, of status (5.6.1590–92). However, her argument is hardly calculated to appease and persuade Roxane. If anything, it only fuels the spurned woman's anger by appealing to the preordained exclusive nature of Bajazet and Atalide's love, and it results in a death pronouncement for them both. And frankly, don't they deserve it? By one code, for duping Roxane; but by the other operative one here, for procrastinating and thinking they could negotiate when they should have acted swiftly and decisively.

Like Bajazet, Atalide releases a candid statement concerning Roxane once she finds herself in the supplicant position, talking not directly with her, but with her slave Zatime. Here again, the scenario of the powerful at the mercy of the powerless is invoked, instantiating perhaps the fantastical fears of the would-be colonizers should they ineptly find themselves in a similar impasse. The noble Atalide is reduced to begging for information from a slave: "Mais de grâce, dis-moi ce que fait Bajazet / ... / Malheureuse, dis-moi seulement s'il respire." (5.8.1648, 1653). ["But have mercy, tell me what Bajazet is doing/ ... / Wretch, tell me if he but breathes."] Zatime is loyal to her mistress Roxane, and refuses to obey Atalide. Atalide's vicious reaction is to lash out at Zatime. The insulting retort "D'une Esclave barbare Esclave impitoyable!" (5.8.1658) ["Pitiless slave of a barbarous slave!"], referring to the shared outsider and lowly status of mistress and servant, only reveals her own prejudice. Profound frustration and equal disdain are communicated in this short exchange. Loyalty lines run along power lines, and here royal blood counts for nothing.

What does count, then, and the all-too-obvious subject of the play, is the failure of communication and the unheeded necessity of swift decisive action. The very first verses have announced the importance of the two basic acts "parler" and "entendre" ["to speak" and "to understand"] (1.1.2), and it has become quickly clear that space and time, that is – context – affect the communication process. Information is never current or reliable (1.1.26–28). During the course of the play, Osmin tells Acomat, who tells Roxane, who tells Bajazet, that the army supports him. But the news is more sure when it reaches Bajazet than it was in Osmin's first telling. Rumors fly (1.1.69–72; 1.2.233–36) and surprises abound (1.1.79–80).

Further, people deliberately mislead one another (1.1.155–56; 1.2.243–46), speak for and in the place of one another (1.3.347–50), and misrepresent one another (1.4.393–94). Profound mistrust (1.1.44; 1.1.183–84) and uncertainty reign (1.3.262–66; 1.4.405–6; 3.7.1075–76). People equivocate (5.5.1564–65) and hypothesize (3.1.819), and they jump to false conclusions (5.10.1672). Faces and gestures are signs to be read (1.3.329–30; 3.1.797–98; 4.4.1221–24), and secrets must be uncovered by observation and shock strategy (3.8.1119–21). Even then, within the individual, information does not flow freely and make sense easily, but must be processed, sometimes successfully and sometimes not. And finally, the characters experience an "Otherness" to themselves, and hence communication even within the individual is fraught (5.2.1461–62).[46] We see this as Roxane interrogates herself on what she has seen, what she should believe, what she must do; as Atalide doubts Bajazet's love; as Bajazet tries to decide if he should challenge or submit to his fate. Thus, while this is a play about the Orient, to be content simply with historicizing the story would be to overlook its broader commentary on communication in general and its particular lessons and predictions for the developing French colonial world.

It is worth pondering Mme de Sévigné's judgment on the play: "Les moeurs des Turcs y sont si mal observées; ils ne font point tant de façons pour se marier."[47] ["Turkish customs are quite badly depicted; they do not make such a fuss about getting married."] What is interesting is not the ambiguity of her pronouncement (how does she mean "se marier"?), but that she apparently feels knowledgeable enough to pronounce at all, and with such assurance. How is it that she can assume enough acquaintance with Turkish ways to discern what is culturally misfitting in this play? In fact, avid reader that she was, she was busily familiarizing herself, even if not thoroughly and accurately, with Turkish customs in the company of her friends.

Along with Madame de Sévigné, the French elite was being educated to know the Ottomans through the many histories and travel journals that were being written and published during the period, texts such as Michel Baudier's *Histoire générale du sérail* (1623), *Les Voyages du Sieur du Loir* (1654), and François de Mézeray's *Histoire des Turcs* (1663) invoked earlier. To her daughter, in 1676, Sévigné wrote: "Je veux vous envoyer par un petit prêtre qui s'en va à Aix, un petit livre que tout le monde a lu et qui m'a beaucoup divertie; c'est *l'Histoire des vizirs*."[48] ["I want to send you, by way of a priest heading off to Aix, a little book that everyone has read and which I greatly enjoyed; it is *The History of the Viziers*."] And in 1689, she reported to her that she and her circle had just finished reading *Mahomet second*.[49] The texts Sévigné read apparently seemed sufficient to encourage her to pronounce with dilettantish authority on this world that she knew only textually and partially, but in which the French were increasingly moving about. Not only sailors and merchants, but the literary elite of France were preparing for a future that would include the "outre-mer" ["overseas"].

There is nothing like a war to draw attention to a particular part of the world. Sévigné's twenty-year-old son Charles had gone off to fight in Crete in 1668, on a bit of a lark – a "fantaisie", but for the mother who stayed behind his departure brought only worry:

J'en ai pleuré amèrement. J'en suis sensiblement affligée. Je n'aurai pas un moment de repos pendant tout ce voyage. J'en vois tous les périls; j'en suis morte. Mais enfin, je n'en ai pas été la maîtresse, et dans ces occasions-là, les mères n'ont pas beaucoup de voix au chapitre.[50]

[I wept bitterly over it. I am deeply distressed by it. I will not have a moment's peace during this whole trip. I see all the dangers; they kill me. But in the end, it was not my decision, and in these instances, mothers do not have much say.]

The French were quietly assisting the Venetians who had been fighting off the Turks since 1646, but in 1669 Crete would fall. However, while it lasted, the war was a glorious outing, a tourist event, and an occasion for learning about that part of the world. Sévigné had friends whose sons were actually killed there. Nevertheless, she would offer curious consolation to her own daughter, Mme de Grignan, when her grandson was about to depart for another front, at Philisbourg: it was a mark of honor (and now a family tradition) to send a son to war.[51] Families would be affected, and would want to know more about where their loved ones were, why they were there, what they were up against, and how the place worked. Hence, beyond or in concert with mercantile interests, books and plays about the Ottoman world and about war sold well and drew crowds.

In order properly to appreciate the full import of the message of Racine's play, then, we must look beyond the problem of communication as dramatized through the telling of the Bajazet story. We must also consider the many circuits of communication that were making available and at the same time obscuring information about the Ottomans to the French. We need to see how this data encouraged them in ways of thinking about these "Others," how the attitudes fostered took hold and misfired, were applied and then cast aside, reworked and selectively retained in this ceaseless process of inventing the Orient and thereby inventing France. Today's French audience can read *Bajazet* on many levels: as a factual or even fictional representation of a historical moment in an exotic setting; as a clue to the construction of taste for a particular seventeenth-century French audience; as a still valid cautionary lesson on the "détours" of communication for all times and all people. But it might also be profitable to consider this play as a timely argument for the need to cultivate the ethos of a double standard (ratifying the act of lying as necessary), and an encouragement to delegated authority to dare to act swiftly, decisively, wisely, without the luxury of consultation, in the name of, in the place of, the king. Further, the play fed into a general perception that French internal class relations could usefully translate, if only in selective ways, into behavioral models for colonialists. These were the lessons in arrogance the French colonialists needed in order to guarantee "successful" relations with local peoples. Hence, Racine's staging of current events.[52]

MITHRIDATE, OR LA COUR DE FRANCE TURBANISÉE

The contingencies of communication, context, and delegated authority as played out in *Bajazet*, where all the characters are subject to the power of the absent Amurat and must reckon with their seeming but, as it turns out, false freedom, are recast in *Mithridate*. Here the absent power, Mithridate, returns home instead, and throws his military weight around directly, but, as it turns out, ineffectually – such behavior is only expedient at the front. In both tragedies, neither fact nor fiction are vitally at stake; the immediate interest resides at a pedagogic level.

If the Bajazet story finds resonance with specific messages regarding
the potential treachery of the written word and lessons for developing
colonial administration, the Mithridate story identifies a related arena of
concern: the vicissitudes of military life and the anatomy of the hero. Both
of these plays far surpass their plots or immediate lessons: the audience
is there not merely to learn, but to rehearse collectively a performance
of its own mindset. These plays are setting a mode of relating for the
French *vis-à-vis* the world – an attitude conducive to the flourishing of
the colonial project, and preparing the way for moving beyond mere
dreams of empire. After all, by 1673, the French were well into their first
major Colonial wave.[53] In order to appreciate this, we need to tease out
a more suggestive than literal correlation between the factual and the
staged in these two plays.

The context for Racine's *Mithridate* in 1673 was not that of the isolated, canonical glory in which it is staged today. The play featured
rather as one of many voices in a politically charged clamor over foreign
policies, alliances, and rivalries – in both the real and the metaphor-
ical senses – that arose in the latter half of the seventeenth century,
as the French forcefully asserted their hegemony in Europe, contested
Habsburg power, and, for this purpose, cultivated a strategic alliance
with the Ottomans.[54]

A curious diatribe, hostile to French interests, affords an oblique entry
into the heated conversation. Titled *La Cour de France turbanisée, et les
trahisons démasquées,* [*The Turbanized French Court, and betrayals unmasked*]
published anonymously in Holland, by a Monsr. LBDEDE, dedicated
just as discreetly to a "Monsieur ***," the pamphlet's opening flourish
attacks French foreign policy:

L'asseurance de vous offrir ce petit ouvrage, et de le mettre sous votre
protection, pour apprendre à la postérité, que la Flandres n'est pas le seul
pays qui ait senti la tyrannie de la France, et qui en ait été ruiné; de sorte
que nous pouvons à bon droit l'appeler turbanisée ... c'est elle, qui met des
Empires et des Royaumes entiers en confusion, qui met par ses intrigues les
membres de chaque Etat dans une malheureuse division, et ce qui est encore
plus déplorable, à la ruine de la chrétienté, et en faveur des infidèles Ottomans
ses alliés.[55]

[The assurance of dedicating this little work to you, and placing it under your
protection, in order to teach posterity that Flanders is not the only country which
has felt the effects of French tyranny, and been ruined by it; in such a way that
we have every right to call it turbanized ... It is she [France], who puts whole
empires and kingdoms into confusion, who by her intrigues puts the members

of every nation into unhappy divisions, and what is even more deplorable, this to the ruin of Christianity and in favor of the infidel Ottomans her allies.]

This pamphlet text followed in the vogue of several others dating from around 1673, excoriating Louis XIV, "Le Grand Turc de l'Ouest,"[56] ["The Grand Turk of the West"] for his under-handed support of the Ottomans.[57] The Pope would add fuel to the pamphlet attack on the disloyal Louis with his own *L'Alcoran de Louis XIV*. [*The Koran of Louis the Fourteenth*].[58] *La France turbanisée* surfaced around 1686, just three years after the French conspicuously failed to come to the aid of the Habsburg stronghold of Vienna, as it was under siege from the Ottomans. Indeed, if Mithridate did not get near Rome through the back door as he planned, the Ottomans did get to the gates of Vienna – altogether too close for comfort, following the marching plans prefigured in Racine's *Mithridate* only ten years before:

> Je sais tous les chemins par où je dois passer: . . .
> Doutez-vous que l'Euxin ne me porte en deux jours
> Aux lieux où le Danube y vient finir son cours,
> Que du Scythe avec moi l'alliance jurée
> De l'Europe en ces lieux ne me livre l'entrée?
>
> (3.1.793, 797–800)

> [I know all the roads which I must take: . . .
> Do you doubt that the Euxine can in two days carry me
> To those parts where the Danube ends its course?
> That the Scythian who has sworn an alliance with me
> Will there grant me entry to Europe?]

Mithridate's goal and the Ottoman one might appear quite a stretch to imagine together were it not for testimony of the time to the effect that theirs were identical: "Le sultan Othman, grand ennemi des chrétiens, n'avait d'autre pensée que de se rendre quelque jour à Rome avec 300.000 ou 400.000 hommes."[59] ["The sultan Othman, a great enemy of the Christians, had no other thought than someday going to Rome with 300,000 or 400,000 of his men."] By this reading, Vienna would have been merely a stopover en route to the heart of Christian Europe, and France hence marked as clearly guilty of consorting with the enemy.

A brief review of events leading up to the printed outburst cited at the outset here not only sets the stage for its occasion, but also for the role of Racine's play, in the general skirmishing that took place on various registers during these charged years. The Ottomans and the Habsburgs, with their territories adjoining, were at each other's throats throughout the century. Louis XIV surreptitiously cultivated relations with the Ottomans; he exploited Ottoman–Habsburg tensions to divert Habsburg attention away from his own expansionist ambitions in Europe. At the same time, Louis's marriage to Marie-Thérèse of Austria and the surface of solidarity that this union represented, along with a more general but firm Christian-based pact, glossed over the French-Habsburg hostility.[60] And so we see that, even with European nations, France looked to her own interests when it came to positioning herself *vis-à-vis* the "outsider."

Meanwhile, in the Mediterranean, as we have just seen, France played a double game with the Ottomans as well. Although they were nominally allies, France protected her maritime commercial interests by challenging the Barbary Republics (under Ottoman rule) and by surreptitiously supporting the Venetians and independent Christian pirates against the Ottomans (see chapter 2 and above). In 1664, nine years before Racine's *Mithridate*, the expansionist Ottomans were driven back from the edges of "Europe" at the fierce battle of Saint Gotthard, mainly by the French. And in 1669, the Ottomans succeeded in wresting the island of Crete from the Venetians, whom the French had discreetly supported – intent all the while on not alienating their Ottoman trading partners. In 1683, ten years after *Mithridate's* first staging, the Ottomans attempted a second and last siege of Vienna: "Kara Mustafa Pasha and his huge army appeared before the gates of the Hapsburg Imperial city on July 14, 1683 . . . European relief of the city was slow in coming. Brandenburg and Saxony contributed some assistance, but Louis XIV of France, who intended to use the discomfiture of the Hapsburgs to further his own anti-Hapsburg cause, delayed."[61] To this day, one still hears, in conversation with the Viennese, that the French did not rally to their assistance. Instead, they deliberately tarried, and the Poles were the ones to bring decisive aid and break the siege. The Ottomans were definitively repelled. But throughout Europe, the French were perceived to be in hand-in-glove alliance with the Ottomans.[62]

Even in the domain of pastry, the Ottoman–French tie is memorialized. In a perverse way, the French have come to be the foremost, if for the most part unwitting, broadcasters of their own duplicitous behavior at this time. Curiously inscribed in gastronomical history, officially dated from around 1689, is the fact that the Viennese invented a pastry, the "Hörnchen," representing the Ottoman emblem of the crescent, to commemorate how they had "eaten" their enemy.[63] That this Viennese delicacy became a prominent feature of the French repertoire, better known as the ubiquitous "croissant," brings together, in ironical fashion, the intertwined stories of the aggressive but failed Ottomans, the besieged but victorious Habsburgs, and the savvy French, passively complicitous with the Ottomans.

Around the time of the production of *Mithridate*, Louis XIV had recently attacked Flanders (1667–68) and was engaged in laying siege to Holland. He stood at the head of his own army after a period of delegation. The Court followed avidly all news from the front, and military heroism was a much sought-after profile. This was the actual occasion of Leibniz's already cited attempt at politicking in his hysterical plea to Louis XIV to undertake a final crusade against the Turks. In Leibniz's diversionary proposal, with promises of saintly as well as political glory, he tried to protect France's near neighbors from Louis's expansionism by directing the king's attention instead toward Constantinople: "Cette expédition délivrera l'Europe de la terreur où elle est plongée, le christianisme qui se déchire lui-même au grand scandale de tant de siècles, les chrétiens de l'Orient gémissant sous le joug des infidèles, le monde devenu barbare, et le genre humain frappé d'aveuglement."[64] ["This expedition will free Europe from the terror in which she is plunged, it will free Christianity which has been tearing itself apart to the great scandal of so many centuries, the Christians of the Orient groaning under the yoke of infidels, the world becoming barbarian, and humankind stricken with blindness."]

Despite, or because of, such vilifications of the Orient, Racine perversely opted to highlight one of its heroes on the French stage. In so doing, he circuitously flouted Habsburg sentiment against the Ottomans and flaunted the murky French allegiance with them. In the figure of Mithridate, the ambiguity inherent in the portrayal of the anti-heroic hero, this great warrior of dubious moral character sums up the ambivalence of French behavior regarding her sometime Ottoman ally. Racine was celebrating France's deployment of the double standard. For other Europeans, that ambivalence needed to be resolved in order to break the French–Ottoman alliance that so threatened their own well-being. They sought solidarity against the Ottomans and assumed it should be a given among Christian countries. France would be reprimanded ("La France a du mal à se souvenir qu'elle est subalterne à l'Empire" ["France has a hard time remembering that she is a subaltern of the Empire"]), and directly taken to task on the grounds of religious treachery:

Elle a plus de soin de la prospérité des Turcs et de la gloire de Mahomet, que de celle de Dieu et du bien de la Chrétienté, et les Mosquées destinées au service du Diable, sont plus avancées par sa protection, que les Eglises où Jésus Christ devrait être prêché. Quel fils aîné de l'Eglise!"[65]

[France has more concern for the prosperity of the Turks and for Mahomet's glory, than for that of God and for the good of Christendom, and the Mosques destined to the Devil's service are more under its protection than the Churches where Jesus Christ's name should be preached. A fine eldest son of the Church, indeed!]

If the story of Mithridate found its way onto the French stage at this time, this gesture could be seen as a discreet way of paying limited homage to France's problematic ally to the east, opportune partner in time of war within Europe, or at the least of taunting the Habsburgs – a gesture of enlightened national self-interest.

Racine's play lends itself to being interpreted as treating or reflecting conflict on several levels. To begin with, *Mithridate* has been seen as an attempt by Racine to outdo his rival Corneille once again in taking on a historical play focused on male hubris. Indeed there is evidence in the play to suggest that Corneille was in Racine's immediate thoughts as he wrote. The mere mention: "Et Rome, unique objet d'un désespoir si beau" (3.1.945–46) ["And Rome, sole object of such beautiful despair,"] echoes Camille's famous line from *Horace*, "Rome, unique objet de mon ressentiment" (4.5.1301) ["Rome, sole object of my resentment"], and the structuring of *Mithridate* around the relations of two brothers to a parent figure, as well as evoking the brothers Curiace and Horace of that same play, summons up memories of the brothers Antiochus and Seleucus in Corneille's *Rodogune*.[66] Further, Mithridate's way of deceiving Monime in order to elicit information from her is reminiscent of Don Fernand's more civil but equally underhanded treatment of Chimène in *Le Cid* (see chapter 2). And let us not forget the overt competition a few years before around the Bérénice story (see chapter 4).[67] Racine can be taken here to be engaging Corneille in a figurative war, as conflict succeeds mere competition during this period, and is conducted on several fronts simultaneously (see chapter 4).

Or one would be justified in reading the play as specifically alluding to the invasion of Holland.[68] The two mentions of "inondations" in Act 3 (3.1.780; 3.1.810) bring immediately to mind the opening of the dikes by the Dutch in desperate self-defense. It seems likely that Racine was responding to a generalized mood of the times and addressing not only current events but standing alliances. The period was fiercely combative, and the public wanted its preoccupations reflected on the stage. Just as Louis was conscious that he was making history in challenging the Dutch, so the Ottomans and the Habsburgs were acutely aware that they were mapping the world as they struggled with each other. And Louis was playing a double strategy against them both.

In all of this struggle, individual reputations as military heroes were made and broken. War narratives were being produced by the myriad participants, similar to Rodrigue's recounting of his victory over the Moors. Combining autobiographical writing, information dissemination, and not a little self-aggrandizement, the genre was becoming popular; witness the following excerpt from the memoirs of the duke of Navailles at the 1669 siege of Crete: "Tout ce qu'on attaqua ensuite fut renversé, la plus grande partie des ennemis se retira en désordre dans la montagne qui est proche; le reste prit la fuite; un grand nombre se jetta dans la mer, et j'en rencontrai plusieurs qui pour me demander la vie, faisaient le signe de la Croix, et criaient, nous sommes Chrétiens." ["All we attacked was overthrown, the greater part of the enemy retreated in confusion to a nearby mountain; the rest fled; a great number threw themselves into the sea, and I came across several who, in begging me for their life, made the sign of the cross and cried, We are Christians."][69]

This was common discourse at and from the front. Racine's play displays his talents for representing the psychological anatomy of the military hero.[70] His portrait of the warrior Mithridate sums up the problematic characteristics that made him such a formidable enemy. At the same time, it sheds light on the psychology of the aggressive "Other" of the East. For the French, the play might be viewed as an important exercise in knowing and assessing one's admirable, but ultimately fallible, enemy and sometime ally. For the Habsburgs, while Mithridate is an anti-hero cast in the unusual role of heroic protagonist, he serves as a cautionary reminder of what they were up against in dealings with their Ottoman neighbors to the east. Certainly, the Viennese elite must have been aware of what was playing on the Paris stage in 1673; the very thought that the French had produced and were attending – that indeed the king favored – a play about that heroic scourge to the east of them, *Mithridate*, cannot have put them at ease. It could only have reminded them of the "backdoor" threat they already felt only too keenly. At the same time, for the European militarized audience generally, Mithridate embodies the problem that any focused warrior faces when he turns his attention to the home front and reads the domestic scene as a war zone.

Racine manages to weight the public and the private profiles of the military hero evenly. Attentive to the final impression, as if he were striking a commemorative medal or decorating a monument, Racine invokes the geography of Mithridate's reach. A litany of names of rivers, mountain ranges, countries, and peoples resounds throughout the play in incantatory fashion, intensifying mystery and allure by conjuring a multiplicity of precisions about the Orient, especially that area that the Ottomans had placed off-limits to the West – the Black Sea.[71] This nautical space, the central site of Mithridate's dominion, was closed to Westerners by the Ottomans in the seventeenth century.[72] The prohibition increased fascination with this part of the world – as we saw in chapter 1, Médée's Colchide was also on the far coast of these forbidden waters – and enhanced the contemporary mystique of Mithridate. The spirit of his greatness is represented concretely on the one hand by the magic of specific place names, and on the other by the two more encompassing terms, "l'Orient" (1.1.11) and "l'Asie" (3.1.771), inviting admiration for the far reach of his power. We can further speculate that the reproduction of his vaunting of dominion over these territories on the Paris stage in incantatory alexandrine verse implicitly appropriates his domain in linguistic terms for the French.

Mithridate's claim over this vast and amorphous expanse signals his stature as great military hero. And his rhetoric is not empty; he commands a wealth of information. He knows the lay of the land and how to get around in it, how to use it to his advantage:

> Quelque temps inconnu j'ai traversé le Phase;
> Et de là pénétrant jusqu'au pied du Caucase,
> Bientôt dans des vaisseaux sur l'Euxin préparés
> J'ai rejoint de mon camp les restes séparés.
>
> (2.3.451–54)

> [Incognito for a time, I crossed the river Phasis
> And from there, reaching to the foot of the Caucasus
> Where the ships lay ready on the Euxine
> I soon rejoined the rest of my camp.]

It is familiar territory to him after forty years of subduing and defending it to his own advantage and against the Romans. Moreover, Mithridate has attached lands and people to his empire (the Greek kingdoms of Ephesus and Ionia [1.3.251]), and mustered allies (the unreliable Parthians, the Scythians, the Sarmatians [1.3.309]). He has made his cause theirs in a sweeping attempt to marshal forces against Rome, and in the process has made them his. France having already identified with Rome (chapter 4), would now also align with Mithridate, and thereby arrange to have it all.

At the moment of Mithridate's entry on stage, he is on the defensive, lucidly aware that fortune does not favor him, that he is embattled by the Romans:

> L'Orient accablé
> Ne peut plus soutenir leur effort redoublé.
> Il voit plus que jamais ses campagnes couvertes
> De Romains que la guerre enrichit de nos pertes.
> Des biens des nations ravisseurs altérés
> Le bruit de nos trésors les a tous attirés:
> Ils y courent en foule, et jaloux l'un de l'autre
> Désertent leur pays pour inonder le nôtre.
> Moi seul je leur résiste. . . .
>
> (3.1.775–81)[73]

> [The overwhelmed Orient
> Can no longer resist their increased effort.
> He sees more than ever his countryside overridden
> With Romans whom the war is profiting from our losses.
> Thirsty for spoils from ravaged nations,
> Rumor of our treasures has drawn them all:
> They are coming in hordes; and jealous one of the other,
> Are deserting their country to flood our own.
> I alone stand against them.]

Cornered as he is, not by an unknown power, but by the Roman general, Pompée – the only figure who approaches him in stature, and who therefore deserves to be named (and therefore the only enemy with a personal identity) – Mithridate makes the audacious decision to break out of his geography, the space that has been his range for forty years, to move from the defensive to the offensive, and to attack Rome directly.

From a monumental vision of the great warrior, Racine shifts to a closer portrait, that of the general in the process of marshaling his forces. Mithridate shares with his sons an immense vision (108 lines), in which he first takes into account his current position of weakness, then harks back to his extraordinary record of snatching victory out of the jaws of defeat. He moves on to a justification for the need to act decisively and radically – is he not in this the very antithesis of the hesitant and indecisive loser, Bajazet? He announces his sweeping plan to take Rome and reduce it to ruin, fixing a timetable and listing probable allies in this venture. Mithridate always speaks as if with a great map before him – vital information at his fingertips – a map that sets his perspective and suggests to him his goals. He is a visionary and a strategist as well, a model military leader. But when his sight falls on more local phenomena, on his domestic scene, then his vision, acute as it is, does him a disservice, for it translates all he sees into a potential battlefield.

As important as the qualities of visionary and strategist are, another trait also most profoundly characterizes him: he is a tactician on the local level. He is a genius of deviousness, a cunning master of the detour. He deliberately plants the false news of his death so as to make his escape; he has frequently fooled his enemy into defeat by feigning to flee (3.1.75), a move that serves him well as a soldier. Mithridate knows how to deploy misinformation to outwit the enemy. This same wiliness does not, however, serve him as well on the home front. In fact, the question must be asked: is there a home front for him?

The human foibles of Mithridate the individual lend themselves well to war, but not to parenting or to wooing. His professional mistrust carries into his domestic life, and he finds no respite from suspicion. While he will reprimand his sons upon his return, he will pretend to accept that they are in Nymphée, where neither of them belongs, for good reason: "Je vous crois innocents, puisque vous le voulez" (2.3.428). ["I believe you innocent, since you wish it so."] But immediately after, he will express his suspicion of them to Arbate: "Ce coeur . . . n'a point d'ennemis qui lui soient odieux / Plus que deux fils ingrats que je trouve en ces lieux" (2.3.458–62) ["This heart . . . has no enemies more odious to him / Than the two ungrateful sons I find here."] He will test Pharnace's good will by ordering him to marry someone he doesn't love, in a remote kingdom to the east. The father, moreover, expresses satisfaction, rather than anger or disappointment, at finding the son out, at successfully ensnaring him and confirming his suspicions: "Ah! c'est où je t'attends!" (3.1.969) ["Ah! I've got you there!"] Marshaling that same tendency to control through deviousness, Mithridate sets a trap for Monime to find out whom she loves: "Feignons; et de son coeur, d'un vain espoir flatté, / Par un mensonge adroit tirons la vérité" (3.4.1033–34) ["Let us feign; and from her heart, flattered by a vain hope, / With a shrewd lie let us extract the truth."]

The soldier's praxis is thus deeply engrained in Mithridate. Even his love is compromised. Monime is not his of her own accord, but of her parents', whose people have concomitantly become Mithridate's subjects:

> Ephèse est mon pays. Mais je suis descendue
> D'Aïeux, ou Rois, Seigneur, ou Héros, qu'autrefois

> Leur vertu chez les Grecs, mit au-dessus des Rois.
> Mithridate me vit. Ephèse et l'Ionie
> A son heureux Empire était alors unie.
>
> (1.3.248–52)

[Ephesus is my country, but I am descended
From ancestors, my Lord, or heroes who in time past
Their virtue among the Greeks placed above kings.
Mithridate saw me: Ephesus and Ionia
Were to his fortunate empire then united.]

The unequal footing of conqueror/conquered precludes the possibility of a love match between Mithridate and Monime. She is reduced to a status of political token – booty for this pirate general. He
has tried to force himself ignobly on her, and to his dubious credit,
unsuccessfully:

> Il la vit . . .
> Il crut que . . .
> Elle lui céderait une indigne victoire.
> Tu sais par quel effort il tenta sa vertu,
> Et que lassé d'avoir vainement combattu,
> Absent, mais toujours plein de son amour extrême,
> Il lui fit par tes mains porter son Diadème.
>
> (1.1.49–56)

[He saw her . . .
He believed that . . .
She would cede to him an ignoble victory;
You know with what effort he tempted her virtue;
And how tired of having combatted in vain,
Absent, but still filled with his great love
He had you with your hands bring her this crown.]

His love for Monime is a soldierly one that cherishes her and keeps her
in his thoughts from a distance, as he is out on his campaigns. She is a
source of comfort and inspiration, an ideal that sustains him as he does
battle:

> Ce coeur nourri de sang, et de guerre affamé,
> Malgré le faix des ans et du sort qui m'opprime,
> Traîne partout l'amour qui l'attache à Monime.
>
> (2.3.458–60)

[This heart fed on blood and starved for war,
Despite the weight of years and of the fate which oppresses me
Drags around everywhere the love that attaches it to Monime.]

But this attachment translates into brusque clumsiness when they are actually together: "Et vous portez, Madame, un gage de ma foi / Qui vous dit tous les jours que vous êtes à moi." (2.4.541–42) ["And you wear, madame, a token of my love / which tells you everyday that you belong to me."] Unequal footing would always interfere with love. This also was a lesson for the French: behavior that might be effective and even called for on the front needed to be curbed at home. In exercising the double standard, the French needed to remember that within France and among their confrères wherever, colonial behavior was inappropriate and self-defeating.

Mithridate has a past and a reputation that precede him on the stage, such that his very name conjures up a ferocious man.[74] He has already eliminated several women in his life: "Tu sais combien de fois ses jalouses tendresses / Ont pris soin d'assurer la mort de ses Maîtresses." (1.1.87–88) ["You know how many times his jealous tenderness / has taken care to assure the death of his mistresses."] As telling is the fact that he has killed two other sons: "Et nous l'avons vu même à ses cruels soupçons / Sacrifier deux Fils pour de moindres raisons." (1.5.349–50) ["And we have even seen him with his cruel suspicions / Sacrifice two sons for lesser reasons."] Pharnace knows him well, as one should know an enemy, even if that enemy happens to be his father. The son does not hesitate to volunteer his father's negative qualities as general aphoristic truths about him: "Plus il est malheureux, plus il est redoutable" (1.5.344) ["The unhappier he is, the more formidable he is."]; "Sa haine va toujours plus loin que son amour" (1.5.354). ["His hatred always goes further than his love."] It is Monime who, as an enlightened Greek, removed from her civilized country (the West) and brought to Mithridate's remote stronghold, will name his world "ce climat barbare" (5.2.1528) ["this barbarous place"] and will call Mithridate himself "barbare" (4.2.1251) ["barbarian"], thus underscoring the cultural, and, by implication, ethical differences between East and West. Mithridate, in his military zeal, has lost touch with "civilization."

Ultimately, Mithridate consists in just that: his name, his reputation – all that the name sums up, a reputation constantly in jeopardy and demanding to be reinforced – lest his status slip from that of king to that of mere marauder and pirate (2.4.563). His ultimate defense against deterioration, to assure the imperviousness of his monumentality, has been to innure himself to poisons by dosing himself, thus preempting the enemy. But this strategy proves ineffectual: he dies not by poison, from without; but by his own sword, by his own choice, in order not to be vanquished. Just as potentially compromising, if in a paradoxical manner, is the fact of his progeny. He cannot have complete control over the ultimate destiny of his body as literally embodied, or of his cause as carried forth by his opposed sons. But for purposes of presenting the psychological profile of a warrior hero, Mithridate's portrait is complete in the play. The staging of this name has required a plot, but the plot is there only to serve as vehicle for communicating the character and the exploits of a great military hero, and the danger of bringing it home.

That Mithridate should be a "barbare" does not exclude him as an exemplar for the French, who were busily refashioning themselves from courtiers into soldiers and colonialists.[75] They needed, though, to be wary of losing touch with "civilization." At the same time, that Mithridate is a "barbare" serves as a timely reminder and rallying cry to the French themselves of the formidable power of the Ottomans to the east of them, even as they exploited the advantages of their uneasy alliance with this "Other." Mithridate on the stage in Paris also serves as a hostile gesture toward the Habsburgs, if they were paying attention, underscoring the precariousness of their position. Mithridate did not reach Rome, but the Ottomans arrived at Vienna, by the route prefigured in Mithridate's marching plan, right up the Danube. The attitudes in Paris that contributed to a successful run of *Mithridate* comport with France's traitorous failure to heed Vienna's call for help ten years later, and explain why she earned the epithet: "turbanisée."[76]

CONCLUSION

The thematics of the two plays *Bajazet* and *Mithridate* suggest the view of the French classical theatre as the locus of a massive misinformation campaign, a devious way of setting the charter for "Frenchness." By routing an unwittingly collusive French audience through a staging of the Ottoman and the Black Sea "Other," by appropriating and manipulating the signs of "Otherness" and at the same time saturating these signs with domestic linguistic and behavioral turns, these worlds were absorbed and incorporated into the French performatory repertoire. The French already had mastered the art of the double standard domestically – with regard to peasants, Jews, protestants – ; and cultivated the same approach with regard to other European powers. Now they had models from which to cultivate this same art with other peoples. At once sensitized and innured to difference by its representation on the stage, confirmed in their propensity to identify and to dis-identify as necessary, the audience could now see their way to claiming preeminence and assuming governance over other worlds. At the beginning of this chapter, I said that the mirroring behavior of the French *vis-à-vis* these other staged cultures produced a simulacrum of merging, but by the end we see that it was only just that, since this was a one-way detour through the "Other" in order to arrive at "France."

Conclusion

On s'imagine vulgairement que les Turcs, les Barbares, et les Sauvages n'y sont
pas si propres [capables des sciences] que les peuples de l'Europe. Cependant,
il est certain que si l'on en voyoit icy cinq ou six qui eussent la capacité ou le
titre de docteur, ce qui n'est pas impossible, on corrigeroit son jugement, et
l'on avoueroit que ces peuples estant hommes comme nous, sont capables des
mêmes choses, et que s'ils estoient instruits, ils ne nous cederoient en rien. Les
femmes avec lesquelles nous vivons, valent bien les Barbares et les Sauvages,
pour nous obliger d'avoir pour elles des pensées qui ne soient pas moins
avantageuses ny moins raisonnables.

[One commonly imagines that the Turks, the Barbarians, and the Savages are
not as fit [capable of learning] as the peoples of Europe. However, it is certain
that if one were to see five or six of them who had the ability or the title of
doctor, which is not impossible, one would quickly change one's opinion, and
one would admit that these same people, being human like us, are capable of the
same things, and if they were educated, they would not cede to us in anything.
The women with whom we live are certainly equal to barbarians and savages,
such as to oblige us to have for them opinions no less favorable and reasonable.]
(Poullain de la Barre, *De l'égalité des deux sexes* [1673])[1]

Ahead of his time, out of step with his own, Poullain de la Barre rhetor-
ically championed the cause of non-Europeans. If women of his own
culture were the main subject of his concern, he did not fail to see the
parallel between prejudices against them and against other "Others."
Ethnocentric and problematically gallant, as his words attest, he was
nevertheless intellectually sensitive to their assigned estate. By listing
Turks at the head of his list of "Others" and, as a group on a nominal
plane with barbarians and savages, Poullain indicates clearly how they
were generally perceived in France. The Ottomans were mighty military
aggressors, wealthy traders, fearful Mediterranean neighbors; hence the
French could entertain only uneasy and volatile relations with them. But,
in addition, the Ottomans represented a highly organized and refined

culture, which the French were obliged to recognize and even, grudgingly or covetously, admire. It was not only the power of this empire then that threatened them; they were unsettled by their own fascination with this world. As with their women, they coped with their conflicted feelings toward the Ottomans by stressing the gap between their worlds – by pronouncing them different and therefore inferior. Over time, they developed convenient self-protective biases against them, that masked more complex feelings. And, in their dealings with them, they cultivated attitudes and techniques of manipulation and domination that would be useful as they developed their colonial identity in other parts of the world.

These positions were both represented and questioned on the French stage. Given the patronage system, literary discourse was significantly dependent on official state policy with its program for French hegemony; hence, there was little leeway for nuanced expression of cultural relativism on the part of France's premier playwrights.[2] Nevertheless, as we have seen, messages, both subversive and supportive of the nation project, circulated in the Parisian world of theatre. Little could Corneille, Molière, and Racine have foreseen the tenacious hold their stagings of the "Other" would have on the French imaginary as their plays were ensconced over time into the core of the nation's cultural canon. Nor could they have appreciated the extent to which their theatrical productions would feed into the more vast enterprise of nation-building.

Any nation's history and cultural production, subjected to similar retrospective scrutiny, would be susceptible to comparable critique, if not, of course, to identical conclusions. My aim has not been to target France as a particularly flagrant example of prejudice. Rather – given my own area of training as a seventeenth-century literary critic, coming to terms with the implications of a rapidly globalizing world and looking to a time in the not-so-distant future when France, with its increasingly multi-ethnic population, will be subsumed as merely a member of the European Union – I seek to find, in the enduring world of the French classics familiar to me and to a still vast number of French citizens today, keys to understanding how France took shape as a nation and how that nationhood might be undone. For if France was constructed in opposition to "Others," the current incorporation (however hesitant) of the excluded – including Islamic populations – into citizenship must surely call into question older notions of French identity. At the same time, I am all too aware that, as with these more gifted seer playwrights, the future eludes us and we cannot know our role in its shaping. The process of demythification can only play out in its own time.

It may indeed be far-fetched to claim that we see in these works the seeds of the colonialism that will come to fruition in the nineteenth century. But if not here, then where? We could indeed go further back in time, and examine the crusader discourse, or we could, as many do, jump ahead to examine that of the "enlightened" eighteenth century. But it is here, in these seventeenth-century works that continue to dominate the French stage, that we can locate basic problems of identity and pinpoint the importance of the "Other" in shaping France's enduring notion of itself. The persistent success of these plays is not only a product of their undeniable genius; it also attests to the persistence of the concerns (including unconscious concerns) they articulate. In today's post-colonial globalizing world, it is imperative to identify and examine these concerns, to put them on the table. This book has attempted to reorient approaches to the plays, while preserving the respect and admiration they so profoundly and deservedly inspire.

At times overtly, at times obliquely, the plays discussed in this book perpetuate anxious and hostile attitudes toward the Ottomans, their culture, and their beliefs, and they continue to legitimate such thinking about all outsiders to France, and about "Others" generally (not to mention women). But they can just as readily be marshaled to expose and highlight both subtle and flagrant instances of prejudice. These plays can operate as touchstones. They can remind us where we have been, where we are, and perhaps even suggest where we are headed. Like all national monuments, they have been placed on pedestals. But unlike words and buildings carved from stone, they are subject to change, open to interpretation. The vast spaces of time that might erode and even obliterate them totally are still, for the moment, beyond our imagination.

Notes

INTRODUCTION

1 Marie de Rabutin-Chantal, marquise de Sévigné to Madame de Grignan, *Correspondance*, III, ed. Roger Duchêne (Paris: Gallimard, 1978), no. 1169.

2 Laurent d'Arvieux, *Mémoires du chevalier d'Arvieux*, IV, ed. Jean-Baptiste Labat (Paris: chez Charles-Jean-Baptiste Delespine, 1735), p. 252.

3 For an introduction to the vast bibliography on the Mediterranean exotic in this period: Alia Baccar, *La Mer, source de création littéraire au dix-septième siècle* (Tûbingen: Biblio 17, 1991); Pierre Martino, *L'Orient dans la littérature française au XVIIe et XVIIIe siècle* (Paris: Hachette, 1906); and Clarence Dana Rouillard, *The Turk in French History, Thought, and Literature (1520–1660)* (Paris: Boivin, 1940).

4 John Lough, *L'écrivain et son public: Commerce du livre et commerce des idées en France du Moyen Age à nos jours*, trans. Alexis Tadié (Paris: Le chemin vert, 1978): according to Lough, while the nobility was an important presence in the theatre, its strong voice did not drown out the opinions of the middle and popular classes, pp. 142, 147. See also Eric Auerbach, "La Cour et la ville," *Le Culte des passions: Essais sur le XVIIe siècle français*, Intro. and trans. Diane Meur (Paris: Macula, 1998), pp. 115–79.

5 Loren Kruger, *The National Stage: Theatre and Cultural Legitimation in England, France, and America* (Chicago: University of Chicago Press, 1992). Kruger speculates about the role of theater in transforming the audience into a nation in the Enlightenment period (3), but I believe this idea can as legitimately apply to the French seventeenth century in the investigation of a less explicit but equally powerful version of the same dynamic.

6 See Jean Duvignaud, *Les Ombres collectives: sociologie du théâtre* (Paris: Presses universitaires de France, 1973), pp. 307–19; and John Lough, *Paris Theater Audiences in the Seventeenth and Eighteenth Centuries* (London: Oxford University Press, 1957), pp. 80–81.

7 However, already at this time, the role of the *Gazette* in shaping news and public opinion was not without importance; see Orhan Kologlu, *Le Turc dans la presse française: des débuts jusqu'à 1815* (Beyrouth: Maison d'édition Al-Hayat, 1971).

8 Marcel Marion, "colonies" in *Dictionnaire des institutions de la France aux XVIIe et XVIIIe siècles* (Paris: Editions Picard, 1989), p. 111.

9 Lisa Lowe, *Critical Terrains, French and British Orientalisms* (Ithaca: Cornell University Press, 1991). According to Lowe, "Orientalism consists of an uneven matrix of orientalist situations across different cultural and historical sites, and . . . each of these orientalisms is internally complex and unstable." (11) However, I also believe that certain orientalist attitudes rehearsed on the seventeenth-century French stage profoundly mark French colonial behavior through its history.

10 Margaret Hodgen, in *Early Anthropology in the Sixteenth and Seventeenth Centuries* (Philadelphia: University of Pennsylvania Press, 1964) points out that during this period, the Turks and the Tartars appear to call for more "ethnological analysis" than more distant peoples, p. 147.

11 Peter France explores various modalities of early modern "Other"ing in his *Politeness and its Discontents: Problems in French Classical Literature* (Cambridge: Cambridge University Press, 1992), taking into account not only "orientals," but peasants and other groups (Russians, English, etc.) who lived on the margins of the continent, or of civilization (Corsica), and with whom the "cultivated" French had contact.

12 Edward T. Hall, "Proxemics," in *Nonverbal Communication: Readings with Commentary*, edited by Shirley Weitz (New York: Oxford University Press, 1974), pp. 205–29, 205–06.

13 Mary Louise Pratt, *Imperial Eyes: Travel Writing and Transculturation* (London: Routledge, 1992), p. 4.

14 Tzvetan Todorov, *On Human Diversity: Nationalism, Racism, and Exoticism in French Thought*, trans. Catherine Porter (Cambridge, MA: Harvard University Press, 1993), p. 384.

15 Again, I refer the reader to the bibliographies of Baccar, Martino, and Rouillard, see note 3; in addition, Racine's *Athalie* and *Esther*, for example, merit consideration as articulations of exoticism, but they relate more readily to immediate domestic pressures (Madame de Maintenon's pedagogical project at Saint-Cyr) and only less directly to the seventeenth-century Mediterranean world.

16 Jean-François Lyotard and Jean-Loup Thébaud, in *Au juste* (Paris: Christian Bourgeois, 1979) go further in claiming a perfect playwright/audience equivalence in the "classical" situation: "un auteur peut écrire en se mettant à la place de son lecteur, peut se substituer à son lecteur, et peut évaluer, juger ce qu'il écrit du point de vue de son lecteur, ce qu'il est aussi . . . Il partage profondément, participe au système de ses lecteurs, de son public." (21) ["an author can write by putting himself in his reader's place, can substitute himself for his reader, and can evaluate and judge what he writes, from the viewpoint of his reader, which reader he is as well . . . He shares deeply in and participates in the system of his readers and his audience."]

17 From a letter (September 3, 1998) of Odile Faliu, chief conservator of the Comédie Française archives.

18 Such as Jean-Marie Apostolidès, *Le Prince sacrifié: Théâtre et politique au temps de Louis XIV* (Paris: Editions de minuit, 1985); *Le Roi-machine: Spectacle et politique au temps de Louis XIV* (Paris: Editions de minuit, 1981); Peter Burke, *The Fabrication of Louis XIV* (New Haven: Yale University Press, 1992).

19 Françoise Pélisson-Karro, in "Sources théatrâles, sources historiques: l'apprentissage de l'histoire de l'Orient sur la scène jésuite," in *Littératures classiques*, 30 (1997), offers a sense of the "Orient" for the seventeenth century: "La Méditerranée, qui sépare les trois parties de la sphère T. O., est à la convergence des traditions mésopotamienne, égyptienne, juive, grecque, romaine, chrétienne, islamique, qui le [l'Orient] déterminent chacune avec son *limes*, zone d'expansion ou d'encerclement elle-même instable dans sa définition:" p. 245. ["The Mediterranean, which separates the three parts of the T. O. sphere, is at the convergence of a variety of traditions (Mesopotamian, Egyptian, Jewish, Greek, Roman, Christian, Islamic) each of which defines the Orient by using its own boundaries, a zone of expansion or encircling which is itself unstable in its definition."]

20 As Ernest Renan pointed out in 1882: "Le Français n'est ni un Gaulois, ni un Franc, ni un Burgonde. Il est ce qui est sorti de la grande chaudière, où, sous la présidence du roi de France, ont fermenté ensemble les éléments les plus divers." ["The French are neither Gauls, nor Franks, nor Burgundians. They are what emerged from the great simmering cauldron of fermenting diversity, presided over by the President of France."], *Qu'est-ce qu'une nation? What is a Nation?* Trans. Wanda Romer Taylor (Toronto: Tapir Press, 1996), pp. 32–33. Also cited in *Nation and Narration*, ed. Homi K. Bhabha (London: Routledge, 1990), p. 15.

21 More precisely, since such plays as *Polyeucte* and *Tartuffe*, *Esther*, and *Athalie* attest to the presence of religious concerns on the stage, it is more accurate to state that the mixing of the sacred and profane was not typical of French classical stage production.

22 Bhabha, "DissemiNation" in *Nation and Narration*, p. 297.

23 Said, *Orientalism* (New York: Vintage Books, 1979), p. 3.

24 Jonathan Dollimore, *Political Shakespeare: Essays in Cultural Materialism*, ed. Jonathan Dollimore and Alan Sinfield (Ithaca: Cornell University Press, 1994), p. viii.

25 Pierre Bourdieu, *Distinction: A Social Critique of the Judgement of Taste*, trans. Richard Nice (Cambridge: Harvard University Press, 1984), p. 1.

26 Conversation with Ross Chambers.

27 Bhabha, *Nation and Narration*, p. 297.

28 But I refer the reader to Julia V. Douthwaite, *Exotic Women: Literary Heroines and Cultural Strategies in Ancien Régime France* (Philadelphia: University of Pennsylvania Press, 1992), where the author systematically performs this important analysis on key early exoticist works.

29 Set forth in *The New Historicism*, ed. H. Aram Veeser (New York: Routledge, 1989), pp. x, 18, 52, 214; this collection of essays comes closest to offering a programmatic overview of the New Historicism.

30 Spelled out in *Political Shakespeare: Essays in Cultural Materialism*, ed. Jonathan Dollimore and Alan Sinfield (Ithaca: Cornell University Press, 1994).

31 See *Cultural Studies*, ed. Lawrence Grossberg, Cary Nelson, Paula A. Treichler (New York: Routledge, 1992), especially the Introduction, pp. 1–22.

32 Especially Homi K. Bhabha, *The Location of Culture* (London: Routledge, 1994); *Nation and Narration* (London: Routledge, 1990); Walter Mignolo, *The Darker Side of the Renaissance: Literacy, Territoriality, Colonization* (Ann Arbor: University of Michigan Press, 1995); Mary Louise Pratt, *Imperial Eyes*; and *Dangerous Liaisons: Gender, Nation, and Postcolonial Perspectives*, ed. Anne McClintock, Aamir Mufti, Ella Shohat (Minneapolis: University of Minnesota Press, 1997).

33 See Said, *Orientalism* for the groundbreaking work that would stimulate important reevaluations of world history and expose the European way of relating to/dominating its "Others," and produce an entire academic industry.

34 *The New Historicism*, p. 17.

35 "The project of a new socio-historical criticism is, then, to analyze the interplay of culture-specific discursive practices – mindful that it, too, is such a practice and so participates in the interplay it seeks to analyze," *The New Historicism*, p. 23.

36 My first acquaintance with the three authors who are the organizing principle of this study came at a Catholic convent school, where we read a cautious selection, notably: Corneille's *Polyeucte*, Molière's *L'Avare* and *Le malade imaginaire*, and Racine's *Athalie* and *Esther*.

ORIENTATION

1 Antoine Furetière, *Le Dictionnaire universel, contenant généralement tous les mots françois tant vieux que modernes, et les termes des sciences et des arts*, II, second edn. (La Haye: Arnoud et Reinier Leers, 1702), p. 1033.

2 Molière, *Dom Juan*, in *Oeuvres complètes*, vol. 2, ed. Georges Couton (Paris: Librairie Gallimard, 1971), 1.1, 33.

3 *Les fourberies de Scapin*, in *Oeuvres complètes*, vol. 2, 2.7, p. 926; see also Charles-André Julien, *Histoire de l'Afrique du Nord* (Paris: Payot, 1964), II, p. 279.

4 Molière, *Les Précieuses ridicules*, in *Oeuvres complètes*, vol. 1, sc. 9, p. 273.

5 Molière, cast of characters, *Le Sicilien*, in *Oeuvres complètes*, vol. 2, cast of characters, p. 325.

6 Molière, *L'Ecole des maris*, in *Oeuvres Complètes*, vol. 1, 1.2, pp. 144–46.

7 Molière, *L'Avare*, vol. 2, 2.4, p. 538.

8 Antoine Galland, *Journal d'Antoine Galland pendant son séjour à Constantinople (1672–1673)*, ed. Charles Schefer, I (Paris: Ernest Leroux, 1881), p. 123.

9 Gérard Tongas, *Les Relations de la France avec l'Empire Ottoman durant la première moitié du XVIIe siècle et l'Ambassade à Constantinople de Philippe de Harlay, Comte de Césy (1619–1640)*, pref. M. Louis Villat (Toulouse: F. Boisseau, 1942), p. 47.

10 Alain Grosrichard, *Structure de sérail: La fiction du despotisme asiatique dans l'occident classique* (Paris: Seuil, 1979), pp. 26–28; Timothy Hampton, "'Turkish Dogs': Rabelais, Erasmus, and the Rhetoric of Alterity," in *Representations* 41 (Winter 1993): 58–82.

11 Lisa Jardine, *Worldly Goods: A New History of the Renaissance* (New York: Doubleday, 1996); Henri-Jean Martin, *Livre, pouvoirs et société à Paris au XVIIe siècle (1598–1701)*, I (Genève: Droz, 1969), p. 485.

12 Donneau de Visé, "Au lecteur," *Suite de l'histoire de Mahomet IV dépossédé* (Paris: Guerout, 1688).

13 For entrancement with travel and travel writing in an earlier period, see Wes Williams, *Pilgrimage and Narrative in the French Renaissance* (Oxford: Clarendon Press, 1998).

14 Jean Thévenot, *Relation d'un voyage fait au Levant dans laquelle il est curieusement traité des Etats Sujets au Grand Seigneur, des Moeurs, Religions, Forces, Gouvernements, Politiques, Langues et Coustumes des Habitans de ce Grand Empire* (Paris: Louis Bilaine, 1664), p. 43.

15 Gabriel Joseph de Lavergne, vicomte de Guilleragues, *Ambassades de M. le comte de Guilleragues et de M. Girardin auprès du Grand Seigneur, avec plusieurs pièces curieuses de tous les Ambassadeurs de France à la Porte, qui font connoistre les avantages que la Religion, et tous les Princes de l'Europe ont tiré des Alliances faites par les François avec sa Hautesse, depuis le Règne de François I, et particulierement sous le Règne du Roy, à l'égard de la Religion; ensemble plusieurs descriptions de Festes, et de Cavalcades à la manière des Turcs, qui n'ont point encore été données au Public, ainsi que celle des Tentes du Grand Seigneur* (Paris: De Luines, 1687), p. 198.

16 François de Mézeray, *Histoire des Turcs*, II: *Contenant ce qui s'est passé dans cet empire depuis l'an 1612 jusqu'à l'année présente 1649* (Paris: Sebastien-Cramoisy, 1663), p. 198.

17 Robert de Dreux, *Voyage en Turquie et en Grèce du R. P. Robert de Dreux, aumonier de l'ambassadeur de France (1665–1669)* (Paris: Pernot, 1925), p. 59.

18 Gottfried Leibniz, "Projet d'Expédition d'Egypte présenté à Louis XIV," in *Oeuvres de Leibniz publiées pour la première fois d'après les manuscrits originaux* (Paris: Firmin Didot Frères, Fils et Cie. 1864), L.

19 Mikhael M. Bakhtin, *Rabelais and his World*, trans. H. Iswolsky (Cambridge, MA: MIT Press, 1968); Natalie Z. Davis, chapter 5 from *Society and Culture in Early Modern France* (Stanford: Stanford University Press, 1975), pp. 124–51; Peter Stallybrass and Allen White, *The Politics and Poetics of Transgression* (Ithaca: Cornell University Press, 1986).

20 Jay M. Smith, *The Culture of Merit: Nobility, Royal Service, and the Making of Absolute Monarchy in France, 1600–1789* (Ann Arbor: University of Michigan Press, 1996), p. 185.

21 Benedict Anderson, *Imagined Communities: Reflections on the Origin and Spread of Nationalism* (London: Verso, 1983).

22 Edward W. Said, *Orientalism* (New York: Vintage Books, 1978), p. 63.

1 MEDEE AND THE TRAVELER-SAVANT

1 Roland Barthes, *Mythologies* (Paris: Seuil, 1957), p. 194; this position stands in opposition to that of the structural anthropologist Claude Lévi-Strauss stressing the eternal fixity of the myth model, which serves as epigraph to Mitchell Greenberg's chapter on *Médée* in *Corneille, Classicism and the Ruses of*

Symmetry (Cambridge: Cambridge University Press, 1986), pp. 16–36. Here I am arguing for the myth as vehicle marking historical change, and am more interested in the adaptations of the myth to time and circumstance than to any "eternal" quality.

2 1606: N. Renouard's translation of Ovid's *Metamorphoses*; 1617: Ch. de Massac's translation of the same; 1635: Pierre Corneille's tragedy, *Médée*; 1659: Pierre Corneille's *La Conquête de la Toison d'or*; 1675: Quinault-Lulli's lyric tragedy *Thésée*; 1693: Thomas Corneille and Charpentier's opera, *Médée*; 1694: Longepierre's tragedy, *Médée*; 1696: J. B. Rousseau and Colasse's opera, *La Toison d'or*. For a complete listing by countries and centuries up to 1981, see Duarte Mimoso-Ruiz, *Médée antique et moderne: Aspects rituels et socio-politiques d'un mythe* (Paris: Edition Ophrys, 1982), pp. 209–18.

3 In medieval France, the classical story was already in circulation: in Duarte Mimoso-Ruiz's list, two novels or "romans" are cited: 1160: B. de Ste More, *Livres de Troie*, and in 1469–74: Lefèvre, *Le Livre de Jason* (Mimoso-Ruiz, *Médée antique et moderne*, p. 212). In the sixteenth century, Buchanan translated Euripides' play into Latin, Baïf made it available in French, and then La Péruse produced one of the first French versions. See Mimoso-Ruiz's list.

4 Marianne McDonald, "Medea as Politician and Diva: Riding the Dragon into the Future" in *Medea: Essays on Medea in Myth: Literature, Philosophy, and Art*, ed. James J. Clauss and Sarah Iles Johnston (Princeton: Princeton University Press, 1997), pp. 297–323.

5 Constance M. Carroll, "Three's a Crowd: The Dilemma of the Black Woman in Higher Education," in eds. Gloria T. Hull, Patricia Bell Scott, and Barbara Smith, *All the Women are White, All the Blacks are Men, but Some of Us are Brave: Black Women's Studies* (New York: The Feminist Press at CUNY, 1982), p. 124.

6 Christa Wolf, *Médée, voix* (Paris: Fayard, 1997).

7 Marie Cardinal, *La Médée d'Euripides*, with a foreword and French text by Marie Cardinal (Paris: Bernard Grasset, 1986).

8 See Pierre Corneille, *Médée*, éd. André de Leyssac (Genève: Droz, 1978); all quotes of the play are taken from this edition and will be cited in the text). And consult Pierre Corneille, *Oeuvres Complètes* I, ed. Georges Couton (Paris: Pléiade, 1980), Notice, 1377 (all quotes for the "Epître" and the "Examen" are taken from this edition and will be cited in the text).

9 Corneille, *Oeuvres complètes* I, ed. Georges Couton, p. xxi, pp. 1379–80; and Elise McMahon, ch. 1. "Witchcraft, Infanticide and the Case of Médée" in *Classics Incorporated: Cultural Studies and Seventeenth-Century French Literature* (Birmingham, AL: Summa Publications, Inc., 1998); Holly Tucker, "Corneille's *Médée*: Gifts of Vengeance," *The French Review* 69 (October 1995): 1–12; Mitchell Greenberg, *Corneille, Classicism and the Ruses of Symmetry*; Hélène Domon, "Médée (ou) L'autre," *Cahiers du dix-septième* I, 2 (Fall 1987): 87–102; Hélène Merlin, *Public et littérature en France au XVIIe siècle* (Paris: Les Belles Lettres, 1994), p. 258; Marc Fumaroli, *Héros et orateurs: Rhétorique et dramaturgie cornéliennes* (Geneva: Droz, 1996), pp. 493–518.

10 *Médée* is not the only "victim" – the recent press has published only seven out of the twenty-five Corneille plays; conversation with the editor of the Petits Classiques Larousse series, Pascale Magni, in June 1998 produced an unsurprisingly circular explanation: *Médée* is not included in the collection because there is not sufficient demand and hence it cannot be financially justified. Magni did add that with recent reforms in the educational system, individual instructors have more say over their class readings, so that plays (like *Médée*) could find their way back into the classroom.

11 Alan Riding, "A Star of the 1600s has waned in the 1900s," *New York Times*, January 3, 1999, theatre section: 5.

12 As mentioned in the Introduction, Edward Said's seminal study *Orientalism* (New York: Vintage Books, 1978), has inspired much debate among literary, cultural, and area studies scholars, and anthropologists – Homi Bhabha, Ali Behdad, James Clifford, Julia Douthwaite, Michael Fischer, Lisa Lowe, to name just a few – not to mention Said himself, who has responded to critiques of his initial work with further refinement of his position, notably in his postface to the 1994 edition, as well as in his continued interventions in his further works.

13 Three "codes" in particular are anticipated in Corneille's play: (1) "le Code de commerce ou Code marchand" of 1673; (2) "le Code de la Marine et des Colonies" of 1681; (3) "le Code Noir" of 1685; from Marcel Marion, *Dictionnaire des institutions de la France aux XVIIe et XVIIIe siècles* (Paris: Editions A. and J. Picard, 1989), p. 108.

14 Richelieu, *Testament politique*, ed. L. André (Paris, 1947); see also Bibliothèque Sainte-Geneviève, ms. 3324; cited in René and Suzanne Pillorget, *France baroque, France classique (1589–1715)* I. *Récit*, pp. 335–36.

15 Laurent D'Arvieux, *Mémoires du Chevalier D'Arvieux*, ed. Jean-Baptiste Labat, I (Paris: chez Charles Jean-Bapiste Delespine, 1735), preface, pp. ix–x.

16 My reading of the play privileges Pollux as the voice of reason and wisdom, whereas Fumaroli, since he is analyzing questions of morality and theatricality together, sees the character Médée as Corneille's vehicle of choice; the two readings do not challenge but rather complement each other, as do Pollux's and Médée's voices.

17 To my knowledge, Pollux is the sole developed stage character to represent this role in the Early Modern French theatre.

18 Fumaroli uses the same quote as his point of departure for discussing the problem of theatre and morality (500).

19 George Marcus and Michael M. J. Fischer, *Anthropology as Cultural Critique* (Chicago: University of Chicago Press, 1986), but especially the introduction to the second edition, 1999.

20 Let us not forget that, for the seventeenth-century audience, Médée's homeland was as far away as ever, since the Black Sea was closed by the Ottomans to all trade and travel except their own. Russia in 1774, Austria in 1784, England in 1799, and finally France in 1802 "obtained the right to ply

the waters of the Euxine"; see A. Uner Turgay, "Trabzon," in *Port-Cities of the Eastern Mediterranean 1800–1914*, special issue of *Review 16* (Fall 1993): 436.

21 The term "barbare" was already explored and articulated, but not resolved, in Greek tragedy; see Edith Hall, *Inventing the Barbarian: Greek Self-Definition through Tragedy* (Oxford: Clarendon Press, 1989).

22 The idea of reciprocal anthropologies has been around even in pre-professional writings and artistic commentaries on the West. See Timothy Mitchell's commentaries in *Colonizing Egypt* (Cambridge: Cambridge University Press, 1988), chapter 1; for West African carvings of Westerners, see Fritz Kramer, *The Red Fez* (London: Verso, 1993); anthropologies both "here and there" have been grounded in postcolonial, diasporic, and transnational conditions of situated knowledges of the past few decades: for explorations by many anthropologists writing about their own as well as other societies, see the journals *Public Culture, Positions*, and the eight volumes of the annual *Late Editions*. Hence James Clifford's questions: "Who is being observed?" and "What are the relations of power?" in anthropological inquiry putting into question many pre-post-modern field studies, are well-explored ones: James Clifford, "Traveling Cultures" in *Cultural Studies*, edited by Lawrence Grossberg, Cary Nelson, Paula A. Treichler (New York: Routledge, 1992), p. 98. In like manner, Michel Leiris's prediction," 'the "objects" of observation' would begin to write back" (256), cited in Clifford's *The Predicament of Culture: Twentieth-Century Ethnography, Literature and Art* (Cambridge: Harvard University Press, 1988), is already anticipated by Corneille as Médée "talks back" in this play. Writing back has especially played out in the response of Arab scholars to Said's representation of their world; see Emmanuel Sivan, "Edward Said and his Arab Reviewers," in *Interpretations of Islam: Past and Present* (Princeton: The Darwin Press, 1985), pp. 133–54.

23 Montaigne, "Des Cannibales," in *Essais* in *Oeuvres complètes*, edited by Albert Thibaudet (Paris: Gallimard, 1967).

24 Antoine Furetière, *Le Dictionnaire universel* (1690; reprinted, Paris: SNL – Le Robert, 1978).

25 Jean Thévenot, *Relation d'un voyage fait au Levant dans laquelle il est curieusement traité des Etats Sujets au Grand Seigneur, des Moeurs, Religions, Forces, Gouvernements, Politiques, Langues et Coustumes des Habitans de ce Grand Empire* (Paris: Lovis Bilaine, 1664), p. 111.

26 Sieur du Loir, *Les Voyages du Sieur du Loir ensemble de ce qui se passa à la mort du feu Sultan Mourat dans le Serrail, les cérémonies de ses funérailles, et celles de l'avènement à l'Empire de Sultan Hibraim son frère qui lui succèda, avec la relation du siège de Babylon fait en 1639 par Sultan Mourat* (Paris: François Clouzier, 1654), p. 166.

27 Robert de Dreux, *Voyage en Turquie et en Grèce du R. P. Robert de Dreux, aumonier de l'ambassadeur de France (1665–1669)* (Paris: Pernot, 1925), pp. 71–72.

28 Jean Chardin, *Journal du voyage du chevalier Chardin en Perse et aux Indes, par la mer noire et par la Colchide, Première partie, qui contient le voyage de Paris à Ispahan* (London: Moses Pitt, 1686), p. 46.

29 Chardin, *Journal*, p. 13.

30 Donneau de Visé, *Histoire de Mahomet IV dépossédé* (Paris: Michel Guerout, 1688), p. 8.

31 Monsieur Ricaut, *Histoire de l'Etat present de l'Empire Ottoman: contenant les Maximes politiques des Turcs; les principaux points de la religion mahometane, ses Sectes, ses Héresies, et ses diverses sortes de Religieux; leur discipline militaire, avec une supputation exacte de leurs forces par mer et par terre, et du revenu de l'état*, trans. M. Briot (Paris: Sébastien Mabre-Cramoisy, 1670), pp. 2–3.

32 Thévenot, *Relation d'un voyage fait au Levant*, p. 107.

33 Robert Mantran, *Histoire d'Istanbul* (Paris: Fayard, 1996), pp. 254–55.

34 European scholarly interest in Islamic erudition was already well marked, especially during the Renaissance and materially evidenced through the circulation of manuscripts and books; see Lisa Jardine, ch. 3. "The Triumph of the Book," in *Worldly Goods: A New History of the Renaissance* (New York: Doubleday, 1996), pp. 133–80.

35 François de Mézeray, *Histoire des Turcs. Second Tome. Contenant ce qui s'est passé dans cet empire depuis l'an 1612 jusqu'à l'année présente 1649. Avec l'histoire de Chalcondyle par Blaise de Vigenere. Les descriptions et figures des habits des officiers et autres personnes de l'Empire Turc et les Tableaux prophétiques sur la ruine du même empire* (Paris: Cramoisy, 1663), p. 185.

36 Gottfried Leibniz, "Projet d'Expédition d'Egypte présenté à Louis XIV," in *Oeuvres de Leibniz publiées pour la première fois d'après les manuscrits originaux* (Paris: Firmin Didot Frères, Fils et Cie, 1864), vol. 5, p. 124.

37 Herbelot de Molainville, Barthélemy, preface to *Bibliothèque orientale ou Dictionnaire universel contenant généralement tout ce qui regarde la connaissance des peuples de l'Orient* (Paris: Compagnie des libraires, 1697).

38 See details of this story in Jean Chardin's *Journal du voyage*, p. 235.

39 Chardin, *Journal du voyage*, p. 2.

40 Despite Richelieu's dictum, although the French nobility was not forbidden from engaging in shipping activities, where agents and middle-men handled the actual affairs, the general act of commerce was considered socially debasing. See Marcel de La Bigne de Villeneuve, *La Dérogeance de la noblesse sous l'ancien régime* (Paris: Sedopols, 1977).

41 Some cite this expression "a nation of shopkeepers" as coined by Louis XIV and alluding to Holland; I have always heard it used in reference to England. See Thomas J. Schaeper, "The Economic History of the Reign" in *The Reign of Louis XIV: Essays in Celebration of Andrew Lossky*, edited by Paul Sonnino (London: Humanities Press International, 1990), p. 37.

42 As the jackets of his *Tristes Tropiques* trumpet: Claude Lévi-Strauss, *Tristes Tropiques* (Paris: Plon, 1955) and *Tristes Tropiques*, trans. John and Doreen Weightman (New York: Penguin Books, 1973).

43 Claude Lévi-Strauss, *Tristes Tropiques*, Fr., p. 436.

44 Lévi-Strauss, *Tristes Tropiques*, trans. John and Doreen Weightman: "My play was called 'The Apotheosis of Augustus' and took the form of a new version of Corneille's *Cinna*" (p. 378).

45 George E. Marcus and Michael M. J. Fischer, *Anthropology as Cultural Critique: An Experimental Moment in the Human Sciences* (Chicago: University of Chicago Press, 1986), p. 34; but *Tristes Tropiques* is not his central anthropological work: that is *The Elementary Structures of Kinship*, *La pensée sauvage*, and the four-volume *Mythologiques*; *Tristes Tropiques* is a lamentation on the effects of colonialism, and so necessarily more lyrical than analytical.

46 Given that the roles of anthropologists, the relations of field work, and the genres of writing anthropology have changed over the past few decades, Corneille and Lévi-Strauss, both tied in to a classical discursive tradition, may have more in common together than either of them with today's discourse on human knowledge; see Marcus and Fischer's Introduction to the second edition (1999) of *Anthropology as Cultural Critique.*

47 Michèle Duchet in *Anthropologie et histoire au siècle des lumières: Buffon, Voltaire, Rousseau, Diderot* (Paris: François Maspero, 1971) claims that reflection of a properly "anthropological" nature does not take place until large collections of travel writings are published together in the eighteenth century, and that hence earlier travel writings cannot properly be considered "anthropology." However, I see both observation and reflection working together in the production and the reception of seventeenth-century writings circulated and produced separately which will later appear in "collected works" form, and don't see how the periodicity she insists on helps to understand the development of the field: "Il faut attendre le moment où les grandes collections de voyages sont constituées . . . tous entre 1700 et 1740 pour que la réflexion prenne le pas sur l'observation" (14). ["It is necessary to wait for the moment when the great travel collections are formed . . . all between 1700 and 1740, in order for reflection to overtake observation."]

48 But see also Roger Célestin, *From Cannibals to Radicals: Figures and Limits of Exoticism* (Minneapolis: University of Minnesota Press, 1996).

49 Margaret T. Hodgen, *Early Anthropology in the Sixteenth and Seventeenth Centuries* (Philadelphia: University of Pennsylvania Press, 1964), p. 8.

50 Ezel Kural Shaw and C. J. Heywood, introduction to *English and Continental Views of the Ottoman Empire 1500–1800* (Los Angeles: William Andrews Clark Memorial Library, UCLA, 1972), pp. v–vi.

51 Pierre Martino, *L'Orient dans la littérature française au XVIIe et au XVIIIe siècle* (Paris: Librairie Hachette et Cie, 1906), p. 44.

52 Here Martino is in agreement with Erica Harth, cited below.

53 An important parallel: the image of the seventeenth century as the century of Europe's "Scientific Revolution" was a result of the erasure of much of the transmission of scientific knowledge into Europe from the Islamic oecumene and Judeo-Islamic Spain, Portugal and Sicily; and also the erasure of such facts as that Newton was an avid alchemist.

54 Lisa Jardine, *Worldly Goods: A New History of the Renaissance* (New York: Doubleday, 1996).

55 Bruno Latour, *Science in Action: How to Follow Scientists and Engineers through Society* (Cambridge: Harvard University Press, 1987), p. 219.

56 For the authoritative account of the Pollux, Jason, Medea stories, see Apollodorus, *The Library*, trans. Sir James George Frazer, 2 vols. Loeb Classical Library (Cambridge: Harvard University Press, 1921).

57 Jean Racine, *Phèdre*, in *Oeuvres complètes*, ed. Georges Forestier, vol. 1 (Paris: Gallimard, 1999), p. 876: "J'ai pris, j'ai fait couler dans mes brûlantes veines / Un poison que Médée apporta dans Athènes" (802). ["I took and let flow in my burning veins / A poison Medea brought to Athens."] This link is also important in Fumaroli's analysis, p. 512.

58 This also brings to mind the Crusaders' quests to bring relics of Jerusalem back to Europe, or more recently US attempts to recover VietNam prisoners of war or any traces of them, all of these qualifying as sacred objects to be repatriated; but it also resonates with seventeenth-century collection expeditions as they sought to obtain and bring home materials from the ancient world, around Troy in particular, since this part of the world featured as the mythic cradle of European civilization according to French founding stories.

59 Henry Laurens, "L'Orientalisme au XVIIe et XVIIIe siècles," in *L'Orient: Concept et images, Civilisations 15*, 15e colloque de l'Institut de recherches sur les civilisations de l'occident moderne (Paris: Presses de l'université de Paris Sorbonne, 1987), p. 39.

60 Gabriel Joseph de Lavergne, vicomte de Guilleragues, *Lettres portugaises suivies de Guilleragues par lui-même*, ed. Frédéric Deloffre (Paris: Gallimard, 1990), p. 137.

61 For example, Grelot, *Relation nouvelle d'un voyage de Constantinople, enrichie de Plans levez par l'Auteur sur les lieux, et des Figures de tout ce qu'il y a de plus remarquable dans cette ville* (Paris: chez la veuve Damien Foucault, 1680), p. 59.

62 Erica Harth, *Ideology and Culture in Seventeenth-Century France* (Ithaca: Cornell University Press, 1983), p. 225.

63 Georges Van Den Abbeele, "Duplicity and Singularity in André Thevet's Cosmographie du Levant," in *Early Orientalisms*, special issue of *L'Esprit Créateur* 32, (Fall 1992): 25–35.

64 Sieur du Loir, preface to *Les Voyages*.

65 Guillaume Joseph Grelot, "Avis au lecteur," in *Relation nouvelle d'un voyage de Constantinople, enrichie de Plans levez par l'Auteur sur les lieux, et des Figures de tout ce qu'il y a de plus remarquable dans cette ville* (Paris: chez la veuve Damien Foucault, 1680).

66 In this one could argue, less interestingly perhaps, but validly, that he was simply following convention for the genre at his time.

67 Corneille, "Discours de l'utilité et des parties du poème dramatique," in *Théâtre complet* I, ed. Georges Couton (Paris: Garnier, 1993), p. 29.

68 Coco Fusco, see "The Other History of Intercultural Performance" in *English is Broken Here* (New York: The New Press, 1995) for a brilliant analysis of the troubled and troubling dynamic the author produces in her audience through her performance as "noble savage behind the bars of a golden cage," her dialogical construction of the "freak," pp. 37–63.

69 Edith Hall, *Inventing the Barbarian*: "The celebration of Greek victory over the inhabitants of Asia Minor must legitimize the actions of the colonizers and express the spirit of the age when Greek cities were beginning to expand self-confidently all over the Mediterranean and the Black Sea" (48). According to Hall's analysis, the inclusion of allusions to this part of the world would be a form of celebration, but certainly the Medea story sounds also a warning of the risks involved in such expansion.

70 In this we see an important difference between France's classical theater, and England's Shakespearean theater, with such characters as Shylock, Caliban, Othello, and plots hinging directly on witchcraft as well as subtexts of freemasonry.

71 Of course, other considerations also determine what can play on the stage, most notably the rules that govern each of the sub-genres of "classical theater" – tragedy, comedy, etc.

72 In this he plays a role frequently assigned to women, who customarily occupy a marginal place in the social order and therefore negotiate more fluidly between fixed males.

73 Hélène Merlin also notes, although only in passing, Pollux's clear grasp of the situation, in *Public et littérature en France au dix-septième siècle* (Paris: Les Belles Lettres, 1994), p. 256.

74 Pollux's and Jason's code is dictated by laws ruling social exchange, as suggested by the terms "ingratitude" and "mal récompensé;" there are serious consequences to violating the principles of gift-giving, as Marcel Mauss has demonstrated in *The Gift: Forms and Functions of Exchange in Archaic Societies* (New York: Norton, 1967), and as Holly Tucker argues in "Corneille's *Médée*: Gifts of Vengeance," *The French Review* 69 (October 1995): 1–12.

75 Corneille hints without claiming that it is Pollux's longer stay in Médée's part of the world, his fieldwork (by early modern standards) that has sensitized him to her ways, the ways of her world.

76 Holly Tucker, "Corneille's *Médée*: Gifts of Vengeance."

77 As with Lévi-Strauss's lamentations on the effects of colonialism in *Tristes Tropiques*.

78 Here again, indebtedness marks the relationship between Médée and Jason along with his argonauts, including Pollux; this further explains Médée's rage, and points up Pollux's respect for the exchange system, while showing Jason as the ungrateful scoundrel who gets his just deserts.

79 Other terms for early travelers, such as "missionary," "crusader," "conquerer" will each have a particular valence and denote specific activities and attitudes; only those mentioned in the text apply appropriately to Pollux.

80 Lévi-Strauss's career trajectory evinces the traits of this model.

81 But, to her credit, she has taken the trouble to ensure that her servant and confidante Nerine has been guaranteed safe haven and protection from Aegée (5.1.1307–8).

82 This is prior to the murder of her children; that act may effectively cancel out this solution for her.

83 "Climat" meant country or location in seventeenth-century French common usage; see Furetière's *Dictionnaire*.

84 Here again, I refer the reader to Fusco's *English is Broken Here*.

85 Hall, *Inventing the Barbarian*; that initially Médée figured as exotic not because she came from foreign lands, but because of her knowledge of pharmacy, points to an early shift in the understanding of what is meant by "exotic" (35, n. 110).

86 See p. 241, but also the entire discussion of the "moi" (pp. 241–55) for a pertinent discussion of the constitution of the ego in Jean Laplanche and J.-B. Pontalis, *Vocabulaire de la psychanalyse* (Paris: Presses universitaires de France, 1967).

87 See also Wes Williams, *Pilgrimage and Narrative in the French Renaissance: The Undiscovered Country* (Oxford: Clarendon Press, 1998).

88 On this subject, see also Fumaroli's astute discussion where he analyzes the "robe de soleil" as "une robe de théâtre," part of the magic of the stage that highlights the contrast between the splendor of the telling of the story of Médée and the crime that is at the heart of that story (pp. 503–04).

89 This passage would benefit from a historicizing application of Gérard Genette's "Vraisemblance et motivation" argument in *Figures II* (Paris: Editions du Seuil, 1969), pp. 71–99.

90 See Karl Marx, *Das Kapital: A Critique of Political Economy*, ed. Friedrich Engels, condensed by Serge L. Levitsky (Washington, DC: Regnery Publishing Company, 1998), pp. 33 and 68 especially; and of course we have seen with Mauss and Tucker that the gift is a key element of human sociality, and produces its own economy of indebtedness.

91 "Creux" m. / "creuse" f. means "empty" in French.

2 STAGING POLITICS: *LE CID*

1 Pierre Corneille, *Oeuvres complètes*, ed. Georges Couton, vol. 1 (Paris: Gallimard, 1973); all citations are taken from this edition of the 1637 text except when there are significant variants, in which case I cite also from the 1660 edition. References are to act, scene, and line.

2 See also Christopher Braider, "Cet hymen différé: The Figuration of Authority in Corneille's *Le Cid*," *Representations* 54 (Spring 1996): 28–56, 35; and Mitchell Greenberg, *Corneille, Classicism and the Ruses of Symmetry* (Cambridge: Cambridge University Press, 1986), p. 39.

3 Corneille's *Médée* can be read as a challenge to anti-"barbarian" prejudice, whereas it is more difficult to read *Le Cid* without being reminded of a racist discourse. Here I suggest that the artist is not necessarily merely a self-conscious ideologue, but also a translator into aesthetically pleasing artifacts of material that is circulating in the air, and he is sensitive as well to his own career requirements.

4 Fernand Braudel, Preface to *La Méditerranée et le monde méditerranéen à l'époque de Philippe II: La Part du milieu* (Paris: Armand Colin, 1990), pp. 16–18.

5 To this date, tide tables for the Guadalquivir River are published daily in the Seville newspaper.

6 In 1636 the Spanish crossed the northern border of France in the Spring and by August had arrived at Corbie, within a hundred or so kilometres of Paris, but this overland aggression took time and the French measured the progress of the Spanish on a daily basis. Surprise attacks by land were highly unusual; word as a rule moved faster and preceded them. See Milorad R. Margitic, *Le Cid: Tragi-comédie* (Amsterdam: John Benjamins Publishing Company, 1989), p. xxxiii.

7 J. B. Diamante would "correct" Corneille's error and reset the play in Burgos when he would rewrite it in 1657; see Suzanne Guellouz, "Une nouvelle lecture des '*Mocedades*' et du '*Cid*': '*El Honrador de su padre*', in *Pierre Corneille*, edited by Alain Niderst (Paris: Presses universitaires de France, 1985), pp. 83–92, 88.

8 Guillén de Castro, *Las Mocedades del Cid* (Madrid: Ediciones Alfil, 1960), p. 68.

9 According to this interpretation, then, the fact that Corneille's Rouen featured an up-tide river might have played some inspiring role, but only insofar as it participated in a greater vision than a mere one-to-one correlation (see Couton).

10 Charles-André Julien, *Histoire de l'Afrique blanche des origines à 1945* (Paris: Presses universitaires de France, 1966), pp. 102–03.

11 Charles-André Julien, *Histoire de l'Afrique du Nord: Tunisie, Algérie, Maroc de la conquête arabe à 1830* (Paris: Payot, 1961), p. 277.

12 While many studies, among them: Serge Doubrovsky's *Corneille et la dialectique du héros*, pp. 89–132; Mitchell Greenberg's *Corneille, Classicism and the Ruses of Symmetry*, pp. 37–65; Judd D. Hubert's *Corneille's Performative Metaphors* (Charlottesville: Rockwood Press, 1997); Marie-Odile Sweetser's *La Dramaturgie de Corneille* (Paris: Droz, 1977), to mention only a few, offer superb readings of *Le Cid*, most do not consider the perspective developed here.

13 *The Cid; Cinna; The Theatrical Illusion*, trans. John Cairncross (Harmondsworth: Penguin, 1975), 3.6.1073–78; all translations of *Le Cid* are taken from this edition; verses are indicated in the notes.

14 Gérard Tongas, *Les Relations de la France avec l'Empire Ottoman durant la première moitié du XVIIe siècle et l'Ambassade à Constantinople de Philippe de Harlay, Comte de Césy (1619–1640)*, preface by M. Louis Villat (Toulouse: Imprimerie F. Boisseau, 1942), p. 159.

15 Tongas, *Les Relations*, p. 162; see also Paul Masson, *Histoire du commerce français dans le Levant au XVIIe siècle* (New York: Burt Franklin, 1967).

16 D'Arvieux, *Mémoires* 5, p. 121.

17 Ibid.

18 Charles-André Julien, *Histoire de l'Afrique du nord*, pp. 279–80.

19 D'Arvieux, *Mémoires*, 5, p. 109.

20 Tongas, *Les Relations*, p. 165.

21 Robert Mantran, *L'Empire Ottoman du XVIe au XVIIIe siècle: Administration, Economie, Société* (London: Variorum Reprints, 1984), p. 325.

22 Robert de Dreux, *Voyage en Turquie et en Grèce du R. P. Robert de Dreux, aumonier de l'ambassadeur de France (1665–1669)* (Paris: Pernot, 1925), p. 60.

23 Antoine Galland, *Histoire de l'esclavage d'un marchand de la ville de Cassis, à Tunis*, ed. Catherine Guénot and Nadia Vasquez (Paris: Editions de la Bibliothèque, 1993).

24 Her own salty refrain, "Et vogue la galère!" would announce regularly in her writing that she was about to hit the open seas of her imagination, to give free rein to her pen, and be inhibited by no qualms or distractions.

25 Madame de Sévigné, *Correspondance* 1, edited by Roger Duchêne (Paris: Gallimard, 1972), lettre 306, p. 572.

26 Gabriel Joseph de La Vergne, vicomte de Guilleragues, *Ambassades de M. le comte de Guilleragues et de M. Girardin auprès du Grand Seigneur, avec plusieurs pièces curieuses de tous les Ambassadeurs de France à la Porte, qui font connoistre les avantages que la Religion, et tous les Princes de l'Europe ont tirés des Alliances faites par les français avec sa Hautesse, depuis le règne de François Ier et particulièrement sous le règne du Roy, à l'égard de la Religion; ensemble plusieurs descriptions de Festes. et de Cavalcades à la manière des Turcs, qui n'ont point encore été données au Public, ainsi que celles des Tentes du Grand Seigneur* (Paris: De Luines, 1687), pp. 269–71.

27 Grelot, *Relation nouvelle d'un voyage*, p. 217.

28 Robert de Dreux, *Voyage en Turquie et en Grèce*, p. 59.

29 See Galland, *Histoire de l'esclavage*, p. 28.

30 Charles-André Julien, *Histoire de l'Afrique du Nord*, p. 280.

31 Chardin, *Journal du voyage*, p. 3.

32 D'Arvieux, *Mémoires* 1:22; *pace* Mantran.

33 Orhan Kologlu, *Le Turc dans la presse française: des débuts jusqu'à 1815* (Beyrouth: Maison d'édition Al-Hayat, 1971), pp. 119, 125.

34 For the complete context, see, Charles-André Julien, *Histoire de l'Afrique du nord*, p. 286.

35 *Histoire nouvelle du massacre des Turcs faict en la ville de Marseille en Provence, le 14 de mars, mil six cents vingt, par la populace de la ville, justement indignée contre ces barbares, avec la mort de deux chaoulx de la Porte du Grand Seigneur, ou ambassadeurs pour iceluy. Avec le récit des occasions qui les y ont provoquez et les préssages de la ruine de l'empire des Turcs*, edited by Henri Delmas de Grammont (1620; reprint, Paris: H. Champion, 1879), p. 25.

36 *Les Capitulations renouvelées entre Louis XIV Empereur de France et Mehemet IV Empereur des Turcs. par l'entremise de M. Charles François Ollier, Marquis de Nointel, Conseiller du Roy en tous ses Conseils, et en sa Cour de Parlement de Paris, et son Ambassadeur en Levant (1673)* (Paris: Frederic Leonard, 1689), p. 10, no. 33: fifty-eight terms of agreement, concerning above all commerce and the protection of diplomats, merchants, and translators.

37 Tongas, *Les Relations*, p. 47; and the crusades didn't end there; as late as the eighteenth century, even Rousseau would militate for one.

38 Paul W. Bamford, *Fighting Ships and Prisons: The Mediterranean Galleys of France in the Age of Louis XIV* (Minneapolis: University of Minnesota Press, 1973), p. 141.

39 Bamford, *Fighting Ships*, p. 138.

40 Chardin, *Journal du voyage*, p. 2.

41 Kologlu, *Le Turc*, p. 109.

42 This absence could be simply dismissed as a consequence of Corneille's loyalty to Aristotle's classical *Poetics*, but, had he been truly loyal to the program of these tenets, he would not have appropriated such a relatively recent, unclassical plot or produced so problematic an intrigue at all. Indeed, witness his need, in both the *Avertissement* and the *Examen*, to defend his many supposed infractions against the rules. We can remember that this is a tragi-comedy, and therefore not subject to the same aristotelian constraints as pure tragedy, but then it is even less evident why Corneille so thoroughly avoided the obvious question of religion.

43 See Benedict Anderson's *Imagined Communities: Reflections on the Origin and Spread of Nationalism* (London: Verso, 1983) for an exposition of this idea.

44 Corneille, *Oeuvres complètes* 1:1471.

45 Israel Burshatin examines the tacit European understanding of Turks and Moors as all of a kind in his study of earlier Spanish versions of *Le Cid*: "The uneasy master recasts wretched Moriscos as ominous brethren of the Ottoman Turk" ("The Moor in the Text: Metaphor, Emblem, and Silence," in *Race, Writing and Difference*, ed. Henry Louis Gates, Jr. [Chicago: University of Chicago Press, 1985], p. 118). This position is justified to the extent that the Ottoman Porte had jurisdiction over the North African republics, and of course the Moriscos was the name for those few Moors who remained in Spain for only a century or so after the formal expulsion of the Moors, until even they were banished.

46 Corneille, *Oeuvres complètes* 1:1471; see also Hélène Merlins's more recent analysis of the play investigating the dynamic of the tension between "le public" and "le particulier," in *Public et Littérature en France au XVIIe siècle* (Paris: Les Belles Lettres, 1994), pp. 250–51.

47 The scandal of a Chimène enamored of her father's assassin, or the issue of the point of honor as duels were being forbidden by Richelieu are also frequently cited as crowd-pleasers.

48 Based on an earlier articulation of alterity – Joseph Conrad's *Heart of Darkness*.

49 Guillén de Castro, *Las Mocedades del Cid* (Madrid: Ediciones Alfil, 1960), Act 2, pp. 67–68; it is this earlier parent text which makes explicit the direct link between Corneille's Moors and the Ottomans of the period, as well as the theme of piracy. There is of course an important ambiguity lodged in the term "mora"; from the Spanish, it simply means "dark," and it is the Spanish who gave the name "Moor"/"Moro" to this people, so they are known as much as a "race" as a political entity. (My translation in French: L'Espagnol nous a obligé d'abandonner / Dans une journée le projet / Et le butin qui valait / Plus d'or que tout ce qu'engendre le Soleil. / Et dans

sa main conquérante / Tombe notre devise Ottomane, / Sans qu'aucune lance chrétienne ne vienne, / Dépourvue d'une tête maure.)

50 See Corneille's "Examen," pp. 703–04.

51 We will refer to this version as "**a.**"

52 We will refer to this as "**b**". Quotes in the body of the text will be taken from the 1637 "**a**" edition cited in note 1, and **b** will be indicated in the notes, and cited only if the texts differ.

53 Tr. John Cairncross, 2.6.607–09, 59.

54 Tr. John Cairncross, 2.5.542, 57.

55 Or, in the more confident tone of **b:**

> Les Mores ont appris par force à vous connaître,
> Et tant de fois vaincus, ils ont perdu le coeur
> De se plus hasarder contre un si grand vainqueur.
>
> (2.6.610–12)

56 **b** 5.1.1558–59.

57 Tr. John Cairncross v.1.1558–60, 99.

58 See also Couton's "Note sur le texte," 1476.

59 Tr. John Cairncross, 5.7.1825–26, 109.

60 Tr. John Cairncross, 3.6.1084, 81.

61 See also Couton's "Note sur le texte," 1476.

62 Corneille applies here Horace's dictum, which he has cited in another context, but still about *Le Cid* in the "Examen" of 1660: "ce qu'on expose à la vue touche bien plus que ce qu'on n'apprend que par un récit" (706). ["What is brought out to be looked at is much more touching than what is only learned through a narration."]

63 **b** 2.5.535–43.

64 Tr. John Cairncross, 2.5.535–43, 57.

65 Tr. John Cairncross, 2.5.542, 57.

66 **b** 4.3.1304–31. In Declan Donnellan's 1998 production of *Le Cid*, he reinterprets Rodrigue's victory speech in a quite modern manner, attentive to the interiority of his characters: " I think if someone shows off about the people he's killed – it's really fear and doubt speaking," . . . "The louder the abuse the bigger the lie; the louder we shout about our uncertainties, the less people believe. I think even if this scene were done with flags and baroque splendor, the whole baroque thing is really about doubt." Quoted by Alan Riding, "Englishing a French Classic (With Their Approval)," *New York Times*, 4 April 1999, Theatre Section, 6.

67 **b** 4.3.1310–26.

68 **b** 4.3.1310: "Le More voit sa perte et perd soudain courage."

69 **b** 4.3.1222–25.

70 Tr. John Cairncross, 4.3.1222–25, 87.

71 **b** 5.7.1827–28: "A ce nom seul de Cid."

72 Tr. John Cairncross, 5.7.1827–28, 109.

73 **b** 5.7.1823–26, 1829.

74 Tr. John Cairncross, 3.6.1073–76, 80–81.

75 See also Michel Prigent, *Le héros et l'état dans la tragédie de Pierre Corneille* (Paris: PUF, 1986), p. 42; and Timothy Williams, "La menace du héros: A propos du *Cid* de Pierre Corneille," *Cahiers du dix-septième* 4 (Fall 1990): 141–50.

76 **b** 4.3.1213–14.

77 Tr. John Cairncross, 4.3.1213–14, 86.

78 See also Brian Massumi, "Deleuze and Guattari's Theories of the Group Subject, through a Reading of Corneille's *Le Cid*," *Discours social/Social Discourse: The International Working Papers Series in Comparative Literature* 1 (Winter 1988): 423–40.

79 See also Christopher Braider, "Cet hymen différé:" 49.

80 See also Braider, "Cet hymen différé:" 31.

81 **b** 3.6.1073–76: "Croit surprendre la ville et piller la contrée."

82 Tr. John Cairncross, 3.6.1073–76, 80–81.

83 Of course, this point can be contested since, in the "European" view, the Moors had initially invaded Spain and France, attacking "native" Europeans and trying to colonize them; such questions as "who was there first?" will always be fraught.

84 **b** 4.5.1425–32.

85 **b** 4.5.1414.

86 Tr. John Cairncross, 4.5.1414, 93.

87 **b** 3.6.1083–84.

88 Tr. John Cairncross, 3.6.1083–84, 81.

89 John Lough, *L'écrivain et son public: Commerce du livre et commerce des idées en France du Moyen Age à nos jours*, trans. Alexis Tadié (Paris: Le chemin vert, 1978), pp. 136–44.

90 See Homi K. Bhabha, Introduction, and ch. 16: "DissemiNation: Time, Narrative, and the Margins of the Modern Nation" in *Nation and Narration*, ed. Homi K. Bhabha (London: Routledge, 1990), pp. 1–8, 291–322.

91 Alan Riding, "Englishing a French Classic," 6.

92 Riding, *NYT*, 6.

93 *Le Petit Robert* (Paris: Société du Nouveau Littré, 1973), 1648.

94 Henri-Frédéric Blanc, *Sidi: Tragédie Bouffe en cinq actes* (Marseilles: Titanic, 1997).

95 Tr. John Cairncross, 5.7.1840, 109.

3   ACCULTURATING THE AUDIENCE:
LE BOURGEOIS GENTILHOMME

1 This chapter is much indebted to the studies of: Ali Behdad, "The Oriental(ist) Encounter: The Politics of *turquerie* in Molière," *L'Esprit Créateur* 23 (Fall 1992): 37–49; H. Gaston Hall, *Molière's Le Bourgeois gentilhomme: Context and Stagecraft* (Durham, England: University of Durham Press, 1990); Mary Hossain "The Chevalier d'Arvieux and *Le Bourgeois gentilhomme*," *Seventeenth-Century French Studies* 12 (1990): 76–88; Françoise Karro, "La Cérémonie

turque du *Bourgeois gentilhomme*: mouvance temporelle et spirituelle de la foi," in *Le Bourgeois gentilhomme: Problèmes de la comédie-ballet*, ed. Volker Kapp, Biblio 17, 67 (Paris: n.p., 1991), pp. 35–93; Pierre Martino, *L'Orient dans la littérature française au XVIIe et au XVIIIe siècle* (Paris: Hachette, 1906), and "La Cérémonie turque du *Bourgeois gentilhomme*," *Revue d'histoire littéraire de la France* 1 (January–March, 1911): 37–60; my argument does not seek to replace but to complement the above studies, and any analysis of *Le Bourgeois gentilhomme* in the context of seventeenth-century exoticism will take these works into account.

2 Molière, *Le Bourgeois gentilhomme* 4.7.18, in *Oeuvres complètes*, vol. 2, ed. Georges Couton (Paris: Gallimard, 1971). References are to act, scene, and page.

3 Hossain, "The Chevalier d'Arvieux," 76–88, and Martino, "La Cérémonie turque," 54.

4 "Nous travaillâmes à cette pièce de théâtre que l'on voit dans les oeuvres de Molière, sous le titre du Bourgeois gentilhomme, qui se fit Turc pour épouser la fille du Grand Seigneur" ["We worked on the play which can be found in Molière's works under the title of the *Bourgeois gentilhomme*, who made himself into a Turk in order to wed the Grand Lord's daughter."] (D'Arvieux, *Mémoires*, 4:252). This story has been well told and analyzed by several critics, among them Ali Behdad, Mary Hossain, Pierre Martino, not to mention D'Arvieux's editor Jean-Baptiste Labat; their commentaries should be consulted for a full appreciation of the play.

5 Behdad also insists on the function of the play as a "critique of the new bourgeoisie" in "The Oriental(ist) Encounter," 39.

6 Robert Mantran, *La vie quotidienne à Istanbul au siècle de Soliman le magnifique* (Paris: Hachette, 1965), p. 20; and Paul Masson, *Histoire du commerce français dans le Levant au XVIIe siècle* (New York: Burt Franklin, 1967).

7 See Karen Barkey, *Bandits and Bureaucrats: The Ottoman Route to State Centralization* (Ithaca: Cornell University Press, 1994), p. 49, for a discussion of the effect of this "influx of silver from the New World" on the Ottoman Empire.

8 Paul Masson, *Histoire du commerce français dans le Levant au XVIIe siècle* (New York: Burt Franklin, 1967), p. 17.

9 Tongas, *Les Relations*, p. 189 specifically; see also pp. 184–202.

10 See Norman Itzkowitz, *Ottoman Empire and Islamic Tradition* (New York: Alfred A. Knopf, 1972), p. 105; and Bernard Lewis, *The Muslim Discovery of Europe* (New York: W. W. Norton, 1992); however, this view glosses over many instances of Levantine interest and curiosity about the West, and stands in marked contrast to the evidence of exchange supplied in Lisa Jardine's *Worldly Goods*.

11 Barkey, *Bandits and Bureaucrats*, p. 53.

12 Chardin, *Journal de voyage*, pp. 29–30.

13 Peter F. Sugar, *Southeastern Europe under Ottoman Rule, 1354–1804* (Seattle: University of Washington Press, 1977), p. 128.

14 Robert Mantran, *Histoire d'Istanbul* (Paris: Fayard, 1996), p. 271.

15 D'Arvieux, *Mémoires* 4:382.

16 Chardin, *Journal du voyage*, p. 26.

17 For example, Fernand Braudel recounts the tale of "Osman Aga, a Turkish interpreter who learnt German during a long period of captivity," in *The Structures of Everyday Life: The Limits of the Possible*, trans. and ed. Siân Reynolds (New York: Harper and Row, 1981), p. 91.

18 For complete accounts, see Lucien Bély, *Espions et ambassadeurs au temps de Louis XIV* (Paris: Fayard, 1990); William James Roosen, *The Age of Louis XIV: The Rise of Modern Diplomacy* (Cambridge: Schenkman, 1976).

19 Robert Mantran, *L'Empire Ottoman de XVIe au XVIIIe siècle: Administration, Economie, Société* (London: Variorum Reprints, 1984), p. 131.

20 Paul Masson, *Histoire du commerce français dans le levant au XVIIe siècle* (New York: Burt Franklin, 1967), p. 155.

21 D'Arvieux, *Mémoires* 4: 226.

22 Cited in C. J. Heywood, "Sir Paul Rycaut, A Seventeenth-Century Observer of the Ottoman State: Notes for a Study," in Ezel Kural Shaw and C. J. Heywood, *English and Continental Views of the Ottoman Empire 1500–1800* (Los Angeles: William Andrews Clark Memorial Library, University of California, 1972), p. 51.

23 Chardin, *Journal du voyage*, p. 34.

24 Ricaut, *Histoire de l'Etat présent de l'Empire Ottoman*, p. 163.

25 Bernard Lewis, *The Muslim Discovery of Europe* (New York: W. W. Norton, 1982), p. 81.

26 Sugar, *Southeastern Europe*, pp. 128–30.

27 Robert Mantran, *Istanbul dans la seconde moitié du XVIIe siècle: Essai d'histoire institutionnelle, économique, économique et sociale* (Paris: Librairie Adrien Maisonneuve, 1962), p. 529.

28 Cited in Heywood, "Sir Paul Rycaut." Paul Rycaut, secretary to the English ambassador Winchilsea (1660–67), pp. 51–52.

29 See Mary Hossain, "The Employment and Training of Interpreters in Arabic and Turkish under Louis XIV: France," *Seventeenth-Century French Studies* 14 (1992): 235–46; and "The Training of Interpreters in Arabic and Turkish under Louis XIV: The Ottoman Empire," *Seventeenth-Century French Studies* 15 (1993): 279–95.

30 Paul Masson, *Histoire du commerce*, p. 156 (cited from AAI 38); see also Francis Richard, "Aux origines de la connaissance de la langue persane en France," *Luqmaan* (Presses universitaires d'Iran), 3 (1986–87): 38.

31 M. l'Ambassadeur Guellouz, "Discussion" of "La vision de l'Orient aux XVIIe–XVIIIe siècles," in *L'Orient: concept et images* (Paris: Presses de l'Université de Paris Sorbonne, 1987), p. 52.

32 D'Arvieux, *Mémoires* 4: 433–34.

33 Itzkowitz, *Ottoman Empire*, pp. 75–77; Robert Mantran, *L'Histoire de l'Empire Ottoman* (Paris: Fayard, 1989), pp. 236–38; V. J. Parry, *A History of the Ottoman Empire to 1730*, ed. M. A. Cook (Cambridge: Cambridge University Press, 1976), p. 162; but see especially Leslie P. Peirce, *The Imperial Harem: Women and Sovereignty in the Ottoman Empire* (New York: Oxford University Press, 1993), p. 144.

34 Chardin, *Journal du voyage*, p. 14.
35 Both stories are from de la Haye, père's tenure as ambassador (1638–66), and he makes allusions to the incidents, albeit indirect, in his correspondences.
36 Donneau de Visé, *Suite de l'histoire de Mahomet IV dépossédé* (Paris: Guerout, 1688), pp. 201–02.
37 De Visé, *Suite de l'histoire*, p. 235.
38 See Jay M. Smith, ch. 4 in *The Culture of Merit: Nobility, Royal Service, and the Making of Absolute Monarchy in France, 1600–1789* (Ann Arbor: University of Michigan Press, 1996), pp. 125–90.
39 Chardin, *Journal du voyage*, p. 14.
40 Robert Mantran, *L'Empire Ottoman du XVIe au XVIIe siècle: Administration, économie, société* (London: Variorum Reprints, 1984), p. 168.
41 Tongas, *Les Relations*, pp. 170–71.
42 D'Arvieux, *Mémoires* 4: 207–39.
43 "Lettres du Roi à de Nointel, ambassadeur à Constantinople," in *Correspondance administrative sous le règne de Louis XIV*, ed. G.-B. Depping (Paris: Imprimerie nationale, 1852), 3: 533.
44 Chardin, *Journal du voyage*, p. 29.
45 Lucien Bély, *Les Relations internationales en Europe (XVIIe–XVIIIe siècles)* (Paris: Presses Universitaires de France, 1992), p. 343.
46 William James Roosen, *The Age of Louis XIV: The Rise of Modern Diplomacy* (Cambridge: Schenkman, 1976), p. 1.
47 See also Abraham van Wicquefort, *L'Ambassadeur et ses fonctions*, 2 vols. (Cologne: Pierre Marteau, 1690).
48 Chardin, *Journal du voyage*, pp. 31–32.
49 From Molière, *Les Précieuses ridicules*. Couton, sc. 9, 277.
50 Molière, *Les Femmes savantes*, in *Oeuvres complètes*, vol. 2, ed. Georges Couton (Paris: Gallimard, 1971), 2.6, p. 1009.
51 Walter Mignolo (*The Darker Side of the Renaissance*) put forth this concept at a seminar on Identity at the National Humanities Center in March 1998.
52 Homi K. Bhabha in "Of Mimicry and Man: The Ambivalence of Colonial Discourse," in *The Location of Culture* (London: Routledge, 1991), p. 90.
53 Here Behdad and I agree (Behdad, "The Oriental(ist) Encounter," 40–42).
54 Behdad uses the term, "mimicry," as "recuperation of difference by reduction to sameness" in "The Oriental(ist) Encounter," 42; whereas I focus on the "not quite" post-colonialist valence, following Homi K. Bhabha in "Of Mimicry and Man: The Ambivalence of Colonial Discourse," p. 86.
55 Bhabha, "Of Mimicry," p. 91.

4 ORIENTING THE WORLD:
ORGANIZING COMPETITION AND GENDERING GEOGRAPHY

1 D'Arvieux, *Mémoires*, 1, p. 179.
2 See Alain Grosrichard, *Structure du sérail* (Paris: Seuil, 1979), p. 27; Lucette Valensi *The Birth of the Despote: Venice and the Sublime Porte*, trans. Arthur

Denner (Ithaca: Cornell University Press, 1993), p. 46, but here with attention to Venice's role as well.

3 *Voyages de Mr. Dumont, en France, en Italie, en Allemagne, à Malthe, et en Turquie. Contenant les recherches et observations curieuses qu'il a faites en tous ces pays; tant sur les moeurs, les coûtumes des Peuples, leurs différents gouvernements et leurs religions; que sur l'histoire ancienne et moderne, la philosophie et les monuments antiques* (La Haye: chez Etienne Fouque, 1699), (pp. 73–74, emphasis mine).

4 For a concise history, see Philip Mansel, *Constantinople: City of the World's Desire, 1453–1924* (New York: Saint Martin's Press, 1996).

5 See Jean-Marie Apostolidès, ch. 4, "La Mythistoire," in *Le Roi-machine: Spectacle et politique au temps de Louis XIV* (Paris: Les Editions de minuit, 1981), pp. 66–92; Harriet Stone, *The Classical Model: Literature and Knowledge in Seventeenth-Century France* (Ithaca: Cornell University Press, 1996), pp. 77–93; and René Jasinski, *Vers le vrai Racine*, vol. 1 (Paris: Librairie Armand Colin, 1958), pp. 394–95.

6 Guillaume Joseph Grelot, *Relation nouvelle d'un voyage de Constantinople, enrichie de Plans levez par l'Auteur sur les lieux, et des Figures de tout ce qu'il y a de plus remarquable dans cette ville* (Paris: chez la veuve de Damien Foucault, 1680), p. 73

7 On this subject, see my chapter: "Constantinople: The Telling and the Taking," in *Mediterranean Thinking: Toward a New Epistemology of Place* (forthcoming Durham, NC: Duke University Press, 2002).

8 Antoine Galland, *Journal d'Antoine Galland pendant son séjour à Constantinople (1672–73)* II, ed. Charles Schefer (Paris: Ernest Leroux, 1881), Appendice (letter from Colbert to Galland), p. 275.

9 See Gérard Defaux, "The Case of *Bérénice*: Racine, Corneille, and Mimetic Desire," *Yale French Studies* 76, "Autour de Racine: Studies in Intertextuality," ed. Richard E. Goodkin (1989): 211–39.

10 For another perspective, see René Jasinski, *Vers le vrai Racine*, vol. 1 (Paris: Librairie Armand Colin, 1958), pp. 364–82.

11 Contemporary critics who especially take this essentializing gesture to task are Emmanuel Sivan, *Interpretations of Islam: Past and Present* (Princeton: The Darwin Press, 1985) especially ch. 5: "Edward Said and his Arab Reviewers," pp. 133–54; Lisa Lowe, *Critical Terrains: French and British Orientalisms* (Ithaca: Cornell University Press, 1991), especially ch. 1: "Discourse and Heterogeneity," pp. 1–29; Aijaz Ahmad, *In Theory: Classes, Nations, Literatures* (London: Verso, 1992), especially ch. 5: "Orientalism and After: Ambivalence and Metropolitan Location in the Work of Edward Said," pp. 159–219; Ali Behdad, *Belated Travelers: Orientalism in the Age of Colonial Dissolution* (Durham: Duke University Press, 1994), pp. 11–13.

12 Edward Said, *Orientalism*, pp. 208–09; here he is referring to Orientalism in a broader context, but his analysis is pertinent to the essentializing that takes place on the French classical stage.

13 Pierre Corneille, *Tite et Bérénice*, in *Oeuvres complètes*, ed. Georges Couton, vol. 3 (Paris: Gallimard, 1980) and Jean Racine, *Bérénice*, in *Oeuvres complètes*,

ed. Georges Forestier, vol. 1 (Paris: Gallimard, 1999). References are to act, scene, and verse.

14 Here I am thinking of the influence of women's salons and of the role of female leadership during the Fronde; see Faith Beasley, *Revising Memory: Women's Fiction and Memoirs in Seventeenth-Century France* (New Brunswick: Rutgers University Press, 1990); Joan DeJean, *Tender Geographies: Women and the Origins of the Novel in France* (New York: Columbia University Press, 1991); Carolyn Lougee, *Le Paradis des femmes: Women, Salons, and Social Stratification in Seventeenth-Century France* (Princeton: Princeton University Press, 1976).

15 Mantran, *L'Empire Ottoman*, p. 162

16 Ibid., pp. 162, 165.

17 Paul Ricaut, *Histoire de l'etat present de l'Empire Ottoman: contenant les maximes politiques des Turcs; les principaux points de la religion mahometane, ses sectes, ses heresies, et ses diverses sortes de religieux; leur discipline militaire, avec une supputation exacte de leurs forces par mer et par terre, et du revenu de l'etat,* trans. Monsieur Briot (Paris: chez Sébastien Mabre-Cramoisy, 1670), p. 278.

18 Mantran, *L'Empire Ottoman*, pp. 162, 165.

19 Unlike seventeenth-century European practices, where rulers delighted in accumulating and flaunting multiple titles and crowns.

20 On the "exemplum," see John D. Lyons, *Exemplum: The Rhetoric of Example in Early Modern France and Italy* (Princeton: Princeton University Press, 1989), pp. 3–34.

21 Itzkowitz, *Ottoman Empire*, p. 37.

22 See also Harriet Stone, *The Classical Model: Literature and Knowledge in Seventeenth-Century France* (Ithaca: Cornell University Press, 1996), p. 81.

23 See Roland Barthes, *Sur Racine* (Paris: Editions du Seuil, 1960), pp. 94–99.

24 See Mitchell Greenberg, ch. 5 "Racine's *Bérénice* and the Allegory of Absolutism," in *Canonical States, Canonical Stages: Oedipus, Othering and Seventeenth-Century Drama* (Minneapolis: University of Minnesota Press, 1994), especially pp. 145 and 158.

25 Ricaut, *Histoire de l'etat présent de l'Empire Ottoman*, p. 86.

26 Roland Barthes, *Sur Racine* (Paris: Seuil, 1963), p. 99.

27 Like Oreste in Racine's *Andromaque* (1667), as he pined for and then came to Epirus in search of Hermione.

28 Leibniz, *Oeuvres* 5: L.

29 Guilleragues, *Lettres portugaises*, p. 49.

30 Ricaut, *Histoire de l'etat présent de l'Empire Ottoman*, p. 16.

31 *Ibid*, pp. 87–88.

32 Leibniz, *Oeuvres* 5: XLII.

33 Leibniz, *Oeuvres* 5: LXIV.

34 Louis de Rouvroy, duc de Saint-Simon, *Le Duc de Saint-Simon, Louis XIV et sa cour: portraits, jugements et anecdotes; Extraits des mémoires authentiques du Duc de Saint Simon (1694–1715)*, 3rd edn. (Paris: Hachette, 1863), pp. 56–79.

35 W. H. Lewis, *Levantine Adventurer: The Travels and Missions of the Chevalier d'Arvieux, 1653–1697* (London: André Deutsch, 1962), p. 27.

36 To the extent that women in the theatre audiences were or were not male-identified, they would have experienced less or greater comfort with this world-view.

5 THE STAGING OF FRANCE: *BAJAZET, MITHRIDATE*, COMMUNICATION AND THE DETOUR

1 Racine, *Bajazet* and *Mithridate* in *Oeuvres complètes*, ed. Georges Forestier (Paris: Gallimard, 1999). References are to act, scene, and line.

2 My subtitle cites Richard Goodkin on *Bajazet* in "The Performed Letter, or How Words Do Things in Racine," *Papers in French Seventeenth-Century Literature* 17.32 (1990): 85–102.

3 *Correspondance administrative sous le règne de Louis XIV entre le Cabinet du Roi, les secrétaires d'état, le chancelier de France et les intendants et gouverneurs des provinces, les présidents, procureurs et avocats généraux des parlements et autres cours de justice, le gouverneur de la Bastille, les évêques, les corps municipaux, etc.*, ed. G. B. Depping, vol. 3 (Paris: Imprimerie nationale, 1852), pp. 508–09.

4 On the importance of the material letter or the seal both to the Ottomans and to the French, see Alain Grosrichard, *Structure du sérail: La fiction du despotisme asiatique dans l'occident classique* (Paris: Seuil, 1979), pp. 81–86, 117.

5 On ciphers and cryptography, and on correspondence in seventeenth-century French diplomatic affairs, see Roosen, *The Age of Louis XIV*, pp. 129–38; also, for a slightly later period, see Bély, *Espions et ambassadeurs*, pp. 134–62.

6 A page from the correspondence of Philippe Harlay, comte de Césy (French ambassador to the Porte, 1634–39) in code and in ciphers, from the *Etat numérique des fonds de la correspondance politique de l'origine à 1871*, *Archives du ministère des affaires étrangères* (Paris: Imprimerie nationale, 1936), CP p. 394, microfilm p. 2.13, no. 442.

7 Some of whose diplomatic gaffes were recounted in ch. 3.

8 Chardin, *Journal du voyage*, p. 16.

9 Ibid., p. 17.

10 Sieur du Loir, *Les Voyages*, p. 254.

11 Eugène Vaillé, *Histoire générale des Postes (1668–1691)* (Paris: Presses universitaires de France, 1951), vol. 4, pp. 123–24.

12 See Michèle Longino Farrell, *Performing Motherhood: The Sévigné Correspondence* (Hanover: University Press of New England, 1991), pp. 111–14.

13 See Eva Posfay, "Ecrire l'Utopie au féminin en 1660," *Cahiers du dix-septième* 6.1 (1992): 221–34.

14 For other useful readings, see Maurice Descotes, "L'Intrigue politique dans *Bajazet*," *Revue d'histoire littéraire de la France* 71.3 (1971): 400–24; Sylvie Romanowski, "The Circuits of Power and Discourse in Racine's *Bajazet*," *Papers in French Seventeenth-Century Literature* 19 (1983): 849–67; Ali Behdad, "The Eroticized Orient: Images of the Harem in Montesquieu and His

Precursors," *Stanford French Review* (Fall–Winter 1989): 109–26; Harriet Stone, chap. 5: "Oriental Reflections: *Britannicus* and *Bajazet*," in *Royal Disclosure: Problematics of Representation in French Classical Tragedy* (Birmingham, Ala.: Summa Publications, 1987), pp. 99–116. Katie Trumpener, "Rewriting Roxane: Orientalism and Intertextuality in Montesquieu's *Lettres persanes* and Defoe's *The Fortunate Mistress*," *Stanford French Review* 11 (Summer 1987): 177–91.

15 I do not mean to examine all possible sources of Orientalist discourse circulating in France around the time of the production of *Bajazet*; to do so would simply reproduce René Jasinski's study *Vers le vrai Racine* (Paris: Armand Colin, 1958), vol. 2, pp. 1–109, or in "Deux notes sur *Bajazet*," in *A travers le XVIIe siècle: Sur Racine* (Paris: Nizet, 1981), pp. 22–34.

16 Terence Cave, in *Recognitions: A Study in Poetics* (Oxford: Clarendon Press, 1988), focuses on many of the same features of the play, but with an eye to demonstrating the way knowledge circulates, surfaces, only to disappear, forever deferring the full and crucial moment of "recognition" as first articulated in the Oedipus story (348–58).

17 See Jean-Marc Moura, *Lire l'exotisme* (Paris: Dunod, 1992), pp. 58, 149.

18 Pierre Corneille, *Segraisiana*; cited in Pierre Martino, *L'Orient dans la littérature française au XVIIe et au XVIIIe siècle* (Paris: Hachette, 1906), p. 36.

19 In this way, Racine honored Aristotle's prescription for the tragic hero who would be at once distant from and similar to the spectator; see Thomas Pavel, *L'Art de l'éloignement: Essai sur l'imagination classique* (Paris: Gallimard, 1996), in particular ch. 5, "L'ici et le maintenant," and the "Epilogue."

20 For example, Eugene Ionesco flies in the face of and explodes today's bourgeois narcissism with his *Rhinocéros* or with *Les Chaises*; audiences are forced to come to terms with his views of them, and yet manage not to.

21 See Mark Gross, "*Bajazet* and Intertextuality," in special issue of *Yale French Studies* 76 (1989): 146–61.

22 As Pierre Martino points out in his discussion of *Bajazet* in *L'Orient dans la littérature française*, pp. 196–214, Segrais invented his *Floridon ou l'amour imprudent* (1656) out of much the same material, but with quite different results (197–99); and Mairet (*Solyman*, 1630) and Tristan l'Hermite (*Osman*, 1656) also mined the same general vein for inspiration (190).

23 For an example of the practice of the detour in Ottoman palace governance, see Itzkowitz, *Ottoman Empire*, p. 54.

24 *Le Mercure galant*, vol. 4, 1673.

25 Kologlu, *Le Turc*, p. 149.

26 See Louis Montrose, *The Purpose of Playing: Shakespeare and the Cultural Politics of the Elizabethan Theatre* (Chicago: University of Chicago Press, 1996).

27 Benedict Anderson, *Imagined Communities: Reflections on the Origin and Spread of Nationalism* (London: Verso, 1983), pp. 37–38.

28 However, on this subject, see Philippe Lane, *La Péripherie du texte* (Paris: Nathan, 1992).

29 Anderson, *Imagined Communities*, p. 30.

30 See Jacques Huré, "A la recherche de l'Orient racinien dans *Bajazet*," *Travaux de linguistique edités par le centre de philologie et de littératures romanes de l'Université de Strasbourg* 24.2 (1986): 57–71.

31 Of course, we could also understand these prefaces in the more conventional manner. The publication history of the play would explain the need for the two and would resemble the preface stories for other plays. The first preface would accompany original editions and often be defensive and polemical in tone; the second, produced for the *Oeuvres* (1676) would be more detached and philosophical, like Corneille's retrospective *Examens*.

32 See Peter France, *Politeness and its Discontents* (Cambridge: Cambridge University Press, 1992), pp. 5–6.

33 Not that they hadn't developed the double standard in their relations with members of other classes and ethnic groups within the European community over the centuries.

34 Bajazet's mother had approved their childhood love and destined them to each other from that time (1.4.361–63).

35 However, this generalization is problematic, given that many "Turks," the Janissaries for example, not only Roxane, are of unclear origin (1.1.98–99), so how to explain a shared trait, unless as a shared perception instead?

36 Chardin, *Journal du voyage*, p. 8.

37 Ibid., p. 52.

38 Ricaut, *Histoire de l'état présent de l'Empire Ottoman*, pp. 17–18.

39 For a complete discussion of the Fronde, see Orest Ranum, *The Fronde: A French Revolution, 1648–1652* (New York: W. W. Norton and Company, 1993); the "Sultanate of the Women" dates roughly 1640–56.

40 Mehmet III ruled only briefly, as did many of his predecessors and successors. His portrait here seems most apt for the inscription below that expresses sentiments that must have been experienced by both Mahomet IV and Louis XIV in their minority.

41 A. D. S. M, *La Cour Othomane ou l'interprète de la Porte, qui explique toutes les charges et la fonction des officiers du Serrail du Grand Seigneur, de la milice, de la religion de Mahomet et de la loy des Turcs* (Paris: chez Estienne Loyson, 1673), p. 185.

42 For an explanation of the Ottoman "politics of reproduction" and of the provenance of the Sultanes, see Leslie P. Peirce, *The Imperial Harem: Women and Sovereignty in the Ottoman Empire* (New York: Oxford University Press, 1993), pp. 28–90.

43 Ricaut, *Histoire de l'Empire Ottoman*, p. 71.

44 On this point, see Michel Baudier, *Histoire générale du Serail et de la Cour du Grand Seigneur où se voit l'image de la grandeur ottomane, le tableau des Passions humaines, et les exemples des inconstantes prosperités de la Cour* (Paris: Cramoisy, 1623), pp. 51–52; and Ricaut in his *Histoire de l'état présent de l'empire ottoman*, pp. 274, 279–80.

45 On the idea of unruliness in the seventeenth century, see Pierre Ronzeaud, "La femme au pouvoir ou le monde à l'envers," *Dix-septième siècle* 108 (1975): 9–33; but also see Bakhtin and Davis, noted in the "Orientation."

46 On self-alienation, see Julia Kristeva in *Strangers to Ourselves*, trans. Leon S. Roudiez (New York: Columbia University Press, 1991).

47 Marie de Rabutin-Chantal, marquise de Sévigné to Madame de Grignan, *Correspondance*, vol. 1, ed. Roger Duchêne (Paris: Gallimard, 1972), no. 254.

48 Ibid., vol. 2, no. 516.

49 Ibid., vol. 3, no. 1169.

50 Sévigné to Bussy-Rabutin, *Correspondance*, vol. 1, no. 85.

51 Sévigné to Mme de Grignan, *Correspondance*, vol. 3, no. 1015.

52 As recently as 1996, a blockbuster movie produced in Ankara, *Istanbul under My Wings* – featuring the same seventeenth-century Ottoman Sultan, Mourad IV, whose reign occasioned the murder of his unfortunate brother Bajazet and inspired the ambassador de Césy's initial relaying of the event to France – stirred up controversy in Turkey. Reported by the Associated Press in the *Durham Herald-Sun* of June 14, 1996, the headline reads: "Turks up in arms over film they say hints Ottoman sultan was bisexual." The preferred medium for the story now has passed from the "outsider" French classical stage to the "insider" local popular cinema of twentieth-century Turkey, and the film targets a different audience with new purpose. It feeds into a politically charged debate pitting Turkish fundamentalists (who object to what they view as aspersions cast on the Ottoman past – Mourad is portrayed as in love with a young man) against secularists (who are more at ease with freedom of interpretation and relaxed about social mores). Questions of communication and context appear to be as fraught as they were three hundred years ago. How is one to evaluate this piece of contemporary news reported by the Associated Press (hardly a Turkish source) from Ankara? Today we have a new response available: "See the movie" (if possible; the Turkish "blockbuster" was swiftly and decisively withdrawn from the popular circuit). In our day, the cinema has succeeded the play as a genre, and competes as purveyor of at least virtual truth for a greater number of people, since fewer and fewer viewers are likely to consult newspaper articles, histories, or correspondences in search of corroboration, factuality or accuracy; and in any case there they would find only information and opinion. Even then, which of any sources has the final word? But, suppose a trusted friend were to send us a detailed letter from Istanbul recounting and assessing the movie and its local effects – then again, what if this letter were to be intercepted? And what if the message were found to be seditious?

53 The second would come in the nineteenth century, with Napoleon's expedition into Egypt, further moves into West Africa, Indochina, and then the taking of Algeria.

54 See also René Jasinski, *Vers le vrai Racine*, vol. 2 (Paris: Librairie Armand Colin, 1958).

55 M. L. B. D. E. D. E, preface to *La Cour de France turbanisée, et les trahisons démasquées*, 3rd edn. (The Hague: chez Jacob van Ellinckhoysen, 1690). Although 1690 is cited as the date of the third edition of this work, other allusions within the text itself indicate that the work appeared and circulated

earlier, around the general time indicated above. Jasinski alludes in passing to this same piece of propaganda against Louis XIV's political maneuvering and assigns it a date: "Un Pamphlet, répandu à profusion un peu plus tard [shortly after 1672] dans l'Europe entière ne lui reprochera que trop de 'turbaniser' la France" ["A pamphlet, widely distributed a bit later in all Europe, reproaches him severely for 'turbanizing' France."] (162); however, it should be noted that in the bibliography of Nicole Ferrier-Carivière's *L'Image de Louis XIV dans la littérature française*, the anti-Louis XIV pamphlet is listed as anonymously published in Cologne in 1686; in *Louis XIV d'après les pamphlets répandus en Hollande* (Paris: A. Nizet, 1936), P. J. W. Van Malssen, dates *La Cour de France* from 1686; 23, 192. Thus, this particular pamphlet would be an angry response to French non-participation in the Siege of Vienna. It can possibly be attributed to François-Paul de Lisola (whose writings were all published anonymously) because of its similarity in title and content to a pamphlet known to be his (*La France démasquée, ou Ses irregularitez dans sa conduite, et maximes* (The Hague: chez Jean-Laurent, M. DL. XX. [sic: should read M. D. C. L. XX]). See Karro, "La Cérémonie turque," pp. 72, 92–93.

56 See P. J. W. Van Malssen, *Louis XIV*, p. 61.

57 Notably, *Het France Turckye* and *Vervolgh Van't Franse Turckye*, see Van Mallsen, *Louis XIV*, pp. 23, 61, 196.

58 Van Malssen, *Louis XIV*, p. 61.

59 That this citation is attributed to an Italian, hence partisan, traveler, Pietro della Valle, makes it a little suspect, but his belief does attest to a deep-seated suspicion and fear of the Turks; Tongas, *Les Relations*, p. 7.

60 The Christian Europeans were "supposed" to present a united front in face of the Moslem Ottomans, as expressed in Le Révérend Père Jean Coppin: *Le bouclier de l'Europe, ou la guerre sainte contenant des avis politiques ... aux Rois et aux Souverains ... pour garantir leurs Estats des incursions des Turcs ... Avec une relation des voyages faits dans la Turquie, la Thébaïde et la Barbarie* (Lyon, 1686).

61 Itzkowitz, *Ottoman Empire*, p. 81.

62 In fact the French would seize full advantage of this diversionary moment; see G. Burrell Smith, *France, 1598–1715* (London: Edward Arnold and Co., 1940), p. 136.

63 Robert, *Le Petit Robert*, p. 385; apparently this curious fact has also caught the attention of Philippe Sollers. See his *Femmes: Roman* (Paris: Gallimard, 1983), p. 419.

64 Leibniz, *Oeuvres de Leibniz*, p. 260.

65 M. L. B. D. E. D. E, *La Cour de France turbanisée*, preface, p. 55.

66 See Richard Goodkin, "The Death(s) of Mithridate(s): Racine and the Double Play of History," *PMLA* 101 (March 1986): 203–17.

67 Corneille, *Oeuvres complètes* 3:1608.

68 Volker Schröder argues that *Mithridate* is an artistic response to the French wars with Holland, hence for a correlative interpretation, in "Racine et l'éloge de la guerre de Hollande: De la campagne de Louis XIV au 'dessein'

de Mithridate," *XVIIe siècle*, no. 198 (50e année, no. 1) (1998): 113–36, and "La place du roi: Guerre et succession dans *Mithridate*," in *Actes du 29e congrès annuel de la North American Society for Seventeenth-Century French Literature*, University of Victoria (Tubingen: Narr, 1998), pp. 147–58.

69 Le Duc de Navailles, *Mémoires du Duc de Navailles et de la Valette, Pair et Maréchal de France et Gouverneur du Monseigneur le Duc de Chartres* (Paris: chez la veuve de Claude Barbin, 1701), p. 241.

70 See Harriet Stone who reads the hero Mithridate as paradox in "Inheriting the Father's Image with His Blood: Mithridate's Legacy to Xipharès and Thésée," *Papers in French Seventeenth-Century Literature* 25, no. 48 (1998): 267–78.

71 Mantran, *L'Empire Ottoman*, p. 382, and see chapter I.

72 The occasional adventurous merchant got through, but passage required a passport from the Sultan, and was uninviting for other reasons as well. The sea was difficult to navigate, and the people who lived around it were considered hostile, hence the particular bravura of Jean Chardin's account of his itinerary through this forbidden and forbidding territory (*Journal du voyage*). In fact, "The Black Sea even became, or rather became once more, in the sixteenth century, Istanbul's private property and only opened once again to Christian traders at the end of the eighteenth century." From Fernand Braudel, vol. 2, *The Wheels of Commerce*, of *Civilization and Capitalism, 15th–18th century*, trans. Siân Reynolds (New York: Harper and Row, 1979), p. 163. Commercial privileges in the Black Sea area would be extended to the French only in 1802; also see Turgay, "Trabzon," 436.

73 Under other circumstances, Racine might just as easily have used the verb "envahir." That he didn't suggests (as Schröder demonstrates) that he was taking at least into semantic account events of the day in Holland.

74 See also, on Mithridate's character, Henry Phillips, *Racine: Mithridate* (London: Grant and Cutler, Ltd., 1990), p. 76.

75 Nor should the usefulness of Xipharès as a model-hero, both as warrior and as lover, be overlooked; but since the play is "about" Mithridate in his title-page prominence, my aim here is to focus on the value of the representation of this character.

76 The Racinian gesture of commemorating Mithridates continues even to this day, not only on the classical stage, but in the world of numismatics. In a recent issue of *Coin World*, Mithridates materially won over the Roman general Pompey, and over time as well. Several large highly prized/priced commemorative coins featuring his profile, and dating from his era, advertise his greatness, from then and for now. While, in the bottom right-hand corner of the ad, a few small and inexpensive pieces stamped with his Roman enemy Pompey's profile are also advertised for sale. The entire detailed blurb of the ad tells the Mithridates story, and only a word – almost an afterthought – on the Roman hero is tacked on at the end: "Finally, we also have a denarius struck in the name of Pompey the Great." The coined legend of Mithridate has accrued material value over the centuries. This is the great hero Racine and his audience looked to in 1673 as model of

military tactics and strategy, cunning, a force to be reckoned with. And these are the values that have endured. Indeed, coins like these were collected by Monsieur Vaillant for Louis XIV. *Coin World*, Monday, March 29, 1993, p. 11.

CONCLUSION

1 Francois Poullain de la Barre, *De l'égalité des deux sexes* (Paris: Fayard, 1984), p. 38.
2 Christian Jouhaud, *Les pouvoirs de la littérature: Histoire d'un paradoxe* (Paris: Gallimard, 2000), p. 22.

Bibliography

A. D. S. M. *La Cour Othomane ou l'interprète de la Porte, qui explique toutes les charges et la fonction des officiers du Serrail du Grand Seigneur, de la milice, de la religion de Mahomet et de la loy des Turcs*. Paris: chez Estienne Loyson, 1673.

Ahmad, Aijaz. *In Theory: Classes, Nations, Literatures*. London: Verso, 1992.

Anderson, Benedict. *Imagined Communities: Reflections on the Origin and Spread of Nationalism*. London: Verso, 1983.

Apollodorus. *The Library*. 2 vols. Trans. Sir James George Frazer. Loeb Classical Library. Cambridge: Harvard University Press, 1921.

Apostolidès, Jean-Marie. "La Mythistoire." Ch. 4 in *Le Roi-machine: Spectacle et politique au temps de Louis XIV*. Paris: Editions de minuit, 1981.

   Le Prince sacrifié: Théâtre et politique au temps de Louis XIV. Paris: Editions de minuit, 1985.

Auerbach, Eric. "La Cour et la ville," *Le Culte des passions: Essais sur le XVIIe siècle français*. Intro. and trans. Diane Meur. Paris: Macula, 1998.

Baccar Alia. *La Mer, source de création littéraire au dix-septième siècle*. Tûbingen: Biblio 17, 1991.

Bakhtin, Mikhael M. *Rabelais and his World*. Trans. H. Iswolsky. Cambridge, MA: MIT Press, 1968.

Bamford, Paul W. *Fighting Ships and Prisons: The Mediterranean Galleys of France in the Age of Louis XIV*. Minneapolis: University of Minnesota Press, 1973.

Barkey, Karen. *Bandits and Bureaucrats: The Ottoman Route to State Centralization*. Ithaca: Cornell University Press, 1994.

Barthes, Roland. *Mythologies*. Paris: Seuil, 1957.

   Sur Racine. Paris: Seuil, 1963.

Baudier, Michel. *Histoire générale du Serail et de la Cour du Grand Seigneur où se voit l'image de la grandeur ottomane, le tableau des Passions humaines, et les exemples des inconstantes prosperités de la Cour*. Paris: Cramoisy, 1623.

Beasley, Faith E. *Revising Memory: Women's Fiction and Memoirs in Seventeenth-Century France*. New Brunswick: Rutgers University Press, 1990.

Behdad, Ali. *Belated Travelers: Orientalism in the Age of Colonial Dissolution*. Durham, NC: Duke University Press, 1994.

   "The Eroticized Orient: Images of the Harem in Montesquieu and His Precursors." *Stanford French Review* (Fall–Winter 1989): 109–26.

"The Oriental(ist) Encounter: The Politics of *turquerie* in Molière." *L'Esprit Créateur* 23 (Fall 1992): 37–49.

Bély, Lucien. *Espions et ambassadeurs au temps de Louis XIV*. Paris: Fayard, 1990.

    Les Relations internationales en Europe (XVIIe–XVIIIe siècles). Paris: Presses Universitaires de France, 1992.

Bhabha, Homi K. "Of Mimicry and Man: The Ambivalence of Colonial Discourse." In *The Location of Culture*. London: Routledge, 1994.

    ed. *Nation and Narration*. London: Routledge, 1990.

Blanc, Henri-Frédéric. *Sidi: Tragédie Bouffe en cinq actes*. Marseilles: Titanic, 1997.

Bourdieu, Pierre. *Distinction: A Social Critique of the Judgement of Taste*. Trans. Richard Nice. Cambridge, MA: Harvard University Press, 1984.

Braider, Christopher. "Cet hymen différé: The Figuration of Authority in Corneille's *Le Cid*," *Representations* 54 (Spring 1996): 28–56.

Braudel, Fernand. *Civilization and Capitalism, 15th–18th century*. Vol. 2 of *The Wheels of Commerce*. Trans. Siân Reynolds. New York: Harper and Row, 1979.

    La Méditerranée et le monde méditerranéen à l'époque de Philippe II: La Part du milieu. Paris: Armand Colin, 1990.

    The Structures of Everyday Life: The Limits of the Possible. Trans. and ed. Siân Reynolds. New York: Harper and Row, 1981.

Burke, Peter. *The Fabrication of Louis XIV*. New Haven: Yale University Press, 1992.

Burshatin, Israel. "The Moor in the Text: Metaphor, Emblem, and Silence." In *Race, Writing and Difference*, ed. Henry Louis Gates, Jr. Chicago: University of Chicago Press, 1985.

Les Cpitulations renouvelées entre Louis XIV Empereur de France et Mehemet IV Empereur des Turcs. par l'entremise de M. Charles François Ollier, Marquis de Nointel, Conseiller du Roy en tous ses Conseils, et en sa Cour de Parlement de Paris, et son Ambassadeur en Levant (1673). Paris: Frederic Leonard, 1689.

Cardinal, Marie. *La Médée d'Euripides*, with a foreword and French text by Marie Cardinal. Paris: Bernard Grasset, 1986.

Carroll, Constance M. "Three's a Crowd: The Dilemma of the Black Woman in Higher Education," in *All the Women are White, All the Blacks are Men, but Some of Us are Brave: Black Women's Studies*. Ed. Gloria T. Hull, Patricia Bell Scott, and Barbara Smith. New York: The Feminist Press at City University of New York, 1982.

Castro, Guillén de. *Las Mocedades del Cid*. Madrid: Ediciones Alfil, 1960.

Cave, Terence. *Recognitions: A Study in Poetics*. Oxford: Clarendon Press, 1988.

Célestin, Roger. *From Cannibals to Radicals: Figures and Limits of Exoticism*. Minneapolis: University of Minnesota Press, 1996.

Chardin, Jean. *Journal du voyage du chevalier Chardin en Perse et aux Indes orientales, par la mer noire et par la Colchide. Première partie, qui contient le voyage de Paris à Ispahan*. London: Moses Pitt, 1686.

Clifford, James. *The Predicament of Culture: Twentieth-Century Ethnography, Literature and Art*. Cambridge, MA: Harvard, University Press, 1988.

"Traveling Cultures." In *Cultural Studies*. Ed. Grossberg, Lawrence, Nelson, Cary, and Treichler, Paula. New York: Routledge, 1992.

Coin World, Monday, March 29, 1993, 11.

Coppin, Le Révérend Père Jean. *Le bouclier de l'Europe, ou la guerre sainte contenant des avis politiques . . . aux Rois et aux Souverains . . . pour garantir leurs Estats des incursions des Turcs . . . Avec une relation des voyages faits dans la Turquie, la Thébaïde et la Barbarie.* Lyon, 1686.

Corneille, Pierre. *La Conquête de la Toison d'or.* In *Oeuvres complètes*. Vol. 3. Ed. Georges Couton. Bibliothèque de la Pléiade, no. 19. Paris: Gallimard, 1980.

   Le Cid. In *Oeuvres complètes*. Vol. 1. Ed. Georges Couton. Bibliothèque de la Pléiade, no. 19. Paris: Gallimard, 1980.

   "Discours de l'utilité et des parties du poème dramatique." In *Théâtre complet*. Vol.1. Ed. Georges Couton. Paris: Garnier, 1993.

   The Cid; Cinna; The Theatrical Illusion. Trans. John Cairncross. Harmondsworth: Penguin, 1975.

   Médée. Ed. André de Leyssac. Geneva: Droz, 1978.

   Médée. In *Oeuvres complètes*. Vol. 1. Ed. Georges Couton. Bibliothèque de la Pléiade, no. 19. Paris: Gallimard, 1980.

   Oeuvres complètes. 3 vols. Ed. Georges Couton. Bibliothèque de la Pléiade, no. 19. Paris: Gallimard, 1980.

   Rodogune. In *Oeuvres complètes*. Vol. 1. Ed. Georges Couton. Bibliothèque de la Pléiade, no. 19. Paris: Gallimard, 1980.

   Segræisiana. In Pierre Martino, *L'Orient dans la littérature française au XVIIe et au XVIIIe siècle.* Paris: Hachette, 1906.

   Tite et Bérénice. In *Oeuvres complètes*. Vol. 3. Ed. Georges Couton. Bibliothèque de la Pléiade, no. 19. Paris: Gallimard, 1980.

D'Arvieux, Laurent. *Mémoires du chevalier d'Arvieux, Envoyé Extraordinaire du Roy à la Porte, Consul d'Alep, d'Alger, de Tripoli, et autres échelles du Levant.* 6 vols. Paris: chez Charles-Baptiste Delespine, 1735.

Davis, Natalie Z. Chapter 5 from *Society and Culture in Early Modern France*. Stanford: Stanford University Press, 1975, PP. 124–51.

Defaux, Gérard. "The Case of *Bérénice*: Racine, Corneille, and Mimetic Desire." *Yale French Studies* 76, 1989. "Autour de Racine: Studies in Intertextuality." Ed. Richard E. Goodkin: 211–39.

DeJean, Joan. *Tender Geographies: Women and the Origins of the Novel in France*. New York: Columbia University Press, 1991.

Depping, G. B., ed. *Correspondance administrative sous le règne de Louis XIV.* 4 vols. Paris: Imprimerie nationale 1850–55, 1872.

Descotes, Maurice. "L'Intrigue politique dans *Bajazet*." *Revue d'histoire littéraire de la France* 71.3 (1971): 400–24.

Dollimore, Jonathan, and Sinfield, Alan, eds. *of Political Shakespeare: Essays in Cultural Materialism.* Ithaca: Cornell University Press, 1994.

Domon, Helene. "*Médée* (ou) L'autre." *Cahiers du dix–septième* 1 (Fall 1987): 87–102.

Doubrovsky, Serge. *Corneille et la dialectique du héros*. Paris: Gallimard, 1963.

Douthwaite, Julia. *Exotic Women: Literary Heroines and Cultural Strategies in Ancien Régime France*. Philadelphia: University of Pennsylvania Press, 1992.

Dreux, Robert de. *Voyage en Turquie et en Grèce du R.P. Robert de Dreux, aumonier de l'ambassadeur de France (1665–1669)*. Paris: Pernot, 1925.

Duchet, Michèle. *Anthropologie et histoire au siècle des lumières: Buffon, Voltaire, Rousseau, Diderot*. Paris: François Maspero, 1971.

du Loir, Sieur. *Les Voyages du Sieur du Loir ensemble de ce qui se passa à la mort du feu Sultan Mourat dans le Serrail, les cérémonies de ses funérailles, et celles de l'avènement à l'Empire de Sultan Hibraim son frère qui lui succèda, avec la relation du siège de Babylon fait en 1639 par Sultan Mourat*. Paris: François Clouzier, 1654.

Dumont, Monseigneur. *Voyages de Mr. Dumont, en France, en Italie, en Allemagne, à Malthe, et en Turquie. Contenant les recherches et observations curieuses qu'il a faites en tous ces pays; tant sur les moeurs, les coûtumes des Peuples, leurs différents gouvernements et leurs religions; que sur l'histoire ancienne et moderne, la philosophie et les monuments antiques*. The Hague: chez Etienne Fouque et François l'Honoré, 1699.

Durham Herald-Sun, June 14, 1996.

Duvignaud, Jean. *Les Ombres collectives: Sociologie du théâtre*. Paris: Presses universitaires de France, 1973.

Euripides. *La Médée d'Euripide*. With a foreword and French text by Marie Cardinal. Paris: Bernard Grasset, 1986.

Farrell, Michèle Longino. *Performing Motherhood: The Sévigné Correspondence*. Hanover: University Press of New England, 1991.

France, Peter. *Politeness and its Discontents: Problems in French Classical Literature*. Cambridge: Cambridge University Press, 1992.

Fumaroli, Marc. *Héros et orateurs: Rhétorique et dramaturgie cornéliennes*. Geneva: Droz, 1996.

Furetière, Antoine. *Le Dictionnaire universel*. 1690. Reprint, Paris: SNL – Le Robert, 1978.

Fusco, Coco. *English is Broken Here*. New York: The New Press, 1995.

Galland, Antoine. *Histoire de l'esclavage d'un marchand de la ville de Cassis, à Tunis*. Ed. Catherine Guénot and Nadia Vasquez. Paris: Editions de la Bibliothèque, 1993.
　　Journal d'Antoine Galland pendant son séjour à Constantinople (1672–1673). Ed. Charles Schefer. Paris: Ernest Leroux, 1881.

Genette, Gérard. *Figures II*. Paris: Editions du Seuil, 1969.

Goldberg, Jonathan. *Sodometries: Renaissance Texts, Modern Sexualities*. Stanford: Stanford University Press, 1992.

Goodkin, Richard. "The Death(s) of Mithridate(s): Racine and the Double Play of History." *PMLA* 101 (March 1986): 203–17.
　　"The Performed Letter, or How Words Do Things in Racine." *Papers in French Seventeenth-Century Literature* 17.32 (1990): 85–102.

Greenberg, Mitchell. *Corneille, Classicism and the Ruses of Symmetry*. Cambridge: Cambridge University Press, 1986.

"Racine's *Bérénice*: Orientalism and the Allegory of Absolutism." In *Canonial States, Canonial Stages; Oedipus, Othering and Seventeenth-Century Drama*. Minneapolis: University of Minnesota Press, 1994.

Subjectivity and Subjugation in Seventeenth-Century Drama and Prose. Cambridge: Cambridge University Press, 1992.

Grelot, Guillaume Joseph. *Relation nouvelle d'un voyage de Constantinople, enrichie de Plans levez par l'Auteur sur les lieux, et des Figures de tout ce qu'il y a de plus remarquable dans cette ville*. Paris: chez la veuve de Damien Foucault, 1680.

Grosrichard, Alain. *Structure du sérail: La fiction du despotisme asiatique dans l'occident classique*. Paris: Seuil, 1979.

Gross, Mark. "*Bajazet* and Intertextuality." *Yale French Studies* 76 (1989): 146–61.

Grossberg, Lawrence, Cary Nelson, Paula Treichler, eds. *Cultural Studies*. New York: Routledge, 1992.

Guellouz, M. l'Ambassadeur. "Discussion" of "La vision de l'Orient aux XVIIe–XVIIIe siècles." In *L'Orient: concept et images*. Paris: Presses de l'Université de Paris Sorbonne, 1987.

Guellouz, Suzanne. "Une nouvelle lecture des *Mocedades* et du *Cid*: *El Honrador de su padre*." In *Pierre Corneille*, Ed. Alain Niderst. Paris: Presses universitaires de France, 1985, pp. 83–92.

Guilleragues, Gabriel Joseph de Lavergne, vicomte de. *Ambassades de M. le comte de Guilleragues et de M. Girardin auprès du Grand Seigneur, avec plusieurs pièces curieuses de tous les Ambassadeurs de France à la Porte, qui font connoistre les avantages que la Religion, et tous les Princes de l'Europe ont tirés des Alliances faites par les français avec sa Hautesse, depuis le règne de François Ier et particulièrement sous le règne du Roy, à l'égard de la Religion; ensemble plusieurs descriptions de Festes. et de Cavalcades à la manière des Turcs, qui n'ont point encore été données au Public, ainsi que celles des Tentes du Grand Seigneur*. Paris: De Luines, 1687.

Lettres portugaises suivies de Guilleragues par lui-même. Ed. Frédéric Deloffre. Paris: Gallimard, 1990.

Hall, Edith. *Inventing the Barbarian: Greek Self-Definition through Tragedy*. Oxford: Clarendon Press, 1989.

Hall, Edward T. *Nonverbal Communication: Readings with Commentary*. Ed. Shirley Weitz. New York: Oxford University Press.

Hall, H. Gaston. *Molière's Le Bourgeois gentilhomme: Context and Stagecraft*. Durham, England: University of Durham Press, 1990.

Hampton, Timothy. " 'Turkish Dogs': Rabelais, Erasmus, and the Rhetoric of Alterity." In *Representations* 41 (Winter 1993): 58–82.

Harlay, Philippe, comte de Césy (French ambassador to the Porte, 1634–39). *Etat numérique des fonds de la correspondance politique de l'origine à 1871, Archives du ministère des affaires étrangères*. Paris: Imprimerie nationale, 1936. CP p. 394, microfilm p. 2.13, no. 442.

Harth, Erica. *Ideology and Culture in Seventeenth-Century France*. Ithaca: Cornell University Press, 1983.

Histoire nouvelle du massacre des Turcs faict en la ville de Marseille en Provence, le 14 de mars, mil six cents vingt, par la populace de la ville, justement indignée contre ces barbares, avec la mort de deux chaoulx de la Porte du Grand Seigneur, ou ambassadeurs pour iceluy. Avec le récit des occasions qui les y ont provoquez et les préssages de la ruine de l'empire des Turcs. Edited by Henri Delmas de Grammont. 1620; reprint, Paris: H. Champion, 1879.

Hodgen, Margaret T. *Early Anthropology in the Sixteenth and Seventeenth Centuries.* Philadelphia: University of Pennsylvania Press, 1964.

Hossain, Mary. "The Chevalier d'Arvieux and *Le Bourgeois gentilhomme.*" *Seventeenth-Century French Studies* 12 (1990): 76–88.

——. "The Employment and Training of Interpreters in Arabic and Turkish under Louis XIV: France." *Seventeenth-Century French Studies* 14 (1992): 235–46.

——. "The Training of Interpreters in Arabic and Turkish under Louis XIV: The Ottoman Empire." *Seventeenth-Century French Studies* 15 (1993): 279–95.

Hubert, Judd D. *Corneille's Performative Metaphors.* Charlottesville: Rookwood Press, 1997.

Hull, Gloria T., Patricia Bell Scott, and Barbara Smith, eds. *All the Women Are White, All the Blacks Are Men, but Some of Us Are Brave: Black Women's Studies.* New York: The Feminist Press at CUNY, 1982.

Huré, Jacques. "A la recherche de l'Orient racinien dans *Bajazet.*" *Travaux de linguistique edités par le centre de philologie et de littératures romanes de l'Université de Strasbourg* 24.2 (1986): 57–71.

Itzkowitz, Norman. *Ottoman Empire and Islamic Tradition.* New York: Alfred A. Knopf, 1972.

Jardine, Lisa. *Worldly Goods: A New History of the Renaissance.* New York: Doubleday, 1996.

Jasinski, René. "Deux notes sur *Bajazet.*" In *A travers le XVIIe siècle: Sur Racine.* Paris: Nizet, 1981.

——. *Vers le vrai Racine.* 2 vols. Paris: Armand Colin, 1958.

Jouhard, Christian. *Les pouvoirs de la littérature: Histoire d'un paradoxe.* Paris: Gollinard, 2000.

Julien, Charles André. *Histoire de l'Afrique blanche des origines à 1945.* Paris: Presses universitaires de France, 1966.

——. *Histoire de l'Afrique du Nord: Tunisie, Algérie, Maroc de la conquête arabe à 1830.* Paris: Payot, 1961.

Karro, Françoise. "La Cérémonie turque du *Bourgeois gentilhomme*: mouvance temporelle et spirituelle de la foi." In *Le Bourgeois gentilhomme: Problèmes de la comédie-ballet,* ed. Volker Kapp. Biblio 17, vol. 67. Paris: n.p., 1991.

Kologlu, Orhan. *Le Turc dans la presse française: des débuts jusqu'à 1815.* Beyrouth: Maison d'édition Al-Hayat, 1971.

Kramer, Fritz. *The Red Fez.* London: Verso, 1993.

Kristeva, Julia. *Strangers to Ourselves.* Trans. Leon S. Roudiez. New York: Columbia University Press, 1991.

Kruger, Loren. *The National Stage: Theater and Cultural Legitimation in England, France, and America.* Chicago: University of Chicago Press, 1992.

Lane, Philippe. *La Péripherie du texte.* Paris: Nathan, 1992.

Laplanche, Jean, and J.-B. Pontalis. *Vocabulaire de la psychanalyse*. Paris: Presses universitaires de France, 1967.

Latour, Bruno. *Science in Action: How to Follow Scientists and Engineers through Society*. Cambridge: Harvard University Press, 1987.

Laurens, Henry. "L'Orientalisme au XVIIe et XVIIIe siècles." In *L'Orient: Concept et images, Civilisations 15*. 15e colloque de l'Institut de recherches sur les civilisations de l'occident moderne. Paris: Presses de l'université de Paris Sorbonne, 1987.

Leibniz, Gottfried. "Projet d'Expédition d'Egypte présenté à Louis XIV." In *Oeuvres de Leibniz publiées pour la première fois d'après les manuscrits originaux*. Paris: Firmin Didot Frères, Fils et Cie, 1864.

Lévi-Strauss, Claude. *Tristes Tropiques*. Paris: Plon, 1955.

Tristes Tropiques. Trans. John and Doreen Weightman. New York: Penguin Books, 1973.

Lewis, Bernard. *The Muslim Discovery of Europe*. New York: W. W. Norton, 1982.

Lewis, W. H. *Levantine Adventurer: The Travels and Missions of the Chevalier d'Arvieux, 1653–1697*. London: André Deutsch, 1962.

Lisola, François-Paul de. *La France démasquée, ou Ses irregularitez dans sa conduite, et maximes*. The Hague: chez Jean-Laurent, M. DL. XX. (sic: should read M. D. C. L. XX).

Longino, Michèle. "Constantinople: The telling and the Taking." In *Mediterranean Thinking: Toward a New Epistemology of Place*. Forthcoming. Durham, NC: Duke University Press, 2002.

Lougee, Carolyn C. *Le Paradis des femmes: Women, Salons, and Social Stratification in Seventeenth-Century France*. Princeton: Princeton University Press, 1976.

Lough, John. *L'écrivain et son public: Commerce du livre et commerce des idées en France du Moyen Age à nos jours*. Trans. Alexis Tadié. Paris: Le chemin vert, 1978.

Paris Theater Audiences in the Seventeenth and Eighteenth Centuries. London: Oxford University Press, 1957.

Louis XIV. "Lettres du Roi à de Nointel, ambassadeur à Constantinople." In *Correspondance administrative sous le règne de Louis XIV*, ed. G.-B. Depping. Vol. 3. Paris: Imprimerie nationale, 1852.

Lowe, Lisa. *Critical Terrains: French and British Orientalisms*. Ithaca: Cornell University Press, 1991.

Lyons, John D. *Exemplum: The Rhetoric of Example in Early Modern France and Italy*. Princeton: Princeton University Press, 1989.

Lyotard, Jean-François, and Thébard, Jean-Loup. *Au juste*. Paris: Christian Bourgeois, 1979.

Malssen, P. J. W. van. *Louis XIV d'après les pamphlets répandus en Hollande*, Paris: A. Nizet, 1936.

Mansel, Philip. *Constantinople: City of the World's Desire, 1453–1924*. New York: Saint Martin's Press, 1996.

Mantran, Robert. *L'Empire Ottoman du XVIe au XVIIIe siècle: Administration, Economie, Société*. London: Variorum Reprints, 1984.

Histoire d'Istanbul. Paris: Fayard, 1996.

L'Histoire de l'Empire Ottoman. Paris: Fayard, 1989.

Istanbul dans la seconde moitié du XVIIe siècle: Essai d'histoire institutionnelle, économique, économique et sociale. Paris: Librairie Adrien Maisonneuve, 1962.

La vie quotidienne à Istanbul au siècle de Soliman le magnifique. Paris: Hachette, 1965.

Marana, Giovanni P. *Letters Writ by a Turkish Spy.* 1684. Reprint, New York: Temple University Publications, 1970.

Marcus, George and Fischer, Michael M. J. *Anthropology as Cultural Critique.* Chicago: University of Chicago Press, 1986.

Margitic, Milorad R. *Le Cid: Tragi-comédie.* Amsterdam: John Benjamins Publishing Company, 1989.

Marion, Marcel. *Dictionaire des institutions de la France au XVIIe et XVIIIe siècles.* Paris: Editions Picard, 1989.

Martin, Henri-Jean. *Livre, pouvoirs et société à Paris au XVIIe siècle (1598–1701).* Geneva: Droz, 1969.

Martino, Pierre. "La Cérémonie turque du *Bourgeois gentilhomme.*" *Revue d'histoire littéraire de la France* 1 (January–March, 1911): 37–60.

L'Orient dans la littérature française au XVIIe et XVIIIe siècle. Paris: Librairie Hachette et Cie, 1906.

Marx, Karl. *Das Kapital: A Critique of Political Economy.* Ed. Friedrich Engels, condensed by Serge L. Levitsky. Washington, DC: Regnery Publishing Company, 1998.

Masson, Paul. *Histoire du commerce français dans le Levant au XVIIe siècle.* New York: Burt Franklin, 1967.

Massumi, Brian. "Deleuze and Guattari's Theories of the Group Subject, through a Reading of Corneille's *Le Cid.*" *Discours social / Social Discourse: The International Working Papers Series in Comparative Literature* 1 (Winter 1988): 423–40.

Mauss, Marcel. *The Gift: Forms and Functions of Exchange in Archaic Societies.* Trans. Ian Cunnison. New York: Norton, 1967.

McClintock, Anne, Mufti, Aamir, Shohat, Ella, editors. *Dangerous Liaisons: Gender, Nation, and Post-colonial Perspectives.* Minneapolis: University of Minnesota Press, 1997.

McDonald, Marianne. "Medea as Politician and Diva: Riding the Dragon into the Future." In *Medea: Essays on Medea in Myth: Literature, Philosophy, and Art.* Ed. James J. Clauss and Sara Iles Johnston. Princeton: Princeton University Press, 1997, pp. 297–323.

McMahon, Elise. "Witchcraft, Infanticide and the Case of *Médée.*" Ch. 1 in *Classics Incorporated: Cultural Studies and Seventeenth-Century French Literature.* Birmingham, Ala.: Summa Publications, 1998.

Merlin, Hélène. *Public et littérature en France au XVIIe siècle.* Paris: Les Belles Lettres, 1994.

Mézeray, François de. *Histoire des Turcs. Second Tome. Contenant ce qui s'est passé dans cet empire depuis l'an 1612 jusqu'à l'année présente 1649. Avec l'histoire de Chalcondyle par Blaise de Vigenere. Les descriptions et figures des habits des officiers et autres personnes de l'Empire Turc et les Tableaux prophétiques sur la ruine du même empire.* Paris: Sébastien Cramoisy, 1663.

Mignolo, Walter. *The Darker Side of the Renaissance: Literacy, Territoriality, Colonization.* Ann Arbor: University of Michigan Press, 1995.

Mimoso-Ruiz, Duarte. *Médée antique et moderne: Aspects rituels et socio-politiques d'un mythe.* Paris: Edition Ophrys, 1982.

Mitchell, Timothy. *Colonizing Egypt.* Cambridge: Cambridge University Press, 1988.

M. L. B. D. E. D. E. Preface to *La Cour de France turbanisée, et les trahisons démasquées.* 3rd edn. The Hague: chez Jacob van Ellinckhoysen, 1690.

Molainville, Barthélemy d'Herbelot de. Preface to *Bibliothèque orientale ou Dictionnaire universel contenant généralement tout ce qui regarde la connaissance des peuples de l'Orient.* Paris: Compagnie des libraires, 1697.

Molière, Jean-Baptiste Poquelin. *L'Avare.* In *Oeuvres complètes.* Vol. 2. Ed. Georges Couton. Paris: Librarie Gallimard, 1971.

— *Le Bourgeois gentilhomme.* In *Oeuvres complètes.* Vol. 2. Ed. Georges Couton. Paris: Librarie Gallimard, 1971.

— *Dom Juan.* In *Oeuvres complètes.* Vol. 2. Ed. Georges Couton. Paris: Librairie Gallimard, 1971.

— *L'Ecole des maris.* In *Oeuvres complètes.* Vol. 1. Ed. Georges Couton. Paris: Librairie Gallimard, 1971.

— *Les Femmes savantes.* In *Oeuvres complètes.* Vol. 2. Ed. Georges Couton. Paris: Librarie Gallimard, 1971.

— *Les Fourberies de Scapin.* In *Oeuvres complètes.* Vol. 2. Ed. Georges Couton. Paris: Librairie Gallimard, 1971.

— *Les Précieuses ridicules.* In *Oeuvres complètes.* Vol. 1. Ed. Georges Couton. Paris: Librairie Gallimard, 1971.

— *Le Sicilien.* In *Oeuvres complètes.* Vol. 2. Ed. Georges Couton. Paris: Librairie Gallimard, 1971.

Montaigne, Michel de. "Des Cannibales." In *Essais* 1:31, in *Oeuvres complètes.* Ed. Albert Thibaudet and Maurice Rat. Paris: Gallimard, 1967.

Montrose, Louis. *The Purpose of Playing: Shakespeare and the Cultural Politics of the Elizabethan Theatre.* Chicago: University of Chicago Press, 1996.

Moura, Jean-Marc. *Lire l'exotisme.* Paris: Dunod, 1992.

Navailles, Le Duc de. *Mémoires du Duc de Navailles et de la Valette, Pair et Maréchal de France et Gouverneur du Monseigneur le Duc de Chartres.* Paris: chez la veuve de Claude Barbin, 1701.

Parry, V. J. *A History of the Ottoman Empire to 1730.* Ed. M. A. Cook. Cambridge: Cambridge University Press, 1976.

Pavel, Thomas. *L'Art de l'éloignement: Essai sur l'imagination classique.* Paris: Gallimard, 1996.

Peirce, Leslie P. *The Imperial Harem: Women and Sovereignty in the Ottoman Empire.* New York: Oxford University Press, 1993.

Pélisson-Karro, Françoise. "Sources théâtrales, sources historiques: l'apprentissage de l'histoire de l'Orient sur la scène jésuite." In *Littératures classiques,* 30 (1997).

Le Petit Robert. Paris: Société du Nouveau Littré, 1973.

Phillips, Henry. *Racine: Mithridate.* London: Grant and Cutler, Ltd., 1990.

Posfay, Eva. "Ecrire l'Utopie au féminin en 1660." *Cahiers du dix-septième* 6.1 (1992): 221–34.

Pratt, Mary Louise. *Imperial Eyes: Travel Writing and Transculturation.* London: Routledge, 1992.

Prigent, Michel. *Le héros et l'état dans la tragédie de Pierre Corneille.* Paris: PUF, 1986.

Racine, Jean. *Bajazet.* In *Oeuvres complètes.* Vol. 1. Ed. Georges Forestier. Paris: Gallimard, 1999.

    Bérénice. In *Oeuvres complètes.* Vol. 1. Ed. Georges Forestier. Paris: Gallimard, 1999.

    Mithridate. In *Oeuvres complètes.* Vol. 1. Ed. Georges Forestier. Paris: Gallimard, 1999.

    Oeuvres complètes. 2 vols. Ed. Georges Forestier. Paris: Gallimard, 1999.

    Phèdre. In *Oeuvres complètes.* Vol. 1. Ed. Georges Forestier. Paris: Gallimard, 1999.

Ranum, Oreste. *The Fronde: A French Revolution, 1648–1652.* New York: W. W. Norton and Company, 1993.

Renan, Ernest. *Qu'est-ce qu'une Nation? What is a Nation?* Intro. Charles Taylor, trans. Romer Taylor. 1882. Toronto: Tapir Press, 1996.

Ricaut, Monsieur. (See also Rycaut, Paul.) *Histoire de l'etat présent de l'Empire Ottoman: contenant les maximes politiques des Turcs; les principaux points de la religion mahometane, ses sectes, ses hérésies, et ses diverses sortes de religieux; leur discipline militaire, avec une supputation exacte de leurs forces par mer et par terre, et du revenu de l'état, traduit de l'anglais de M. Ricaut, ecuyer, secretaire de M. le Comte de Winchelsey, ambassadeur extraordinaire du Roy de la Grande Bretagne Charles II vers Sultan Mahomet Han quatrième du nom, qui règne à présent, par M. Pierre Briot.* Trans. M. Briot. Paris: Sébastien Mabre-Cramoisy, 1670.

Richard, Francis. "Aux origines de la connaissance de la langue persane en France." *Luqmaan* (Presses universitaires d'Iran), 3 (1986–87): 38.

Richelieu, Armand du Plessis, Cardinal de. *Testament politique.* Cited by Pillorget, René and Suzanne in *France baroque, France classique (1589–1715) I. Récit*, 335–36.

Riding, Alan. "Englishing a French Classic (With Their Approval)." *New York Times*, April 4, 1999. Theater Section, 6.

    "A Star of the 1600s has waned in the 1900s." *New York Times*, January 3, 1999, theatre Section: 5.

Robert, Paul. *Le Petit Robert* (dictionary). Paris: Société du Nouveau Littré, 1973.

Romanowski, Sylvie. "The Circuits of Power and Discourse in Racine's *Bajazet.*" *Papers in French Seventeenth-Century Literature* 19 (1983): 849–67.

Ronzeaud, Pierre. "La femme au pouvoir ou le monde à l'envers." *Dix-septième siècle* 108 (1975): 9–33.

Roosen, William James. *The Age of Louis XIV: The Rise of Modern Diplomacy.* Cambridge: Schenkman, 1976.

Rouillard, Clarence Dana. *The Turk in French History, Thought, and Literature (1520–1660).* Paris: Boivin, 1940.

Rycaut, Sir Paul. (See also Ricaut, Monsieur.) *History of the Turkish Empire from 1623 to 1677: an exact Computation of their Forces both by Land and Sea. Illustrated with divers Pieces of Sculpture representing the variety of Habits amongst the Turks. In three books.* Translated from the English into French by M. Pierre Briot. London: printed for John Starkey and Henry Brome . . . , 1668.

Present State of the Ottoman Empire Containing the Maxims of the Turkish Politie, the most material points of the Mahometan Religion, their Sects and Heresies, their Convents and Religious Votaries. Their Military Discipline, with The History of the Turkish Empire From the Year 1623. to the Year 1677. Containing the Reigns of the three last Emperours, viz. Sultan Morat or Amurat IV. Sultan Ibrahim, and Sultan Mahomet IV. his Son, The XIII. Emperour now Reigning. By Paul Rycaut, Esq.; late Consul of Smyrna. Trans. from the English into French by M. Pierre Briot. London: printed by J. M. for John Starkey at the Mite in Fleet Street near Temple Bar, 1666.

Said, Edward. *Orientalism.* New York: Vintage Books, 1979.

Saint-Simon, Louis de Rouvroy, duc de. *Le Duc de Saint-Simon, Louis XIV et sa cour: portraits, jugements et anecdotes; Extraits des mémoires authentiques du Duc de Saint Simon (1694–1715).* 3rd edn. Paris: Hachette, 1863.

Scheeper, Thomas J. "The Economic History of the Reign." In *The Reign of Louis XIV: Essays in Celebration of Andrew Lossky.* Ed. Paul Sonnino. London: Humanities Press, 1990.

Schröder, Volker. "La place du roi: Guerre et succession dans *Mithridate*." In *Actes du 29e congrès annuel de la North American Society for Seventeenth-Century French Literature, University of Victoria.* Tubingen: Narr, 1998.

"Racine et l'éloge de la guerre de Hollande: De la campagne de Louis XIV au 'dessein' de Mithridate." *XVIIe siècle* no. 198 (50e année, no. 1) (1998): 113–36.

Sévigné, Marie de Rabutin-Chantal, marquise de. *Correspondance.* 3 vols. Ed. Roger Duchêne. Bibliothèque de la Pléiade. Paris: Gallimard, 1972.

Shaw, Ezel Kural, and C. J. Heywood. Introduction to *English and Continental Views of the Ottoman Empire 1500–1800.* Los Angeles: William Andrews Clark Memorial Library, UCLA, 1972.

Sivan, Emmanuel. "Edward Said and his Arab Reviewers." In *Interpretations of Islam: Past and Present.* Princeton; The Darwin Press, 1985.

Smith, G. Burrell. *France, 1598–1715.* London: Edward Arnold and Co., 1940.

Smith, Jay M. Ch. 4. In *The Culture of Merit: Nobility, Royal Service, and the Making of Absolute Monarchy in France, 1600–1789.* Ann Arbor: University of Michigan Press, 1996.

Sollers, Philippe. *Femmes: Roman.* Paris: Gallimard, 1983.

Stallybrass, Peter, and White, Allen. *The Politics and Poetics of Transgression.* Ithaca: Cornell University Press, 1986.

Stone, Harriet. *The Classical Model: Literature and Knowledge in Seventeenth-Century France.* Ithaca: Cornell University Press, 1996.

"Inheriting the Father's Image with His Blood: Mithridate's Legacy to Xipharès and Thésée." *Papers in French Seventeenth-Century Literature* 25, no. 48 (1998): 267–78.

"Oriental Reflections: *Britannicus* and *Bajazet*." Ch. 5 in *Royal Disclosure: Problematics of Representation in French Classical Tragedy*. Birmingham, Ala.: Summa Publications, 1987.

Sugar, Peter F. *Southeastern Europe under Ottoman Rule, 1354–1804*. Seattle: University of Washington Press, 1977.

Sweetser, Marie-Odile. *La Dramaturgie de Corneille*. Paris: Droz, 1977.

"Refus de la culpabilité: Médée et Corneille." In *La Culpabilité dans la littérature française*, in *Travaux de littérature*. Paris: Klincksieck, 1977.

Tavernier, Jean-Baptiste. *Nouvelle relation de l'interieur du serrail du Grand Seigneur: contenant plusieurs singularitez qui jusqu'icy n'ont point est mises en lumière*. Paris: Barbin, 1675.

Thévenot, Jean. *Relation d'un voyage fait au Levant dans laquelle il est curieusement traité des Etats Sujets au Grand Seigneur, des Moeurs, Religions, Forces, Gouvernements, Politiques, Langues et Coustumes des Habitans de ce Grand Empire*. Paris: Lovis Bilaine, 1664.

Todorov, Tzvetan. *On Human Diversity: Nationalism, Racism, and Exoticism in French Thought*. Trans. Catherine Porter. Cambridge, MA: Harvard University Press, 1993.

Tongas, Gérard. *Les Relations de la France avec l'Empire Ottoman durant la première moitié du XVIIe siècle et l'Ambassade à Constantinople de Philippe de Harlay, Comte de Césy (1619–1640)*. Preface by M. Louis Villat. Toulouse: Imprimerie F. Boisseau, 1942.

Trumpener, Katie. "Rewriting Roxane: Orientalism and Intertextuality in Montesquieu's *Lettres persanes* and Defoe's *The Fortunate Mistress*." *Stanford French Review* 11 (Summer 1987): 177–91.

Tucker, Holly. "Corneille's *Médée*: Gifts of Vengeance." *The French Review* 69 (October 1995): 1–12.

Turgay, A. Uner. "Trabzon." *Port Cities of the Eastern Mediterranean (1800–1914)*, special issue. *Review* 16 (Fall 1993): 435–66.

Vaillé, Eugène. *Histoire générale des Postes (1668–1691)*. Vol. 4. Paris: Presses universitaires de France, 1951.

Valensi, Lucette. *The Birth of the Despot: Venice and the Sublime Porte*. Trans. Arthur Denner. Ithaca: Cornell University Press, 1993.

Van Den Abbeele, Georges. "Duplicity and Singularity in André Thevet's Cosmographie du Levant." In *Early Orientalisms*, special issue of *L'Esprit Créateur* 32 (Fall 1992): 25–35.

Veeser, H. Aram, editor. *The New Historicism*. New York: Routledge, 1989.

Villeneuve, Marcel de La Bigne de. *La Dérogeance de la noblesse sous l'ancien régime*. Paris: Sedopols, 1977.

Visé, Donneau de. *Fuite del'histoire de Mahomet IV dépossédé*. Paris: Michel Guerout, 1688.

Le Mercure galant (Paris), January 9, 1672. (Newspaper written and published by Donneau de Visé.)

Suite de l'histoire de Mahomet IV dépossédé. Paris: Guerout, 1688.

Wicquefort, Abraham van. *L'Ambassadeur et ses fonctions.* 2 vols. Cologne: Pierre Marteau, 1690.

Williams, Timothy. "La menace du héros: A propos du *Cid* de Pierre Corneille." *Cahiers du dix-septième* 4 (Fall 1990): 141–50.

Williams, Wes. *Pilgrimage and Narrative in the French Renaissance: The Undiscovered Country.* Oxford: Clarendon Press, 1998.

Wolf, Christa. *Médée, voix.* Paris: Fayard, 1997.

Index

CAMBRIDGE STUDIES IN FRENCH

GENERAL EDITOR: Michael Sheringham, (*Royal Holloway, London*)

EDITORIAL BOARD: R. Howard Bloch (*Columbia University*), Malcolm Bowie (*All Souls College, Oxford*), Terence Cave (*St John's College, Oxford*), Ross Chambers (*University of Michigan*), Antoine Compagnon (*Columbia University*), Peter France (*University of Edinburgh*), Christie McDonald (*Harvard University*), Toril Moi (*Duke University*), Naomi Schor (*Harvard University*)